Multiple Modernities

Multiple Modernities

Cinemas and Popular Media in Transcultural East Asia

EDITED BY

Jenny Kwok Wah Lau

TEMPLE UNIVERSITY PRESS

PHILADELPHIA

Temple University Press, Philadelphia 19122
Copyright © 2003 by Temple University
All rights reserved
Published 2003
Printed in the United States of America

♾ The paper used in this publication meets the requirements of
the American National Standard for Information Sciences—Permanence
of Paper for Printed Library Materials, ANSI Z39.48-1984

Library of Congress Cataloging-in-Publication Data

Multiple modernities : cinemas and popular media in transcultural East Asia /
edited by Jenny Kwok Wah Lau.
     p.   cm.
  Includes bibliographical references and index.
  ISBN 1-56639-985-8 (cloth : alk. paper) — ISBN 1-56639-986-6 (pbk. :
alk. paper)
    1. Motion pictures—East Asia. 2. Popular culture—East Asia.
I. Lau, Jenny Kwok Wah, 1954–
  PN1993.5.E9 M75 2002
  791.43′095—dc21

                      2002020339

To Andrew

Contents

Preface and Acknowledgments

The concept and frame of investigation for this book came to me as a response to the imminent reannexation of Hong Kong to China in the mid 1990s, the breakdown of the socialist structure worldwide, and the rise of the East Asian economic zone.[1] Obviously, a new world order was looming. Furthermore, during my trips back to Hong Kong in 1996 and 1997, I viewed a number of local television shows whose level of enmeshment with the visual presentation and programming of American mass media surprised me. At the same time, conversations held in public places, such as grocery stores, restaurants, the Art Center, and the Cultural Center, revealed a rather self-preoccupied medley of concerns ranging from the stock market to the unfolding "history of disappearance" of the city. Perplexing questions arose. What would a new "transnational" world order be like? What distinguishes this form of "Asian modernity" from that of Europe and the United States, especially that being revealed and created by popular media?

This book is primarily derived from the international conference "Asian Cultures at the Crossroads: An East-West Dialogue in the New World Order" held in Hong Kong in the fall of 1998 and funded by the David C. Lam Institute for East-West Studies. Taking mass media as the most conspicuous statement of contemporary life, I asked: How should we look at modern culture when the cold-war dichotomy no longer exists? What kind of cultural negotiation is taking place if the new world is monopolized by a single center? How do cinema and other popular media reflect and create such a negotiation?

As I write this preface, the September 11 attack on New York and Washington, D.C., has just taken place. This epic tragedy, which arguably manifested a serious cultural clash, sent a clear message that a new world discourse is badly needed and at the same time is already in its inception. It clearly signaled to us the urgency to formulate views that can center-stage the multiplicity of cultures. The investigation of these perspectives will continue to be one of the most significant intellectual dialogues of the new century. Whether we are ready for it or not, reality is biting us all.

Most of the essays in this book are based on the conference papers. Much appreciation is due to all of the writers. By working at the cutting edge of their own fields, they have generously shared their insights both through their writing and through numerous conversations about the project. Along the way, a number of colleagues offered invaluable professional advice, comments, and support. Among them I am especially indebted to Professors Chuck Kleinhans, David Desser, George Semsel, and Patricia Erens for their continuous encouragement and for their faith in the ultimate fruition of this prolonged endeavor.

Thanks are also due to Aaron Gerow and Jing Wang, who, in translating two of these very penetrating essays, accomplished the unenviable task of making complicated material understandable in another language. I am also grateful to Whitney Huber for her typing and editing skills, not to mention her utter dependability; to John Lent for the pictures from his encyclopedic collection; and to the staff and editors at Temple University Press, who exhibited the highest standards of efficiency and professionalism. The author and the publisher would further like to thank Duke University Press for the kind permission to reprint Jeroen de Kloet's article as Chapter 2 of this book.

As Trinh-T Minh-ha so aptly observed, "Substantial creative achievement demands . . . time, . . . [but most women's writing is] incessantly interrupted, deferred, denied, at any rate subordinated to family responsibilities."[2] This process of writing has been a challenge to me. Without the faithful support of all my friends, this project would have resulted in what Tillie Olsen describes as "atrophy; unfinished work; minor effort and accomplishment; silences."[3] I thank all the people around me, especially my family and my children, who have been patient, understanding, and simply all-enduring.

Notes

1. The transcriptions used in the essays on mainland Chinese and Hong Kong media are in pinyin except for cases when a different romanization is already commonly used. The transcriptions in the article on Taiwan television follow the Wade-Giles system. A filmography is included in each of the articles on Korean cinema, which is relatively less well-known in the United States.

2. Trinh-T Minh-ha, *Women, Native, Other: Writing Postcoloniality and Feminism* (Bloomington: Indiana University Press, 1989), p. 7.

3. Quoted in ibid.

Multiple Modernities

Introduction

Jenny Kwok Wah Lau

Western modernity has traveled to the East.[1] On the societal side, it has brought about colossal institutional changes, such as market economies, bureaucratic states, and modes of popular government. These transformations became especially noticeable on a global scale after the cold war. The rapid economic change in the East Asian countries has created a so-called new Asian generation—an affluent condition that is a source of both pride and anxiety for modern Asia. The pride of success in the restructuring of society, and in the resulting capacity to create material abundance compatible with that of the contemporary West, is accompanied by the anxiety of recognizing that such material advancement involves an unprecedented receptiveness toward Western ideas, manifested via financial and technological investments. This is particularly problematic in parts of Asia, such as China, that have struggled fiercely with Western colonization in the past and are trying to establish postcolonial status.[2]

The legacy of Western modernity is not restricted to the economic realm but inevitably has spilled over to Asia's cultural structures, symbols, and expressions. It is common knowledge that most of Asia's contemporary visual culture—television, films, magazines, fashions, and so forth—is, at least superficially speaking, either a direct imitation or a kind of "mutation" from Euro-America. As the renowned German film director Wim Wenders pointed out in his 1987 documentary *Tokyo-Ga:* "The Japanese continue to make televisions for the whole world to see America." This change in the arena of the symbolic is accompanied by a change in the concrete lifestyle of ordinary people. A seemingly minor but actually indicative example is the uniform nine-to-five work shift found everywhere in industrialized countries before the spread of computer technology. This apparently insignificant practice posed a challenge to China in the beginning of its post-Mao modernization. As a result China quickly canceled its national policy of afternoon siestas, just one indication of the transculture evolving in East Asia as it formulates responses to specifics of Westernization. A more general and crucial issue that could be raised is how and where Asians spend their time and money after work during this process of change.

These examples, only the tip of the iceberg of the massive movements of technology, trade, and media persuasion, also demonstrate the power of modernity to standardize life practice. Based on this notion, universalists project a future convergence of all cultural activities into one global form, basically led by the Euro-American center.[3] Yet, such a belief tends to selectively focus on the "Westernized" elements of Asian life and to ignore the differences. Discourses thus created favor categories already popular in the West, such as self-identity, gender, nation, boundaries, genres, the postmodern, and so on. Usually ignored are categories such as human connectedness, cross-gender issues, transcendental existence, and so forth. A "new Asia," by this interpretation, is nothing more than an entity to be absorbed into the great tide of transnationalism built by global corporations and media productions.

Those who are more conscious of the complexity of human issues believe that although modernity may be Western in origin and global in reach, the transformation of a vast collection of people (the entire non-West) could hardly be uniform. A historical precedent in the West itself can demonstrate the point. Both the Renaissance and the Enlightenment benefited from the impact of Greek culture but were assimilated in different ways by northern and southern Europe. The Nordic, French, and English societies each responded differently to the impact of neoclassical studies and generated its own version of Renaissance and modernity. Similarly, contemporary modernization in East Asia, as a product of modern encounters with the West, has resulted in a variety of cultural manifestations. This points to the fact that a Weberian societal/institutional modernity epitomized by a market economy and democratic polity, when transplanted to the various cultures of East Asia, does not necessarily create an identical cultural modernity.

Asian societies entered modernity at different points in their histories. Some encountered the West during the height of their accomplishments; others encountered it at a time of relative weakness. Some exchanges took place through trade, others through intellectual interchange, politics, or even war. Thus, each society has had to negotiate its relationship with this new reality from the standpoint of its own sociohistorical context. In this sense, modernity was (and still is) full of divergent potential, and because of its ability to elicit responses was (and still is) an agent not only of homogenization but also of heterogenization.

In the arena of cinema and media, the contemporary power of technology in creating simulated cultures has no doubt valorized the impact of the West. However, the seemingly universal signs transmitted through media, such as images of love and luxury in the film *Titanic* or freedom and rebelliousness in rock and rap music, may work differently than in their places of origin. These symbols, potent as they may be, are always recast within the local context, which is constantly shaped by the "habitus"—the life patterns, the structures of response—of each community.[4] While *Titanic* may be a fantastic love story for many, rumor has it that the Chinese prime minister Jiang Zemin, after viewing the film, was moved by its message to "never overburden oneself with a wishful or oversized project," an interpretation quite different from that of most Americans. A more serious case in modern world affairs is the 1989 Tiananmen Square protest staged by the people of Hong Kong and Taiwan. In terms of information, both societies received similar news from CNN and other international news agencies. But in Hong Kong there was a massive demonstration by two million people (out of five million residents) against China's action, while in Taiwan the response was scanty or lukewarm, at best. Local conditions strongly shaped reactions toward the same "reality." This multiplicity of responses to shared images points to the diverse or even fragmented nature of cross-cultural, cross-boundaries communication.

If modernity is an attitude rather than an epoch, "a mode of relating to contemporary reality," as Foucault puts it, a major part of modernity in East Asian countries involves their different cultural/historical relationships to the presence of the contemporary West.[5] These relationships represent the many possibilities of the dialectics of the converging, homogenizing, transcultural impulses and the diverging, heterogenizing, multicultural effects that operate within modern societies. The new Asia that is currently in formation will consist of not one uniform modernity but multiple modernities that defy both the prescriptions of the globalists/universalists and the descriptions of the localists/indigenists. Consequently, it is important now to ask what these "multiple modernities" are and how they may continue to define Asian identities.

The goal of this book is to explore the cultural terrain of several major East Asian societies, namely mainland China, Hong Kong, Taiwan, South Korea, and Japan, in regard to their response to Western modernization. It looks at modern/postmodern popular culture as both a generator and a product of different cultural forces. Through the examination of the very tools that organize and articulate modern lived experiences on a mass level—the media of film and other forms of popular culture—it delineates different artifacts and asks how they reflect and create the idea of different modernities.

Unlike the first three-quarters of the twentieth century when a single mass medium, such as film and, later, television, could dominate a society, in the last two decades Asia has been subjected to multiple media experiences. For example, cinema may be popular in one Asian society (South Korea) and less popular in another (Taiwan). The inquiry carried out here focuses on culturally reflexive media and does not hesitate to cross the boundary of the still very popular medium of cinema to broaden its scope of studies when necessary. In doing so, it avoids drawing broad cultural conclusions based on narrow studies of only one medium.

Furthermore, this anthology avoids the orientalist convention of seeing East Asia either as a single uniform block (except Japan) or as a set of discrete entities to be examined separately. East Asian societies largely share similar cultural and ideological roots, a recent history of colonization and decolonization (with the exception of Japan, to a certain extent), and an experience of Westernization. The area is now even more closely connected via technology, trade, and mass media. In this sense, East Asian societies do share important commonalities. At the same time, individual societies exhibit significant differences. Besides its linguistic and economic-political uniqueness, each society has its own history of modernization. For example, Westernization in Japan (since the Meiji period) pre-dated that of the rest of Asia.[6] China has a history of discontinuous or inconsistent relations with Western modernization in the twentieth century. South Korean modernization was a forced process until the 1990s, governed by a military dictatorship and marked by violent protests. Hong Kong was a British colony with a policy of relative openness and a laissez-faire economy. Taiwan, which reemerged from the yoke of Japanese colonization after World War II, was brought under yet another military government, which was also instrumental in its modernization. Thus, East Asia is also a collection of separate societies whose intercultural connections do not eradicate their uniqueness. To put together an anthology of this kind is a way to allow this new paradigm to take hold, to allow each individual society to speak for itself so that the picture of uniqueness and multiplicity can emerge. To present each of their pictures side by side is to allow them to mirror, reflect, and dialogue with each other in terms of their interpretation and experience of modernity.

Because it takes a number of interdisciplinary scholars to build such a mosaic, this book had to be, almost by definition, an anthology. Many of the writers are leaders in their fields, and their articles reflect a cutting-edge quality in terms of both their subjects of investigation and their poignant conceptualizations. Most of these articles also share a critical-descriptive methodology that begins with a set of close readings and arrives at conclusions only when there is strong supporting evidence for them. This approach avoids imposing rigid or preconceived frameworks that tend to produce formulaic readings, as are found in some current writings on film or cultural interpretation. Rather, the writings emphasize reflexivity that is pragmatically and empirically verifiable. These richly documented observations are valuable both for understanding the cultural scene itself and for drawing conceptual conclusions. In addition to the traditional categories of class, gender, ethnicity, and nationality, many of the writers develop previously ignored social parameters, such as lifestyle, personal taste, age, and status. They thus extend beyond existing critical categories and even challenge established perspectives, such as the East/West, modernist/postmodernist, or globalist/regionalist dichotomies.

The study of East Asian media from a transnational critical perspective began to gain attention during the 1990s. Some of the major works include the two books *Melodrama and Asian Cinema* and *Colonialism and Nationalism in Asian Cinema*, edited by Wimal Dissanayake, and part of *In Pursuit of Contemporary East Asian Culture*, edited by Xiaobing Tang and Steven Snyder. These studies address the issues of nationhood, gender, and identity in various national and transnational contexts. *Global/Local: Cultural Production and the Transnational Imaginary*, edited by Rob Wilson and Wimal Dissanayake, offers stimulating discussion on the global/local interface of popular cultures as found in tourism, film, computers, and newspapers in different parts of the world, including Japan, Korea, and Taiwan. In addition, John Lent has supplied the field with useful information; his edited book *Asian Popular Culture* also includes brief critical surveys on East Asia. Other published works focus more on a single society, in the last few years especially on China. Sheldon Lu's *Transnational Chinese Cinemas: Identity, Nationhood, Gender* offers textual readings that consider Western and transnational impacts. Rey Chow's *Primitive Passions* consists of critiques of Chinese films from a transnational feminist perspective. Both *Chinese Modernism in the Era of Reforms* by Xudong Zhang and *Chinese Modern: The Heroic and the Quotidian* by Xiaobing Tang include discussions of Chinese cinema and popular culture from a modernist perspective. Recently, a number of books on Hong Kong cinema have taken a transnational perspective in their discourses, such as *At Full Speed: Hong Kong Cinema in a Borderless World,* edited by Esther C. M. Yau, *and The Cinema of Hong Kong: History, Arts, Identity,* edited by Poshek Fu and David Desser. David Bordwell's *Planet Hong Kong,* although Hollywood centered in its comparative references, is well aware of the global implication of its framework. While all of these quality works are conscious of globalism, many do not intend to question the notion of modernity itself. *Postmodernism and China,* edited by Arif Dirlik and Xudong Zhang, provides an intriguing examination of the popular culture of China in an attempt to map and match the Chinese postmodern condition in relation to the West. (Both Dai Jinhua and Chuck Kleinhans discuss the strengths and limits of such an approach in this book.) Single-medium/single-society studies usually achieve a certain depth but cannot provide a broader view in the context of the connectedness or distinctiveness of each of these East Asian cultures. This book sees the necessity of a broader understanding of East Asia without losing sight of the specifics of its societies. It aims at providing a common ground for an inter/intracultural dialogue.

The book is divided into three parts. "States of Modernities" shows the role that various modernizing elements play in the cultural formation of modern China, Japan, and South Korea. Jenny Kwok Wah Lau's article on the Chinese sixth-generation filmmakers points to the inadequacy of the cold-war paradigm—the "free" world versus the "dictatorial/socialist" world, and "free" market versus state-controlled market. She argues for a contextualized global-local model and searches for detailed pictures of the cultural versus the political, and the local versus the international. Drawing upon Chinese contemporary art movements, Lau notes that many of the sixth-generation films replace socialist heroes with ordinary people, reflecting an interest in the "reality" of banal situations and a concern for "immediate presence."

Jeroen de Kloet's discussion of Chinese rock music continues and expands the investigation of China's response to "modern" or "Western" culture. De Kloet challenges music critics who took Chinese rock either as mimicry of the West or as a tool for subversion. Like Lau, he refutes the clichéd cold-war dichotomies of commercial versus political (dissident) readings of Chinese rock music. Instead, he identifies a fragmentation after the mid-nineties when the medium can best be understood as a site of interaction between commerce, personal taste, and lifestyle. These two essays form a useful background for the later essay by Dai Jinhua, a poignant interrogation of the so-called Chinese postmodernist culture. She probes the arena of contemporary theater, poetry, postmodernist performance art, fiction, documentary films, popular sixth-generation films, and various discourses regarding these cultural practices in China, providing an overview of the cultural situation of Beijing. The three essays together present a rich and heterogeneous picture of the internal dynamics that shape China's cultural mutation and its response to the West.

Sharing a similar interest in the "present" and in the concrete reality of ordinary living, certain sectors of the media in Hong Kong surprisingly resemble their mainland Chinese counterparts, even though their expressions are vastly different. In "The Fragmented Commonplace," Hector Rodriguez emphasizes the inadequacy of the single-medium approach for understanding Hong Kong and proposes an analysis of various media that taken together provide a better picture of the multimedia, multicultural milieu of this cosmopolitan city. His study focuses on the formal construction and subject matter of avant-garde theater, experimental video, short novels, and short films. Given that the audience of mainstream media such as television and films is in rapid decline, this article proposes a new view of the undercurrents of a highly heterogeneous culture. The interest in ordinary living stands in sharp contrast to the earlier colonial (official) discourse, which tends to exoticize Hong Kong. From this perspective, the similarities between Hong Kong and mainland China become less surprising, for the latter's avant-garde movements also contrast with official (socialist) discourse that idealizes certain aspects of China. Yet while the "present" of both Hong Kong and China involves a heightened sense of the local culture, in the former this interest results from that culture's "disappearance" (due to its reannexation to China in 1997), while in the latter it comes from an influx of differences from the outside world.

Although the Japanese film industry resembled that of Hong Kong, Taiwan, and China in that it suffered an almost irreversible collapse and subsequent fragmentation in the 1990s, its sporadic comebacks were quite different. The modernist realism of the Beijing and Hong Kong media projects a picture unlike the hypermodernist futuristic imagery of Japanese films. Yomota Inuhiko's analysis of a number of highly popular 1990s Japanese films presents a trans-/bi-gender, multiethnic, postnational, post-high-tech society that destroys Japan's illusion of itself as a "pure nation." His discussion reveals a cinema filled with surreal and sometimes nightmarish stories of the city of "Tokyo." These futuristic or even prophetic cityscapes of "Tokyo," which resemble none of the contemporary world cities such as Tokyo itself, Hong Kong, Amsterdam, or London, are at the same time representing all of them. This cinema reflects not the transnational picture found on the Chinese scene, but a sense of postnationalism, a product of globalization that erases the distinctive features of every culture. Unlike those who search for an alternative reality grounded in the "present," the futuristic Japanese films Yomota discusses are critical of the technological/transnational presence. While Hong Kong media assimilate world culture in terms of technique, language, and the modernist notion of self-identity, Japanese films postulate a world haunted by multiethnic conflicts and high-tech mishaps.

Mitsuhiro Yoshimoto's article on Tanizaki Jun'ichiro, a popular and controversial Japanese writer, reveals that an East-West dichotomized discourse is an orientalist construct that has skewed understanding of Japan's relationship to the rest of the world. The erroneous notion of dichotomy confuses ethnic or cultural variations with social variations such as age, education, experiences with the outside world, personal temperament, and so forth. What is labeled "Western" or "Japanese" could simply be a reflection of personal differences. Yoshimoto proposes that instead of the "Japanese" elements or their lack in Jun'ichiro's work, critical readings would do better to focus on a combination of the self-reflective analysis of the writer himself and on general group differences not necessarily racial or national in origin. His essay demonstrates what is tacitly implied in others in this collection: The formation of contemporary East Asian culture is not a one-way response to the "West."

Yomota's description of a Japanese cinema concerned with the futuristic aftermath of modernism and postmodernism through images of destruction, gender transgression, and postnational racial segregation offers a gray picture of high postmodernity, an apocalyptic sense of history and critique of technology not commonly found in the media of Hong Kong or China. Yet, at the same time, as exemplified in Jun'ichiro's popular novels, there is the search for the "real as experienced," regardless of what was previously essentialized as "Japanese." In this sense, some Japanese media share a concern with the Chinese who are seeking "reality" from the concrete immediacy of presentness, despite the state's mythology.

In his discussion of the history of modernization in South Korea, Han Ju Kwak shows how such factors as the idealism of the student movements of the eighties, the nostalgia for the disappeared Korea, and a strong sense of entrapment by modernity have contributed to an evolving Korean cinema. Kwak analyzes four filmic responses: movement, tradition, present-tradition, and decontructionist films. Similar to Japan's, Korea's cinema of the eighties and nineties expresses dissatisfaction with modernization and industrialization. Scenes of environmental decline in mining towns, landscapes of cheap karaoke bars and motels, and the sound of sirens in Seoul are reminiscent of desolate images of Tokyo in the aftermath of (fictional) nuclear war.

Along similar lines, Frances Gateward focuses on the reaction of the young toward the results of the modernization imposed on the Korean people by their dictatorial leaders. Tracking the history of Korean cinema and its traditional prohibition of dealing directly with political issues, a prohibition similarly imposed on the cinema of Hong Kong, Gateward turns to melodramas to explore the gender and class problems faced by Korean youth in the nineties. Both Kwak and Gateward maintain that the new Korean cinema of the eighties and nineties represents, through various thematic strategies, a political critique of modernization. Among these strategies: the retold history of the democratization protest carried out by a decade-long student movement; the recovery of the "lost" Korea signified by traditional social ceremonies, folk arts, and folksongs; and the despair of postmodern city life. Thus, both Korean and Hong Kong media responded to the "loss" of the traditional or authentic past through nostalgic remembrance. But the Koreans are much more critical of the modernization and industrialization process, while Hong Kong retains its ultrametropolitan fragmentation. The Korean images of melodramatic realism also contrast with the futuristic, science fiction–like destruction of postnational Tokyo. While Korean cinema, especially the movement films as classified by Kwak, is engaged in political issues, the Chinese sixth-generation films actively seek alternative stories and disengage themselves from politicized discourse.

To broadly summarize, East Asia's response to technology and transnationality may differ from one society to another, yet all share an almost Baudelairean aesthetic of daily life.

The second section of the collection, "Postmodernism and Its Discontents," comprises essays that directly critique three of the most popular views on the relation of modern Asian culture with the West. David Desser, in "Consuming Asia," argues that the established assumption about cultural flow—that "the East always learns from the West"—is erroneous. In fact, Hollywood for decades has been borrowing significantly from both Japan and Hong Kong. The Japanese influence was not limited to the art film master best known in the West, Akira Kurosawa, but affected American popular media as early as 1954 with the Japanese creation of Gojira (Godzilla), which generated waves of science fiction monster films in the United States. An ongoing impact was evident in Japanese-made toys, animation films, and electronic games, and in karaoke bars. Similarly, Hong Kong martial-arts films have attracted attention since the 1970s. The action hybrids Ninja Turtles and Power Rangers exemplify the way Hong Kong expertise has molded the U.S. imagination. Through detailed documentation Desser establishes his thesis and repudiates the one-way myth of colonial discourse.

Chuck Kleinhans, in "Terms of Transition," begins with observations on popular Hong Kong–Hollywood action-packed movies and questions the Jamesonian correlation frequently cited by cultural analysts between these Asian cultural products and postmodernity. He objects that such analyses mainly track and identify the differences between the so-called premodern, modern, and postmodern phases and ignore the overlap and constant fluctuation among them. For instance, aesthetically speaking, the realist narrative of these action movies falls well within the tradition of the romantic rather than the modern. Thus, using a postmodernism framework alone neglects important contradictions generated by other traditions and practices that coexist within the same culture, such as the old capitalist economy, whereby Asia is usually the exploited.

Dai Jinhua's essay continues the argument against the simple use of the postmodernist framework to interpret the culture of modern China. She points to the political use of the "postmodern" itself, which ignores contradictions that accumulated and erupted in China at the end of the eighties, a time that some may prefer to forget. Dai elaborates extensively on the cultural scene in the 1990s, covering modernist performance arts, popular theater, personal/documentary films, popular literature, commercial films, and so forth. To interpret this new phenomenon she proposes an alternative framework that intertwines history, state politics, creative ideas, commerce, and world politics. These discussions in the second part of the book substantiate both the content and the methods proposed in the first part and further describe the multiplicity and the complexity of the pictures of modernity revealed in critical close readings.

The two essays in the third section of the book, "Women in Modern Asia," challenge myths concerning contemporary Asian women. Augusta Palmer, Jenny Lau, and Lin Szu-Ping all suggest that one of the biggest contradictions of modernity lies in its treatment of women, an issue that remains largely unresolved despite its centrality for human progress. Palmer and Lau analyze the contradiction between the popular belief that women in Hong Kong enjoy unusually high status and its insubstantial images in Hong Kong cinema. Under the triple binds of capitalism, patriarchy, and paternalism, cinematic characters of women, especially in the "art" films directed by the first and second new-wave directors, are mostly unidirectional, elusive, and sometimes even misogynistic. This, surprisingly, contrasts with the more traditional or popular action films, which may seem less sophisticated but portray women in more progressive terms.

Lin Szu-Ping's almost anthropological analysis of a Taiwan television series reveals how the modernist sensitivities of its female audience can significantly reframe a traditional local soap opera. This unusual media-related story involves a community that, in reflecting on its own culture, creatively formulates an alternative that fits its own experience of modernity. The incident repudiates the picture of passivity on the part of the "modernized," who in reality rise to meet and negotiate both tradition and modernity on their own terms. While both essays focus on the gender inequality that remains intact in modern Asia, each describes a unique response to it.

One recent commentator has pointed out that modernity is signified by "a mood of distance, a habit of questioning and an intimation of what Baudelaire calls the 'marvelous' in the midst of the ruins of our tradition."[7] The self-reflexive critical engagement to one's "hybrid" culture is detectable in post-Tiananmen China, postnational Japan, and the post–martial law, new democratic culture of South Korea and Taiwan. This book investigates and presents a scenario of multiple modernities in which each society mobilizes its own cultural resources, less for "coping" with Westernization, as the West may view it, than for a double negotiation between social and cultural modernity.

These studies taken together form a mosaic of Asian modernities. However, it would be pretentious to think that one book can map out the entire East Asian picture. Omissions are inevitable due to space limitations. For example, the media culture of Taiwan and women's issues warrant more detailed attention. Nevertheless, this anthology draws out some of the complexities of the configuration as reflected in the many facets of Asian popular cultures. Through a deeper understanding of Asia's many responses to the challenge of different ideas and technologies, one may begin to appreciate the ingenuity of communities who continue to create their own versions of civilization.

Notes

1. I specify "Western modernity" versus simply "modernity" in recognition of recent debates in sociology that suggest the West should not monopolize the term "modernity." Even within the Western tradition, definitions of modernity differ. I use the word in its broad sense to describe the general mode of rational thinking and living since the Enlightenment in Western Europe. This definition does not negate the existence of other forms of modernity generated by non-European cultures.

2. Although China was never fully colonized by any European country, its history in the past two hundred years was still one of massive economic, military, and territorial concessions.

3. See the vigorous discussion in Featherstone, Lash, and Robertson, *Global Modernities*.

4. For a gloss on the term "habitus," see Bourdieu, *In Other Words*.

5. See Michel Foucault, "Ethics: Subjectivity and Truth," in *Essential Works of Foucault, 1954–1984*, vol. 1, ed. Paul Rabinow (New York: New Press, 1997), 303–320.

6. Notice that modernization is not the same as Westernization, although Westernization has functioned as a catalyst for some quantum changes in Asia. This, in a sense, is similar to what happened in Europe, where "modernization" would not be viewed as "Grecianization."

7. Gaonkar, *Alternative Modernities,* 23.

Selected Bibliography

Barlow, Tani E., ed. *Formations of Colonial Modernity in East Asia.* Durham, N.C.: Duke University Press, 1997.

Bourdieu, Pierre. *In Other Words: Essays Towards a Reflexive Sociology.* Translated by Matthew Adamson. Stanford, Calif.: Stanford University Press, 1990.

Featherstone, Mike, Scott Lash, and Roland Robertson, eds. *Global Culture: Nationalism, Globalization, and Modernity.* London: Sage, 1990.

———. *Global Modernities.* London: Sage, 1995.

Gaonkar, Parameshwar Dilip, ed. *Alternative Modernities.* Durham, N.C.: Duke University Press, 2001.

Goldman, Merle, and Andrew Gordon, eds. *Historical Perspectives on Contemporary East Asia.* Cambridge: Harvard University Press, 2000.

Jameson, Fredric, and Masao Miyoshi, eds. *The Cultures of Globalization.* Durham, N.C.: Duke University Press, 1998.

Robertson, Roland. *Globalization: Social Theory and Global Culture.* London: Sage, 1992.

Schroedor, Ralph, ed. *Max Weber, Democracy, and Modernization.* London: Macmillan, 1998.

Tomlinson, John. *Globalization and Culture.* Chicago: University of Chicago Press, 1999.

Wilson, Rob, and Wimal Dissanayake, eds. *Global/Local: Cultural Production and the Transnational Imaginary.* Durham, N.C.: Duke University Press, 1996.

Part I

States of Modernities

CHAPTER I

Globalization and Youthful Subculture: The Chinese Sixth-Generation Films at the Dawn of the New Century

Jenny Kwok Wah Lau

A new generation of filmmakers from China has taken the world by surprise. Their work differs radically from that of their immediate predecessors, the world-renowned fifth-generation directors, such as Zhang Yimou and Chen Kaige.[1] Contrary to the fifth-generation directors, who employed an elegant craft to narrate subversive folklore and enjoyed the last moment of the state-supported studio system, these sixth-generation directors are unfortunate (or fortunate?) enough to be caught in a transitional period when significant changes are happening both in the cultural world and in the filmmaking industry. The sixth-generation filmmakers are the first group to grow up when China's open-door policy was full-fledged. In addition, while they were students at the Film Academy, the film industry of China was already changing from a socialist industry to a semi-market-driven business. This colossal structural transformation resulted in directors losing their stable production environment and working within a system that is still forming, a twilight zone of film production where no channels are proper or improper, clearly legal or illegal. The young sixth-generation directors are challenged to carve out unique ways of production simply to ensure their survival. Sometimes even the most elemental practice, such as location shooting in the city of Beijing, which involves city rules that no one really is clear about, can raise many bureaucratic eyebrows. At this confused stage the Chinese system has no clear way of funding or distributing and exhibiting these films; money from outside China finances many.

To complicate this political problem, the filmmakers of this new generation, with no nostalgia for the recent Chinese past, are modernist or even postmodernist in their view. Their films are literally products of the streets, steeped in realism and offering a raw and unprecedented look at attitudes and lifestyles in post-Tiananmen China. Such content does not encourage officials (the cultural police) to favor their works either. Some of their films are not shown in China. Without a large local audience the only hope of public recognition is through winning international prizes, and many have done so.

China's move toward a market economy has meant a substantial cutback of government support for the film industry, and the sixth-generation directors have had to garner financial and technical resources from outside the country. But the larger cultural-industrial question is: What does it mean to have a great number of the most energetic and creative filmmakers producing films that will not be shown to the Chinese?

This essay explores the cultural landscape that has shaped the life, art, and production practices of this group of filmmakers to discover the reasons behind and the effects of the incongruence between China's cultural system and its political system.[2]

Critics who tend to retain the cold-war paradigm champion the sixth-generation films as "dissident" by focusing on China's "oppressive" practice toward these cultural workers. While some of the films may have controversial content, categorizing them as dissident privileges a narrow political reading and neglects the multifaceted elements at work in them. Such pigeonholing reduces a complex real-life situation to a simplistic political narrative of the socialist world versus the "free" world.[3] Consequently, I prefer not to classify these works under the highly politicized category "dissident film" and take a more wholistic approach, attending to the details of their context and inquiring into other sources that contribute to the disharmony between the filmmakers and their cultural supervisors.

These films are best seen as a reflection of the cultural metamorphoses that China is experiencing at this juncture of centuries; an "uneven globalization" that has created sets of unsynchronized movements between its local cultural world, the economic world, and the political world, is among the most important factors that defines the dilemma of the sixth-generation filmmakers. Considering other major cultural movements in China, such as the arts and literature, helps demonstrate how the transnational factor shapes the formation of China's contemporary culture, and how modern lifestyles are reflected in the films and the filmmaking of this young generation.

Zhang Yuan and Legal Films in China

Among the sixth-generation filmmakers Zhang Yuan could be considered the first and leading director. His filmmaking career epitomizes the experience of the group, and an exploration of his filmmaking sheds light on the contemporary film world in the post-socialist economy and culture of China. Since Zhang graduated from the Beijing Film Academy in 1989, he has made about one film per year. The West has recognized him partly because his films consistently garner awards at international film festivals.[4] In particular, his film *East Palace, West Palace* caused an international dispute between the Cannes Film Festival and China. From the Chinese officials' point of view, the production procedure of this film was considered illegitimate (as was that of most of his films and many other sixth-generation films), and therefore neither his film nor he could participate at Cannes; the Chinese officials confiscated his passport. However, since the content of the film, which portrays gay life in China, was intolerably out of line with the Chinese official stand, one cannot but suspect that the real reason for China's rejection of the film was its content rather than its production process. The Cannes Film Festival committee insisted that it was a Chinese film and on the night of its screening staged a protest.

The issue of legality in filmmaking in China has been fluid, especially at the beginning of the 1990s. In the socialist past, the central government not only initiated and controlled film production but also owned the production, distribution, and exhibition networks. The Culture Ministry set annual production goals for the number and themes of films and their budgets. Creative personnel, mostly each studio's directors and writers, would plan films that adhered to these goals. A final script went first to the head of the studio, then to the China Film Bureau, which operated under the Culture Ministry and supervised all operations related to the filmmaking industry. Once it approved a script, the bureau would grant a permit for production; with the permit came the funds assigned to the film. The (government-owned) studio directly supervised and lent technical support to the production. The completed film then went to the bureau's Censorship Department for approval, a prerequisite for permission to show the film publicly. The film's next destination was the Distribution Department, another branch of the Film Bureau. A flat rate (about 1,000 rmb per copy before the Cultural Revolution, 30,000 rmb per copy during the early nineties) would be paid to the studio. Once permission for exhibition was granted, the entire distribution and profit-making end of the business was of little concern to the director, since his or her rewards were not related to the box office. Sometime before the film even went into distribution, the major creative personnel such as the director, scriptwriters, and actors received a "prize," not a bonus, whose amount depended on their rank. Whether or not the filmmaker would make another film and receive funding for his or her next film, depended not so much on the film's commercial success as on the production goals set by the central government, the director's political relationship with the studio head, the China Film Bureau officials, and the political climate.

In 1982 a new system joined the existing system, similar except for the method of funding some films. Each year the central government's Culture Ministry still set modest goals for themes and production quotas. However, the government would fund only some of these envisioned films and encouraged studios to raise money from outside investors. The permit-seeking process for production and distribution remained similar, although the shooting permit now went not to the individual filmmaker but to a government studio under which the film could be produced. The filmmaker could either seek full technical support from the studio through which the permit was granted or shoot the film with outside equipment and personnel, a freedom made possible by high-tech facilities newly available on the open market.

It is clear then that since the early eighties, China has been gradually abandoning the socialist system of production. Capitalistic economic practices were introduced in the form of encouraging private investment and allowing production activities outside of the government studios, but the China Film Bureau remained the sole distributor of all the films produced in China until 1989, when distribution was opened up to private companies. The significance of the new system of filmmaking lay in the greater production freedom it allowed.

What remains intact from the old system is state control over the content of films shown to the public. Even when money is available, the filmmaker still has to secure a permit from the China Film and Television Bureau (the former Film Bureau) through one of the government-owned film studios, whose producer has to submit the script for approval. With prior censorship by the China Film and Television Bureau, the film may be shown both inside and outside of China. Without it, a film may still be produced, but its public screening is banned.

Such were the complex conditions under which Zhang Yuan worked after he graduated from the Beijing Film Academy. When he was planning his first film, *MaMa* (Mother, 1990), a story about disabled people in China, his major financial support came from the China Association of the Handicapped. This film was made with the permission of the bureau and then lost its distributor, who presumed that it would not appeal to a general audience. Its sole screening occurred at the Beijing Film Academy until it was sent outside China, where it immediately drew attention from international critics. The film won the Jury Award and a Special Mention at France's Festival des Trois Continents in Nantes. Later, when the film was shown on China's television, it was well received.

While *MaMa* was a "legal" film, Zhang's next film, *Beijing Bastards* (1992) was not. *Beijing Bastards*, written by Tang Danian, starred China's most popular rock singer, Cui Jian, who was allowed to perform but banned from broadcasting in China. A collage of the lives of a number of Beijing underground artists, the film was largely funded by Zhang and Cui himself. Knowing that this theme would not be easily accepted by the bureau, Zhang decided not to pursue a production permit but shot the film on location throughout Beijing with no studio involvement. Postproduction was done in France, with help from the French Cultural Council. Yet the film was considered illegal by China and was never shown there.[5] Distributed in France and other Western countries, it won prizes at various festivals. Its international distribution offended China, which prohibited Zhang from shooting films nationwide. But it is hard to suppress the artistic impulse.

After *Beijing Bastards*, Zhang shot *The Square* (1994), a feature documentary about Tiananmen Square, which won a Jury Award at the Hawaii Film Festival. Production money came from Hong Kong and France. *Sons*, in 1995, won the Tiger Award at Rotterdam. Then came the clash with Chinese officialdom over the showing of *East Palace, West Palace* (1996) at Cannes.

Zhang Yuan is one of a group of some thirty young filmmakers suppressed by the authorities that includes scriptwriters, photographers, sound engineers, actors, and so forth. Most graduated from the Beijing Film Academy and have been actively pursuing every possible avenue to make films that, based on my conversations with them, express their views, even when they contradict the official line.

Filmmakers often disagree with their governments, and in China this disagreement is not unique even to the sixth-generation filmmakers. Films with content unacceptable to the government began with the fifth-generation directors, among them *Judou* by Zhang Yimou, *Blue Kite* by Tian Zhangzhang, and *Farewell My Concubine* by Chen Kaige. Nor was foreign investment in production new with the sixth-generation filmmakers. A number of fifth-generation directors, especially Zhang Yimou and Chen Kaige, attracted money from outside China after their international success, most notably from Japan, Taiwan, and France. However, with the exception of *Blue Kite,* all of the fifth-generation films were "legally" made with Film Bureau permits through an official film studio; they were nevertheless banned in China for awhile because of their content. Yet many of the sixth-generation film directors cannot even secure a permit to start "proper" production. What is it about these films that prevents the Chinese government from issuing them permits?

What Sets the Sixth-Generation Films Apart

While both the fifth- and sixth-generation filmmakers question a worldview overdetermined by political discourses and attempt to reinvestigate the reality of life, striking differences separate them.

No Epics

The classical form of larger-than-life heroes that characterized many fifth-generation films made before the mid-nineties (perhaps with the exception of Huang Jianxin)—tragic or otherwise (albeit much reduced in scale compared to the heroes of the Cultural Revolution formulaic films)—disappeared in the sixth-generation films.[6] Gone are not only the traditional heroes, but also the idea of heroism itself, the traditional form of storytelling, and the fifth-generation international trademark epic that conveys an almost prophetic insight through the use of spectacle. In my conversation with some sixth-generation filmmakers, it became clear that they did not appreciate this kind of formalism but had turned their interest to the truly ordinary. Visually, they strive for utter realism. Narratively, they make no attempt to create extraordinary characters. (Fifth-generation films, even in stories of ordinary folk, such as farmers, regular citizens, or villagers, made them unusual or heroic characters.) But by rejecting the "grand themes"

Beijing Bastards, directed by Zhang Yuan, 1992.

approach, the sixth generation rejects a major premise of traditional socialist art; they are sometimes labeled nihilists.[7]

An example of these nonepic films is *Beijing Bastards,* freely structured around the daily life of a few young men. With the exception of the rock singer Cui himself, who can be considered the main character in a loose narrative centered around his music career and his problems with his girlfriends, none of the other men participate in any dramatic plot. The film depicts some minor encounters between them as they spend leisurely time together drinking, playing chess, chatting, skirmishing over money, and so forth. There is no traditional protagonist or antagonist, neither the high drama of a hero trope nor the journey trope of an ordinary man. As one of the young men, Tang, mutters: "I just want to live in an ordinary way. I do not want to be in the mainstream [of trying to be idealistic or extraordinary]." This scene, shot in a documentary interview style, conveys a preference for the naked reality of living, however unstructured, over the mythologized grand narrative of a heroic/villainous life.

Cinematically, the film is full of apparently unrelated documentary footage of the streets of Beijing: crowds surging, bicycles rolling by, children running around. But it is exactly because of these "unrelated" shots and scenes that the film requires a reading distinct from that of the fiction film typical of China's traditional socialist cinema. The film as a whole tells no story but creates an impression of "simply living." In some parts, it resembles a diary, a collage of not necessarily related events in the lives of its characters. In other parts, the film resembles music video, where much of the meaning must be deduced from the lyrics.

Films such as *The Postman* (a postman who secretly reads the letters that he delivers), *The Beads* (the lives of asylum patients), and *The Days* (the lives of some artists) share a common theme: people living in ways that are a combination of what is imposed on them, what they desire, and what they can afford. No individual necessarily has any preconceived, unified, or consistent high ideal or goal (freedom/propriety, capitalism/socialism, traditional/anti-traditional). For example, in *The Postman,* while the main character's mundane job of sorting and delivering mail allows him to sneak into other peoples' lives, nothing dramatic happens. His indecorous practice is interrupted only by a few unexciting sexual encounters, and the sound track echoes with the mechanical thumps of a postal clerk stamping an endless pile of letters, an apt accompaniment for the postman's monotonous life.

As in *The Postman,* so in *Beijing Bastards,* which neither champions the rock singer's sexual life as free love (positive or Westernized?) nor criticizes it as irresponsible (negative)—few of these films pass judgment on their characters. Again, not only is the didactic model of the socialist hero versus the selfish villain absent, but also the score's lyrics (a major part of the film) repeatedly reject the heroism of the revolution. In place of the sacred socialist mission and the grand ideal of good overcoming evil is a return to the reality of one's experience, what one can truly know. The film ends with the lyrics from Cui's song: "Year upon year the wind blows, changing in form but never going away. How much pain to how many people, revolution after revolution. . . . Suddenly there is a mass movement in front of my eyes. Changing my life like a revolution. A girl gives her love to me. And it's like wind and rain in my face." This is the apparent point of the film.

Stream of Life and Disengagement

Some scholars label this new form of film "stream of life" cinema, a term attributed to the new trend in art and literature that began in the mid-eighties in China. As described by Maria Galikowski, author of *Art and Politics in China,* "stream of life" art offered "intimate and personal portrayals of 'low-key' non-political subjects" and was a reaction against the overt politicization of the traditional socialist art/media.[8] Even though the fifth-generation films are untraditional and critical, their themes—heroic patriotism (*One and Eight*), transcendental faith or loss of faith in communism (*Yellow Earth*), transgression of the thousands of years of Confucian social rules (*Judou*), and so on—remain associated with the grand theme of reflecting on cultural roots or socialist tradition. The sixth-generation films, on the other hand, have developed a variety of alternative narratives.

A subplot in *Beijing Bastards* raises the issue of creative freedom. In the beginning of the film a landlord is asking a rock band in the middle of a practice session to move out. Their apparent financial problem is later aggravated by city officials' unwillingness to provide a performance site for their concert. The scaffolding that the musicians themselves put up for the show is torn down by police during a rehearsal. But the plot, full of conflict potential, does not develop in the direction of epic drama. Nor is there a moralistic delving into whether the police or the artists are right or wrong. The camera continues to capture the ordinariness of life; the artists continue to sing whenever and wherever they can, sometimes on a stage, sometimes along the streets. This theme of creative freedom is new in Chinese cinema. *The Postman* is another film that addresses unusual themes—privacy, a double life led in a supposedly moral society, and the boredom of ordinary living—in a nondramatic and intimate way.

The sixth-generation films, by leaving the socialist discourse behind, also affirm their belief in its irrelevance for the daily life of contemporary China. Unlike the fifth-generation films made before the early nineties, which criticized the mythologies created by the central political discourse, the sixth-generation films are outright oblivious to these mythologies. If the Film Bureau appears open-minded in allowing the critical fifth-generation films to be shown, it faces a different challenge with the sixth-generation filmmakers—not criticism but disengagement from the official political discourse. It is this disengagement, accompanied by a "disorganized" (or fragmented) variation of narratives, that has befuddled the officials.

Free Market or Globalization

The Chinese film theorist and critic Wu Kat was partly correct in pointing out that the sixth-generation films are more "personal" because "a free market economy has enabled the filmmakers to use their personal experience to interpret reality rather than following a party interpretation."[9] But by collapsing the controversial issues of the sixth-generation films into a matter of "personal" versus "party" expression, Wu does not go far enough. The sixth-generation films are personal in that they usually represent the filmmakers' own vision and do not pretend to convey grand universal truths, as some of the traditional socialist films did. But these films also stand out in their wide variety of subject matter, perspectives, and style. Most significantly, they represent an important cultural product resulting from the most central social change in China in the past twenty years, the process of globalization. The sixth-generation films not only reflect China's modernization but also participate actively in its production. Unfortunately, the slower pace of change in the state's political world has created tremendous tension with its new cultural world. Perhaps by sorting out the social conditions that produced filmmakers with a significantly new interpretation of reality, one can begin to understand the crux of the dispute between the artists and the state.

Social Environment

Most of the sixth-generation filmmakers graduated from the Beijing Film Academy around 1989, young people born at the end of the Great Cultural Revolution who never experienced the direct impact of its idealism and heroism. By the time they hit their teenage years, China in 1979 had already opened its doors to the "free" world. Their adolescence and early adulthood were filled first with popular songs and TV (and later movies) from Hong Kong, and later with the Western media that brought in Hollywood movies, CNN News, BBC News, and other North American and European cultural expressions. As a result of transnational communications the young filmmakers shared significant global experiences and memories with the rest of the world, such as the demolition of the Berlin Wall, the collapse of the Soviet Union, and the economic boom and later downturn of East Asia. As the authors of *Global Modernities* predicted, the globalization of the media has created a heightened sense not only of the "outside world" but also of "the world as one community." Obviously, this has had tremendous impact on how these young people interpret their immediate surroundings. For example, *Beijing Bastards,* a film filled with songs that question traditional interpretations of history, also affirms the relation between Chinese and Western culture. *The Days* is framed within the larger context of interlocational economics, namely art sales between Hong Kong and mainland China.

During their university years, most of the sixth-generation filmmakers spent their time in the by then metropolitan capital, Beijing, and visited nightclubs and bars frequented by Westerners. The Film Academy began to screen many foreign films. For example, between 1985 and 1989, when these filmmakers were trained, the Film Academy staged a Japanese Film Festival of more than forty films, a Latin American Film Festival, an East European Film Festival, and so forth.[10] These events not only introduced students to foreign films but helped them establish personal friendships with foreign artists, administrators, film scholars, and critics who followed or represented these festivals in China. One result of such intercultural interaction is, as described by Jan Pieterse, an "intensification of world wide social relationships (which will influence even the most local or even personal matters)."[11] Rock star Cui Jian, who broke away from traditional orchestral music, or Zhang Yuan, who would not have been able to finish the postproduction of his film *Beijing Bastards* without the help of the French Cultural Ministry, are evidence of the concrete impact of this global momentum in China. The translocational (or transnational) factor is important in the sixth-generation films, for many were made or screened with the help of international connections.

The central story of *Beijing Bastards* epitomizes the transnational condition of the city. Obviously, rock music itself is a quintessential symbol of the West. Other references—the ubiquitous international television news in the house, the mention of business contracts with pop-song producers in Taiwan, and so forth—point to the connections between life in Beijing and the rest of the world. This sensitivity to and integration with the world community did not begin with the sixth-generation filmmakers but with their predecessor artists and writers. During the eighties, when these filmmakers were growing up, a number of significant cultural movements resulted from the extensive exchanges between China and the outside world, mostly the West—large-scale museum or gallery exhibitions of foreign arts and scholarly visits that introduced foreign philosophies, critical thinking, literature, and so on—that flooded China with untraditional ideas.[12] At the same time, within China's own art and literary world, daring political commentary began to appear as early as 1979. The sensation created by the first unofficial artists' group, Stars, which held its first (scar art) exhibition in Beijing in 1979, is an indication of the Chinese public's interest and their anticipation (under the promise of Deng Xiaoping) of a new cultural era. The political commentaries on the scar art of 1979 quickly spawned a spectrum of interests, including an interest in ordinary life and the life of minorities, as well as powerful avant-garde movements in the eighties. The first was the '85 Movement, also known as the New Wave, which reflected a patriotic desire to evaluate the Chinese traditional cultural ethos and the reality of the immediate, ordinary environment as opposed to that described by the government. In 1989, the China/Avant-garde Exhibition, held in the China Art Gallery in Beijing, continued to question Chinese tradition while creating new concepts and new arts. Both art movements were heavily influenced by Western techniques, ideas, and philosophies.[13]

The spirit of experimentation and radical thinking in the arts continued despite official interference, and by the early 1990s the new avant-garde movement included experimental theater, behavioral (or performance) art, and installation art, creating unprecedented variety on the Chinese art scene. Historians of Chinese art, such as Chris Driessen and Heidi van Mierlo, consider the eighties to be the period when Chinese art made a decisive break with centuries-long tradition; by the early nineties, contemporary Chinese art was born.

Yet the avant-garde art of the nineties departed from that of the eighties: The collective memory of history, especially of the Cultural Revolution, and the examination of national cultural tradition disappeared. Instead, art was characterized by individualism and irreverence for classical heroism.[14]

China's reconnection with the rest of the world and its promise for more intellectual and economic freedom in the early eighties created a utopian mood in the post–Cultural Revolution era. Scar literature or wounded literature began simultaneously with scar art, a reassertion of humanistic thinking that recanted and condemned the heresy of the Cultural Revolution. This movement quickly metamorphosed into the much acclaimed reflective literature and later the root-searching literature of the mid- and late eighties. Again, as in the art world, the literature of this time differed from traditional socialist literature in both techniques and themes, searching for cultural origins and tradition and focusing on reality as experienced by ordinary people. Nevertheless, as the economic plan suffered setbacks time and again, and as intellectual freedom was cut back throughout the decade, the idealism of the artists and writers began to wane. Even before the Tiananmen Square incident in 1989, it was obvious that awareness of the "progress" of the outside world, both materially and "culturally," and the fading hope of similar progress in China had brought a widespread disillusionment. The nineties turned out to be an era of obliviousness toward both history and culture.

Although the sixth-generation filmmakers, at that early point of their careers, may not have been aware of the first experimentation, the continuous influx of arts and ideas from the outside and the vehement response of the Chinese artists and writers toward new thinking fueled the entire creative world. The indigenous movements in the arts and literature had a profound effect on the younger filmmakers, partly because of their personal relationships with some of the contemporary artists, and partly because of the tra-

dition of Chinese filmmakers, who consider themselves artists (as opposed to pure en-
tertainers), sharing with the other arts a cultural mission of having something to say to
the audience. It is, therefore, not surprising that the Chinese film world followed the
artists' path, and that the fifth-generation made reflective or root-searching films. Examples are *Red Sorghum* and *Judou,* which, among many themes, reassessed traditional
and socialist thinking on sexuality. The sixth-generation films bear some resemblance
to both the avant-garde and the "stream of life" art and literature. This accounts for the
unique condition in China in which opening up to the outside world, especially to Western media, has not created a hegemonic form of Hollywood entertainment filmmaking.
In fact, although there is obvious commercial imitation, the major products of the sixth-
generation filmmakers display a much more serious cultural concern.[15]

The filmmakers' interaction with the outside world obviously encouraged alternative
ways of thinking. However, as Roland Robertson has noted, the increasing interaction
between different cultures, which constitutes the very dynamics of globalization, does
not necessarily generate cultural homogenization or a cultural hegemony from the West
alone, but also heterogenization or heightened sensitivity to one's local culture.[16] This
description is particularly relevant to the current film culture in China. Although some
sixth-generation films have decidedly international themes, such as the issue of gay
rights in *East Palace, West Palace,* or humanitarian issues in *The Beads,* these films also
reflect local elements. In *Beijing Bastards,* the extensive documentary footage of Beijing
streets—traffic, street peddlers, two people fighting for a public telephone, old women
looking out for small children playing outside their homes in the evening, bicycles cruis-
ing across Tiananmen Square with the Forbidden City as background, rainy days and
sunny days, daytime and nighttime scenes, and so forth—strongly anchors the narrative
in a specific locale. Similarly, the film's characters are highly familiar with their environment. In one scene, Tang sits by the side of the street next to the shoemaker, who is
fixing one of his shoes. When his friend sees him, they holler across the street at each
other. Soon Tang hops over with one foot shoeless to meet his friend. In another scene,
two friends come out of a bar slightly drunk and get into a skirmish. Then they wander
idly around the city all night. From the ease with which they interact with each other
and their surroundings, the audience can believe that they are the city's true natives. The
film itself raises the issue of localness and foreignness directly near its end, when a new
band appears in a bar, which makes the rock singer (Cui) and his friends jealous. They
bitterly criticize the new singer as "a Chinese coming back from overseas [the United
States]," claiming that "if he had been good enough, he would not have had to come
back." With this subtle and clever twist, the film not only says that rock music is not
the sole property of the West but also identifies the new singer's problem as being from
the West and therefore lacking localness.

In this sense, *Beijing Bastards* takes the world as a whole and does not divide it up
according to the old East-West dichotomy. The only categories are the local and the non-
local. Similarly, *East Palace* depicts the very specific local Chinese police view of homo-
sexuality, and *The Beads* the idea of insanity and the medical profession. This scenario

of a global culture within a localized context, which first appeared in the art movements during the eighties, has impacted the sixth-generation filmmakers, some of whom later produced films of similar orientation.

Another experience that separates the fifth-generation filmmakers from their younger colleagues is that although the former grew up in different parts of China, because of the structural and ideological uniformity of society at that time, they shared similar experiences and were fed similar interpretations of them. For instance, many had been sent to rural parts of China during the Cultural Revolution. The fifth-generation films, especially between 1982 and the early 1990s, such as *One and Eight, Yellow Earth, Children's King, Red Sorghum, On the Hunting Ground, Horse Thief, Sacrifice Youth, Old Well,* and *Judou,* like scar literature and reflective literature, share common political and cultural themes. This is not the case with the sixth-generation filmmakers, who grew up in the open-door-policy era when a much more variegated scene quickly replaced cultural uniformity. The influx of different cultures and the relative freedom to pick and choose created a collection of subcultures. These changes are also reflected in the young filmmakers' films, which vary in theme and style, although they are unified in their interest in the urban (as opposed to the fifth-generation 1980s films' focus on the rural) and grouped under the umbrella term "sixth-generation films." This variety also accords with their metropolitan environment, in which plurality is the norm.

Judging from the cultural environment, there is reason to believe that the sixth-generation filmmakers did not necessarily set out to abandon socialist idealism and become "dissidents," a description to which they themselves strongly object. Rather, in their environment, socialist idealism is only one of many ideas that they can choose to respond to, and one that has not caught much of their interest. Instead of seeing their films as antagonistic to socialist ideals, one can view them as reflecting a kind of nonrecognition of such ideals. Thus, the dispute between the filmmakers and the authorities could be interpreted less as a conflict than as a miscommunication in which the authorities cannot see the irrelevance of their own paradigms. It is a combined ideological and generational gap between the cultural world of the young, the pluralistic, and the globally local, and the established, the uniform, and the traditionally local. While the cultural world has moved beyond what socialism can contain, the political/economic system has not kept pace. The shift from a state-supported film industry to one supported by private investments has not changed the socialist nature of the medium, for the state still has substantial control over exhibition, the ultimate purpose of making a film. This peculiar situation has created difficulties for some cultural workers in Beijing whose immediate subculture is largely composed of elements unrelated to socialist practices.

When I talked to some of the sixth-generation filmmakers, it was obvious that they did not consider themselves to be "dissident" filmmakers. Nor did they admire the heroism implied in that label. Similar to the tenor of their films, these filmmakers simply relate their impression or comment on life in their immediate environment. But the naked realism exposed in the description of some truly ordinary people whose lives do not fit into any set discourse or grand Party narrative becomes part of the filmmakers' problem. Consequently, even the most inoffensive film, such as *The Postman,* can become offensive to the government.

As a temporary solution, the sixth-generation filmmakers can show their films outside China. But while international distribution becomes their major source of revenue, there is no established international distribution network for their works. Even winning international awards may not help unless these come from big-name festivals. With such a bleak future looming, some of these young filmmakers have tried to strike a compromise. One example is the film *Growing Up* (or *How Steel Was Tempered,* 1998), produced by the fifth-generation director Tian Zhangzhang, which secured a production permit through the Beijing Film Studio. Although the finished film was eventually screened in China, its final version required seven reeditings to satisfy the Film and Television Bureau.[17] According to some of the sixth-generation filmmakers, the Film and Television Bureau has added a new set of policies that govern the publicity of their films, in addition to censorship. For example, for a category called "films of doubtful content," the bureau issues "permission for screening, but not for publicity, or minimal budget for publicity." Since without publicity a film is almost doomed to fail financially, this policy will seriously affect the careers of filmmakers. Another category, "permission for screening but not for entering international film festivals," includes *Growing Up.* For some sixth-generation filmmakers, this little crack in the wall of bureaucratic control provides no working ground for their creations.

Perhaps now is the time to ask why the Chinese government seems so out of sync with its cultural workers. Without applying the cold-war presumption of total dictatorship in a socialist country, one can view this as a conflict between the economic need for stability and the metropolitan need for liberalization. Ever since the late seventies, as China focused on improving its material condition, three economic classes have arisen that at times may have different or conflicting interests: the rich business class, who reside mostly in urban or semi-urban areas; the middle class of the large metropolitan cities; and the very poor of the rural areas. On the issue of political homogeneity, the very rich and the very poor seem to share the same need, stability, for the sake of economic opportunity. Members of the metropolitan middle class are different. Having earned their position in society mostly by learning skills and knowledge via an institutional education, having achieved some material security, and being relatively sophisticated in cultural matters through both education and exposure to the outside world, they want more intellectual freedom. Most of the sixth-generation filmmakers fit into this category. Yet, China, a country of considerable size and complexity, must strive for a balance even in view of the existing tension. The challenges China faces are enormous and constant. However, one need not see liberal thinking as a threat to economic growth. In fact, depending on the ingenuity of the entrepreneurs and the politicians, liberal thinking can stimulate such growth. One could interpret the unpretentious reality portrayed by the sixth-generation filmmakers as not only a criticism of society but also an insightful recommendation of what could be done for society's betterment. One could see their sensitivity and creativity as a resource that will help move the nation forward.[18]

At this moment a significant number of films made by sixth-generation filmmakers are floating around planet earth, waiting for an audience; they are hard to come by even for anxious critics. In spite of *Cahier du Cinema*'s substantial 1999 review and a relatively extensive retrospective of their works at the Lincoln Center for Performing Arts in 2001, their unavailability to general audiences renders these films unknown to most of the world.[19] Will the sixth-generation filmmaker succumb to the immense pressure of restriction? Should one predict a disappearance of the sixth-generation underground films due to political pressure and distribution problems? In light of Zhang Yuan's continuing success in international festivals, will China consent to show at least some of the sixth-generation award-winning films? Whatever the future holds, this group of uncompromising films comprises one of the most valuable documents on the cultural conditions of contemporary China.

Notes

1. Although there are debates around the terms "fifth generation" and "sixth generation," the genealogical division is still recognized in the Film Academy. See note 6.

2. Not all of the sixth-generation films were banned. Some that were screened, including *Weekend Lover* (1994) and *Fogged Youth* (1996), attracted a fair level of attention from the critics in China.

3. Obviously, some sixth-generation films involve themes and comments that may not be to the taste of some government officials. However, I have shown some of these films at a number of conferences, and most mainland Chinese, quite perplexed by the government's ban, agreed that they do not seem to have a strong and explicit political agenda or to be offensive. But at a conference I attended, it seemed that some European scholars disagreed and labeled them political "dissident films."

4. Zhang Yuan feature films are *MaMa* (1990), *Beijing Bastards* (Beijing Za Zhong, 1992), *The Square* (Guang Chang, documentary, 1994), *Sons* (Er Zi, 1995), *East Palace, West Palace* (Dong Gong Xi Gong, 1996), *Crazy English* (Feng Kuang Ying Yu, 1998), and *17 Years* (Guo Nian Hui Jia, 1999). In addition, Zhang has shot a number of short films and videos.

5. The 1998 Fulbright senior scholar from the China Film Achieve, Wang Rui, who was the visiting scholar at the Film School of Ohio University, told me he had not seen or heard of the film before.

6. The corpus of the fifth-generation films used for comparison here and in the rest of the essay refers to those made before the mid-nineties. Since then there have been some changes in their story form and style, for example, *Not One Less* (1998) by Zhang Yimou.

7. This "grand themes" policy (*ticai jueding lun*), which began during the Great Leap Forward movement in the 1950s, has always generated role models, heroes, and epics in films.

8. Galikowski, *Arts and Politics in China*, 199.

9. Wu Kat, "Trends of Films in the Time of Change: Chinese Films 1996–97," *Contemporary Chinese Film Forum*, 1998, 11–22. (The *Forum* is an internal journal of the China Film Achieve.)

10. I have an account of these festivals from my student Wang Weiyen, a student in the Film Academy during the same period.

11. Jan Nederveen Pieterse, "Globalization as Hybridization," in Featherstone, Lash, and Robertson, *Global Modernities,* 48.

12. On the gallery and museum exhibitions, see Noth, Pohlmann, and Reschke, *China Avant-garde,* and Driessen and van Mierlo, *Another Long March.*

13. See Driessen and van Mierlo, *Another Long March.*

14. Ibid. Chinese literature scholar Wang Jing presents a useful description of the political environment that caused the emergence of Chinese avant-garde literature that could also apply to the rise of the avant-garde movement in arts and film. See Wang, *China's Avant-garde Fiction.*

15. China has recently signed an extensive U.S. trade agreement that includes an increase of the import quota for foreign films from ten to fifty. This may adversely affect China's "cultural" filmmaking and encourage Hollywood-type entertainment filmmaking.

16. Roland Robertson, "Globalization: Time, Space, and Homogeneity-Heterogeneity," in Featherstone, Lash, and Robertson, *Global Modernities,* 25–44.

17. My student Wang Weiyen, who was in the sound crew, said she could hardly recognize the story in the final version.

18. Here I am merely commenting on how the Chinese government could value the country's own artists, not suggesting that these artists themselves need a nationalistic reason for their art.

19. *Cahiers du Cinema,* special issue, "Made in China," May 1999.

Selected Bibliography

Andrew, Julia, and Kuiyi Shen. *Modernity and Tradition in the Art of Twentieth Century China.* New York: Guggenheim Museum, 1998.

Driessen, Chris, and Heidi van Mierlo, eds. *Another Long March: Chinese Conceptual and Installation Art in the Nineties.* Breda, Netherlands: Fundament Foundation, 1997.

Featherstone, Mike, ed. *Spaces of Culture: City Nation.* London: Sage, 1999.

Featherstone, Mike, Scott Lash, and Roland Robertson, eds. *Global Modernities.* London: Sage, 1995.

Galikowski, Maria. *Arts and Politics in China.* Hong Kong: Chinese University Press, 1998.

Giddens, A. *The Consequences of Modernity.* Stanford, Calif.: Stanford University Press, 1990.

Noth, Jochen, Wolfger Pohlmann, and Kai Reschke, eds. *China Avant-garde: Counter Currents in Art and Culture.* Hong Kong: Oxford University Press, 1994.

Tomlinson, John. *Globalization and Culture.* Chicago: University of Chicago Press, 1999.

Wang, Jing. *China's Avant-garde Fiction.* Durham, N.C.: Duke University Press, 1998.

——. *High Culture Fever: Politics, Aesthetics, and Ideology in Deng's China.* Berkeley: University of California Press, 1996.

Zhang, Xudong. *Chinese Modernism in the Era of Reforms.* Durham, N.C.: Duke University Press, 1997.

CHAPTER 2

Marx or Market: Chinese Rock and the Sound of Fury

Jeroen de Kloet

Strike a Pose

More than fifteen years have passed since "Nothing to My Name" by China's first rock star, Cui Jian, marked the beginning of the rise of a spectacular youth subculture in China. The old Mao suits—then signifying conformity to Party rule—were replaced by leather jackets, Communist revolutionary classics were transformed into punk. Music was turned into a site of political struggle. It is not a coincidence that documentaries about the Beijing rock scene always include images of the 1989 June 4 demonstrations. The provocative poses struck by the artists were warmly welcomed as the first signs of China's path to democracy. The anger of a government official who in 1987, after hearing Cui Jian's version of the revolutionary classic "Southern Muddy Bay" (Nanniwan), banned his performances and thus forced Cui Jian to perform underground, strengthened the impression that rock symbolizes the struggle to free oneself from the Communist burden on the way toward a democratic society.[1] Cui Jian was the first of many rock singers who daringly challenged the dominant culture. The ban of his music in 1987 was to be followed by many other incidents. In the spring of 1989, singer He Yong expressed his anger while performing on the streets of Beijing. He screamed (from "Garbage Dump"):

The world we are living in	What they eat is conscience
Is like a garbage dump	What they shit are thoughts
People are just like worms	Is there hope is there hope
Fighting and grabbing	Is there hope is there hope.

Originally published as Jeroen de Kloet, "Let Him Fucking See the Green Smoke Beneath My Groin: The Mythology of Chinese Rock Music," in *Postmodernism and China*, ed. Arif Dirlik and Xudong Zhang, pp. 239–274. Copyright 2000, Duke University Press. All rights reserved. Reprinted with permission.

His radical sarcastic nihilism is politically subversive in a country where one is supposed to support the construction of a healthy socialist society. That these lyrics passed censorship in 1994 is still considered a miracle by the record company. That the accompanying video clip, depicting He Yong caught in a cage desperately trying to escape, was banned in China was no surprise at all.

The military tanks that violently ended the student protests in 1989 did not crush the rock culture. On the contrary, the first part of the 1990s showed a rapid growth of Chinese rock, accompanied by conflicts and repression. After bursting into tears while reporting the June 4 massacre, China's Central Television reporter Wei Hua was fired and became China's first female rock singer. A stadium tour of Cui Jian was cut short in 1991 after government officials got scared of the enthusiastic response of the audience. Bands constantly censored their lyrics in order to get approval from the Ministry of Culture. After making fun of the Communist model worker Li Suli at the end of 1996, He Yong was not allowed to perform for three years. These examples reflect the subversive history of Chinese rock. The singers are true heroes, fighting for a democratic China, disturbing Party bureaucrats with their electric guitars. It is hardly surprising that Chinese media condemn the local rock culture, which is considered "unacceptable for Chinese society."[2] Rock is seen as a sign of unhealthy spiritual pollution from the West and as a cultural form that by its very nature remains incompatible with Chinese culture.[3] Deng Xiaoping had already warned that "capitalist lifestyles should not run wild in our country. It is unbearable to corrupt the younger generation with the declining culture from the West."[4] In October 1997 the Party launched a new set of regulations to strengthen its control over artistic performances, in order "to advance the construction of our socialist spiritual culture . . . and improve the excellent culture of our nation and enrich the people's spiritual life."[5] The new regulations further limited the freedom of rock musicians.

It goes without saying that not only the musical content but also the imagery and lifestyles of the rockers are considered by the Party to be anything but enriching to the spiritual life of the common people. The red-dyed hair of punk singer Gao Wei, the drug use of female star Luo Qi, the mysterious death of guitar player Zhang Ju of the rock group Tang Dynasty—all are miles away from the idealized lifestyle of the familiar Communist model soldier. From the fringe of society, Chinese rock challenges, subverts, disturbs, and maybe even changes contemporary Chinese culture. The dissonant voices stirred up the tranquil waters of Chinese politics in the 1990s. To quote China's controversial writer Wang Shuo: "What didn't happen through June 4th will happen through Rock."[6]

This highly selective, romantic reading of Chinese rock corresponds with popular notions of rock as a countercultural movement. It suits our desire to see dominant ideologies subverted. It strengthens the stereotypical image (among other stereotypes) of China as a severely repressive society with a cruel political regime, and in doing so it indirectly celebrates liberal Western society. It is a product of what I call rock mythology.[7] This mythology, as I argue, functions as the glue that binds producers, musicians, and audiences together. It is the basis of the production of the rock culture. In this essay I aim to deconstruct this mythology and search for different readings of this culture. In doing so, I employ an eclectic approach in which I combine theories of subcultures, popular music studies, and Chinese writings—both popular and academic—on rock music, as well as my own observations in Beijing. This is a modest attempt to develop a de-mythologized reading—or, better, readings—of the Chinese rock culture that will give special attention to its fragmented nature and the perceived ideological opposition of rock and pop.

Rock Mythology

Chinese rock can easily be read as genuinely subversive and oppositional. "Since its release, the wide availability of this music of anger and frustration has continued to empower opposition to the regime. Yaogun yinyue's [Chinese rock] role as an objectification of anti-government feeling—as a resource for use in political opposition—has intensified."[8] Chinese rock is said to subvert Chinese politics, just as rock from communist countries is said to have resulted in the collapse of communism.[9] Václav Havel, former president of Czechoslovakia, even claimed that the revolution began in the rock scene.[10] Apart from being a projection of the researcher's romantic desire to see ideologies subverted, rock mythology, as it appears in both academic and journalistic discourses, is based on several assumptions.

It's Subcultural . . .

"Rock culture" is seen as a monolithic whole, whereas the opposite is the case. The bias in theories of subcultures toward the deviant, countercultural, and masculine is also prevalent in accounts of the Beijing rock culture.[11] I consider it a highly fragmented subculture, with multiple relations to its wider cultural milieu and with constantly shifting, permeable boundaries. It is a fragmented cultural practice in both style and degree of commitment of musicians and audiences. Music styles range from folk music to heavy metal. Some address wider social issues and others are very introspective. It is a fluid cultural practice; personal as well as collective identities are constantly being negotiated.

It's Political . . .

In journalistic and political discourses in the West, Chinese politics is often interpreted as ideologically uniform, as absolutely totalitarian.[12] However, Chinese politics is characterized by factional struggles within the Party. At the very least, one can distinguish progressive factions, who desire further modernization of the political system; conservative factions, who have a strong nostalgia for "real" communism; and liberal factions, who have a strong focus on economic growth.[13] Party hegemony is therefore by no means homogeneous and internally uncontested.

It's Controversial . . .

Rock's controversiality seems to be "proven" by the numerous examples of its censorship by the Party. Yet, like Chinese politics, censorship is too easily considered total and consistent, whereas in practice it is constantly being contested and negotiated by artists, producers, and publishers.

It's Still Political . . .

By definition, rock is seen as incompatible with socialism. There are no reasons to believe this to be true. Rather than criticizing socialism, rock often challenges broader societal norms. According to Jolanta Pekacz, in Eastern Europe the state actually succeeded in domesticating rock, and relations between the state and rock were more often symbiotic than hostile.[14] There is no state funding in China for rock, nor do presidents express their appreciation of it (as did Gorbachev). But state officials are not by definition hostile toward rock. The Ministry of Culture sponsored an antipiracy concert in October 2000 at which Cui Jian performed, rock band Hei Bao was allowed to perform in Tibet in 1995,[15] musicians are allowed to leave the country for performances, and even a rock music school is permitted to operate in Beijing.

It's Cultural . . .

Chinese rock is sometimes interpreted and valued in relation to the high-culture versus low-culture dichotomy. Partly because of its strong links with other cultural practices, such as avant-garde art and modern literature, rock is often conceived as belonging to the "liberating," "enlightening" high arts as opposed to the "oppressing" low arts, such as Gangtai pop (the commercial pop music from Hong Kong and Taiwan). It is a pertinacious yet false approach, based on outdated theories of the Frankfurter Schüle.[16] Cantopop is too often reduced to an overtly commercial, noncreative expression, which ignores its musical and textual complexities, its diversity, its reception by audiences, and the contradictory dynamics of commodification.

It's Authentic . . .

Closely related to the last point is the issue of authenticity. Artists are often considered gifted, highly talented persons who are always ready to express their authentic emotions. From this perspective, rock, in contrast to pop, is generally considered an authentic expression of personal feelings, a musician's testimony to his or her anger, sufferings, and personal struggles. However, I will contend with Becker that "works of art . . . are not the products of individual makers, 'artists' who possess a rare and special gift. They are, rather, joint products of all the people who cooperate via an art world's characteristic conventions to bring works like that into existence."[17]

It's Globalized . . .

The rock culture is interpreted in the context of globalization and seen as being at the forefront of the deconstruction of that final relic of the past, communism, in favor of the new global ideology, capitalism. This interpretation is as one-sided as its inversion, namely the accusation (rather than celebration) that rock symbolizes China's path to "Westernization," thereby indicating a profound cultural loss. In the latter interpretation, "the exotic Other" comes scarily close to "the Self," clear-cut boundaries gradually dissolve in sounds of electric guitars. Earlier research has shown that processes of globalization increase rather than decrease cultural heterogeneity.[18] Chinese rock musicians constantly negotiate different cultural flows (different in both time and space); the music both reflects and reinterprets processes of creolization. One should not view the rock culture as a representation or a cause of global popular culture. According to Fabian (1997), "the local is the global under the conditions of globalization that obtain at this moment in history."

It Remains Political . . .

The tendency toward politicized readings of rock is even more apparent for China, as both modern China studies and media coverage show a strong bias for the political. Chinese society is frequently reduced to the political sphere. One should not focus solely on the tensions between the musicians and the state. "A stark dichotomy between virtuous artists and an oppressive state no longer goes very far in explaining the multiple stresses to which China's artists must respond."[19]

Finally, the audience's reception and use of the music is usually dismissed. Audiences are too often seen as uniform. Texts are polysemic, and seemingly controversial lyrics might be "read" in a different way, just as Party propaganda can be and is being read in a subversive way.[20]

There is a need to interrogate rock mythology, to go beyond unidirectional interpretations. I opt for a fluid, dynamic, and most probably contradictory analysis of this cultural practice, an analysis freed from dichotomies such as East/West, local/global, communism/capitalism, high/low, rebellious/compliant, rock/pop, and art/commercialism. The challenge does not lie in a complete deconstruction and rationalization of rock as a commodity; this would too easily guide us to a Marxist interpretation in which rock, as part of commercial mass culture, is viewed as yet another product to stupefy and silence the masses. Neither do I wish to deny the potential political subversiveness of Chinese rock. Rather, the challenge lies in illuminating the complex and contradictory processes at work in the production, creation, and reception of rock music, while at the same time grasping, and thus doing justice to, the feelings being expressed and shared with audiences.

Deconstructing Boundaries: Rock Contra Pop

The perceived dichotomy of pop versus rock is worth further analysis, since it dominates both academic and journalistic discourses on Chinese rock. This dichotomy can also be found in discourses on Western popular music, especially around the 1960s. Frith distinguishes three music worlds: art (or bourgeois), folk, and pop (or commercial); in contrast to pop, "the assumption is that rock music is good music only when it is not mass culture, when it is an art form or a folk sound."[21] Therefore, rock lyrics mattered more than pop lyrics, rock verse was said to be poetry.[22] With the rapid differentiation into various music scenes in the West, the distinction seems to have lost its value, but rock's underlying legitimizing narrative still prevails. Rock is said to be sincere and authentic. The desperate screams of Kurt Cobain signify a truly tormented soul, whereas the sweet voice of Mariah Carey carries a mass-produced product. Frith opts for a reverse of this narrative: "If, for example, the standard line of rock 'n' roll history is that an authentic (that is, folk) sound is continually corrupted by commerce, it could equally well be argued that what the history actually reveals is a commercial musical form continually being recuperated in the name of art and subculture."[23] These processes of commodification are not restricted to rock. On the contrary, all sorts of music are being commodified. Frith therefore concludes that "a comparative sociology reveals far less clear distinctions between music worlds than their discursive values imply."[24] The value distinctions made between "commercial" and "authentic" are debatable. There is no reason to believe that the emotional impact of a song is reduced by its commodification, nor that a song considered "authentic" automatically leads to a stronger reception by the listener.

The two major publications on Chinese rock, *Like a Knife* by Andrew Jones and *Der Lange Marsch des Rock 'n' Roll- Pop- und Rockmusik in der Volksrepublik China* by Andreas Steen, use a typology from Ray Pratt based on the presumed function of the music for audiences:

1. The conservative, hegemonic use, strengthening the existing status quo and supporting those in power.
2. A negotiated use, in which the music functions as a safety valve. According to Pratt, "instead of taking action to change fundamentally the repressive existence of daily life, one is offered a substitute world of music, a 'negotiated' form of consciousness."[25]
3. The emancipatory use, in which music functions as a tool to emancipate suppressed people. An obvious example used by Jones is Cui Jian's hit "Nothing to My Name," one of the anthems of the 1989 democracy movement.[26]

However, this typology could be problematic. It tends to lead to unidirectional interpretations of the meanings of music. It has inspired both Jones and Steen to consider rock emancipatory as long as it is not yet commodified. As I have shown, this assertion is part of rock mythology and ignores the contradictory processes at work. Whereas rock can be emancipatory, pop music, if not part of the hegemonic structure, is at most a safety valve for Chinese youth, according to Steen.[27] Jones argues for a more positive reading for negotiated uses by stressing the struggle in production, linked to larger struggles in society—but "the outcome of these negotiations, because of their imbrication with the apparatus of [pop] music production and dissemination, are by definition never emancipatory."[28] Also for Jones, it is only rock that can be emancipatory. His typology, which resembles Hall's typology for different forms of reception—preferred, negotiated, and oppositional—classifies rather than clarifies.[29] It strengthens the rock versus pop dichotomy, ignores the fluidity of musical meanings, and reinforces rock mythology.

The difference between rock and pop is emphasized by Asian record producers in order to position rock. In their marketing, rock is labeled authentic music, in contrast to the commodified, "canned" pop music, especially from Hong Kong and Taiwan. Rock mythology is thus crucial for, and therefore strengthened by, the professional marketing of the rock culture.[30]

Deconstructing boundaries does not mean denying differences. If one looks at the production side, there are indeed differences in the production of pop and rock on the mainland. Pop singers in China usually belong to a working unit (*danwei*). They sing lyrics written by others, and the music is also written and played by others. The case for pop singers in Hong Kong and Taiwan is similar, as it is for bands that are often considered rock, such as Beyond, disbanded in 2000, although to a lesser extent. On the other hand, rock singers in China usually write their own songs and lyrics and do not belong to a working unit. To point out the differences between rock and pop is interesting, but more significant is why one chooses to look at the differences. What is relevant is the ideology behind the dichotomy, the way in which it invents rock as a specific music world essentially different from that of pop.

Behind the Scenes

So far, the literature on Chinese rock culture has treated it chronologically.[31] Instead, I opt for an overview based on different scenes I distinguish within the rock culture, which has become too fragmented for a neat chronology. As with subcultures, boundaries are only momentarily fixed and scenes frequently overlap. In my opinion, the idea of a music scene corresponds closely with Fabian's interpretation of a genre.

> A concept such as genre can help us better understand the role which popular culture may play in situations where power meets with resistance. . . . Genre channels authority and creativity, it erects boundaries and thereby creates identities . . . [it] allows us to conceptualize the process that produces, through differentiation of forms, a particular domain of popular culture and to locate, as it were, sites where struggle with and for power take place. Nevertheless . . . genre remains a concept which is associated with classifying such that it is easy to forget its kinship with generating.[32]

What interests me is neither a neat classification of rock culture nor the creation of an order that provides us with an illusionary understanding or yet another typology, but rather the processes that produce different scenes, and the related articulation of identities. "The strategy of comparison implies an awareness of difference as its epistemological stimulus while at the same time, in its very requirement of juxtaposing at least two realities, being a guard against exaggerated notions of uniqueness and incommensurability."[33] As such, it might reveal moments of both struggle and compliance with the cultural, economic, and political realities of China and thus do justice to the fragmented, fluid nature of the rock subculture. To illustrate this, I will further analyze two scenes, the underground bands and heavy-metal bands.[34] While both have moments of rebellion and compliance, underground bands tend to be more oppositional, at least in intent, and heavy-metal bands show more compliance to nationalism and the status quo. Ethnographic observations guide me to theoretical interventions. In my view, interpretation of "field data" implies a critical, theoretical interrogation of ethnographic reports. In the following ethnographies of three underground bands (NO, the Fly, and Zi Yue) and one heavy-metal band (Tang Dynasty), I describe how they negotiate place (that is, the symbolic and linguistic articulation of Chineseness), what aesthetics they employ, and what their position is within both the cultural landscape of China and rock culture. Rather than dealing with these issues separately, I aim to stress their intertwining by presenting them as a whole.

The Underground Bands (Formed Around 1993)

Summer 1997, Beijing. The serene sounds of the Gu Zheng (a traditional Chinese string instrument) fill the room. Zu Zhou, the twenty-six-year-old singer of the band NO, is playing his demo tape. But soon the listener starts to wonder; something is different. The string sounds are full of disturbing dissonances, far from the tranquillity the ancient instrument is reputed to exude. Zu Zhou sees the surprise in my eyes and stops the tape. He starts playing the Gu Zheng, this time in the familiar way. Now I recognize the peaceful sound used by classical musicians and by other rockers in Beijing such as Cui Jian and Wang Yong.[35] "You know, I can play the instrument in a classical way, like they do. But what's the point? It makes no sense!" Then he puts a pair of scissors between the strings and starts to pull them more violently. The sound transforms; gone is the myth of the peaceful, deep Chinese traditional culture. What remains is a disturbing noise in which anger competes with confusion. In my opinion, Zu Zhou's use of the Gu Zheng symbolizes the predicament of today's Chinese youth: When the (traditional) past restricts rather than liberates, when communism has long lost its appeal, what else is there to do but radically change the culture, deconstructing the past in a search for a better future?

Singer Feng Jiangzhou from the punk-noise band the Fly is also fascinated by "characteristic" Chinese sounds, which he aims to combine with computer samples and sounds from electric drills: "I am most interested in using Chinese instruments as well as revolutionary songs. . . . But I would definitely refuse to make them sound beautiful, I would try to make them sound uncomfortable. I like uncomfortable things." This conscious distortion of musical expressions considered "traditionally Chinese" forms one important marker of difference used by underground bands (*dixia yinyue,* as the genre is also labeled in China) such as NO and the Fly. The transformation of sounds considered stereotypically Chinese alters rather than completely subverts the connotations attached to it. These connotations are, in the case of the Gu Zheng, mainly quietness and depth, signifying Chinese history, and in the case of the communist songs, the heroic revolutionary past.

Zu Zhou's refusal to use traditional musical instruments in a classical way sets him apart from musicians in other scenes, who use the traditional sound to construct an "authentic" Chineseness. However, in both cases, the use of traditional instruments proves that this is indeed Chinese rock.[36] This perspective is rooted in the rigid local versus global dichotomy I have already criticized. What distinguishes Chinese rock from, say, Western rock or even rock from Taiwan, is indeed its locality, the mainland. Nevertheless, this does not imply that one can or should discover its locality in specific sounds or words. Its locality at the same time encompasses the global. The local and the global are intertwined categories, rather than mutually exclusive ones.

The negotiation of the past, by either a conventional or a "distorted" use of traditional instruments, can be interpreted as an act of self-orientalizing. Even though the dissonant sounds of Zu Zhou's Gu Zheng might not create the tranquil, peaceful, mysterious China that is created by Wang Yong, they still mark a difference from "the West." It can be considered an act of "Othering" done by the "Other" himself, albeit unconsciously, thus informing an essentialized Chinese identity.[37] The articulation of "Chineseness" corresponds with two dominant images of China, namely Ancient China and Communist China. Their clothing styles also often stress this Chineseness: the Mao cap of Cui Jian and the Communist Youth League shawls that singers were wearing during a punk performance I attended are just two examples. Here, one can see links between the rock culture and the avant-garde painters, among whom Mao suits have been tremendously popular (not to speak of the imagery used in the paintings themselves, often closely linked to the style of Communist propaganda art). While the rock of NO employs sounds, words, and imagery that construct the music as specifically Chinese, they use other symbols to stress its international, cosmopolitan character. The paradox is that, apart from a fascination with being Chinese, Chinese rock musicians are at the same time deeply fascinated by the West. Bands refer frequently to such sources of inspiration as the Beatles and U2. The use of English for both bands' names (the Fly and NO), as well as for song titles, gives their CDs an international aura. Through these seemingly contradictory dynamics, place is being negotiated, a place that is both local and global, and, depending on the moment, either may be articulated. The Western journalist is happy to find traditional sounds in the music; the Chinese youngster is attracted by the sense of cosmopolitanism that the music provides him. Markers of sameness (the shared Chinese tradition) as well as of difference (the Communist past) are both employed in relation to Hong Kong and Taiwan. The negotiation of place does not equal the construction of the local. Rather, place needs to be interpreted as "a borderland, a crossroads—that is, a space where the boundaries between inside and outside are blurred, a space characterized by a multiplicity of crisscrossing forces rather than by some singular and unique, internally originated 'local' identity."[38]

Besides being a musician, NO singer Zu Zhou is a writer, poet, and painter and has participated in several performance art activities. Links with other "art worlds" become obvious, especially in the underground scene. Feng Jiangzhou from the Fly is also an avant-garde painter. His first CD was released in 1997 by a small Taiwanese label and appeared on the mainland market only in 1999 on the Beijing-based Modern Sky label. He released in the same year two NO CDs on the mainland market. The Fly's controversial jacket design—depicting copulating couples and naked men—had to be changed to pass the censors. Interestingly, song titles such as "I Don't Like You Cummin' a Lot" and "Educated from Ugly Life" remained intact. A mainland critic concluded after listening to the CD: "Chinese avant-garde art is usually impotent art. Chinese rock is usually hollow. What kind of chemical reaction will happen if we put these two things together? . . . The Fly has set new standards for Chinese rock and made us realize how hypocritical and senseless the "so-called" avant-garde rock music was. . . . Grunge, punk and noise are really the best ways to express avant-garde art because they are extreme. The lyrics of this album are controversial, they tried hard to use filthy words to improve their dirty, noisy and bad aesthetics."[39]

As the avant-garde of the rock culture, underground bands have close ties with the cultural avant-garde of China.[40] The review just quoted was published before the CD was allowed on the mainland market, for despite government control, CDs find their way to music critics, who are allowed to publish their reviews nationwide, thus indirectly promoting government-banned CDs. Party hegemony, it seems, is far from absolute and uncontested. This quote also shows how critical the Chinese discourse on rock can be. Assessments are based on comparisons over time (with references to the Chinese rock classics) or over place. Reviews of new Chinese releases appear along with reviews of the latest CD of the Chemical Brothers or Beck. The reviews of Chinese rock are based on comparisons with Western rock, which more often than not comes out ahead.

For Zu Zhou and Feng Jiangzhou, music functions as a site to negotiate feelings of anger and frustration that young people are hardly allowed to express in Chinese culture. Both Confucian and Party ideology stress the importance of conformity, of obedience to parents, educators, and bosses. As Feng Jiangzhou said: "I am actually very angry about a lot of things in China, like disrespect among people, the whole political system, but I do not have the courage to confront people directly, so when I write I can be very angry and aggressive." As Hebdige puts it, "The subcultural response . . . is both a declaration of independence, of otherness, of alien intent, a refusal of anonymity, of subordinate status. It is an insubordination."[41] The danger is that by focusing solely on the subcultural identity one overlooks or ignores other identities that are being explored in other spheres of life by the musicians. By romanticizing the provocative poses, rock mythology ignores the more mundane aspects of a musician's life.

Besides the negotiation of expressions considered "Chinese" and the strong ties with other cultural domains such as the visual arts, underground musicians are vocal in their criticism of contemporary Chinese society. In an article on the post–Cui Jian generation, Chinese academic He Li quotes from rock critic Kong: "Zu Zhou's uniquely penetrating tenor, like a knife stained with blood and sperm, tears off everything. . . . His purely despondent bass divulges the loneliness towards the future and the destruction of the will to live. Their simple and weird minor-scale progression embeds anxiety and emptiness. It is not only a musical language, but also a spiritual wandering guided by some old instinctive language. Their irregular and airy sound texture constructs some kind of imaginary space." He Li himself states that "NO is like a group of sadists from hell."[42] Zu Zhou's critique of contemporary Chinese society is more a radical denial of meaning: "I am disgusted by Marxism. In my opinion, it has cheated me. . . . This is a senseless age, maybe the true age hasn't come yet."

He expresses his alienation and fatalism in his song "Let Me See the Doctor Once More":

> Let this rickshaw take me to the home of the surgeon
> Let him fucking see the green smoke beneath my groin
> Let me see you once more—doctor
> I want to find back my
> Left thigh, left rib, left hand, left lung, and my right-wing dad.

This song is, in its reference to the singer's lost right-wing dad, obviously political, but at the same time alienating and confusing. The listener wonders what is meant by the green smoke beneath his groin. Dadaist elements characterize Zu Zhou's music and lyrics. In my view, the impact of his lyrics can be illuminated not by in-depth semiotic analysis, but rather by its direct impact. As a puzzled listener, I am left with questions rather than with understanding. The Chinese audience, when entering the music world of Zu Zhou, can be expected to start feeling *unheimlich* in a society that constantly celebrates its economic success and the glorious future of its youth.

The dadaist tactics applied by Zu Zhou show similarities with those applied by Feng Jiangzhou. In a Taiwanese review, the music from the Fly was compared to the guerrilla tactics of Chairman Mao: Instead of launching a frontal attack, the critic pointed out, the Fly was employing sideways movements to oppose the dominant culture. Rather than writing about politics, Feng Jiangzhou prefers to write about sex. Sex—another topic difficult to discuss in China—signifies the political. But Feng's criticism goes beyond the political:

> What would be considered beautiful by a lot of people is just a very popular notion of beauty. I don't think my lyrics are dirty at all, I want people to rethink what is beautiful and what is dirty. . . . The other reason why I choose sex as the subject matter is as a reaction to the pop music of China. The government seems to, if not encourage, at least condone pop music, whereas it gives so many problems to rock 'n' roll. I find pop music so superficial, but it represents its own vulgar aesthetics. It would be very difficult for me to write very sophisticated lyrics as its critique. The only way to do so is to find another subject matter which could be as vulgar for the general people, and sex seems to be very appropriate to counter Chinese pop music. . . . Everything [in China] is just so covered up. In the past there have been extremely erotic books, pornographic materials, but people would hide them and present themselves as gentlemen. We have a song entitled "Gentleman." In China, everyone would like to be that gentleman, and I would like them to tear off that mask. Because if you are always wearing a mask, you don't exist. People should be real.

In his elucidation, some aspects of rock mythology reappear in a sophisticated way. Feng Jiangzhou aims to subvert the ideology of pop by using provocative, vulgar lyrics. The implicit accusation of pop as being in line with the dominant ideology and the superficial remains important for his positioning as a rock musician. Also, the idea of tearing away the masks people wear to reveal their true, authentic identity is closely linked to the belief that his music—in being open about sex—is an example of authenticity. What remains unsaid by Feng Jiangzhou is how subversive the "vulgar" aesthetics of pop in practice can be—which would lead to a blurring of boundaries between rock and pop—and what is meant by "real people."

Nevertheless, the mirror the Fly offers the audience is far from comforting. The lyrics are characterized by directness and absurdity, as this fragment from the song "Nirvana" shows:

> Because there is no electric light in this village hut
> Because today is not the day of full moon
> Because tonight I cannot fall asleep
> Because tonight I want to play with myself
> . . . .
> Under my bottom shines the first ray of sun
> I want to bring with me this entire hut of the fragrance of shit
> I am in Nirvana
> In Nirvana.

I interpret the tactics applied by both Feng Jiangzhou and Zu Zhou as tactics of symbolic inversion, which Barbara Babcock defines as an aesthetic "negation of the negative." This aesthetic negation confronts the audience with the lineaments of Chinese culture. It questions the normal in its focus on what is considered abnormal. It destabilizes the illusory symbolic order. "Such 'creative negations' remind us of the need to reinvest the clean with the filthy. . . . The modus inversus does more than simply mock our desire to live according to our usual orders and norms; it reinvests life with a vigor and a Spielraum attainable (it would seem) in no other way."[43] In a text written as part of promotional material for the Fly, mainland rock critic He Li points out the significance of these tactics of symbolic inversion: "Flies are not lovely creatures. Their connotations in our language are negative: multiple-eyed, dirty, sickness-spreading, full of pus . . . and we are expecting a more hygienic, more civilized, more elegant, more orderly time of money-making. The flies and we are enemies! In major cities of China, punk, I am afraid, enjoys only a very limited audience, because we are always concerned about hygiene, neat clothes, civilization, politeness. But it is also because of this that flies bear special meaning for our life." The dissonant sounds, the negation of daily life, and the focus on what usually remains unsaid sets the Fly apart from other rock bands. The similarities with Zu Zhou are clear: Both are transforming the sounds of the past, both share links with other art worlds. With the band Zi Yue, the Fly shares a very articulate critique of contemporary Chinese society. It shows that rock mythology and the discourse of rebelliousness it produces are not essentially false, but, as will become clear in my discussion of heavy metal, this does not mean that one can equate rock with rebellion.

The music of Zi Yue ("it says" or "the master speaks," a reference to the Chinese philosopher Confucius) is produced by Cui Jian. Qiu Ye, more than the Fly or NO, focuses on making Chinese rock. He criticizes those who in his eyes copy Western music and stress the Chinese character of his music. Again, stereotypical indicators of "Chineseness" are used to mark the music's difference from "Western" rock. Qui Ye's music has been labeled "opera rock," a reference to his vocals, which strongly resemble those used in Beijing opera. The jacket of their album released in 1997 mixes Chinese symbols such as a temple and a classic Chinese painting with cosmopolitan images such as high apartment blocks and oil barrels. It symbolizes and criticizes the modernization of China, a shift from the peaceful temples to concrete urban landscapes and environmental pollution. Buddhist elements can be found in the lyrics as well as in the music. Qiu Ye claims to be very much inspired by Buddhist culture and to strive for the perfection of Buddhism in his daily life. The Chinese characteristics in the music apparently travel well to the West: Zi Yue performed in Canada in 1999 and in Italy in 2000.

A closer look at Qiu Ye, his music, and his lyrics, reveals that he is not losing himself in an uncritical celebration of the past. In the promotional material provided by the record company, Qiu Ye elaborates on his opinion of contemporary Chinese culture: "Too many shadows of our ancestors are enshrouding our culture and our life. The so-called morality serves only one class. It has only one aim: to enslave, to overthrow and to enslave again. . . . Looking at the so-called process of human history, whether it's religion, politics, laws or economy, they are all closed cans suppressing and constraining human instincts, like putting you into a vacuum and suffocating you. They call it unity." Not only does he criticize Chinese society and the suffocating bonds of the past, but also he touches upon the development of popular music in China: "The so-called jazz, rock and roll, punk and pop music were all products of emotions—at the very beginning. But now when we are appreciating it, praising it and then practicing it, we discover at the same time that it is also a can, and you still cannot run away from it! God! Is it what's called consciousness? And is it this consciousness which has created so many 'musicians'? And the 'music culture'?" Now in his early thirties, Qiu Ye has been active in the rock culture for more than ten years. Following the 1990s trend of starting one's own business, Qiu Ye started his own company in 2000 and aims to release a second CD in 2002. Meanwhile he makes a living by performing frequently in the rock venues of Beijing, such as the Rhine Bar, and by giving guitar lessons to music students.

Although Qiu Ye ended up in prison for two weeks in 1997 after criticizing the driving style of what turned out to be an undercover agent (Zu Zhou also spent the summer of 1997 in prison, for reasons he did not want to say), his lifestyle is not that of "sex, drugs and rock 'n' roll"—a cliché that fits only some musicians in the rock culture. He lives with his wife in the center of Beijing in a small, old house, together with other families. His home, consisting of two rooms, seems to represent the schism between his personal life, symbolized by a girlish, tidy bedroom with neat pink sheets and a big color TV, and his professional life, symbolized by a chaotic living room with musical instruments, walls full of Taoist phrases combined with words such as "rock 'n' roll" and "Sex Pistols." He went in debt to buy an old Russian car: Acting like a rock star before you become one is not cheap. His CD was released almost a year after the recording of the master tape was finished. This tape did not pass the scrutiny of the Censorship Department of the Ministry of Culture. Finally, one song had to be omitted. The reason for these problems is less political than it seems. The mother of Zi Yue's drummer, Zhang Yue, who is a director of a Beijing TV station, accused Qiu Ye of being a counterrevolutionary after she found out that her son was using marihuana; she forced the Ministry of Culture to pay extra attention to their master tape. In the end, her complaints were proven to be false, but the release was delayed. This incident shows how much the censorship procedure depends upon arbitrary personal factors. Qiu Ye's problems were caused by one enraged mother, who used the formal procedures for her own ends.

I met Qiu Ye a few days before the release of his CD. His anger toward Chinese society goes hand in hand with disillusionment toward the rock culture, reminding me of his words in 1995: "As a rocker, they often treat me like a dog, as the dregs of society. Why? I only want to make music, I only live for music. I am not interested in money, nor in business. Music is an instrument for me to express my feelings, my thoughts." After being a musician for so many years, nothing seems to have changed; on the contrary, things have become worse. For Qiu Ye, bands only copy these days, they do not express any thoughts in their music. Qiu Ye is controversial in the rock culture because of his strong opinions. After he refused to play together with some punk bands whose "thoughtless" music he cannot stand, his relationship with Feng Jiangzhou cooled. He says that, within the rock culture, he only likes Cui Jian and Zu Zhou, who sometimes joins the performances of Zi Yue with his violin.

Zi Yue's CD was praised as the best Chinese album of 1997 by one of China's leading music magazines, *China Broadway* (*Zhongguo Bailaohu*). According to rock critic Shang Guan: "Just when we are lamenting the decline of Chinese rock and roll, Zi Yue brings us this delightful album. It is not only a pleasant surprise, but also a comfort—a comfort to all the hearts which have cooled down for such a long time. . . . This album, which is a bit psychedelic and full of punk spirit, enshrines the band members' (mainly its vocalist Qiu Ye's) sharp insights to the world as well as deep and painful metaphors to reality.[44]

Metaphors are crucial to understanding the music of Zi Yue. Lyrics are very dominant in his music because of Qiu Ye's declaiming, raplike singing style. In his song "My Dear Good Child," Qiu Ye sings about the conflicts between a son and his father:

> I have a lot of words in my heart
> Actually I should have told my dad earlier
> But every time before I open my mouth
> Dad will give me a piece of candy

His father, annoyed by this spoiled new generation, responds angrily:

> That's why I tell you: my child, I am contented, so should you be happy
> Don't knit your eyebrows and pretend to be deep in thoughts

The nice things you eat, you drink, you wear are what your old man, me, has
   spent his whole life to get
Understand?

And the son replies:

I try to bear it but it's unbearable
I have to tell you right away
But before my words come close to my lips
You give me
You give me a big mouth
Then you look at me, angrily
And say: what do you actually want, you bastard!
I say: the piece of candy you give me, dad,
Is not sweet at all.

A classic generational conflict unfolds. But at the same time the personal intersects
clearly with the political. The song can be considered a reflection on the relationship between the Party (the father) and today's youth (the son). Tired of all the stories about
the sufferings of the past, before the liberation of China, severely disappointed by that
candy called communism, the youngsters want to scream to the Party, talk about their
disappointments, their dissatisfactions, their dreams. But they will be silenced.

The underground bands entered the stage of commodification in the late nineties, not
without some self-questioning. NO was contracted by Modern Sky. According to He Li,
NO's fear is that whatever is expressed is destined to be consumed by greedy commercialization and the superficial "modern" audience. He quotes Zu Zhou, who stated in
an interview in 1994: "We want to be famous. But then one day, when we are indeed
famous, when our music becomes popular, that implies we are so bad."[45] Based on the
problematic perception that only noncommercial music can be sincere, authentic, and
thus good, Zu Zhou feels caught in the paradox of both desiring and condemning fame.
Ironically, what he fears to lose are precisely the selling points used by record companies to promote rock. The dialectics of commodification, grounded in rock mythology,
constantly reinvent rock as a specific music world.

Both Zi Yue and the Fly challenged the rock culture with their releases in 1997. The
reviews speak of a rebirth of Chinese rock. Characteristic of the bands is their discontent with rock culture. In the words of Feng Jiangzhou: "In China, from 1986 to 1996,
for ten years, Chinese rock remained quite the same. It is basically hard rock. So I believe that from 1997 there should be something new. But I can't jump too far—otherwise there would be a displacement. What I am trying to do is to create something that
is just beyond the existing rock 'n' roll, that is the avant-garde in China."

Other markers of difference are their subversive use of traditional Chinese instruments, their articulate criticism of Chinese culture, for which tactics of both inversion
and metaphor are used, as well as their strong ties with other art worlds. These crucial
markers have generated (to put it tautologically) a specific genre in the rock culture. In
their wake, other underground bands have followed, such as Wooden Horse, Tongue,

and Chen Dili. But the extreme sounds of these bands—Zi Yue is the only exception—mean that most occupy a marginal position on the mainland music market. However, "what is socially peripheral is often symbolically central, and if we ignore or minimize inversion and other forms of cultural negation we often fail to understand the dynamics of symbolic processes generally."[46] Expressions from the margin are often crucial symbolic sources that affect, and sometimes challenge, more "mainstream" cultures. But here lies a paradox, since by centering the peripheral we tend to push the center to the periphery.[47] In theorizing about what is peripheral, we ought to avoid juxtaposing it with a center but interpret it as always already a crossroads, an intersection of center/periphery, a fluid borderland.[48]

In their lyrics, their sounds, and their imagery, the bands generate moments of opposition. As I have shown, their methods are indirect and encompass more than the political. In their music they express an anger and dissatisfaction with contemporary Chinese society, feelings they can hardly express in other ways. The dadaist aesthetics of NO, the vulgar aesthetics of the Fly, as well as the metaphorical aesthetics of Zi Yue all challenge dominant political and cultural values.

At the same time, I question the construction of "Chineseness" in the music and imagery, the "Othering" vis-à-vis the non-Chinese world (that is, nonmainland). Qiu Ye's aspiration to create a pure Chinese rock is an attempt to essentialize cultural differences. As such, it strengthens the illusion of a fixed cultural identity, an illusion that corresponds well with dominant Chinese perceptions. It accommodates rather than challenges the notion, dominant both in China and in the West, of the uniqueness of China. Subversion goes hand in hand with compliance. These contradictions become even more apparent if we look at the heavy-metal scene.

Heavy Metal

Ding Wu, born in 1962, used to play with Hei Bao. Unable to express his love for heavy metal (*zhong jinshu*), he left the band and together with Zhang Ju and two American overseas-Chinese students, including Kaiser Kuo, formed Tang Dynasty in late 1988. The name encompasses the band's longing for China at its most glorious. During the Tang Dynasty (618–907), Chinese civilization reached its highest point. As the record company Magic Stone describes it in promotional material: "While Western Europe struggled through the hardships of the middle ages, Chinese culture flourished during the Tang Dynasty as the center of world trade and the highest point of world civilization." In a comparison with the West, the record company states in the promotional material: "The most important thing is, here you will hear the self-confidence of the Chinese, because they have done what you thought only Westerners could have done."[49]

But another reading is even more obvious. A strong longing for the past is expressed in Tang Dynasty's imagery (the CD jacket features traditional calligraphy and the band's name written on two red flags), music (the compositions contain clear references to the past, such as Beijing opera, Xinjiangese folk music, and the use of traditional instruments) and lyrics. This celebration of the past and its related criticisms of the present form the main philosophy of Tang Dynasty. In their songs, they express their solitude in modern times, their despair, and their search for a better world. Contemporary life is believed to be superficial, gray, and sad.[50] A music critic comments on the band: "In their music, they express their true feelings towards life and their understanding of the world. . . . They express in their own way a longing for a strong and influential China: a return to the Tang Dynasty."[51]

In line with rock mythology, their criticisms of modern times are considered authentic. In the real world, the search for a different life has been far from unproblematic. The band has gone through hard times. After being contracted by the Taiwanese label Magic Stone they became successful overnight. Their CD is said to have sold more than one million copies, and within a few months after its release more than ten pirated versions were on the market.[52] Unable to cope with their instant success, problematic years followed the debut. Addiction to drugs lasted for years, and in May 1995 guitarist Zhang Ju died in a motorcycle accident. The rest of the group split with Magic Stone, who, according to the band, did not support them during their hard times. Only in 1997 did the band start up again, with manager Dickson Dee from Hong Kong. American-born Kaiser Kuo, who had left the band in 1989, replaced Zhang Ju on the guitar. His return was severely criticized by other rock musicians. Whereas Zhang Ju played the guitar in a Chinese way, Kaiser is said to play it in an American way, unsuitable for Chinese rock. Besides, he is said to be a bad guitar player. This hostility toward foreign elements illustrates the attempt to make rock with "Chinese" characteristics.

The importance of Tang Dynasty for the Chinese rock culture can hardly be overestimated. They introduced heavy metal to China, and the piercing, high voice of Ding Wu could be heard in the streets all over the cities in the winter of 1993. With their long hair, their upper bodies naked on MTV, their motorcycles and leather jackets, they corresponded closely to the stereotypical rock image. Boys were impressed by their masculinity. The archaic language further strengthens the chivalric aesthetics, which correspond to the tradition in China of ancient martial-arts heroes (*wuxia xiaoshuo*). In addition, their compositions were powerful, some almost military, with strong melodies and unexpected twists. Aware of their market potential, they were looking for a record company and wanted to set up their own. According to Kaiser Kuo, "The company should have an art director, a manager, and the members of Tang Dynasty. It is financially advantageous for Tang Dynasty to have a corporate identity, to define priorities."

Gradually, Chinese rock has become more professional and at the same time more commercial. The artists themselves refer to the music as a product to be marketed. Tang Dynasty was contracted in 1998 by a mainland Chinese record company, Jingwen, who released their second album, *Epic*, which featured aesthetics similar to their earlier work. However, this release failed to reestablish the nationwide popularity the band had won after their first release. Instead, other heavy-metal bands have gradually taken over the scene, such as Overload, Iron Kite, and, in particular, the Cold Blooded Animals.

The symbolism in the music and the video clips of Tang Dynasty, full of references to the past, express a pervasive sense of cultural loss.[53] Jones quotes Lao Wu, at that time the bass player for Tang Dynasty: "Rock is based on the blues, and we can never play the blues as well as an American. It's just not in our blood. We can imitate it, but eventually we'll have to go back to the music we grew up with, to traditional music, to folk music."[54] His dogmatic and essentialist approach is questionable. First, rock has more sources than just the blues. Second, these sources cannot all be traced to the United States, but also, for example, to African rhythms. Finally, and most importantly, the search for origins is debatable, for even instruments considered "traditionally" Chinese will contain elements of instruments from other cultures. The irony is that Lao Wu's statement resembles Western discourses, in which rock is also frequently linked to folk music in order to differentiate it from commercial pop music.

According to singer Ding Wu, the band indeed feels a longing for the old China, for the cultural richness of the past. But, he continues, this does not reflect discontent with the present. It is just a longing. This longing is expressed in their song "A Dream Return to the Tang Dynasty," which in its reference to the grievances (of today's youth) also criticizes the present:

Wind—cannot blow away our grievances
Flowers—cannot color over our longing for home
Snow—cannot reflect the mountain stream
Moon—cannot fulfill the ancient dream
Following the patterns on my palm
Branded there by fate
Following fate I fall into a trance
In dream I return to the Tang Dynasty.[55]

Kaiser Kuo stresses that they do not want to oppose politics: "We are not rebellious at all, we are actually pro the present administration. Because of the open-door policy we can exist. China is such a huge country that it needs a strong leadership." He agrees that they are in a way actually patriots. Kaiser basically sees their music as a kind of safety valve, as a way for youngsters to release their emotions and energies, as a way to rediscover the Chinese culture, to be proud to be Chinese. In his celebration of Chinese culture he draws a comparison with Japan: "[Japanese history] is going to be dwarfed by China. . . . Chinese culture is a mine, there is such a lot to do. There are people who go crazy for these Japanese samurai stories, but there is so little of it, there is such a well of it in China." In their promotional material, Magic Stone quotes from a talk between bass player Lao Wu and a Japanese record company: "I often watched the performance of Japanese Rock and Roll bands on TV. They all have good techniques but I can't feel or find the Japanese culture and creativity. Can you tell me which bands are worth listening to and which bands can represent Japan's own culture?"[56]

The philosophy of the band strongly resembles the nationalist ideology expressed by the Party. The strong feelings against Japan are dangerously chauvinistic. Kaiser Kuo believes the band to be pro-establishment. He, as well as the record company in its promotion, voices populist notions on the supremacy of Chinese culture above Japanese culture. Kaiser Kuo left the band in 1999 after conflicts with Ding Wu over NATO's bombing of the Chinese embassy in Belgrade. As an American-born Chinese, Kaiser Kuo was said to accept NATO's apologies to China, whereas Ding Wu—and most Chinese—saw it as a deliberate attack on their country. It is of course ironic that, despite his patriotic opinions, Kaiser Kuo had to leave the band over such an issue.[57]

More than underground bands, Tang Dynasty's music—in its celebration of the past—can be considered an attempt to essentialize cultural differences. It not only accommodates but also celebrates the dominant Communist Party notion of the uniqueness of China. The act of "Othering" can also be considered a commercial strategy. "The band is an avowedly commercial venture, and in this light, its nativism . . . is perhaps less an ideological stance than a marketing device."[58] The affiliation between Tang Dynasty and both political and economic realities is, however, not solely characterized by compliance. The chivalric aesthetics of Tang Dynasty, as reflected in the bombastic music compositions, the archaic, mysterious lyrics, the religious charisma of vocalist Ding Wu, and the critique of modern culture in the lyrics, all create a music world that seems to challenge the current celebration of economic progress and rapid modernization in China. But it is in fact a contradictory space that accommodates today's political realities. As such, it shows that rock culture can never be interpreted as solely oppositional or solely in compliance with dominant culture.

By Way of Conclusion

The "music world" of Chinese rock consists of producers, musicians, audiences, academics, journalists, and politicians. Each of them plays part in the production of the rock culture. The underlying rock mythology, as outlined in this essay, functions as the glue that binds these worlds together. If we aim to grasp the meanings of Chinese rock music, there is a need to think beyond rock mythology and search for a more subtle analysis in which we trace the moments of opposition against as well as compliance with the political, social, and economic system. Such an analysis needs to question fixed dichotomies such as pop-rock, high-low, commercial-alternative, East-West, local-global, in favor of a more fluid approach. This implies stepping beyond the dominant subcultural paradigm, in which subcultures are "read" vis-à-vis a certain dominant culture, and their "symbolism" is solely interpreted within that paradigm. The red scarf of Cui Jian can be read as an ironic, symbolic act of resistance. This interpretation, while valid, could dismiss broader processes at work. Postcolonial studies help us to think further, to unravel the context that produces such an "act of rebellion." Chinese rock emerged in a rapidly globalizing world. Thus, the context in which it emerged includes not only the mainland, but also the region ("Greater China") and the world, in particular the West. Place is being negotiated, a place that is local in its focus on Chineseness, as well as global in its adaptation of a global sound and cosmopolitan imagery. The self-orientalizing practices as traced here resemble the Party politics of the 1990s, in which nationalism plays a dominant role. The heavy-metal band Tang Dynasty is a particularly salient example of the expression of strong nationalistic sentiments. I have shown that this does not imply that rock carries no critique at all. I outlined different aesthetics used by the bands—dadaist, metaphorical, vulgar, and chivalric—that can be considered challenging to dominant cultural and political values. But rather than seeing these practices as purely subversive, it is fair to say that in China the subcultural response of the rock musicians to contemporary Chinese society is neither simply affirmation nor total refusal or "genuine revolt." I believe it is necessary to point to the other side of the coin. One should avoid romanticizing rock at the expense of pop and recognize moments of conformity within the rock culture.

Notes

Acknowledgments: I thank Chow Yiufai for his critical encouragement and help with the translation of lyrics, and Qin Liwen for her support in Beijing.

1. On images of the demonstrations in documentaries about the Beijing rock scene, see Lanning, *Voices of the World*; Sackman, *Beijing* and *Uit De Schaduw*. On the official's banning of Cui Jian's performances, see Jones, *Like a Knife*. The authorities considered it intolerable to turn a revolutionary classic into a rock song, which has not kept others from following Cui Jian's example. In 1992, along with the Mao craze that swept the country, a tape appeared with rock covers of revolutionary classics. See Geremie R. Barme, "The Irresistible Fall and Rise of Mao Zedong," in *Shades of Mao: The Posthumous Cult of the Great Leader,* ed. Barme (New York: M. E. Sharpe, 1996): "Now that everyone was 'toying' (*wan'r*) with Party tradition there was nothing particularly risky about the music: repackaged revolutionary rock was just another part of the cultural landscape. Mao was also very popular among the stylishly naughty boys and girls of the Beijing rock demimonde, so much that pro-Mao machismo was endemic to the scene" (46). However, Tang Dynasty, another rock group, has a heavy-metal version of the "International" that was not officially released in the mainland, whereas it was released in Taiwan and Hong Kong.

2. X. Chen, "MTV."

3. Song, "Zhongguo yaogunyue yao xiang hefang?"

4. X. Chen, "MTV."

5. *Renmin Ribao* (People's Daily), "Yingyexin Yanchu Guanli Tiaoli."1997.

6. My translation. Quoted in Maren Eckhardt, "Ich Haben Nichts, Wir Haben Nichts." In *Yaogun Yinyue: Jugend-, Subkultur Und Rockmusik in China, Politische Und Gesellschaftliche Hintergrunde Eines Neuen Phanomes,* ed. T. Heberer. Vol. 1 of *Ostasien-Pazific,Trierer Studien zu Politik, Wirtschaft, Gesellschaft, Kultur* (Hamburg: Lit Verlag, 1994).

7. By using the term "mythology," I do not wish to suggest the existence of a "reality" that lurks behind the mythology. I believe rock mythology to be an important discourse that produces rock culture as a music world. My aim in deconstructing the mythology does not lie in revealing a "truth" about the rock culture as such, but rather in analyzing how the rock culture is constructed. I aim to develop a different perspective on this cultural practice in which discussions frequently overlooked are included.

8. Tim Brace and Paul Friedlander, "Rock and Roll on the New Long March: Popular Music, Cultural Identity, and Political Opposition in the People's Republic of China," in *Rockin' the Boat: Mass Music and Mass Movements,* ed. Reebee Garofalo (Boston: South End Press, 1992), 127.

9. Timothy W. Ryback, *Rock Around the Bloc: A History of Rock Music in Eastern Europe and the Soviet Union* (Oxford: Oxford University Press, 1990).

10. Havel presided over a government between 1989 and 1992 with a heavy representation of rock musicians. See Sabrina Petra Ramet, "Rock: The Music of Revolution (and Political Conformity)," in *Rocking the State: Rock Music and Politics in Eastern Europe and Russia*, ed. Ramet (Oxford: Westview Press, 1994), 55, 1.

11. In *Subculture: The Meaning of Style* (Suffolk: Chaucer Press, 1979), Dick Hebdige deconstructs oppositional styles (like punk) that challenge dominant culture. In later works (*Hiding in the Light* [London: Routledge, 1988]), he questioned his previous assumption that subcultures were intentionally challenging dominant culture, and he developed a more nuanced approach by adopting Foucault's ideas of power and surveillance. The idea of surveillance is useful to emphasize that Chinese youngsters have to respond to multiple stresses: They are expected to be the good son, the hard-working, obedient student, and the model citizen. According to Angela McRobbie in *Feminism and Youth Culture: From "Jacky" to "Just Seventeen"* (London: Macmillan Education, 1991): "The classic subculture does provide its members with a sense of oppositional sociality, an unambiguous pleasure in style, a disruptive identity and a set of collective fantasies" (33). It is crucial to trace and analyze the moment this happens, while at the same time searching for its reverse, that is, the moment rock does support today's political realities in China.

12. Jolanta Pekacz makes a similar point regarding Eastern Europe; see "Did Rock Smash the Wall? The Role of Rockin Political Transition," *Popular Music* 13, no. 1 (1994): 42.

13. See Andrew Nathan, *Chinese Democracy* (New York: Knopf, 1985), and *China's Crisis*.

14. Pekacz, "Did Rock Smash the Wall?" 44.

15. Liang, "Zai shijie wuji shang."

16. Adorno, *Einleitung in Die Musiksoziologie*.

17. Howard S. Becker, *Art Worlds* (Berkeley: University of California Press, 1982), 35.

18. See Ulf Hannerz, "The World in Creolisation," *Africa* 57, no. 4 (1987): 546–559, and Arjun Appadurai, "Disjuncture and Difference in the Global Cultural Economy," *Public Culture* 2, no. 2 (1990): 1–24.

19. Richard Kraus, "China's Artists Between Plan and Market," in *Urban Spaces in Contemporary China: The Potential for Autonomy and Community in Post-Mao China*, ed. Deborah S. Davis, Richard Kraus, Barry Naughton, and Elizabeth J. Perry (New York: Cambridge University Press, 1995), 190.

Tensions between music cultures and the state are of course not restricted to China. Illustrative of this is the Criminal Justice Law passed by the English Parliament in 1995 that aimed to ban (1) playing music with loud repetitive beats and (2) gatherings of more than ten persons at unsuitable places (thereby aiming to impede techno parties). Consequently, a new genre emerged, labeled Chemical Beats (named after the band the Chemical Brothers). The music is even more psychedelic, aggressive, and provocative than "common" techno, yet the beats are less repetitive. See Hester Carvalho, "Niet Te Verbieden Ritmes," *NRC Handelsblad*, 18 April 1997, 6.

20. See Friedman, "Oppositional Decoding," 132, and Stuart Hall, "Encoding-Decoding," in *Culture, Media, Language*, ed. S. Hall, D. Hobson, A. Lowe, and P. Willis, 157–162 (London: Hutchinson, 1980).

21. Simon Frith, *Sound Effects: Youth, Leisure, and the Politics of Rock 'n' Roll* (London: Constable, 1982), 41; see also 32–38, and Simon Frith, *Performing Rites, On the Value of Popular Music* (Oxford: Oxford University Press, 1996), 42. The concept "worlds" comes from Howard Becker. In *Art Worlds*, Becker describes the art world in a tautological way as consisting "of all the people whose activities are necessary to the production of the characteristic works which that

world, and perhaps others as well, define as art. Members of art worlds co-ordinate the activities by which work is produced by referring to a body of conventional understandings embodied in common practice and in frequently used artifacts" (34). The vagueness of the concept provides space for multiple interpretations, yet inherent to the idea of a "world" are its boundaries. The concept tends to ignore the processes at work. In fact, my criticisms of the concept of subculture also apply to this concept. The advantage of the idea of a "music world" is that its connotations include both producers and audiences, whereas "subculture" mainly refers to the musicians and their fans.

22. Frith, *Sound Effects*, 34.

23. Frith, *Performing Rights*, 42.

24. Ibid., 43.

25. Steen, *Der Lange Marsch*, 14.

26. Jones, *Like a Knife*, 46.

27. Steen, *Der Lange Marsch*, 14.

28. Jones, *Like a Knife*, 47.

29. Hall, "Encoding-Decoding."

30. The marketing slogan of Magic Stone indicates the strong ties between rock mythology and the marketing of the music: "The worst times, the best music" (zui huaide shidai, zui haode yinyue), as if rock automatically emerges in a repressive society.

31. See Jones, *Like A Knife*, and Steen, *Der Lange Marsch*.

32. Fabian, *Moments of Freedom*.

33. Ien Ang, "Doing Cultural Studies at the Crossroads: Local/Global Negotiations," *European Journal of Cultural Studies* 1, no. 1 (1998): 27.

34. For a comprehensive encyclopedia of Chinese popular music, see Huang et al., *Shi nian Zhongguo liuxing yinyue jishi*; for a detailed account of the early history of Chinese rock and the first bands, see Steen, *Der Lange Marsch*; for a brief overview of contemporary bands, including music fragments, see http://www.geocities.com/SunsetStrip/Studio/2418/cubl.html.

35. The quotes that follow in the text are drawn from my interviews with the musicians, carried out between July and December 1997.

36. Steen, *Der Lange Marsch*.

37. An interesting case in point is the music of Sister Drum (DaDaWa). Her "world music," presumably strongly influenced by Tibetan folksongs, is one of the rare examples of Chinese voices that succeed in the Western market. Its popularity outside China (both in East and Southeast Asia, as well as in the West) can partly be explained by its strong exotic flavor, which corresponds well with stereotypical images of Tibet as a mythical place with a long and rich history. Both the music and the jacket imagery depicting a veiled, mysterious woman construct an exotic place, far from the modern world. This critical review appeared in China: "The singer does not express the spirit and philosophy successfully . . . this music copies a lot from Tibetan folk music in an unnatural way. In some songs, the background vocals are more unstable than mysterious. The electronic instruments merely belong to superficial and snobbish modern culture" (Dai, "Miandui xinling" [Face the heart]). Instead of questioning the exoticism in the music, this critic refers to the incompatibility of folksongs and pop music. Of course, the adjectives he uses to describe modern culture and the related mystification and celebration of either the past or other ("traditional") places are not unfamiliar. Rather than following his accusation of Sister Drum's cheap cultural adaptation, I prefer to name it self-imposed orientalism as part of a carefully planned commercial strategy.

38. Ang, "Doing Cultural Studies," 24.

39. An, review of CD "The Fly": 42.

40. The same holds for their Western counterparts like the German industrial band Einssturzende Neubauten, which also participates in other cultural fields such as theater. Both NO and the Fly admit to having been strongly influenced by Einssturzende Neubauten.

41. Hebdige, *Hiding in the Light*, 35.

42. He, "Yaogun 'Guer,'" 88. He Li also quotes critic Sun Mengpu, who describes the music of NO as: "A soul is bleeding in the butchery. A man, cursing the cultural garbage, cruelly exposes his anger, his tears and his despair. Rock and roll is music beyond limits. I see, in the darkness of fear, a pair of eyes, stunned, and a heart, floating in the air, dying."

43. Barbara B. Babcock, introduction to *The Reversible World: Symbolic Inversion in Art and Society*, ed. Babcock (London: Cornell University Press, 1978): 19, 32.

44. Shan Guan, review of CD Zi Yue, *Zhongguo Bailaohui* (Chinese Broadway), no. 2 (1998).

45. He, "Yaogun 'Guer.'" The interview was by Mingpao, Hong Kong, 8 August 1994.

46. Babcock, introduction, 32.

47. For example, in their fascination for Chinese rock, Western academics usually ignore or downplay the value of pop music and, in their writings, push the center—pop has a far greater audience in China—to the margin.

48. Ang, "Doing Cultural Studies," 25.

49. Steen, *Der Lange Marsch*, 165.

50. Ibid., 164–175.

51. Dao, "Wuyue huainian Zhang Ju."

52. Interview with Niu Jiawei, manager of Magic Stone, September 1997.

53. Several authors (Anagnost 1997, Chow 1995, Wang 1996, and Zha 1995) refer to this current zeitgeist, characterized by a strong sense of loss. They point to a longing for the past, where one could still distinguish good from bad, a nostalgia rooted in an urgent need for certainties. What strikes me is that these interpretations are primarily given by analysts with a Chinese background, by those who are positioned in this elusive space in between cultures. Without doubt, "projective identification" plays a role.

54. See Andrew F. Jones, "The Politics of Popular Music in Post-Tiananmen China," in Perry and Wasserstrom, *Popular Protest*, 161, 159. Jones, who was the first to analyze the complicity of rock with CCP politics, refers to a 1991 article in *China Youth News* that stated the government should tolerate rock to oppose the dominance of Cantopop. "There is not just a little irony here: an oppositional subculture based on an Anglo-American musical form that originally sprang from a repudiation of traditional Chinese culture is nationalistically invoked in the official press as a domestic alternative to foreign products."

55. Ibid., 160.

56. After conflicts with vocalist Ding Wu, Lao Wu left Tang Dynasty. Jones (ibid.) quotes Lao Wu in his critique of Western society: "I've been westernized almost my whole life. I spent twenty years absorbing anything Western that I could get my hands on. I never knew anything about my own tradition. And now I really hate anything from the West. I resent its influence . . . modern Chinese culture has never lived up to the tradition because it's been ruined by all the Western influence. We have to get back to our roots, . . . that's what the mission of [Chinese rock] should be all about."

57. The rumor within the rock culture was that the conflict was far less related to ideology than to conflicts within the personal sphere.

58. Jones, "The Politics of Popular Music," 161.

Selected Bibliography

Adorno, Theodor W. *Einleitung in Die Musiksoziologie: Zwölf Theoretische Vorlesungen.* Frankfurt: Suhrkamp Verlag, 1962.

Anagnost, Ann. *National Past-Times: Narrative, Representation, and Power in Modern China.* London: Duke University Press, 1997.

An, Ning. Review of CD "The Fly." *Zhongguo Bailaohui* (Chinese Broadway), no. 9 (1997): 42.

Befu, Harumi, ed. *Cultural Nationalism in East Asia: Representation and Identity.* Berkeley: University of California Press, 1993.

Chen, Xiaomei. *Occidentalism: A Theory of Counter-Discourse in Post-Mao China.* New York: Oxford University Press, 1995.

Chen, Zhi Ang. "MTV zai zhongguo boran xingqi" (MTV thrives in China). *Renmin Yinyue* (People's music), no. 4 (1994).

Chow, Rey. *Primitive Passions: Visuality, Sexuality, Ethnography, and Contemporary Chinese Cinema.* New York: Columbia University Press, 1995.

Dai, Cheng. "Miandui xinling" (Face the heart). *Zhongguo Yinxiang* (China audiovisual monthly), no. 12 (1995).

Dao, Zui. "Wuyue huainian Zhang Ju" (Remember Zhang Ju in May). *Dangdai getan* (Modern music field), 5, no. 41 (1997): 27.

Fabian, Johannes. *Moments of Freedom: Anthropology and Popular Culture.* Charlottesville: University of Virginia Press, 1998.

Foucault, Michel. "The Subject and Power." In *Michel Foucault: Beyond Structuralism and Hermeneutics*, ed. H. L. Dreyfus and Paul Rabinow. Chicago: Harvester Press, 1983.

Friedman, Edward. "The Oppositional Decoding of China's Leninist Media." In *China's Media, Media's China*, ed. Chin-Chuan Lee, 129–146. Boulder, Colo.: Westview Press, 1994.

Gelder, Ken, and Sarah Thornton, eds. *The Subcultures Reader.* London: Routledge, 1997.

Hall, Stuart, and Tony Jefferson, eds. *Resistance Through Rituals: Youth Subcultures in Post-War Britain.* London: Hutchinson, 1976.

He, Li. "Yaogun 'Guer'" (Rock 'n' roll "orphans"). *Jinri Xianreng* (Today's avant-garde), no. 5 (1997): 66–94.

Huang, Liaoyuan, et al., eds. *Shi nian Zhongguo liuxing yinyue jishi* (Chronicle of ten years of Chinese pop music, 1986–1996). Beijing: Zhongguo dianying chubanshe, 1997.

Jin, Zhaojun. "Zongguo yaogunyue zhi wo jian" (How I see the Chinese rock culture). In *Xue Ji, Yaogun mengxun: Zhongguo yaogunyue shilu* (In search of dreams in rock music: A catalogue of Chinese rock). Beijing: Zhongguo Dianying Chubanshe, 1993.

Jones, Andrew F. *Like a Knife: Ideology and Genre in Contemporary Chinese Popular Music.* Ithaca, N.Y.: Cornell University Press, 1992.

Kong, Bu. "NO yuedui zhongjiao ben de zhiwo cingjiu" (NO's religiouslike self-salvation). *Jinri Xianfeng* (Today's avant-garde), no. 5 (1997): 66–94.

Lanning, Greg, director. *Voices of the World: Cui Jian.* London: BBC, 1991. Documentary.

Lee, Gregory B. *Troubadours, Trumpeters, Troubled Makers: Lyricism, Nationalism, and Hybridity in China and Its Others.* London: Hurst, 1996.

Liang, Liang. "Zai shijie wuji shang juxing de yaogunyue" (Rock concert on the ridge of the Roof of the World). *Zhongguo Yinxiang* (China audio-visual monthly), no. 9 (1995): 33–34.

Nathan, Andrew. *China's Crisis: Dilemmas of Reform and Prospects for Democracy.* New York: Columbia University Press, 1990.

Perry, Elizabeth, and Jeffery Wasserstrom, eds. *Popular Protest and Political Culture in Modern China*. 2d. ed. Oxford: Westview Press, 1994.

Pratt, Ray. *Rhythm and Resistance: Explorations in the Political Uses of Popular Music*. New York: Praeger, 1990.

Sackman, Peter. *Beijing: Rock Buiten Westen*. Hilversum: VPRO TV, 1997. Documentary.

———. *Uit De Schaduw*. Hilversum: IKON TV, 1992. Documentary.

Shang, Guan. Review of *Cd Zi Yue*. *Zhongguo Bailaohui* (Chinese Broadway), no. 2 (1998).

Song, Xiao. "Zhongguo yaogunyue yao xiang hefang?" (Where will Chinese rock music rock to?). *Zhongguo Yinxiang* (China audio-visual monthly), no. 5 (1997).

Steen, Andreas. *Der Lange Marsch des Rock 'n' Roll- Pop- und Rockmusik in der Volksrepublik China*. Berliner China-Studien no. 32. Hamburg: LIT Verlag, 1996.

Wang, Gungwu. *The Revival of Chinese Nationalism*. IIAS Lecture Series, no. 6, ed. Paul van der Velde. Leiden: International Institute for Asian Studies, 1996.

Xue, Ji. *Yaogun mengxun: Zhongguo yaogunyue shilu* (In search of dreams in rock music: A catalogue of Chinese rock). Beijing: Zhongguo Dianying Chubanshe, 1993.

Zha, Jianying. *China Pop: How Soap Operas, Tabloids, and Bestsellers Are Transforming a Culture*. New York: New Press, 1995.

CHAPTER 3

Reexamining the East and the West: Tanizaki Jun'ichiro, "Orientalism," and Popular Culture

Mitsuhiro Yoshimoto

Globalization is now a ubiquitous phenomenon. Regardless of where we are located geographically, socially, and economically, we feel the impact of globalization in one way or another. Movement of capital, information, and people across national and other borders is increasingly accelerated, resulting in the formation of a global space whose contradictions, not homogeneity, cannot but affect all of us on the planet. It is therefore no surprise that globalization has become a new buzzword in academia. Yet the astonishingly fast and unpredictable expansion of transnational networks of circulation of all kinds presents a formidable challenge to the existing academic disciplines, many of which are now struggling to reconfigure themselves to cope with the new economic, political, and social reality of global inequalities and contradictions.

Despite its undeniable significance, however, globalization may not be an all-purpose concept for explaining the contemporary world. Many world historians and world-system theorists argue, for instance, that the world was globally interconnected well before the emergence of modern nation states. According to Andre Gunder Frank, "Globalism (even more than globalization) was a fact of life since at least 1500 for the whole world, excepting a very few sparsely settled islands in the Pacific (though only for a little while)."[1] Moreover, despite all the commotion about its newness, it seems globalization as a critical discourse has yet to present a genuinely alternative model of the world. No matter how many boundaries are crossed, ignored, or destroyed, the way the world is conceptualized is still closely linked to the centrality of nation states and no less dependent on such problematic geographical units as Asia and Europe or such geocultural notions as East and West. Even if we come to realize that the ascendance of Europe to the hegemonic position in the world system was a relatively recent phenomenon, it is excruciatingly hard for us to shake off the general Eurocentric framework within which the world is imagined. As the discourse of globalization gains popularity, it becomes more urgent for us to think through still dominant geocultural categories such as East and West, whose hold over our imagination and cognitive capacity to map the world is far from over.

Another important issue that needs to be addressed in any examination of globalization as a geocultural question is the role of audio-visual images and popular culture. Popular culture is one of the privileged topics for discussions and analyses of globalization. The global circulation and consumption of films, fashion, popular music, and television programs are certainly changing national, cultural, and ethnic identities and the surfaces of everyday life; that is, more than just a sign or indicator of globalization, popular culture is now one of the major propelling forces behind the process of globalization. Yet, again, we need to proceed cautiously to avoid falling into a trap of believing in the absolute newness of the phenomenon or seeing the border-crossing power of popular culture from an either/or perspective: that is, either merely celebrating popular culture's liberating potential or dogmatically condemning its role in global homogenization. For example, the ubiquitous presence of Japanese televisual images in Taiwan and Hong Kong or the popularity of Chinese and other Asian films in Japan is undoubtedly a significant new development since the 1990s. What it exactly means is, however, far from clear, and it remains to be seen if the new transnational networks of circulation of popular culture would contribute to the dismantling of problematic geographical or geocultural categories, or on the contrary, reinforce their hold over our ability to imagine a global space.

The purpose of this essay is to scrutinize the geocultural dichotomy of East and West and articulate the possibilities of popular culture as an agent of problematizing this dichotomy. Instead of philosophically deconstructing the categories of East and West or analyzing transnational flows of contemporary audio-visual images, I shall take a detour by approaching these problems through an examination of the work of one prominent Japanese writer of the twentieth century, Tanizaki Jun'ichiro (1886–1965). Neither a philosopher nor a scholar, Tanizaki is a fiction writer whose treatment of geocultural categories and popular culture is serious, sophisticated, and above all imaginative. Given that a mere philosophical understanding of how the geocultural dichotomy of East and West lacks a conceptual coherence or factual basis has not had much impact on the popular conceptualization of the contemporary world, it is important for us to explore other ways of changing our perception. Tanizaki's work constitutes one such alternative body of discourse in which the problematic of East and West is not logically explained but figuratively treated through the power of literary imagination. By examining Tanizaki's work, we may be able to learn how to overcome the hegemonic framework by simultaneously using and destroying these geocultural categories.

What makes the work of Tanizaki particularly useful for our purpose is his use of popular culture as a means of problematizing a dominant geocultural imagination. As one of the few prominent modern Japanese writers who were seriously interested in and engaged with popular culture, Tanizaki not only talked about it in his essays but also actively participated in its production as a script writer/executive consultant for Taikatsu, a film production company established in 1920 to produce a new type of film whose quality would match that of Hollywood and European movies. Throughout his career, Tanizaki carefully avoided asserting a great divide between high art and popular culture, and his sensitivity to the complexity of the relationship between them is closely related to his refusal to use the East-West dichotomy as a self-evident truth. Given globalization's propensity for blurring a boundary between high art and popular culture, the work of Tanizaki is more relevant than ever.

Geocultural Matrix

Any attempt to summarize Tanizaki's accomplishment as a writer cannot avoid the question of periodization, and any attempt to divide his career into distinct stages or phases must deal with the problems concerning the power of geocultural imaginations and the position of popular culture in a modern consciousness. Critics have proposed different ways of dividing Tanizaki's career into distinct stages or periods, and they all reveal the basic critical assumptions about the relation of East and West and that of high art and popular culture. One such model posits three periods of diabolism, modernism, and traditionalism. Another model sees seemingly more neutral four periods of early, early-middle, middle, and late.[2] What is commonly assumed in these models is Tanizaki's radical transformation from a hedonistic modernist to a staunch traditionalist. It is widely believed that Tanizaki started as an enthusiastic admirer of Western modernism and mass culture, and many of his early works displayed his penchant for things Western. But sometime in the 1920s, particularly after his move to the Kansai area because of the destruction of Tokyo by the Great Kanto earthquake, Tanizaki's attention increasingly turned away from the West, modernism, and the culture of mass consumption as he rediscovered and became an ardent defender of the beauty of traditional Japanese culture. Many critics who hold this view tend to dismiss Tanizaki's earlier works, since for them the radical change marks two stages in the development of Tanizaki as a writer. These critics argue that Tanizaki did not simply change but matured by shedding the shallow influence of Western modernism and American mass culture. To underline the superficiality of Tanizaki's "diabolic" or "exotic" modernism, some of them even claim that Tanizaki was from the beginning a traditionalist after all. Concomitant to this strategy of emphasizing Tanizaki's lifelong interest in traditional Japanese culture is an attempt to preserve the unity of Tanizaki's career by ultimately dismissing the writer's late works, which do not fit with his image as a classicist. Thus, whereas *The Key* (Kagi, 1956), a twisted tale of psychological manipulation and masochistic play centered around an old university professor and his much younger wife, is dismissed as an aberrant and schematic novel without much real substance, *Diary of a Mad Old Man* (Futen rojin nikki, 1961–62) is accepted because as "comedy" it creates a distance between Tanizaki, the author, and the novel's protagonist, a seventy-seven-year-old man, who is, in spite of his deteriorating health, sexually obsessed with his daughter-in-law's feet.[3] Carefully excluding works that seem to be corrupted by Westernized values, mass culture, and journalistic sensationalism protects Tanazaki's evolutionary development.

It is often dangerous to see in a writer's career such an evolutionary development from a beginning to a mature period, and particularly in the case of Tanizaki; the concrete specificity of his work betrays the evolutionary model. If it is misleading to claim that Tanizaki became interested in Japanese tradition only after his move to the Kansai area or the "West" of Japan, it is equally questionable to label Tanizaki's interest in modernism and American mass culture the mere passing phase of a pretentious young writer. Tanizaki's fascination with the West cannot be dismissed simply as a masquerade. Or, if it can, then it is equally possible to say that his interest in Japanese tradition is also nothing more than a masquerade. "There is no doubt that Tanizaki was interested in the Western culture," one critic writes, "but that does not mean he was imitating Western masters. With the knowledge of the Western art, literature, and philosophy, he tried to create the Eastern literary art. He struggled throughout his life to create his own literature based on the Eastern tradition."[4] I agree with this critic's view that Tanizaki was not a mere imitator of Western art and literature. However, his argument does not make much sense because he does not explain why Tanizaki first needed to learn the literature and culture of the West before creating what he calls "Eastern literary art." (Is he implying that despite its name, "Eastern literary art" is not autonomous but dependent on "Western literary art"?) We can debate the relative artistic value of Tanizaki's two late works, The Key and The Bridge of Dreams (Yume no ukihashi, 1959), and may conclude that the former is an exception that does not belong to the canon of Tanizaki's work after all. However, this hypothetical conclusion still cannot explain why Tanizaki was interested in creating a novel like The Key late in his alleged evolutionary process at the age of seventy. What made him produce until the very end of his life "impure" texts such as The Key, in which American literature, Hollywood movies, and a Polaroid camera appear as important textual details and narrative motifs? Was it just a mistake? Did Tanizaki lapse into his former "pretentiously Westernized" self? Or, does this "exception" tell us that there is something wrong with the evolutionary view of Tanizaki's career based on the dichotomy of East and West?

There is no question about Tanizaki's infatuation with the West and cultures of modernity early in his career. Many of his works of the 1910s and 1920s feature the West as an object of overwhelming attraction. Then, in the late 1920s and early 1930s, Tanizaki wrote a series of works that did not seem to share any apparent similarities with these earlier works. The settings of such stories as Quicksand (Manji, 1928–1930), Some Prefer Nettles (Tade kuu mushi, 1928–1929), Arrowroot (Yoshino kuzu, 1931), The Reed Cutter (Ashikari, 1932), and A Portrait of Shunkin (Shunkin sho, 1933) are no longer Tokyo and Yokohama but Kyoto, Osaka, Kobe, and their surrounding areas. The stories often allude to classical Japanese texts and incorporate other traditional Japanese arts as an integral part of milieus and characters. Yet, these obvious changes in thematic content do not automatically lead to the conclusion that Tanizaki changed from a hedonistic modernist blindly pursuing Western culture to a conservative culturalist admiring old Japan. At the same time, an alternative view that Tanizaki nonchalantly embraced traditional Japan and the modern West may be too general to fully account for the specificity of Tanizaki's engagement with Western modernism and traditional Japanese culture.[5] The "return to Japan" was probably not a monolithic phenomenon, as is often argued, but it still needs to be carefully examined in order to grasp the historical specificity of Tanizaki's career and individual works.[6]

One of the leading literary critics who warn us not to encase Tanizaki in the cliché of the "return to Japan" discourse is Nakamura Mitsuo. The central point of Nakamura's argument is that the concrete specificity of Tanizaki's individual experience makes it impossible to reduce his change in the 1920s to another example of the conversion of modern Japanese intellectuals, many of whom became infatuated with Western culture in their youth and then returned to Japan as they got older. Tanizaki's return to "old Japan" through his move to the Kansai area of Kyoto, Osaka, and Kobe was not a manifestation of the pattern of circular movement from the East to the West, and then back to the East again, but a "radical transformation of self, which was carefully planned and accomplished on the level of both art and personal life."[7] Nakamura claims that when Tanizaki moved to Kansai, he shook off influences of Western thought and returned to his true self of childhood nurtured in an old merchant milieu of Tokyo's downtown (*shitamachi*), which he was reminded of by antediluvian districts and customs of Kyoto and Osaka. As he escaped from Western influences, Tanizaki abandoned the fundamental tenets of civil society and embraced instead the ethos of traditional townspeople. According to Nakamura, what made this about-face easy for Tanizaki was the superficiality of Western influences on him. Despite his infatuation with things Western, Nakamura asserts, Tanizaki never understood Western thought, literature, and art deeply. What appears to be a radical disjunction in Tanizaki's career was in fact part of his continuous evolution as a writer who was less interested in intellectual thinking and analysis than in sensuous forms and phenomena of a superficial kind.

According to Nakamura, the West was for Tanizaki first and foremost an idealized object of exoticism. When Tanizaki talks about the West in his works, it frequently appears as Hollywood movies, modern cityscapes, scenes of urban life and mass consumption, white women, clothing, and food. On the surface, Tanizaki's biographical information seems to confirm Nakamura's claim that the writer's understanding of the West was tragically shallow and simplistic. Many of his fellow writers and predecessors were attracted to the West, but none went to the extent of immersing himself in the simulated world of the West as Tanizaki did. The lifestyle of Tanizaki, who completely identified himself with the Westerners, was in fact extreme. In 1920, with his wife, Chiyoko, and their daughter, he moved to Yokohama, a port city west of Tokyo. In the following year, after their house was destroyed by a typhoon, the Tanizakis moved to a house in the Bluff, Yokohama's foreign settlement. The style of this new house was truly Western. The previous owner was British and left for the Tanizakis furniture and even a cook, whom they continued to employ. For about two years, Tanizaki lived in this Western-style house, which did not have a single Japanese room with tatami mats except one room for a Japanese maid; wore Western clothes and shoes all day long; ate Western food; took lessons in Western dancing and English conversation; and mingled with foreign residents of this semicolonial enclave. Tanizaki continued to maintain his outrageously Western lifestyle, which is reflected in many of his works of the 1920s, until September 1, 1923, when the Great Kanto earthquake hit the Tokyo-Yokohama area, killing more than 100,000 people. His house destroyed by the earthquake, Tanizaki moved to the Kansai region, where he allegedly realized the superficiality of his Westernized life, and began to embrace a rapidly disappearing old Japan.

Nakamura argues that when Tanizaki discusses the West, his expressions tend to be turgid and anachronistic, and Tanizaki's understanding of the West seems, compared to other modern Japanese writers' genuine appreciation, too naïve and sometimes even infantile. In one of his essays Tanizaki observes that children naturally prefer Western food and art to their Japanese counterparts because the former are more direct and straightforward than the latter. Nakamura, however, points out that there must be many children who prefer sashimi and *chawanmushi* to steak and fried oysters, and suggests that it is not children in general but Tanizaki himself who likes things Western. If Tanizaki's observation proves anything, it is not some natural affinity of children and Western culture but his own infantilism. Tanizaki cannot comprehend Western thought and the nature that gave rise to that thought because of his childlike mind. While conceding that Tanizaki's view of the West is not completely wrong, Nakamura still stresses that it is too simplistic and one-dimensional. To illustrate his point further, Nakamura compares Tanizaki's naive infatuation with Western material culture to another Japanese writer Nagai Kafu's deeper understanding of Western thought. Unlike Tanizaki, who never visited Europe or the United States, Kafu spent 1903 to 1908 years in the United States and France. Because he lived in various parts of the United States for five years, when he moved to France, Kafu was not naively attracted to modern technology and material culture anymore. Instead, he came to appreciate "the beauty of tradition permeating French society."[8] Like Kafu, Nakamura also lived in Europe and experienced what underlies the development of technology and civilization in the West. Nakamura seems to believe that his superiority over Tanizaki comes from his ability to differentiate a true West and a commercialized West. For Nakamura, the West is European literature and intellectual tradition, while for Tanizaki it is what Nakamura considers a debased version of Europe or the West called America. Nakamura thinks that it is this difference between Europe and America that Tanizaki never understood. In his words, "Tanizaki's view of the West as a whole is Americanism."[9] The ability to distinguish a genuine West from a commercialized West is crucial. Without it, one can never understand the West and its tradition correctly, and therefore progress in the broadest sense becomes impossible. For Nakamura, as for many other modernists, the West embodies universality, so that Tanizaki's inability to understand the true logic of the Occident cuts him off from the universal way of thinking shared by all human beings.[10] Tanizaki is ultimately dismissed by Nakamura as a colonial intellectual who could not distinguish the superficial fashions and consumer culture of Western capitalism from the deep philosophical and ethical principles underlying the West's civil society, with at its core the autonomy and freedom of individuals. According to Nakamura, Tanizaki never comprehended the truth of the West. Nor was he even interested in it seriously. Fascinated with material culture and technology yet never really attracted to the deep-seated philosophical foundations of Western civilization, Tanizaki embraced, Nakamura claims, only the superficial, material aspects of Western civilization most typically found in Western colonies.

Even though it contains some interesting observations, Nakamura's study of Tanizaki is in the end not particularly convincing. The problem with Nakamura's argument is clearly evidenced, for instance, by his reading of *A Fool's Love* (Chijin no ai, 1924–25), which for him sums up Tanizaki's infatuated relation to the West. The protagonist Joji's masochistic idolization of Naomi is at the same time his paralyzing admiration for the West that Naomi embodies. For Nakamura, this is ludicrous because what is called for is not blind adoration of the West as the object of sensuous experience but an intellectual understanding of Western culture and thought from a critical distance. Moreover, according to Nakamura, what Naomi embodies is not a genuine West of high art and cultural refinement but a false West of mass culture and consumerism. Nakamura contends that Joji is literally a surrogate figure for Tanizaki, and the lack of critical distance between the protagonist and the author makes the latter blind to how pathetically comical Joji's myopic infatuation with the false West is. Yet, there is nothing in the text that indicates the author's uncritical identification with the protagonist. Nakamura's claim that Joji is Tanizaki seems to be arbitrary speculation unsupported by textual evidence. Furthermore, *A Fool's Love* is full of ironic passages where the person who jeers at the other's shallow imitation of Western manners turns out to be as ridiculous as the ridiculed other. As Tomi Suzuki observes, Nakamura's "harsh attack on *Chijin no ai* from the point of view of someone with a more profound knowledge of 'true' Western modernity than the objects of his criticism makes him part of the chain of ridiculers and the ridiculed that *Chijin no ai* effectively dramatizes."[11]

Nakamura's charge of infantilism against Tanizaki is also suspect. He refers to passages from the writer's essays that celebrate the healthy vitality and straightforward cheerfulness of Western culture. For Nakamura, they are proof of Tanizaki's infantile view of the West, the complexity of which eludes the simple mind of this writer with the *shitamachi* merchant's sensibility. It is, however, worth reminding ourselves that Tanizaki started as a "diabolic," "decadent" writer who found his mentors in Charles Baudelaire, Edgar Allan Poe, and Oscar Wilde. Given this background, it is necessary to take what Tanizaki said in the late 1920s and early 1930s with a grain of salt. Nakamura's persistent attempt to portray Tanizaki's mind as underdeveloped, simple, and childlike seems equally unsuccessful. As Nakamura correctly points out, Tanizaki excels in the depiction of children, and this might be because he is to some extent a writer of childlike sensibilities. Even if this in fact is the case, it does not automatically lead to the conclusion that Tanizaki is therefore innocent and naïve. What makes his works on children so compelling is his refusal to perpetuate popular images of children as simple, straightforward, uncomplicated beings. They pursue serious sadomasochistic play (*Early Youth* [Shonen 1911) and even create a little secret kingdom ruled by a child president who is much more adept at manipulating and wielding power over his subordinates than are the adults around him (*The Little Kingdom* [Chiisana okoku, 1918]). Since there is nothing childlike about Tanizaki's children in an ordinary sense, his argument on the "superiority" of the West is far more complex than the way it is summarized by Nakamura. It is probably more infantile to accept Tanizaki's remarks at face value without first considering various self-contradictions and rhetorical irony in his texts.

The West Tanizaki is attracted to is to a large extent a product of his imagination. At the same time, the West Nakamura believes in is also for the most part nothing but his own construct. Whereas from the perspective of Nakamura Tanizaki's West may appear too shallow, Nakamura's West is at least equally one-dimensional. It is baffling to see Nakamura mentioning the references to Hollywood movies and American film magazines in Tanizaki's writings as evidence for the latter's naïve view of the West. He refers to Tanizaki's involvement in film production in 1920 only in passing, interpreting it as just another manifestation of the writer's penchant for contemporary cultural trends and fashion.[12] But Tanizaki's interest in the cinema was far more significant than Nakamura and other Tanizaki critics have argued. What is lacking in Nakamura's caricatured portrayal of Tanizaki's obsession with the West is an attention to the concrete situations of the West in the 1920s and 1930s. It was the age of modernism, speed, and mass consumption. What constituted art in the age of mechanical reproduction was irreversibly changed by photography and, more importantly, by film. When we read Nakamura's criticism, we cannot help thinking that, for him, to understand Western culture correctly is to read Baudelaire and Flaubert in French. Any mention of mass culture is automatically equated with a lack of intellect and superficiality. But Baudelaire is not some "classic" poet whose work epitomized a fossilized Western tradition, but a flâneur on the streets of "Paris, capital of the nineteenth century."[13] The cinema, which Nakamura ignores as some frivolous, commercialized residue of Western civilization, was at the forefront of the contemporary cultural transformation of the West in the twentieth century. The West he urges us to study and comprehend correctly does not exist even in the so-called West; instead, it can be found only in the mind of Nakamura. By dismissing mass culture as a mere degradation of Western cultural tradition, Nakamura's criticism fails to see Tanizaki's works as what the writer Oda Sakunosuke called a "literature of possibilities."

Nakamura fails to recognize not only how fundamentally new technology and mass culture have transformed the concept of art, but also how much his "Europe" and "high culture" are already a product of the mass commodification he despises. In the aftermath of World War I, the strong yen made it much easier for Japanese intellectuals to stay in Europe and buy books in bulk. Travel to Europe, which had been reserved for a limited number of the elite, became possible for those with reasonable financial resources. "Europe" was therefore not an abstract entity but tangible objects and experiences that could be purchased, exchanged, and consumed with money. To the extent that he does not scrutinize this socioeconomic basis of the newly attainable "Europe," Nakamura's use of the notion of the West in his criticism seems in the end more naïve than Tanizaki's.

"Orientalism" and the Decolonization of the Mind

"Garrulous Jottings" (Jozetsuroku), which was serialized in a highbrow magazine *Kaizo* from February to December 1927, is mostly known as an essay in which Tanizaki debated the significance of the "plot of the novel" with Akutagawa Ryunosuke. But

Tanizaki's essay is more than just a rebuttal of Akutagawa's position on what the novel should be. Besides the formal characteristics of the novel, it touches upon many different subjects, including cultural differences between the East and the West. In fact, "Garrulous Jottings" is a crucial text for our understanding of Tanizaki's treatment of these two geocultural categories and the problematic of Tanizaki's so-called *Nihon kaiki* or "return to Japan." As a text, however, it has often been misread or simply dismissed in Tanizaki criticism. Some critics claim that the purpose of the essay is to demonstrate that "the Occident was superior to the Orient," while others assert that Tanizaki attempts to demonstrate the superiority of the Orient over the Occident, or "to define and exemplify the nature of Orientalism and the Oriental tradition."[14] But these summaries do not do justice to the complexity of Tanizaki's argument. A close reading of *Garrulous Jottings* reveals that Tanizaki did not either simply "return to Japan" or remain infatuated with the West.

On the surface, Tanizaki may seem essentialist, since he does not shy away from asserting certain cultural dispositions allegedly unique to the Orient. He starts his speculative reflection with the following passage on *Toyoshugi* or "Orientalism":

> First of all, it is not clear even to me what exactly *Toyoshugi* is. But, in brief, it refers to Oriental taste, ways of thinking, physical build, character. I am not quite sure how to articulate myself, but I can sense in the Orient something uniquely different from the Occident, not only in literature and art but also in politics, religion, philosophy, and even the ordinary experiences of everyday life and the small details of clothing, food, and shelter. At least Orientals must know what I am talking about. Perhaps it is not appropriate to use the expression *shugi* [-ism]. In English it is Orientalism or something, but what it is called is not particularly important. What I am trying to say will become clearer as I explain more.[15]

Immediately after this passage where he asserts the existence of a positive difference between the Orient and the Occident, Tanizaki introduces a hierarchical order in their relationship; he argues that the Occident is superior to the Orient. To illustrate his point, he draws on his childhood experiences and uses one of his favorite topics, food. When he was five or six living in Tokyo's Nihonbashi, he had occasion to eat Western food (*yoshoku*). He could not believe there was such a delicious food as steak and fried oysters. Even when the same ingredients such as eggs were used, an omelet was much tastier than Japanese-style fried eggs (*tamagoyaki*) or scrambled eggs (*iritamago*). According to Tanizaki, the reason he liked Western food better than Japanese food is that "the taste of Oriental food—or at least Japanese food—is too subtle, and does not appeal to children's taste. In contrast, that of Occidental food is strong, so that children can appreciate it without any difficulty."[16] Tanizaki then discusses the difference between Japanese and Western paintings to clarify his argument further. Although as a child he never found any beauty in Japanese paintings, when he saw a Western-style painting of the Virgin Mary, he was struck with its "indescribable nobility, fearfulness, and beauty." Tanizaki claims that to impress and move children, a painting must be drawn realistically, using linear perspective and chiaroscuro techniques. The painting of the Virgin Mary he admired was probably not a great work of art, but at least it was more realistic than Japanese-style painting. For Tanizaki, his observation that children prefer things Occidental to things Oriental is significant because the mind of the child is a tabula rasa. Although they may not comprehend things related to the complex web of human emotion, specialized knowledge, or sexual desire, children can understand as well as adults those aspects of art and culture that are not related to these subjects. Because their sense of perception has not yet lost freshness, children are sometimes better evaluators of works of art. While Oriental culture tends to be warped, subtle, subdued, complex, and dark, Occidental culture, which honest and pure children prefer to the former, is more straightforward, energetic, positive, realistic, and above all healthier. To the extent that healthy culture is more beneficial for the progress of human society, Occidental culture is better than Oriental culture.

Yet, for Tanizaki the superiority of the Occident over the Orient is not absolute. Although he is greatly attracted to it, Tanizaki cannot embrace Occidental culture without reservation. He admits that at the moment of his writing he prefers Oriental to Occidental culture. He finds, for example, Western food the least palatable of all cuisines; the best cuisine is Chinese, and then Japanese.[17] His attraction to Hollywood movies is countered by his admiration for classical Chinese poetry. Tanizaki does not believe that healthy Western art is essentially superior to unhealthy Eastern art, since "healthiness" is not necessarily the same as "superiority." We often deliberately choose "unhealthiness" over "healthiness," and what appears to be irrational choice may be what constitutes culture in the first place.

What is at stake in the comparison of Occidental and Oriental culture is contemporary geopolitics and Japan's position in the international power structure. Tanizaki argues that the objective situations of the world do not allow him and other Japanese to freely choose Oriental culture over Occidental culture. Regardless of what it really is, Occidental culture is much more direct and accessible than Oriental culture. If we understand Occidental and Oriental culture thoroughly, we may conclude that in the end Oriental culture is more suitable for Japanese. But the majority of the Japanese do not have enough financial and other resources to patiently go through the arduous training necessary to fully appreciate the subtlety of Oriental culture. Since they can see only the surface of Oriental and Occidental culture, for most Japanese the latter is much more attractive and accessible than the former. Superficially, Occidental culture, which is straightforward and energetic, is easier to understand and appreciate; thus, people are naturally drawn to it. At issue is the question of immediate attraction and accessibility for the masses, not that of the inherent superiority of either Occidental or Oriental culture. Tanizaki notes that the openness of Occidental art does not necessarily indicate its crudity. To become an artist of the first rank in Occidental art is as difficult as to achieve the same goal in Oriental art; however, the former is more accessible than the latter to ordinary people who are interested in art only as amateurs. Moreover, it is undeniable that in terms of technology and the material conditions of society, the Occident is far more advanced than the Orient. Even if Tanizaki personally decides to stick to Oriental culture, in a small country like Japan, there is no place where he can hide himself from railroads and factories, that is, the material civilization of the Occident. Thus,

Tanizaki's dilemma is the following. On the one hand, because it is healthier and tech-
nologically more advanced, Occidental culture is more suitable for human society. On
the other hand, Occidental culture cannot be celebrated simply as a better choice for the
Japanese and Orientals. The Orient will be spiritually colonized by the Occident unless
it seriously tries to preserve and protect its unique culture. Torn between the East and
the West, Tanizaki wonders how the old tradition of the East can be harmonized with
the contemporary social system borrowed from the West.

So many modern Japanese intellectuals like Tanizaki constructed a dyadic relationship of East and West, finding irreconcilable differences between the two. What distinguishes Tanizaki from many others is that he does not in the end try to create harmony
between East and West. Instead, he chooses to reexamine and problematize these two
notions thoroughly. One of the widely accepted images that Tanizaki scrutinizes is the
dichotomy of the spiritual East and the materialistic West. Although "it is often said that
Western civilization is materialistic, and Eastern civilization spiritual," he does not see
any substance behind this common assertion.[18] According to Tanizaki, one of the well-
known figures who propagate this dichotomous view is Rabindranath Tagore, whose
argument he criticizes as too simplistic.[19] There is obviously a great tradition of Buddhist philosophy in India, but then, argues Tanizaki, in the West, there is similarly an il-
lustrious history of philosophy dating back to the times of ancient Greeks. Contemporary Japanese would not be able to name on the spot any great Oriental philosophers
comparable to Plato or Kant, and in fact it is easier for Japanese to understand Greek
philosophy than Indian philosophy. Moreover, even in the United States, which is regarded as the most materialistic country in the world, there is Henry David Thoreau, a
"sage of Walden's forest." Tanizaki concludes that the reason why the East is often said
to be more spiritual than the West is the former's underdevelopment as a civilization; that
is, it is because the material aspects of its civilization is less advanced that the East appears to be more spiritually oriented than it actually is.

By criticizing Tagore, Tanizaki seems to assert the superiority of the West over the East
because the former is much more advanced in material aspects and at the same time
boasts a great philosophical tradition. But Tanizaki has no intention of perpetuating the
myth of Western superiority over the non-West. While the spirituality of the East is exposed as a modern myth, the identity of the West is simultaneously problematized.
Tanizaki argues that "there is no real basis for the claim that the East is more spiritual
than the West, except for the fact that Shakyamuni, Christ, and Mahomet, the founders
of the three great religions, were all born in Asia."[20] In this nonchalantly sarcastic remark, Tanizaki simultaneously exposes the spirituality of the East as a modern myth and
excludes the West from the realm of religiosity. He pokes fun at the alleged superiority
of the West by pointing out that the West is after all not so "Western," because the spiritual foundation of Western civilization, Christianity, originated in the East. The Middle East is of course an essential part of Western history and identity. By saying that
Christ was born in *toyo* (東 洋), which means the Orient or more specifically "Japan's
Orient," Tanizaki tries to reclaim the category of the East from the foundational myth
of the West.[21] And once we realize how ironic Tanizaki's attitude toward the West can

be, his contrast between Oriental and Occidental culture that we examined earlier begins to signify something other than it ostensibly says. According to Tanizaki, Occidental culture serves better than Oriental culture for the progress of humanity because of its healthiness and accessibility even to children. But the metaphors of adults and children are hardly neutral ones, particularly when they appear in a Eurocentric discourse. As J. M. Blaut points out, Eurocentrism has forged "the dualistic-developmental conception of human rationality": "Non-Europeans . . . were seen as psychically *underdeveloped*, as more or less *childlike*. But, given the psychic unity of mankind, non-Europeans could of course be brought to adulthood, to rationality, to modernity, through a set of learning experiences, mainly colonial. . . . It was not simply a case of "the natives are like children." The idea of non-European nonrationality was a definite, putatively scientific principle, widely accepted: non-Europeans think somewhat like children, and will be led toward adulthood by Europeans."[22] Given Eurocentrism's construction of non-Westerners as children to be educated by Westerners, Tanizaki's association of the Occident with children subverts his positive remarks on Occidental culture and the logic of Eurocentrism itself.

The Japanese idea of toyo is derived from what is called the Orient by Westerners, yet there is a fundamental positional difference implied in it. The idea of toyo was invented in the late nineteenth century as an alternative to the Western construction of the objectified Orient. Along with the category of toyo emerged a new academic field of *toyoshi* (a history of the Orient), whose objective was to authenticate this category and transform Japan into a subject of history. Toyoshi as an academic discourse rightfully criticized the Eurocentrism underlying the West's version of world history and attempted to create new historical "facts," since as J. M. Blaut reminds us, Eurocentrism is not a mere prejudice or bias. At the same time, however, it also constructed Japan as an exceptionally unique and advanced nation in Asia; in the world of toyoshi, Japan was a modern nation on an equal footing with Europe and superior to China and the rest of Asia. Stefan Tanaka argues that

> unlike the West's Orient, the term *toyo* assumed merely cultural difference, not inherent backwardness. The creation of *toyoshi* thus authorized a particular Japanese view of Europe and Asia as well. It established modern Japan's equivalence—as the most advanced nation of Asia—with Europe, and also the distinction from and cultural, intellectual, and structural superiority over China. While Europe, as the West, became an other, that against which Japan compared itself, *shina* [China] became a different other; it was an object, an idealized space and time from which Japan developed.[23]

Although it resonates with toyoshi, Tanizaki's "Orientalism" or *toyoshugi* does not find anything exceptionally superior about Japanese culture as opposed to either European or Chinese culture. Instead of returning to the alleged origins of unique Japaneseness, by bringing up the somewhat ambiguous and undefinable notion of *toyoshugi*, Tanizaki problematizes the essentialized geocultural identities of the East and the West. His point is not that these categories are mere illusions which people can freely dispense with. Instead, his argument shows that this dyadic pair of categories has no fixed content or meaning outside of a specific historical context. Interested in neither the East nor the West by itself, Tanizaki attempts to trace the tortuously twisted relation between these two value-laden categories, whose practical meanings and functions are inextricably tied to the worldly affairs of imperialism and colonialism.

Earlier we observed that despite his attempt to problematize the widely accepted discourse on Tanizaki's "return to Japan," Nakamura Mitsuo ends up constructing another questionable image of this complex writer. What is specifically missing in Nakamura's criticism of Tanizaki is the awareness of history that is found everywhere in the latter's various treatments of the East-West dichotomy. Nakamura dismisses Tanizaki as an infantile, non-intellectual writer whose shallow understanding of the West makes him a typical example of native intellectuals in European colonies. This caricatured view of natives—which Nakamura does not seem to think caricatured—shows how shallow is his own understanding of the problem Tanizaki struggles to solve. What is remarkably absent in Nakamura's criticism of Tanizaki is any attempt to connect what he takes as the foundational principles of modern Western thought and the fact of colonialism that he uses to question Tanizaki's intellectual ability. But the one who is blind to his own colonized mentality is not Tanizaki but Nakamura. "Garrulous Jottings" and many of his other works indicate that Tanizaki is much more aware of geocultural implications of imperialism and colonialism, and the impossibility of talking about art and literature outside of the contemporary geopolitical situations controlled by the dominant Western powers. Why is it necessary to understand the West correctly? Do Europeans eagerly try to understand the East correctly, too? If they do not, why is that the case? Is there such thing as the "real" West in the first place? Is Nakamura a neutral observer looking at the West as an object of knowledge? Aren't there concrete social relations between the Westerners and himself? Shouldn't he confront those relations as a problem in his engagement with the West? The fact that Nakamura does not seriously ask any of these questions shows how blind he remains to his own enunciating position.

According to one of the most prevalent clichés concerning the Japanese national character, the Japanese do not understand their own culture very well; it is only after foreigners—that is, Westerners—point out how wonderful a particular example of Japanese art or cultural practice is that the Japanese begin to appreciate its true value. The history of Japanese cinema seems to fit this pattern very well. Another good example is the Japanese woodblock print or *ukiyoe,* which was, as the popular account goes, basically ignored by the Japanese cultural elite until "discovered" by Westerners in the mid–nineteenth century. Until then, the Japanese cultural elite never regarded it as a repertoire of high art with serious artistic value. In his discussion of the West's "discovery" of ukiyoe, Tanizaki puts into question the validity of this "history" of ukiyoe's reception. He argues that Japanese should not feel ashamed of their "ignorance," and that Westerners should not be proud of their superior aesthetic sensibility. The history of ukiyoe's reception does not demonstrate Westerners' superiority over Japanese with regard to their faculty of aesthetic judgment. What the "discovery" tells us instead is that among many types of Japanese art, ukiyoe was the easiest for Westerners to appreciate because of their belief that art should be about "love" and "human affairs." It also shows how ignorant Westerners were about the specific reason why such a superb art as ukiyoe had not been respected by Japanese. Even though many Japanese, including those who belonged to the cultural elite, enjoyed ukiyoe, they did not publicly talk about it because of Confucian moral standards. They merely pretended not to be interested in ukiyoe, and discretion was a key element in their reception of this popular art. Thus, Tanizaki suggests that Westerners in a sense violated the implicit social etiquette of Japanese by celebrating ukiyoe as if it were their greatest discovery.[24]

Tanizaki is critical of both Westerners who objectify Japan through an Orientalist gaze and Japanese who exoticize themselves to adulate Westerners. According to Tanizaki, culture cannot be treated as an example of export goods. If any national culture is highly refined and attractive, people from other countries will try to understand and appreciate it on their own. Therefore, there is no strong need for Japanese to advertise the value of Japanese culture by, for example, translating their own literature into foreign languages. When Japanese literary works are used as a public relations campaign by Japanese themselves, translation is often carried out based on very superficial images of national types. Tanizaki's *The Age of Fear* (Kyofu jidai, 1916) is being translated into Italian, he speculates, because of the translator's assumption that its bloodiness would appeal to the "national character and tastes of Italians."[25] Moreover, even when it is Westerners who initiate the process, the introduction of Japanese culture to non-Japanese can still be a futile endeavor as long as Japan is merely objectified as an exotic other. An example of such a misguided effort is Paul Claudel's attempt to bring a Japanese theater group to Paris, which Tanizaki regards as nothing more than a meddlesome intervention of an Orientalist. Western arrogance and Japanese obsequiousness often go hand in hand. Claudel, who stayed in Tokyo as French ambassador in the first half of the 1920s, was keenly interested in classical Japanese theater and wrote a play incorporating some of its conventions.[26] Even though he did not see the performance of this particular play at the Teikoku Gekijo (Imperial Theater), Tanizaki read the play and found it "nonsensical" (*gunimotsukanai*). He expresses his annoyance with the Teikoku Gekijo's servile response to Claudel, who despite his mediocre play demanded that the best Kabuki actors such as Matsumoto Koshiro and Onoe Kikugoro be cast in the main roles. Why do Japanese need to help Westerners whose understanding of Japanese art is pathetically shallow? Why do Japanese theater owners play up to a globetrotting French ambassador who has written an embarrassingly silly play as a hobby? It is of course nice to see a great Kabuki actor who does not brag about his talent. But why is it necessary for an actor of Koshiro's standing to teach so kindly Kabuki's acting techniques to a not particularly talented actor just because he is American? Tanizaki's point is not that the Japanese should be proud of their unique culture and protect it blindly as their possession. Instead, what emerges in his discussions is his strong suspicion of any assertion of Japaneseness, either by Japanese or Westerners, that remains oblivious to or actively suppresses the geopolitical dimensions of national and cultural identity.

Nations and Popular Culture

Tanizaki was one of the few modern Japanese writers who were not only interested in film but also actively involved in filmmaking at the moment when Japanese cinema was undergoing the process of modernization. His pursuit of film art turned out to be very brief, yet it was intense and serious. None of the films that he produced and/or wrote scripts for has survived, so we must rely on contemporary reviews and the scripts to conjecture what those films were like. Although it is lamentable, the permanent loss of his films is not as devastating as it might seem at first. For film continued to play a major role in his works even after he retired from the world of filmmaking. Tanizaki explored the fundamental impact of the cinema on modern subjectivity, literary narration, and the social construction of reality in many of his works, among which *Some Prefer Nettles* is one of the most interesting.

Some Prefer Nettles is often read as a transitional work for Tanizaki both personally and artistically. One of the dominant modes of reading this novel is to regard it as an example of the modern literary genre called *shishosetsu* or the "I-novel"; that is, critics have tried to determine how accurately this novel reflects Tanizaki's troubled personal life. In the 1920s Tanizaki was locked into a strange love triangle with his estranged wife Chiyoko and his friend/writer Sato Haruo. In 1921, Tanizaki agreed to "give" Chiyoko to Sato, since he was no longer interested in his wife, and his wife and friend were in love with each other. At the last moment, however, Tanizaki changed his mind and refused to fulfill his promise. This so-called Odawara incident led to a rupture in the friendship of Tanizaki and Sato, both of whom then published their own views of the incident and their ambivalent feelings toward one another in the form of fiction, play, and poetry. The two estranged friends finally made up with each other in 1926, and five years later Tanizaki not only "yielded" his wife to Sato but also publicly announced it as a consensual act among the three parties involved. As if to mirror the author's real life, *Some Prefer Nettles* focuses on a failing marriage of the protagonist, Shiba Kaname, and his wife, Misako, because of their sexual incompatibility. Even though he has no interest in Misako, Kaname does not want to actively initiate a legal procedure to end their marriage. Unlike his cousin Takanatsu, who experienced a divorce himself and plays the role of mediator for the estranged couple, Kaname remains passive, waiting for a "natural" resolution of the marriage. He encourages his wife to see her lover, Aso, while he himself secretly goes to see a Eurasian prostitute, Louise, on a regular basis. Despite this unusual arrangement, Kaname is not necessarily advocating a "modern way of life." He can care less about Confucian moral value, yet he is not sure about a new morality, either. The novel does not present any clear resolution; instead, it ends with the scene filled with a vague sense of anticipation.[27]

Artistically, too, *Some Prefer Nettles* is often regarded as a transitional work because it supposedly registers for the first time Tanizaki's return to Japan. The protagonist, Kaname, is in a state of limbo not only in his marriage but also in terms of his cultural identity. A native Tokyoite, Kaname used to dislike Osaka, where people are said to be not modest but crude and aggressive, and its culture less refined and more vulgar than the culture of Tokyo. But he is now increasingly drawn to the charm of Osaka partly because of the influence of his father-in-law, the Old Man. Even though he used to be drawn to things Western, the Old Man, who lives in the ancient capital of Kyoto with his young mistress, O-hisa, now fully embraces the traditional way of life. Kaname finds the lifestyle of the Old Man rather attractive and even accompanies him and O-hisa to see a traditional puppet theater performance on the island of Awaji. Kaname wonders whether the old Japan of the Old Man is more comfortable than the modern Japan of Misako and himself. As if to underline a change in his cultural identity, Tanizaki describes at the beginning and end of the novel the scenes in which Kaname takes a bath in two dramatically different settings. In the opening scene, Kaname takes a quick bath in a brightly lit bathroom of his own modern house, which has a tiled Western-style bathtub. In contrast, in the novel's concluding section, he finds himself in a traditional iron pot–style bathtub at the Old Man's house in Kyoto. The bathroom in this traditional Japanese-style house is so dimly lit that he can hardly see his own body (in O-hisa's words, "He [the Old Man] offers to wash my back sometimes, but it's so dark he can't tell front from back").[28] According to one critic, "Tanizaki is clearly moving toward rejecting a confusing and upsetting sense of a meaningless foreign 'modernity' for the more comforting experience of a meaningful native antiquity."[29] Similarly many others argue that *Some Prefer Nettles* is an early sign of Tanizaki's mature period, when he more fully engaged with classical Japanese literature and traditional aesthetics.

Regardless of critics' judgment of its artistic value, two types of reading dominate the critical writings on *Some Prefer Nettles*. For many, it is an important work because as *shishosetsu* or autobiographical fiction it reflects Tanizaki's personal life faithfully and gives us a glimpse of his interiority. For others it is a flop precisely because it is bad *shishosetsu;* that is, the author's confession of his inner most feelings and thoughts is not truthful enough. Correlatively, cultural commentaries interspersed in the work are taken either positively or negatively depending on the particular critic's taste and personal beliefs. And in either mode of reading, the novel's significance is heavily dependent on its relation to Tanizaki's biography.

But what makes *Some Prefer Nettles* interesting is not its biographical significance but its treatment of large geocultural questions, which Tanizaki raises in such essays as "Garrulous Jottings." Various remarks on cultural practices—old and new, East and West—interspersed throughout *Some Prefer Nettles* are not some dispensable elements decorating its main narrative, and cannot be taken at face value because they are mediated by Tanizaki's literary imagination. If "Garrulous Jottings" is his critical reflection on the hegemony of Eurocentrism and its effect on Japanese cultural identity in the form of an essay, *Some Prefer Nettles* is his attempt to think through similar issues in the form of fiction. Two important thematic motifs Tanizaki uses to interrogate the geocultural issues are geographical locations and different types of popular culture.

To show a structural relation among key locations in the novel, David Pollack constructs a diagram consisting of horizontal and vertical axes.[30] The vertical axis consists of three places, with Tokyo at the top, Osaka in the middle, and the island of Awaji at the bottom. According to Pollack, this is a diachronic axis showing the past (Awaji), the present (Osaka), and the future (Tokyo) of Japan. At the center of the horizontal axis is again found Osaka, with Kobe on the right and Kyoto on the left. Unlike the vertical axis, the relationship of Kyoto, Osaka, and Kobe represents not historical development but the cultural and moral values associated with the three places: traditional morality (Kyoto), ambiguous—half-traditional, half-modern—morality (Osaka), and foreign morality (Kobe). Pollack's diagram is an interesting way of thinking about the crucial roles played by places in *Some Prefer Nettles*, yet in the end it may not clarify the significance of geographical locations as bearers of specific symbolic meanings as much as it is supposed to do. A major problem with this structural mapping of location is that it prematurely fixes what each place symbolizes in the novel. Take, for instance, the case of Tokyo. In the 1920s, particularly after the earthquake in 1923, Tokyo was clearly the center of modernism in Japan, and until the mid-1920s Tanizaki was a leading voice in the ambivalent celebration of modern urban life. Interestingly, what is conspicuously absent in *Some Prefer Nettles* is any overt reference to Tokyo as a city of modernism, urban lifestyle, and mass consumption and entertainment, which were represented by such areas as Asakusa and Ginza. If, as Pollack claims, Tanizaki's intention was in fact to show the vacuity and inauthenticity of modern Japan/Tokyo, it would be all the more necessary to represent the superficiality of *modan raifu* (modern life), which is, however, not concretely depicted in the novel.

To understand the role of Tokyo in *Some Prefer Nettles*, it is important to recognize that Tanizaki is not necessarily interested in Tokyo itself but in its relations to other geographical locations. Tanizaki does not establish a relationship among places with fixed symbolic meanings; instead, he plays with various structural relations and dichotomies between those places, whose symbolic significance emerges only as a result of those relations. Thus, the position of Tokyo is determined, as the following passage shows, only in its relation to another urban center, Osaka.

> He [Kaname] disliked the Osaka samisen, but even more he disliked the uncouth Osaka narrator, the embodiment, it seemed to him, of certain Osaka traits that he, born and reared in Tokyo like his wife, found highly disagreeable, a sort of brashness, impudence, forwardness, a complete lack of tact when it came to pushing one's personal ends. The typical native of Tokyo has a natural reserve. Quite foreign to him is the openness of the Osakan, who strikes up a conversation with a stranger on the streetcar and proceeds—in an extreme case, it must be admitted—to ask how much his clothes cost and where he bought them. Such behavior in Tokyo would be considered outrageously rude. The plain sense of how to comport oneself is no doubt better developed in Tokyo than in Osaka. Sometimes, indeed, it is so well developed that it leads to an excessive concern with appearances and a timid unwillingness to act. But be that as it may, the son of Tokyo can, if he chooses, find in Osaka singing the perfect expression of Osaka crudeness. Surely, he may say to himself, the problem, no matter what strong emotions it stirs up can be taken care of with less grimacing, less twisting of the lips and contorting of the features, less writhing and straining toward the skies. If in fact it cannot be expressed in less emphatic and dramatic terms, then our Tokyo man is more inclined to turn it off with a joke than try to express it at all.[31]

As is evident in this fairly typical example, the crucial point of contrast between Tokyo and Osaka is not necessarily the degree of modernization but concrete cultural traits that make the two cities distinctively different from each other.

The problem with a schematic diagram that assigns fixed—stereotyped—meanings to geographical locations in the novel further becomes apparent when we examine the case of Kyoto, an ancient capital of Japan. On the surface, Kyoto embodies Japanese traditions: There are hundreds of Buddhist temples and Shinto shrines in the exclusive old city, where outsiders are not always welcomed to settle down. While utilizing this popular image of Kyoto, Tanizaki does not simply reaffirm it. A key element in his attempt to problematize the image of Kyoto as a bearer of culturally symbolic meanings is the Old Man. He loves puppet theater, wears traditional kimono, brings to a theater his own lunch in lacquerware, and takes a bath in a traditional bathtub which is "so small that one could hardly sit in it comfortably and so sharp to the touch with its heated metal sides " (193). Yet, despite embracing things traditional, the Old Man is not as traditional as he may seem at first. "The old man's arguments were full of references to 'young people today'" (35), but this admirer of puppet theater was a great fan of movies when he was young. Although he is called the Old Man, he is in reality not so old. The Old Man enjoys playing the role of an old man. ("He was always careful to cultivate in his dress and his manner an impression of advanced years. 'Old men should act like old men,' he was fond of saying, and his choice of clothes today was apparently an application of his dictum that 'old men only look older when they try to wear clothes too young for them.' This constant emphasis on age rather amused Kaname. The old man was not really as old as all that. . . . 'Being old is another of your father's hobbies,' Kaname had once remarked to her" [19–20].) The traditional taste and lifestyle of the Old Man, who is one of the most theatrical characters in the novel, are simulations—not inventions—of tradition. Thus, "what he said was never to be taken entirely at its face value" (35).

The Old Man's youthful fascination with movies and his propensity for acting the role of an old and old-fashioned man are not unrelated to the fact that Kyoto was simultaneously a city of the old and the new. In its own unique way Kyoto was as modern as Tokyo, Yokohama, Osaka, or Kobe. Along with Tokyo, Kyoto was a center of filmmaking, particularly a genre of film called *jidaigeki* or "period film." As somebody who was directly involved in film production himself, Tanizaki was familiar with the cinematic scene in Kyoto, a city dubbed "Japan's Hollywood." When he left Yokohama after it had been destroyed by the Great Kanto earthquake, Tanizaki found refuge in Kyoto. He rented a house in the area called Tojiin, right next to the Makino Kinema studio. Makino was a leading independent production company that made *jidaigeki*, particularly *chanbara*, sword-fight movies. There is no direct reference to Kyoto's filmmaking scene in *Some Prefer Nettles*, but given Tanizaki's own personal background and the popularity of films produced in Kyoto around the time of its publication, it is probably too simplistic to see Kyoto as an embodiment of traditional culture without any irony.

In his extensive discussion of differences between well-known geographical locations in Japan, Tanizaki resorts to the familiar binary pair of East and West. A twist is that these two categories refer not to two putatively unique civilizations (Orient and Occident) but to the division within Japan itself. The dichotomy of Japan's East (the Kanto region of Tokyo and Yokohama) and West (the Kansai region of Kyoto, Osaka, and Kobe) problematizes the semiotic coherence of Japan as a cultural sign, and consequently the identity of Japan as a nation. Moreover, Tanizaki does not simply replace the dichotomy of East and West with that of Japanese East and Japanese West, since each of the terms in this new binary pair contains differences within itself.

Does Kaname's increasing attraction to the puppet theater in Osaka, and then to its older form on the island of Awaji, signify a nostalgic return to an old, mythic Japan? David Pollack writes:

> The central and pivotal episode of *Some Prefer Nettles* is Kanamé's epiphanic return to the soil and the fold roots of his race. . . . Like the ethnologist Kunio Yanagita, Tanizaki is at pains here to recreate a "real folk," celebrating this "peasant art born from the pure soil of village tradition" as "the work of the race" (*minshuteki*). . . . The power of this concept to override distinctions of time, space, and social class permits it to transcend *all* such analytic categories, so that its most powerful effect is to induce a kind of hypnotic state which obliterates all the debilitating oppositions that plague and paralyze modern man—exactly what "modernity" means to Tanizaki. Under its spell are forgotten the troubling differences that have separated what was once an authentic, ancient, Japanese, rustic, popular, and communal *folk* from what has degenerated into the inauthentic, modern, Western, urbane, elite, and civic *individual*. Under the enchantment produced by the warmth, the crowd, and the music, Kaname falls into a drowsy reverie in which the present blends imperceptibly with memories of the past and youth to create a warm public bath of eternal unity.[32]

The pursuit of authenticity and tradition certainly motivates the Old Man to go on a pilgrimage to Awaji, where he watches a more rustic puppet theater performance and tries to obtain an old Awaji puppet. But as we just discussed, his traditional taste and lifestyle are nothing more than a veneer, and Kaname's attraction to the Old Man too is more than just a simple rediscovery of traditional Japan. Rather than signifying "race," the word *minshuteki* is used to refer to the idea of "popular" in the novel. And a close examination of his text shows that Tanizaki introduces the idea of popular precisely to problematize a clear dichotomy of Japan and the West.

According to Pollack, what characterizes the authentic Japan that Kaname rediscovers is the sense of communality, the opposite of Western individualism. He finds compelling evidence for his argument in the notion of *kata*, which means a type, form, or model.

> Tanizaki somehow manages to amass a host of small details to achieve an effect whose power—compounded of sunlight, music, crowd noises, children, candy, smells—is entirely sensual. In this blurring and melting (*toketeiru*), the most important distinction obliterated is that between particular details and overall effect, and so between individuals and the communal whole. The means by which this is achieved is the replacement of the troublesome entity of the individual with conventionalized types, or *kata*. As each puppet is a type whose features and movements conform to a pattern established centuries ago, exactly the same can be said about the human beings who come to participate as performers and observers at this rustic gathering; even the distinction between "performer" and "audience" is obliterated in this welter of participant actor-farmers. The old man and O-hisa, too, "appointed like a doll on the stage, accompanied by a doll, in search of an old doll to buy," are just as clearly types. Authenticity, far from involving any notion of "free choice" or "individuality," here implies the ability to fulfill one's role; "to conform to a type, to be the captive of a form [*kata ni*

hamaru toka kata ni torawareru] . . . requires a necessary and entirely positive abandonment of self."[33]

But kata is not just conventionalized types, models, or forms that replace the unique individuality. Tanizaki does not necessarily introduce the idea of kata to dissolve the individual self into the communal whole. Nor does he make use of it to demonstrate how unique Japanese puppet theater is. Instead of reaffirming Japanese uniqueness or communal ethos, Tanizaki focuses on the difference between professionals and amateurs, or specialists and ordinary people, and tries to show how kata as a type of popular knowledge bridges a gap between the two. Because of kata, nonprofessional actors, singers, narrators, and puppeteers can act, perform, or stage Kabuki and puppet plays in a presentable manner. Kata makes these performing arts available to a number of people who do not have easy access to theaters in urban centers. The significance of kata does not lie in its Japaneseness but in its democratic impulse, whose embodiment in the arts of the twentieth century is of course movies. Thus, Tanizaki writes in *Some Prefer Nettles*: "In the days before motion pictures, there was thus a happy substitute for them: a few hands and a little equipment, and a puppet theater could be put together to wander lightly over the country" (144). Tanizaki does not take up puppet theater, Kabuki, and other kinds of traditional popular culture to authenticate the centuries-long tradition of the Japanese "race." His purpose is in fact the opposite; that is, he valorizes popular culture precisely because it problematizes the dyadic scheme of cultural interpretation that posits the East against the West as mutually complementary entities. From Tanizaki's perspective, the possibility of popular culture lies in its ability to cross national, geographical, and geocultural boundaries. Popular culture is an active site of interaction, hybridization, and contestation, where Japaneseness and Westernness finally lose any fixed meanings.

Conclusion

For Tanizaki, to paraphrase Rudyard Kipling's pronouncement, "East is not East, West is not West; and never the twain shall meet." If any fruitful encounter of East and West is impossible, it is not because the two differ essentially on some alleged level of civilization. Constructed as two opposite terms of a dichotomy, East and West cannot meet yet complement each other in a geopolitical scheme. A major effect of the East-West binarism as it has been used in the past few centuries is to justify the West's colonial interests on a global scale. As a response to this ideological imposition, the East has appropriated the same dyadic pair of geocultural categories to assert its own autonomy and even superiority over the West. What distinguishes Tanizaki's work from this common response is that instead of simply reversing the hierarchical order of East and West, he constantly problematizes the identities of both and refuses to give any fixed cultural attributes to either. Tanizaki obsessively posits East against West to demonstrate the fundamentally imaginary nature of the signs. Tanizaki's move to and embrace of Osaka or "the West" of Japan cannot be equated to his alleged "return to Japan." Instead, it is an overdetermined strategic move through which Tanizaki not only foregrounds the arbitrariness of the West as a signifier but also develops his implicit—sometimes overt—critique of the nostalgic celebration of Edo (Tokyo) as a prelapsarian cultural space outside of history. What appears to be an essentialist statement in his writings is almost always undermined on a rhetorical level, and as we observed earlier, the rhetoric of a text often gives a completely different meaning to that statement. When many critics take Tanizaki's traditionalist turn—his masquerade as a cultural essentialist—too seriously, it becomes nothing more than a convenient ploy that enables them to dodge questions which may undermine the foundations of exceptionalism, both Western and Japanese.

The continuous use of such modern geocultural categories as East and West would not help us understand our contemporary world more clearly. Nor would they be an effective theoretical basis for any practical action to change it. However, at this juncture in history, it seems to be extremely difficult not to use these categories when we discuss geocultural issues. Critical discourses of postmodernism, transnationalism, or globalization may be the beginning of a new paradigm change, but none of them seems able to do away with older geocultural frameworks. If it is not yet possible to discard them completely, then we must continue to problematize and think through the East-West binarism. Given the current state of the world and our critical apparatus to theorize about it, Tanizaki's literary effort and nonparochial view of popular culture can still guide our critical endeavor.

Notes

1. Frank, *ReOrient*, 340.

2. Anthony Hood Chambers, *The Secret Window: Ideal Worlds in Tanizaki's Fiction* (Cambridge: Council on East Asian Studies, Harvard University, 1994), 126.

3. Donald Keene, *Dawn to the West: Japanese Literature of the Modern Era (Fiction)* (New York: Holt, Rinehart and Winston, 1984), 778–780.

4. Tokuhiro Miura, "Tanizaki and the Tradition," in *Tanizaki Jun'ichiro kenkyu,* ed. Ara Masato (Tokyo: Yagi Shoten, 1972), 637.

5. Eiji Sekine, review of *The Secret Window: Ideal Worlds in Tanizaki's Fiction* by Anthony Hood Chambers and *Deadly Dialectics: Sex, Violence and Nihilism in the World of Yukio Mishima* by Roy Starrs, *Journal of the Association of Teachers of Japanese* 30, no. 1 (April 1996): 45–46.

6. Ken Ito, *Visions of Desire: Tanizaki's Fictional Worlds* (Stanford, Calif.: Stanford University Press, 1991), 101–103.

7. Nakamura Mitsuo, "Tanizaki Jun'ichiro ron," in *Nakamura Mitsuo zenshu* (Tokyo: Chikuma Shobo, 1971), 4:275.

8. Nakamura Mitsuo, "Kafu to Jun'ichiro," in *Nakamura Mitsuo zenshu,* 4:122–123.

9. Ito Sei, Usui Yoshimi, Kawamori Yoshizo, and Nakamura Mitsuo, "Tanizaki Jun'ichiro ron: shiso to mushiso sei," in *Tanizaki Jun'ichiro* (Tokyo: Yuseido, 1972), 190.

10. Ara Masato, "Soron," in *Tanizaki Jun'ichiro kenkyu,* ed. Ara (Tokyo: Yagi Shoten, 1972), 51.

11. Tomi Suzuki, *Narrating the Self: Fictions of Japanese Modernity* (Stanford: Stanford University Press, 1996), 172.

12. Nakamura, "Tanizaki Jun'ichiro ron," 269.

13. Walter Benjamin, "Paris, Capital of the Nineteenth Century," in *Reflections: Essays, Aphorisms, Autobiographical Writings,* trans. Edmund Jephcott (New York: Schocken Books, 1986).

14. Keene, *Dawn to the West,* 756; Tokuhiro Miura, "Tanizaki and the Tradition," in *Tanizaki Jun'ichiro kenkyu,* ed. Ara Masato (Tokyo: Yagi Shoten, 1972), 631.

15. Tanizaki Jun'ichiro, "Jozetsuroku," *Tanizaki Jun'ichiro zenshu* [hereafter *TJZ*] (Tokyo: Chuo Koron Sha, 1982), 20:84.

16. Ibid., 20:84–85.

17. Ibid., 20:93; "Yoshoku no hanashi" (1924), *TJZ* (1983), 22:162. See also "Shina no ryori" (1919), *TJZ,* 22:78–83, and "Bishoku kurabu" (1919), *TJZ* (1981), 6:139–189.

18. Tanizaki, "Jozetsuroku," 20:88.

19. It is important to note that Tanizaki's representation of Tagore's discourse itself is also probably too simplistic. Whether he was aware of it or not, the target of his critique is a Tagore constructed more by contemporary Japanese media than by Tagore himself.

20. Tanizaki, "Jozetsuroku," 20:89.

21. Stefan Tanaka, *Japan's Orient: Rendering Pasts into History* (Berkeley: University of California Press, 1993).

22. Blaut, *Colonizer's Model of the World,* 96.

23. Tanaka, *Japan's Orient,* 12–13.

24. Tanizaki, "Ren'ai oyobi shikijo" (1931), *TJZ,* 20:245.

25. Tanizaki, "Jozetsuroku," 20:133.

26. Tanizaki does not mention the play's title, but it must be *The Woman and Her Shadow* (La Femme et son ombre), which was performed at the Teikoku Gekijo in 1922.

27. Kono Taeko, *Tanizaki bungaku no tanoshimi* (Tokyo: Chuo Koron Sha, 1998), 138–167.

28. Tanizaki Jun'ichiro, *Some Prefer Nettles* (New York: Perigee Books, 1981), 194.

29. David Pollack, *Reading Against Culture: Ideology and Narrative in the Japanese Novel* (Ithaca, N.Y.: Cornell University Press, 1992), 72.

30. Ibid., 71–73. Also see Pollack's diagram of geographical locations and their symbolic meanings in *Some Prefer Nettles.*

31. Tanizaki, *Some Prefer Nettles,* 34–35. Succeeding references to this work are cited by page number in the text.

32. Pollack, *Reading Against Culture,* 80–81.

33. Ibid., 81–82.

Selected Bibliography

Bernardi, Joanne. *Writing in Light: The Silent Scenario and the Japanese Pure Film Movement.* Detroit: Wayne State University Press, 2001.

Blaut, J. M. *The Colonizer's Model of the World: Geographical Diffusionism and Eurocentric History.* New York: Guilford Press, 1993.

Frank, Andre Gunder. *ReOrient: Global Economy in the Asian Age.* Berkeley: University of California Press, 1998.

Hodgson, Marshall G. S. *Rethinking World History: Essays on Europe, Islam, and World History*. Cambridge: Cambridge University Press, 1993.

Jameson, Fredric, and Masao Miyoshi, eds. *The Cultures of Globalization*. Durham, N.C.: Duke University Press, 1998.

Miyoshi, Masao. *Off Center: Power and Culture Relations Between Japan and the United States*. Cambridge: Harvard University Press, 1991.

Morley, David, and Kevin Robins. *Spaces of Identity: Global Media, Electronic Landscapes, and Cultural Boundaries*. London: Routledge, 1995.

Said, Edward. *Orientalism*. New York: Vintage Books, 1979.

Treat, John Whittier, ed. *Contemporary Japan and Popular Culture*. Honolulu: University of Hawaii Press, 1996.

Young, Robert. *Colonial Desire: Hybridity in Theory, Culture, and Race*. London: Routledge, 1995.

CHAPTER 4

Stranger Than Tokyo: Space and Race in Postnational Japanese Cinema

Yomota Inuhiko

Translated by Aaron Gerow

"It's funny. You come to something new. And everything looks the same," says John Lurie in Jim Jarmush's *Stranger Than Paradise* after traveling from New York to Cleveland and then finally to Miami. But it is also an excellent expression of the tourist's condition in the consumer society that envelops or, better said, constructs us. Just as someone from Hong Kong would be overwhelmed with a sense of déjà vu upon visiting Tokyo or Seoul, a person from Tokyo traveling to Hong Kong or Seoul would be struck with the same feeling. Before setting foot in a place, we are forced to associate with all sorts of images about that place. At the end of a labyrinth of copies of copies, we finally arrive, tired and exhausted, at the actual city, but it is no longer a heart-pounding adventure, but a simulation of an adventure—a "hyperreal" experience, to borrow Umberto Eco's term. As long as we are in the midst of the structure of déjà vu, we can no longer visit "real" unknown places anywhere on this earth.

Using this as a starting point, I would like to focus on the problem of how present-day Tokyo has been expressed in images within the worldwide boom in tourism by looking at some Japanese films made in the 1990s: several of Oshii Mamoru's animated films, Iwai Shunji's *Swallowtail Butterfly* (*Suwaroteiru*), and Sai Yoichi's *All Under the Moon* (*Tsuki wa dotchi ni dete iru*). All three works were filmed in the mid-1990s and enjoyed both critical and box-office success. They also share some form of analysis or attitude toward the fact that Tokyo, having achieved the status of a high-capitalist society, has rapidly become multicultural and multilingual since the 1980s. One can say that they provide a critical stance against the myth of a homogeneous national identity that Japanese up until now quite naively believed.

Yet the genres that each of these films belongs to, as well as the ideologies they embody, are clearly different. Their reception in Japan was also exceptional. After Japanese cinema peaked around 1960 in terms of both numbers of films made and numbers of tickets sold, it went into a swift decline. Six large film companies employed a studio system in 1960, four in 1971, and in the 1980s Nikkatsu was the only company regularly producing program pictures.[1] Entering the 1990s, the great companies of the past were great in name only; they ceased production and clung to life only through film distribution. This helps explain why directors from the preceding generations, like Kurosawa Akira and Oshima Nagisa, could not raise financial support domestically and had to rely on foreign producers to continue directing.

The dismantling of the program picture system cut off the opportunities for new directors. Aside from Nikkatsu, film companies, with little hope for the future, were lax about nurturing new filmmakers. For example, outside their animation festivals and remakes of *kaiju eiga* (monster films), Toho showed no originality. As for Shochiku, it relied too much on its Tora-san films and had not imagined life without them when the series came to an end in 1997. When Nikkatsu became stagnant on the sex comedy route, they switched to soft-core pornography production; when that too ran its course, the studio ceased production. With low budgets and fast production schedules, only the world of pink films managed to preserve the program picture to the present day, despite their terrible production conditions and lack of prestige.[2]

So where did new directors come from after the 1980s?

In that decade, every kind of industry—publishing houses, television networks, massive corporations, venture capitalists—put money into films. When the bubble collapsed in the 1990s, small-scale, self-produced indie films prospered, which essentially came to support this period of Japanese cinema. Responding to this, television directors, novelists, artists, rock musicians, and "*tarento*" from fields that had nothing to do with cinema up to then, took to directing but have since virtually disappeared.[3] They were different from the generation trained in the studio system as assistant directors. They knew nothing of the ways of the studios and held different kinds of sensibilities about cinema. Their staffs also came from various fields and arrived with various cinematic sensibilities. The period when everyone shared a tacit understanding of cinema was over. One exception is the directors who emerged from the pink film, a number of whom escaped from the general film world, "the place where the sun doesn't shine," and showed a vigorous creative will—directors like Kurosawa Kiyoshi and Suo Masayuki.

The new waves in East Asia are temporally centered on the 1980s—in Hong Kong in 1978, Korea in 1980, Taiwan in 1983, and China in 1984. Only Japan failed to produce a new generation to raise a flag together. If we were to search for a similar moment in Japan, it might be 1989, the year that directors like Kitano Takeshi, Tsukamoto Shin'ya, and Zeze Takahisa made their debut. We should also take into account the international documentary film festival that started that year in Yamagata. With the appearance of Kitano Takeshi as a director and the international praise he garnered, journalists speculated that Japanese cinema had arrived at a third golden age (the first and second golden ages were in the 1930s and 1950s). However, I am not sure to what degree this phrase "third golden age" is appropriate. Of course, there were talented film-makers working in the 1990s. However, if asked how they were interconnected, I could not provide a clear answer.

While the Oshii films considered here are science fiction anime starring a cyborg of uncertain national identity and set in a futuristic city that is neither Tokyo nor Hong Kong, Sai's work is a love comedy centered on a Japan-born Korean and a Filipino that takes place in Kabuki-cho in Shinjuku in the 1990s. Iwai's film could be categorized pro-visionally as an action movie that depicts the marginal illegal residents of a "city lim-its" unlike any part of Tokyo. While the three works may be similar in presenting 1990s Tokyo through some kind of alienation effect, they conflict on other points. Let's take a close look at each of them.

Oshii

Oshii Mamoru was born in Tokyo in 1951. From childhood, he loved war films and es-pecially tanks. In this sense, one could say he is an elder of the *"otaku"* generation. With a nudge from Chris Marker's *La Jetee* (1962), he handed in a graduation film that com-bined still photographs of a vast number of birds in flight. After graduation, he worked in the 1970s in the animation industry, whose harsh working conditions and failure to establish "auteurism" put it, he felt, far behind live-action cinema. He was forced to mass-produce children's animation for television. In Japanese animation, 1984 was a year that will go down in history: Miazaki Hayao's *Kaze no tani no Naushika* (Nausi-caa) and Oshii Mamoru's *Urusei yatsura 2—byutifuru dorima* (Urusei Yatsura 2—beau-tiful dreamer) opened simultaneously, establishing the artist/author for animated films.

After this, Oshii was active in both animation and live-action filmmaking. He made films about the self-reflexivity of cinema, live-action films like Godard's *Le Gai savoir* (1968) in which the main characters argue endlessly, and films that aim at Brechtian re-sults by reproducing the spatial structure of the theater through animation. If Miyazaki is the conductor of ecology and nostalgia for postwar democracy, Oshii is a skeptic in-fatuated with eschatology and anarchism.

The three animated films that Oshii Mamoru produced from the late 1980s to the 1990s have been received enthusiastically by anime fans both at home and abroad. The term "Japanimation" was coined to describe his work and that of Miyazaki Hayao. When *Ghost in the Shell* was released in America, it hit number one on the *Billboard* video-sales chart. Looking at *Patlabor* (*Kido keisatsu Patoreiba*, 1989), *Patlabor 2* (1993), and *Ghost in the Shell* (*Kokaku kidotai*, 1995), one can see that the cities in which the stories are set, which look like constructions of the high capitalist era with their forests of skyscrapers, are at the same time spaces brimming with the nostalgia par-ticular to ruins.

Patlabor takes as its setting Tokyo in the near future, when innumerable giant robots are carrying out the reclamation of Tokyo Bay; at some point, they begin causing acci-dents or deviating from their tasks. The brilliant technician responsible could not stand

Patlabor, directed by
Oshii Mamoru, 1989.

the destruction of the old downtown *(shitamachi)* area of Tokyo where he was born and
raised, so he planted a virus in the robots. The special police force—the hero of the
film—tries to find out more about his birth home and ends up searching throughout
downtown Tokyo. What is interesting about this animated film is not the battle between
robots, but the streets of Tokyo that appear in the background. The police arrive at unknown ruins, passing through canals, the poor, wooden rowhouses of downtown, a
1920s apartment building, graveyards, and landfills. Their journey seems to work its
way through the three transformations that Tokyo has experienced in the twentieth century (the destruction of the 1923 earthquake, the obliteration caused by American air
raids in 1945, and the extensive rezoning prompted by the 1964 Olympics). In the end,
the heroes stand speechless before a huge mountain of rubble and garbage that looms
in front of an avenue of skyscrapers, a metaphor for Japan's final destination. What we
mustn't overlook here is the fact that amidst the images of the city we believed to be
Tokyo, Oshii has inserted views of housing projects that could easily be those of Hong
Kong or China, and that seem natural in this setting. Here nostalgia and exoticism do
not contradict. It is as if Oshii is saying that we have lost these modern city landscapes
in Asia.

Ghost in the Shell, directed by Oshii Mamoru, 1995.

Patlabor 2 portrays a "fake" military coup d'état that takes place in the same Tokyo. Here Tokyo is a metropolis that appears on computer screens in a flood of signs and symbols, as well as a city of abandoned canals and highways; this contrasting double image represents the city. If one unravels the history of Tokyo up until the nineteenth century, one sees that the city, which, like Venice, had a complex and abundant system of canals, thoroughly eliminated water from the landscape as part of the development of modern capitalism, filling in one canal after another until present-day Tokyo was created. Oshii is making an archaeological expedition of Tokyo in this film.

In *Ghost in the Shell,* this passion for canals develops throughout the motion picture. One can no longer say that the setting is Tokyo. It is a cosmopolitan city of the twenty-first century that is not clearly Tokyo, Hong Kong, Venice, or Amsterdam. Here robots in the form of human beings mix with people and walk along the city streets. Since this city is sinking, most of the roads are under water and the residents use boats instead of automobiles when traveling. The female cyborg who is the heroine of the film spends her days automatically receiving information that flows in from the world's computers and loses the foundation for her sense of self as her personal memory becomes ambiguous.

The cities that appear in Oshii's three films originate in the peculiarities of a place called Tokyo, shift toward a possible alternative Tokyo, and finally transform into a nationless metropolis that matches nowhere on earth. These spaces are consistent in that they overflow with technology as well as exist as future societies where a city can look like a gargantuan set of ruins. What is strongly transmitted throughout the films is a sense of nostalgia.

Ghost in the Shell, directed by Oshii Mamoru, 1995.

The moral theme of *Ghost in the Shell* is that one must reencounter the absolute Other that threatens the existence of the self when one loses a sense of that which grounds the self. In order to clarify this theme, Oshii quotes the famous mirror metaphor from the Christian Bible (1 Corinthians 13:12)—"At present we see only puzzling reflections in a mirror"—and makes the heroine experience hallucinations of her own self-image. A Lacanian analyst could probably find an abundance of allusions in this film. What interests us, however, is the kind of utopian cosmopolitanism that Oshii finds at the end of his pursuit of a nostalgic Tokyo.

Iwai

Iwai Shunji, born in 1965, belongs to a generation younger than Oshii and Sai. He is, of course, not from the generation whose experience of the cinema was constructed in movie theaters watching program pictures, and neither is he of the generation that became famous through the route of training as an assistant director within the major film companies. He came out of music-video production, was recognized for his television direction, and advanced into films. Iwai's career path into the 1990s precisely parallels the video industry's advance into cinema. Inspired by Kieslowski's *The Double Life of Veronique* (1991), Iwai's *Love Letter* (1997) gained popularity among the young through nostalgia and sentimentalism. *Suwaroteru* (*Swallowtail Butterfly,* 1996) has a duality that mythically presents Tokyo's ethnic problems while concealing them at the same time.

It is difficult to say where Japanese cinema will go in this new century. We can say only that multiplicities of Japanese films will exist synchronistically. Sai Yoichi and Iwai Shunji have almost nothing in common, and even in the field of animation the worlds of Oshii Mamoru and Miyazaki Hayao are absolutely different. We may need a new category to substitute for the genre we call Japanese cinema that has continued over the last century. It might be a geographical conception such as "East Asian cinema," or just "cinema," which simply indicates the genre of representation.

Swallowtail Butterfly is a tale of the rite of passage of a young girl, set in Tokyo in the near future. The streets of Tokyo, seen in a shot from a helicopter at the film's opening, are presented for a time in sepia. Through off-screen narration in rather expressionless English, we hear an explanation of the period in which the film is set that, like the one at the start of *Star Wars,* makes it seem to have taken place a long time ago. Because the yen was strong "at that time," men and women ambitious to make their fortunes came flooding into Tokyo from all around the world, and Tokyo became a city of innumerable illegal immigrants who called Tokyo "Yen Town." From the perspective of the average Japanese, the way of living of these multinational people who came to make a bundle of yen before returning to their home countries was none other than "*Yen dau*" or "yen stealing." So they were called "yen stealers."

On the surface this narration communicates the message that the mass of illegal immigrants, most of whom are Chinese, truly embodies Tokyo, but that message is misleading. The true stance or ideology of this film is that everything that appears here is presented with a tourist-like curiosity that mixes utopia with fairytales. One must not forget that the lengthy sepia aerial shot at the beginning carries nostalgic connotations. It becomes clearer as the film progresses that this is not a work that realistically depicts the glories and tragedies, the lives and deaths, of illegal immigrants, but rather one that presents them, in an age completely different from the present and in a totally distinct city, through a narrative that is like a magical story or fairytale. The fact that this is supposed to be Tokyo is only abstractly conveyed. Given that no one in Japanese society speaks English every day, the opening narration in English may create an even greater distance from the object being discussed.

Swallowtail Butterfly is more than two hours long, but the story is not very complicated. A young orphan girl, who speaks a smattering of English and Japanese, through chance circumstances ends up living in a colony that is a stomping ground for petty gangsters and Chinese prostitutes. The place is either a landfill or a desert—clearly a marginal space that makes one recall *Baghdad Cafe. Swallowtail Butterfly* is a very abstract film, so this colony has the character of an asylum (a place of refuge) that is both isolated and restful, a kind of utopia. One does not know specifically where this place is. A chaotic space where various ethnicities intermingle similarly appears in Yamamoto Masashi's *Atlanta Boogie* (1996) and *Junk Food* (1998), but in Iwai Shunji, we find little of the actuality of Yamamoto's work. What we do find is a stage exotic enough to satisfy the tourist gaze of the audience.

The girl is called Ageha, or "Swallowtail," in this colony. The residents speak English, Japanese, Mandarin, or Cantonese and view Japanese officials with distrust and

Swallowtail Butterfly, directed
by Iwai Shunji, 1995.

enmity. They devote themselves to committing petty crimes, selling sex, and using Japanese as suckers to con money from. But Ageha takes part in none of this. She is watched
over like a rare and pure being in need of protection. When the song that one of her
friends, a prostitute, sings gains the attention of a Japanese music producer, the friend
instantly becomes both a star and the target of yellow journalism. This gets mixed up
with a Chinese gang war, and by the end almost everyone in the colony is killed except
Ageha, who survives without a scratch. She has thus been initiated and graduates to
womanhood.

The film does not make clear whether or not Ageha is Japanese. She is assumed to be
a girl who does not know what her nationality, real name, or mother tongue is. But to
the degree that she is a "zero sign," she does function perfectly as a metaphor for today's Japan. Just as it is difficult to discover a ground for that society, Ageha is in the
end a being without a foundation, the self-portrait of a Japan that remains forever un-
determined, living free in a strangely cosmopolitan world absent either a tradition that
professes cultural nationalism or the myth of a homogeneous race. The reason young
people were enthusiastic about this film when it was released in 1996 was probably that
they could find in it a simple metaphor for their society.

What envelops Ageha could be called an excessive mass of Others. Men and women
appear before her, one after another, speaking the various dialects of Chinese. They are
no longer pure but live a brutal life in order to survive in a foreign land. However, they
recognize the special purity inside Ageha and protect her, teaching her the meaning of
life. The place where Ageha is located is, in fact, none other than the space of a tourist.
Her experiences resemble the pseudoexperiences of Japanese young people who, protected by the strength of the yen, travel in the East and Southeast and, as in Mark

Twain's *The Prince and the Pauper*, get a peek at poverty and the difficulties of life through exotic glasses, and return home to Japan with the sense of having completed a rite of passage.

What this reminds one of is the pseudodocumentary *Susunu! Denpa Shonen* featuring Saruganseki that was extremely popular on TV in Japan in 1996. In this program, the TV camera humorously recorded in great detail the experiences, including the failures, of two young and ignorant Japanese—the comedy duo Saruganseki—as they travel through Asia without any money, relying on chance and the kindness of the local people they meet. The message of this program is that Asians (not the people of Hong Kong or Vietnam in particular, but Asians) have a sense of human kindness that predates the age of modern alienation and will warmly welcome Japanese in trouble. In the story of *Swallowtail Butterfly*, one can see a dependency on the Other similar to that of the Saruganseki program—that is, the anatomy of dependence.

The great majority of the residents of this asylum are played by Japanese actors. Curiously, while Shanghai and Beijing dialects are loudly spoken here, not one word of Korean is uttered. Considering the history of foreign residents of Japan, this is extremely unrealistic. The number of residents who came to Japan from the former colony of Korea, as well as their children and their children's children, total from 600,000 to one million, a number that dwarfs the number of immigrants from China, Iran, and the Philippines who have arrived over the last twenty years. Nevertheless, *Swallowtail Butterfly* carefully excises all that might remind one of Korea. The reason is clear: The filmmakers judged that Korea is, to the Japanese, not an exotic and ideal destination for tourists as are Hong Kong and Shanghai; combined with the racial discrimination that Koreans have long experienced in Japanese society, it would have been inappropriate to playfully take up their case in this context. To put it simply, things Korean are not fashionable in a narrative of the cosmopolitan atmosphere of contemporary Japan.

One more thing about the characters' use of language: While many languages are spoken here, no speech is mixed—that is, none is hybridized. The kind of pigeonization, the mixture and interpenetration of the lexicon of different languages anyone experiences when living abroad, is not evident in any character. All speak a Beijing or Shanghai dialect. There is no depiction, in any sense, of the kind of warping or metamorphosis of speech that comes with being separated from one's mother tongue. *Swallowtail Butterfly* may line up multiple languages as in a mosaic, but its use of languages remains abstract because, apart from the Japanese language, it recognizes languages not as present-day, living entities, but simply as objects of tourism. When one compares it to Yamamoto Masashi's *What's Up Connection* (*Tenamonya konekushon*, 1989) or *Junk Food* (1997), one can see how static a view of language the director Iwai Shunji has. Not only does a lively form of communication develop in Yamamoto's films, where Cantonese, Japanese, and English intermix, but also the unease and frustration of communication are presented—realistically and with a touch of humor. *Swallowtail Butterfly* is the opposite: The acting by Japanese actors is only superficially inflected by foreign languages, with barely any investigation of the Otherness of language itself.

The movies that most resemble this film—if you leave out the issue of foreigners—are probably the New Action films Nikkatsu made in the early 1970s. They depicted hippies living in the empty spaces of western Shinjuku (which like Manhattan or Central in Hong Kong, is now covered with skyscrapers), young people putting up an anarchistic resistance to the police, civil society, and bourgeois family values. In place of hippies, *Swallowtail Butterfly* offers Chinese illegal immigrants. However, the tourist gaze that rules this film converges in the end on a message that Japan is the only innocent object, the only thing worth protecting. This film was applauded by Japanese youth of the 1990s because it presented onscreen, in a very sweet fashion, their desire to be protected, even in their groundlessness.

Sai

Sai Yoichi was born in 1949 to resident Koreans with Communist sympathies. At the end of the 1960s, he became involved in the student movement and was expelled from school. He entered the film industry, learned lighting at a studio, and spent seven years as an assistant director. When Oshima Nagisa directed *Ai no korida* (*In the Realm of the Senses,* 1976), he was the chief assistant director. Just as Oshima has, since the 1960s, been concerned with Korea, a former Japanese colony, his pupil Sai is concerned with Okinawa, currently a base for the U.S. military. Sai has used this southern island as a stage for four of the films he has made so far.

Sai debuted as a director in 1983, and his first film was a picaresque romance featuring a policeman as the main character. He spent much of the 1980s shooting commercial action films with teenage idols cast in the main roles. Today, if these films were carefully analyzed one after the other, one would realize that he had secretly hidden ethnic minority signs in them. The shooting of *Tsuki wa dotchi ni dete iru* (*All Under the Moon*) in 1993 was a huge turning point for Sai. The first in Japanese cinema to deal with ethnicity head on, this film, which portrayed resident Koreans in a half-humorous, half-cynical light, caused quite a stir. Since then, as well, Sai has used Shinjuku and Okinawa as locations for works whose minority main characters have suffered discrimination. Sai was trained as an assistant director while the old studio system still functioned, so he belongs to its last generation.

As I mentioned, the largest ethnic minority in Japan is composed of people from the former colony of Korea. They are the objects of large-scale discrimination both politically and socially. In the mass media and show business, actors of Chinese ancestry like Judy Ong and Agnes Chan have worked under an English name and Chinese surname, making a selling point of their Chineseness. But it has been the general practice until recently for Koreans to hide their Korean names and present themselves as Japanese; the disparate treatment and social reception accorded Koreans and Chinese in Japan continues. One interesting phenomenon is that since 1945, the percentage of Koreans among the stars and actors working in Japanese films and show business has become

Poster for *All Under the Moon,*
directed by Sai Yoichi, 1993.

quite high. The great majority of Japanese, however, either do not know this or whisper it in secret, as if it is something scandalous and not for public consumption. The situation in which, for example, the calendar of a large bank, warning of financial dealings with Korean residents of Japan, presents the picture of a brightly smiling resident Korean actress as a typical Japanese beauty, has continued for some time.

Until the 1970s, it was largely taboo for Korean residents of Japan to appear publicly in major studios' films. For that reason, several directors of *yakuza* (or gangster) movies had to use various contrivances to present stories of Korean residents without having Korea or one word of Korean appear onscreen. Films like *Nihon boryoku retto: Kei-*

hanshin koroshi no gundan (Yamashita Kosaku, 1975) or *Jingi hakaba* (Fukasaku Kinji, 1975) are typical *yakuza* movies that thrilled the average Japanese spectator, but hidden throughout are secret messages that only resident Koreans can understand. This is very interesting when put together with the fact that from 1960 to *Swallowtail Butterfly* in the present, Chinese have appeared in comedy or action movies whenever the chance presented itself, gaining popularity playing, for instance, humorous and friendly cooks. Since Chinese have been given, in their own way, a positive stereotype in Japanese cinema, they have been able to appear onscreen amidst a conservative order. That has not been the case with Koreans because, if Japanese view Chinese as trustworthy, deeply philosophical, and good cooks, they view Koreans as dirty, poor, liars, and the enemy. In other words, Koreans have been too close a presence for Japanese to build them into a positive stereotype in cinema; Japanese and Koreans have been like doubles looking at each other's images in a mirror, so similar one cannot tell them apart. Oshima Nagisa is the one exception among Japanese film directors who has seen through this problem. From the 1960s, he has been the only one to feature resident Koreans positively in his films, giving him the perspective to criticize the hypocrisy and falsehood of Japan under the emperor system.

Sai Yoichi (known as Choi Yang-il in Korean) produced *All Under the Moon* in 1993, a film that focuses on the problem of foreigners in Japan. In some sense, this was a large gamble, but the film was a success at the box office and became an epoch-making event in the history of Japanese cinema.

The hero of *All Under the Moon* is a young North Korean citizen named Tadao (called Chunnam in Korean). His mother secretly entered Japan as a child in 1948 on the occasion of the massacre of nearly forty thousand on Cheju Island; she currently runs a Philippine bar in Kabuki-cho in Shinjuku. Tadao works as a driver at a taxi company run by a classmate from his days at Korean high school. One of his fellow workers is a former Japanese boxer who always begs Tadao for money, forever psychologically dependent upon him. When he blurts out his stock phrase, "I hate Koreans because they are dirty, stupid liars, but, Tadao, you're different," Tadao always listens to him with tolerance and ends up lending him money. The words of the former boxer are a summary of the negative stereotype that the average Japanese has long held of resident Koreans, and by daring to put that out in the open, this film tries to take a higher, more critical position. (While it has not been produced, in the sequel that the producers imagined, it would become known that this former boxer is also a resident Korean, who desperately spits out those discriminatory epithets to construct his own identity as a Japanese.)

The conditions and worldviews of the various ethnicities living in contemporary Tokyo are presented through Tadao's sober and philosophical eyes. There is the hypocritical businessman who, while liking Korean food and expressing the desire to go to Korea, deep down despises Koreans. There is Tadao's mother, who demands hard work from her Filipino employees yet continues to send Japanese yen to her family that went to North Korea. And there is Tadao's boss, who, in his determination to escape the fate of resident Koreans (supposedly limited to running Korean restaurants or *pachinko* parlors), tries to operate a golf range, only to end up running his taxi company into bankruptcy. Sai also gives us an old man from South Korea, who, infuriated that only songs glorifying North Korea's Kim Il Sung are being sung at the wedding of resident Koreans, demands that the master of ceremony allow him to sing a South Korean folksong. These kinds of Tokyo realities had not once been taken up by Japanese directors living in Japan. Sai's film literally and thoroughly defamiliarizes the official conception of Japan as a state with a homogeneous people and a homogeneous language.

Yet *All Under the Moon* is not a high-class exercise to enlighten the small number of "conscientious" Japanese intellectuals. It is basically a comedy or a romantic drama. At the center of the film is the story of Tadao's falling in love with a Filipina hostess who works at his mother's bar and overcoming various difficulties until the two become united. In the first place, the comedy that pervades the film is carefully thought through, allowing audience members to realize their ideological, cultural, and political positions in their own way. I remember seeing this film one night at a theater in Shinjuku. While most of the spectators were Japanese, I realized there were resident Koreans and Filipinos watching when I heard loud laughter or snickering at small gags that the average Japanese would never get. When the film was over and I left the theater, there was the Kabuki-cho landscape that I had just seen on the screen, with nothing changed at all. That was a very stimulating experience; I felt that my eye for Tokyo had changed.

The films of Oshii Mamoru, Iwai Shunji, and Sai Yoichi were all box-office successes in the 1990s that also received high praise from the critics. However, each takes an entirely different attitude toward the ethnicity of Tokyo. What is important to Oshii is the nostalgia brought about by nationless, cosmopolitan surroundings, one strongly tinged with the symptoms of postmodernism, where the city can be both utopia and ruin. The Other he depicts is a purely speculative or metaphysical entity without a trace of reality. Yet, what lies at the foundation of Oshii's world is a strong feeling that there is something wrong with the Tokyo metropolis that has experienced rapid modernization since the mountains of rubble in 1945. His is an aesthetic rejection of cultural nationalism itself.

In contrast to Oshii, Iwai organizes a festival for the Other, putting many kinds of Chinese on screen. However, these Others are nothing but ideal images constructed after the fact through the gaze of the tourist. The multilingual world repeatedly emphasized throughout the movie remains everywhere superficial, at the level of decoration. While it may seem on the surface as if the concept of Japan has been deconstructed, in reality it remains without a scratch, preserved in a more innocent state. It was for this reason that the film satisfied the tourist-like curiosity of Japan's younger generation.

Sai has attempted something very different from either Oshii or Iwai. He intended to defamiliarize Tokyo in specific ways from a standpoint unrelated to either nostalgia or the tourist gaze, and he succeeded in doing so in a very humorous way. *All Under the Moon* makes spectators conscious again of the ideological positions they inhabit, bringing to light the differences that have been hidden. Here the Other is not a concept meant for play, but a real neighbor, enemy, or family member. In the 1990s, Sai not only effectively represented the multilingual, multiethnic nature of Tokyo. *All Under the Moon* is the first film in the long line of Japanese film comedies to expose laughter itself as a superlative cultural and ideological act, a movie that, against the imagistic manipulation of stereotypes, reveals an entirely different possibility for the image.

In the Japanese film world of the 1980s and 1990s, after the studio system largely collapsed in the 1970s, independent directors began to put Asian foreigners on-screen, as if accommodating themselves to the increasingly multiethnic nature of Japanese society. The three I have discussed are among those directors, and they reveal three very different models. This speaks not only to the variety of contemporary Japanese cinema, but also to the possibilities and limitations surrounding the issue of how Japanese film should face the Other.

Notes

1. Program pictures are films mass produced to fill up the exhibition programs of theaters that have a block booking contract with a producer/distributor. In the heyday of the studio system, when theaters needed two new movies every week or ten days, studios had continually to produce films to fill these bills. These sometimes overwhelming conditions nonetheless provided many opportunities for filmmakers to develop their talent and hone their craft.

2. Pink films are low-budge, adult-rated motion pictures that mostly feature sex as their selling point. Given Japanese censorship restrictions, most are the equivalent of soft-core pornography in the West, but they have served as an important training ground for many contemporary directors.

3. *Tarento* (talent) is the term often used for television personalities or celebrities.

Selected Bibliography

Lee, Bong Ou. Tsuki wa dotchi ni dete iru *o meguru 2, 3 no hanashi* (Two or three stories about *All Under the Moon*). Tokyo: Shakai Hyoronsha, 1994

Monma, Takashi. *Ajia eiga ni miru Nihon* (Japan observed in Asian movies). 2 vols. Tokyo: Shakai Hyoronsha, 1996.

Yomota, Inuhiko. *Ajia no naka no nihon eiga* (Japanese movies in Asia). Tokyo: Iwanami Shoten, 2001.

———. *Nihon eiga no radikaruna ishi* (The radical will of Japanese movies). Tokyo: Iwanami Shoten, 2000.

CHAPTER 5

Discourse on Modernization
in 1990s Korean Cinema

Han Ju Kwak

Given that the unique accomplishment of modern South Korean history and culture is widely considered to be represented by its unprecedented extent and intensity of modernization, modernization can be seen as the major constituent core of South Korean collective experience during the last century. The cinema of South Korea, as a privileged form of social representation, has confronted the modernization process, offering its solid representations by dramatizing the people's current fears, anxieties, conceits, pleasures, and aspirations. Particularly since the deregulation of the film industry in 1987, South Korea has produced various films that dealt with the issue of modernization both directly and indirectly.

In relation to modernization I want to discuss five important South Korean films which have evoked considerable response from both Korean audiences and critics: *Black Republic* (1990), *Sopyonje* (1993), *A Single Spark* (1995), *Festival* (1996), and *The Day a Pig Fell into the Well* (1996).[1] Before examining these films' discourses on modernization, it would be useful and almost necessary to review the historical experience of modernization in Korea and to question its meanings to the Korean people in sociohistorical context.

The Korean Experience of Modernization

South Korea's economic development has been praised as the "miracle on the Han," and its path to industrialization has been acknowledged as an effective model for the "third world."[2] The nation's economic achievements are indeed noteworthy. Less than twenty years after embarking on full-scale modernization in the early 1960s, South Korea transformed itself from one of the world's poorest and least industrialized nations to one of the richest and most successful of the newly industrialized countries.[3] Gross national production per capita soared from $79 in 1960 to $1,597 in 1980 thanks to unprecedented high and sustained economic growth that averaged 7.6 percent a year.[4] The economy continued to expand until the financial crisis that hit Asia in 1997.

Koreans began to experience Western influences in the late nineteenth century, some of them by choice, others by imposition from external forces. Yet the encounter with the West, often through Japan, was generally antagonistic because of Western imperialism and Korea's stubborn closed-door policy, maintained until 1879. Soon afterward, Korea became an arena of struggle for imperialist powers, then went through thirty-five years of Japanese colonization until liberated in 1945, a beneficiary of the Allied victory in World War II.

Korea's first moves toward modernization after liberation suffered a two-pronged setback, caused first by further solidification of the partition of the country in 1948 and then by the Korean War (1950–53). South Korea recovered from the devastation of the war only with extensive U.S. assistance. The dominating presence of the United States during the war and reconstruction period led to massive American influence on Korean life. Korea's yearning for modernization had previously meant Westernization; now it was being equated with Americanization.[5] Beginning in 1961, when General Park Chung Hee took power by a military coup, South Korea headed toward full-scale modernization, as the Park regime sought legitimacy for its military dictatorship by pursuing rapid economic growth. This process was largely accomplished through highly centralized and effective state planning and direction of economic activity, combined with vigorous expansion of family conglomerates called *chaebol*.[6] The eighteen years of the Park regime, ending with the dictator's assassination in October 1979, laid the foundation, if it did not accomplish the completion, of modern Korean society.

After the brutal crackdown against the Kwangju Uprising in May 1980, General Chun Doo Hwan took power and followed his predecessor's model: state-driven economic growth and ruthless suppression of opposition voices. A nationwide people's protest against the authoritarian regime forced the 1987 presidential election to be relatively democratic. Since then, South Korea has witnessed gradual democratization in every field, but with troublesome side effects.

Along the way to modernization, there have been losses as well as gains. Perhaps the most important factors calling South Korea's development into question are political: State power was based on a military dictatorship, and growth was supported and maintained by policies requiring the suppression of most basic political, civil, and labor rights. Growth was accompanied by intense exploitation, and a cycle was created in which the workers' and farmers' strong resistance led to greater repression by the state in its attempt to maintain the conditions necessary for continued growth.[7] Martin Hart-Landsberg sums up the negative aspects of the South Korean experience of modernization: "The South Korean approach to development—by placing exports over domestic needs, profits over wages and working conditions, dependence on the United States and Japan over national independence, and thus by necessity the interests of the few over the rights of the many—demanded unacceptable sacrifices from the South Korean people."[8]

Today, the issue of industrialization, the economic and quintessential aspect of modernization, no longer plays a central role in South Korea's modernization discourse. In this sense, one might argue, the period of "classic" modernization ended around 1988. The discursive agenda concerning modernization then shifted rapidly from industrialization to postindustrial concerns such as structural adjustments, including the creation of a competitive information and media industry and emphasis on the issues of quality of life and culture. Modernization became a question of social meaning. As a multilayered and multifaceted historical process, modernization still haunts the Korean people.

As the crucial and most powerful force in the modern world, modernization above all refers to the transition from a "traditional" agrarian order to a "modern" industrial society. Modernization has two overarching historical roots, both of which originated in eighteenth-century Western Europe: the Enlightenment and capitalist industrialization. Capitalist industrialization was indeed the ultimate driving force of modernity. The Enlightenment project, based on a trust in rationality and progress, was aimed at nothing less than the creation of a new kind of universal culture: secular, rational, humanitarian, republican—in a word, "progressive."[9]

Yet modernization is necessarily ambivalent in at least three ways. First, modernization may achieve material civilization by human intervention in the conditions of social life and nature, but it also generates unanticipated negative effects such as economic polarization, environmental crisis, negation of democratic rights, and the danger of war, conditions that could negate its overall merits. This is the major source of ambivalence toward modernization among people undergoing the transition.

Second, modernization creates another source of ambivalence for non-Westerners. Because of the identity of modernization with Westernization, modernization may be viewed as the imposition of a Western discourse whose essence is the instrumental rationality generated by the logic of capital.[10] The discursive effects of modernization involve a process of internalization of Western values by non-Western people. As this occurs, non-Westerners come to have "the intractable ambiguities of the postcolonial subject position with split loyalties allowing a colonization of consciousness." This phenomenon is particularly relevant to the people of South Korea, who in adopting Western culture have reproduced a colonial pathology of self-denigration and self-marginalization.[11]

The third ambivalence seems to be specific to Koreans. The so-called rush to development that transformed South Korea from a rural to an industrial society exactly overlapped President Park Chung Hee's rule. This period combined the most direct and severe political oppression with the highest economic growth in Korea. Modernization reminds most Koreans of the Park regime, a period of bittersweet memories—though I would say mainly bitter ones.

Korean cinema has evolved amid turbulent social and political realities since the first Korean-made film, *The Righteous Revenge*, was shown on 27 October 1919. Since the

1920s, it has produced realist social films that consistently respond to sociohistorical reality by dealing with people's joy and sorrow in their social context. The most obvious feature of realist social drama is its underlying theme of modernization, regardless of its surface differences, mainly depicting the devastating or destructive force of modernization through realist representations. Many Korean films, including romantic entertainments, are social commentaries with political implications. Even a banal melodrama featuring a bar girl's vicissitudes can be a profound social text that reveals the violent changes occurring in society—for example, the destruction of traditional family structure, the exodus from country to city, and the conflict between old and new values.

The Movement Approach

Considering that Korean cinema previously suffered from severe political censorship, *Black Republic* and *A Single Spark* are notable in having antigovernment activists as their heroes. As rare cinematic representations of the *minjung* movement, they offer an alternative picture of Korean society through a stark critique of the existing order from the perspective of the movement's formerly suppressed underground philosophies.

Udong, the Korean term for movement, has usually meant antigovernment social movements. In this essay, "the movement" designates all South Korean social movements against the existing order, which is characterized by capitalistic exploitation and political authoritarianism. The movement in modern South Korea was a very peculiar and tenacious historical force. Against the authoritarian political regimes and violent social changes in modern Korean history, an opposition movement took shape under the military dictatorship in the 1960s. The movement not only vigorously fought against the authoritarian military regime but also keenly criticized ruthless capitalism. Initially led by college students and intellectuals, the movement was a resistance to the political oppression imposed by the authoritarian government. Since the mid-1970s, however, minjung—the oppressed working people, including laborers, peasants and urban poor— began to emerge as its subject, and the movement evolved to a more comprehensive radical social struggle against the existing capitalist and authoritarian system. It also criticized the United States and Japan as neocolonial powers, especially since the Kwangju massacre in 1980. Thanks to the major role of minjung in the struggle, the movement is often termed the "minjung movement." The movement not only played a decisive role in modern South Korea's trajectory toward democracy through mobilizing minjung's power, but also provided Koreans with an alternative vision and lifestyle. For it made possible the impressive emergence of minjung culture, a populist leftist counterculture that evolved under and against the highly authoritarian regime since the 1970s.[12]

The movement was very critical of the South Korean military government's implementation of an aggressive modernization policy in the form of state capitalism, at the cost of enormous social dislocation, including the widening of class gaps and the further proletarization of the underprivileged class. From the movement view, the whole process of modernization was one of degeneration and more injustice. The strong point of the movement discourse was its moralizing power, not its claim of "scientificity" borrowed from Marxism. The sense of self-sacrifice underlying movement discourse itself has been assumed to have its own value in the process of intensification of injustice. What gives power to the movement's moralizing discourse—for example, extreme, sometimes irrational demands for equality—despite its idealism seems to be the underlying anti-modern(ization) and anti-Western(ization) feelings among much of the population.

Black Republic (1990): Class Conflict and Its Fracture

Black Republic is the second film by director Park Kwang-su, who has shown a consistent interest in social reality. The film focuses on the sociopolitical events in a desolate mining town and the love between Ki-young, an ex–student activist on the run, and Young-sook, a local prostitute. Filmed mostly in the Kohan-Sabook region, a typical coal-mining area in South Korea, *Black Republic* offers a realistic rendering of a declining mining town that, cut off from the outside, provides a microcosm of Korean society. This very space succinctly represents the social ills of Korean society as it pursues modernization via capitalism.

First, capitalists directly exploit laborers. The boss of the briquette factory delays paying wages. Miners are threatened by the owner's move to close down the coal mine without any advance notice. Second, a sense of moral decay motivated by vulgar materialism prevails. The waitresses of a tearoom—Young-sook is one of them—are virtually prostitutes. In contrast to the bleak landscape of the town, karaoke bars and motels bustle. The film also shows the ugly complicity between capital and political power. Whenever the interests of capital are threatened, Detective Kang reinstates the existing order by suppressing laborers and the weak. Moreover, the town is visibly declining because coal use is decreasing. This is the space of exploitation, decadence, marginality, and discontent.

The film depicts a dichotomy—the capitalist and the laborer, the oppressor and the oppressed. The domination and exploitation of laborers by capitalists is typified by the relationship between the boss, Lee, and his employee Chung. While Chung is heavily in debt to his wealthy boss, Lee prepares to move to Seoul, where new opportunities for profit arise. Without exception, labor is exploited by capital and oppressed by those in political power. *Black Republic,* above all, is firmly constructed on the discourse of class conflict. The hero, Ki-young, who under a false identity manages to find a job as a worker at a briquette factory, sincerely sympathizes with the plight of laborers. The strikers' rally scene, in which Ki-young cheers them on by clapping, implies that he reaffirms his conviction in the capability of minjung to achieve social change.

The negativity of the ruling group is symbolized in the relationship between Boss Lee and his son Sung-chul, the antihero at the forefront of capitalist exploitation and degradation. Sung-chul, the son of a capitalist, however, turns out to have a pathological fixation on his dead mother. The film's sympathetic descriptions of him attribute his misbehavior to his father, who abandoned Sung-chul's mother to take a second wife after

Black Republic, directed by
Park Kwang-su, 1990.

becoming rich. With this attribution, the film depicts Sung-chul as a necessary outcome
of bourgeois greed, selfishness, and decadence: Modernization is nothing but a deepen-
ing of alienation and a restructuring of power relations in favor of the centralization of
capital, ensuring the marginalization of other sectors.

Although *Black Republic* has many elements of melodrama, such as women's suffering and the emphasis on true love, the film's discourse, based on the movement perspective, differentiates it from ordinary melodrama. Its focus on the negativity of the ruling class rather than on the positivity of the movement makes it an effective critique of
the social reality of modern South Korea. The absence of violent manifestations of class
antagonism, however, implicitly contradicts the film's movement discourse. Laborers in
this film are no longer the subjects of proletarian class-consciousness and social change.
Despite its ostensible subversive quality through its treatment of class conflict, *Black Republic* does not proceed to revolutionary practices. To be sure, Ki-young brings hope to
this marginalized space, but it eventually turns out to be a romantic, not a political,
hope—he falls in love with Young-sook. The film incorporates the movement perspective in critiquing social reality, but it abandons it by failing to investigate the possibility
of social transformation.

A Single Spark *(1995): Resistance as Memory*

On November 13, 1970 a twenty-two-year-old textile worker, Jeon Tae-il, immolated
himself at Seoul's Peace Market, shouting as the flames consumed him, "Comply with
the Labor Standards Act!" and "We're not machines!" This suicide, which shocked the
entire nation, became the touchstone of the labor movement. Jeon's self-immolation,
coupled with the opposition leader Kim Dae Jung's mass support in the 1971 presidential election, was a key reason for the Park regime's introduction of the notoriously authoritarian Yushin system in 1972.[13]

A Single Spark offers a rare serious examination of South Korean society in the 1970s, during which the modernization drive gained momentum and took off, and both its achievements and contradictions became clear. In the film, a fugitive with an intellectual activist background, Young-soo, looks back on the life of Jeon. The film thus interweaves two story lines: the flashbacks depicting Jeon's life and the present activities of Young-soo and his laborer wife, Jung-soon, in 1975. The film, on the one hand, demonstrates Jeon's efforts and struggles to improve the working conditions in Peace Market sweatshops through Young-soo's reconstruction of Jeon's career, and, on the other hand, depicts the distressingly dark reality of the mid-1970s through Young-soo and Jung-soon's organizational activities.

The discursive agenda of *A Single Spark* can be summarized in two strands: a realistic representation of the extremely inhumane working conditions in the 1970s, and a sympathetic portrayal of the movement. We see the earlier intolerable conditions of garment industry workers in the Peace Market, as well as management and the authorities' current ruthless suppression of a new trade union in Jung-soon's factory. The film uses black-and-white cinematography to show the deplorable working conditions in the Peace Market, where teenage laborers work more than sixteen hours a day in a claustrophobic space without proper ventilation. At work, sleep-deprived workers often take injections in the arm to keep themselves awake. They are thoroughly controlled by the management in terms of time and space. In the most striking scene, a female worker spits tubercular blood, the result of the polluted air in the workplace. Jeon gives her first aid with his handkerchief and takes her to a bathroom to wash her. When she realizes that she cannot wash her bloodstained hands (the film suggests the faucet does not work), she cries in despair, "There's no place to wash my hands." When Young-soo looks around the Peace Market in 1975, we see that the present conditions are no better than those of five years before. Further, when Jung-soon, one of the new trade union's founders, returns from an organizing meeting, a factory manager tries, in front of her house, to intimidate her into stopping her activities. Jung-soon's colleagues, who are staging a sit-in to protest the failure by the Office of Labor Affairs to authorize her union, are brutally dispersed by the police. These descriptions reaffirm the movement's conviction that the state apparatuses are merely tools of labor oppression in favor of capital.

In a reality where "no vague light of hope is found," the movement provides a potential source of hope. The film counterbalances the negativity of modernization with the movement in the 1970s, symbolized by Jeon, the incarnation of genuine humanity, a quality that is emphasized throughout the film. For example, Jeon returns home from the factory on foot, because he spends his bus fare feeding the girl workers who cannot afford lunch. His efforts and struggle for the betterment of his coworkers are so self-sacrificing that he looks unreal, devoid of human needs and mundane desires. The film in fact elevates Jeon to the status of saint, although we also see his fragility and earthiness.

When Jeon becomes tired of hard work and grows hopeless caring for young workers, he heads for a remote road construction site, where he regains his previous qualities and "resurrects" himself from deadly despair and anxiety. At the end of a sequence

A Single Spark, directed by Park Kwang-su, 1995.

in which Jeon lies like a dead body for awhile in a ditch, Jeon's voiceover states: "I have to come back to my little brothers and sisters in the Peace Market. I'm going to give myself up, kill myself, and come back beside you." In this superbly photographed and emotionally charged sequence, Jeon miraculously "resurrects" himself from the symbolic grave to become a Christ figure. This dramatically existential commitment and shift from despair to determination is linked to Jeon's subsequent self-immolation. Jeon's death protesting injustice turns into a sacrifice for salvation; in fact, Young-soo says, "Jeon's death is martyrdom in a religious sense." Moreover, Jeon is also a revolutionary. He achieves social consciousness by himself and acts to change undesirable situations. He organizes workers' meetings to discuss working conditions and does research to find out what the workers need. His will to change the unjust reality culminates in his tragic self-immolation. In short, Jeon is an ideal figure for the movement: a saintly revolutionary.

It is by necessity, *A Single Spark* suggests, that Jeon metaphorically resurrects the social consciousness of the oppressed workers. It is also suggested that those who struggle against the capitalist authoritarian regimes in essence resemble Jeon: pure, unselfish, and self-sacrificing. In a scene depicting Young-soo and Jung-soon in bed, Young-soo tells his wife, "You're a Jeon Tae-il." The ending, in which Young-soo finds a young worker carrying a book written by him, *A Critical Biography of Jeon Tae-il,* who surprisingly and significantly looks like Jeon, symbolizes the metaphorical resurrection of

Jeon in numerous ordinary people. In this way, Jeon as a real historical figure becomes a myth with the power to mobilize minjung, the oppressed people. The film adroitly makes Jeon a living myth, despite the twenty-five years that have elapsed since his suicide, by bringing his magnetism to the present through realistic representations. Thanks to Jeon, the pure, humane, and self-sacrificing image of the activists of the movement is firmly constructed.

It is significant that no negative description of Jeon and participants of the movement occurs in the film, which ignores Jeon's human pain and weakness in both body and soul. He is first and foremost "beautiful," the ultimate signifier of human sincerity (the original Korean title of the film means "a beautiful youth, Jeon Tae-il"). The participants are not only morally pure and superior, but also so cautious that they make no mistakes. Such "structuring absences" clearly reveal this film's discursive orientation. Jeon's humanity offers a sharp contrast to the behavior of the factory owners and government officials. The film consistently contrasts the avaricious bourgeoisie to miserable laborers, bureaucratic government officials to altruistic student activitists, and ugly reality to the semi-religious morality of the movement. The overtone of the movement's morality serves to condemn the social reality.

Jeon's self-immolation of course offers the most powerful critique of modernization in *A Single Spark,* the culmination of his resistance to the demonic face of modernization. By setting fire to a Labor Law book as well as to himself, Jeon declares that the Labor Law, the (by)product of modernization for the improvement of workers' conditions, is useless, nothing but an ideological tool to hide the contradictions of modernization. The burning of a Labor Law book thus becomes the highest metaphor for the falsity of modernization.

Reality in this film is first of all depicted as economically structured. The bourgeoisie exploits the laborer for profit. The laborer is increasingly alienated from the process of labor. The conflict between these two classes is irreconcilable. The film implies that, at least at that point, there can be no reconciliation between the bourgeoisie and the working class, and that the only means to achieve humanity lie not in disavowing class conflicts, but in overcoming them by collective effort. In this way, the dichotomy that *A Single Spark* constructs is more classic than that of *Black Republic.*

A Single Spark does not reflect the material affluence achieved through modernization (from which the present audience unquestionably benefits) because the cinematic space is the 1970s. It accentuates instead the cause and morality of the movement and in this way constructs a discourse in favor of the movement, the stronghold of social struggles for freedom, equality, and decolonization in Korea. While the film lacks a description of the militancy of the movement organized under the banner of various Leftisms,[14] it lauds the morality and existential decisions of individuals, as vividly shown by Jeon's self-immolation.

Nevertheless, *A Single Spark* represents a regressive reaction to the modernization process. It reveals an inability to bridge the huge gap between the 1970s and the present, clinging to the 1970s and closing its eyes to the radical changes brought about by modernization. Social reality has changed so much that starvation has disappeared and

Koreans have a democratic government. The movement has disintegrated and faction-alized to the point that it is no longer a source of hope for most Koreans. Under these circumstances, the film loses its connection to reality, becoming merely a nostalgic ren-dition of memories. Despite the film's great value as a sociological document on 1970s Korean society, the question of what Jeon's life and death mean to the present audience remains unanswered. Manifesting nostalgia for a past in which the divide between right and wrong was distinct and clear, the film ironically pushes the movement discourse into memory.

These two films that deal with the movement theme offer a powerful critique of Korea's modernization. Both view modernization as a socioeconomic phenomenon, primarily the result of capitalist industrialization. It is primarily represented as negative, resulting in the deplorable alienation of labor and the oppression of humanistic aspirations; its most crucial feature is the intensification of labor's alienation. This negativity is pre-sented by the ruthless exploitation of labor by the capitalist and the collusion between capital and political power.

Both *Black Republic* and *A Single Spark* adopt an intellectual's viewpoint by making a former student activist as their hero. Like Ki-young in *Black Republic,* Young-soo in *A Single Spark* is the central character in terms of the film's point of view, acting as nar-rator at times. The heroes of both films are also outsiders. Because of the instability of their position—both are wanted by the police—Young-soo and Ki-young do not par-ticipate in any organized activity for social change. Although both films' adoption of the intellectual outsider's point of view is very instrumental for the critique of social reality, it also seems to hamper any further investigation of positive alternatives. Since the op-pressed people are not presented as the subject, the films do not show the disruptive and subversive power of the minjung discourse as the major voice contending against the dominant language, the language of the state. In adopting the point of view of an intel-lectual outsider—a member of a marginal group in the movement discourse that puts minjung at its center—both films fail to provide a vision for the future. The movement theme necessarily has a retrospective quality rather than a progressive one. The discur-sive effect of these movement theme films seems to contain a necessary dilemma: Their critique is meaningful, but their relevance is doubtful. Both leave unexamined the ques-tion of the splitting of the self caused by modernization.

The Tradition Approach

The tradition of national culture is often in opposition to modernization, whose uni-versalizing effects tend to push it into oblivion or, at best, into the realm of collective memory. The Korean people have had an uneasy relationship with their past, largely due to the unprecedented intensity and comprehensiveness of their modernization experi-ence. Tradition has been a strong object of ambivalence for most Koreans. On the one hand, it was an obstacle to modernization that had to be removed as soon as possible.

On the other hand, the immense impact of the modernization process forced Koreans to discard their heritage, on which national identity is anchored. *Sopyonje* and *Festival,* the films made by the most acclaimed Korean director, Im Kwon-taek, are noteworthy in that they adopt the "tradition approach," foregrounding the issues of traditional culture in the context of modernization.

Sopyonje (1993): The Bitter Defeat of Tradition

Sopyonje is acknowledged as an epoch-making film in South Korean cinema in that despite being a low-budget art film it became the biggest box-office success in history. *Sopyonje* is a film about itinerant Korean folk artists performing *pansori,* the near-defunct Korean indigenous art of dramatic singing. A man in his thirties, Dong-ho, roams the rural hinterlands, ostensibly to buy herbal medicines but actually in search of Song-hwa, his stepsister. They were both orphans adopted by and apprenticed to a pansori master, Yu-bong, who pressured them to sacrifice everything for their art. Dong-ho rebelled and ran away. Song-hwa stayed, lost her sight at the hands of her stepfather, and outlived him.

Sopyonje emphasizes the artists' discord with the changing social reality of modernization. In this respect, the art in the film is an important signifier with a social dimension, and the film can be read as a discourse of modernization. By and large, the process of modernization is invisible in the film. Instead, through the description of the artists' hapless resistance to the marginalization of pansori, the film subtly suggests modernization's destructive effects on a traditional art. The decline of pansori is vividly presented by the sharp contrast between Yu-bong's performance at a squire's birthday party and subsequent performances by Song-hwa and Yu-bong. In the former, Yu-bong masterfully demonstrates the artistry of pansori, receiving a warm response from the audience. Years later, in a performance in the market, Song-hwa sings pansori in front of a very small audience of children, whose attention wanders to a cheerful brass band advertising a Westernized show. In fact, Yu-bong's family loses its means of living when confronted by Western culture. Having supported themselves by performing pansori to promote a peddler's products in the street, Yu-bong's family is eventually cast out by the peddler. The employer, doubtful of the popularity of pansori, decides instead to employ a violinist to provide an exotic cultural experience for the Korean audience. When Dong-ho shouts to his stepsister, "Now we can't make our living only by pansori in this world!" he succinctly expresses the marginalization of pansori.

However, Yu-bong disavows modernization by denying pansori's obvious decline. Song-hwa has become so otherworldly that modernization has no meaning in her life. The escape from the modernizing social reality culminates in Yu-bong's blinding of Song-hwa. He later confesses to his stepdaughter that he intentionally blinded her by giving her a poisonous herb to implant *han* (deep grief) into her and thus improve her singing. Here his act is a desperate attempt to overcome the marginalization of pansori through the sublimity of his stepdaughter's singing.

Sopyonje, directed by Im Kwon-taek, 1993.

The unprecedented box-office success of *Sopyonje* demonstrates the film's enormous emotional resonance for the Korean audience. This enthusiastic response stems from the close connection of the film's content to the Korean collective experience. The decline of pansori signifies to them the whole process of marginalization of Korean/traditional/spiritual values by the painful process of modernization.[15] The audience possibly realizes that it has paid a price for favoring Western/material civilization. Like the pansori artists, we as a Korean audience have been marginalized and victimized by Western discourse, alienated from our traditional culture. Our way of life and our system of values have been eroded and replaced by Western customs and values, which modernization necessarily introduces. As an audience, we cannot help sympathizing with the characters who desperately try to escape from the totalizing power of modernization. In short, Yu-bong and Song-hwa are our father and sister, while pansori is a metaphor for the past that we lost in the modernization process.

Unlike Yu-bong and Song-hwa, Dong-ho reaches a compromise with reality. He is the alter ego of any ordinary Korean, typifying the modern Korean experience. Tired of poverty and maltreatment, he runs away from his stepfather. The same exodus occurred en masse in Korea from the 1950s to the 1970s. After years of striving, Dong-ho successfully settles in a city and can afford to look back upon the past. He journeys in search of his sister, Song-hwa, a journey also toward pansori and the past he deserted.

His longing for reunion with Song-hwa, pansori, and the past also implies that he is not totally satisfied with the present, the result of modernization. Historical change produced by modernization drove him to run away. However, the more he gets immersed in modernized reality, the greater his alienation. What Dong-ho finds in modernization is not progress, but ambivalence. His departure from, and subsequent return to, Song-hwa, pansori, and the past manifests his ambivalence toward modernization.

Sopyonje's phenomenal success can be interpreted as a result of the audience's reconciliation with the past, which most Koreans were ruthlessly forced to ignore, forget, and negate in pursuit of modernization. In a sense, viewing *Sopyonje* seems to have provided an interaction with the audience's collective memories and the whole social and national identity. One might say that the film made members of the audience come to terms with their own bitter memories. *Sopyonje* offers a superb example of the cinematic response to, or confrontation with, modernization in South Korea, mainly through its underlying critique of the imposition of Western discourse in the context of modernization.

Festival *(1996): Tradition in the Present*

Im's other film, *Festival*, which also addresses the subject of traditional culture, takes a far different approach from *Sopyonje*'s.[16] While *Sopyonje* describes its bitter defeat in the recent past, *Festival* represents a victory of tradition in the present through Joon-sup's family members, who come to terms with each other through the ritualistic funeral of the mother.

The most impressive aspect of *Festival* is its detailed documentation of the traditional Korean funeral. The film, like an ethnographic documentary, reenacts complicated funerary procedures now nearly forgotten—from witnessing the last moment of life to the burial of the coffin. The filmmaker, in fact, makes evident his documentary approach to the ceremony by inserting subtitles that label and explain each procedure, no doubt to help young audiences understand the social meanings of traditional funeral formalities.

This is a major key to reading the film's discourse on tradition. In it, the traditional funeral is meaningful in two respects. First, as the subtitles explain, every formality has significant meanings based on the traditional value system, an amalgam of Confucianism, Buddhism, and shamanism. They are not annoying conventions and inconveniences that should be discarded, but prayers for the peace of the deceased and for the descendants' happiness. Thus the ritual formalities have their own meanings and rationale, which modern Koreans, like foreigners, usually do not know. Second, the tradition has the positive effect of dispelling antagonism between individuals. It magically turns a ceremony of mourning for the deceased into a festival of reunion and harmony for the living.

To emphasize the festival-like quality of the traditional funeral, the film initially shows all kinds of human conflict. Among them, the conflict between family members, the most serious, is primarily represented by Yong-soon. Her unexpected appearance creates tension within the family. It is learned that, as an illegitimate daughter of Joon-sup's brother, she had experienced severe maltreatment from her stepmother and had run off

Festival, directed by Im Kwon-
taek, 1996.

with some money stolen from her stepsister. Along with the uncomfortable memories,
her gaudy looks—inappropriately colorful makeup, black sunglasses, and white clothes
—and her bold behavior reinforce the others' repulsion. Thanks to the reconciliatory
power of the traditional funeral, however, all conflicts are exposed and subsequently resolved. The harmonious finale is symbolized by the taking of a family picture that includes Yong-soon.

Yet the harmonious victory of tradition in *Festival* is quite problematic, because it is
attained only through the temporary suspension of modernity made possible by the
combination of a rural location, the existence of a benevolent mother and her natural
death, and a traditional funeral. The film, in short, describes a utopia where modernization does not display its overwhelming effects, and where present lives and tradition
intermingle to form a whole. *Festival* lacks the power of negation that *Sopyonje* prominently effects, offering little critical reflection on what tore the family apart and then
made them reconcile. The film does not interrogate the discursive effect of moderniza-

tion. It does not question why and how we Koreans have discarded our splendid traditional values and institutions, although they provided us with the social meanings by which human beings live. Rather, we see the bright side of modernization, typified by material affluence and increased leisure time. What matters in the film is the fact that we do not know the deep meanings of tradition—thus the explanatory subtitles. This implies that the disappearance of tradition is due not to the totalizing effect of Westernization, but to our negligence. In this way, tradition's negative power is absent in the film, and tradition becomes a mysterious abstraction which we should preserve and celebrate. Furthermore, by claiming that through tradition, community may be symbolically restored, the film suggests that traditional culture can coexist with Western customs and values. Whereas *Sopyonje* acknowledges the necessary and tragic defeat of traditional culture in the course of modernization, *Festival* claims the triumph of tradition in the present.

In doing so, *Festival* ignores reality: National-cultural identity arises only in response to a challenge posed by the Other, so that any discourse of national-cultural identity is always and from the outset oppositional, although not necessarily conducive to progressive positions.[17] By failing to capture the tension stemming from the opposition of national culture to modernity, *Festival*, despite its realistic rendering, remains a romantic fantasy film.

The Postmodern Approach

The Day a Pig Fell into the Well *(1996): Deconstructing "Korean" Modernity*

Against the rapidly changing sociocultural terrain of the 1990s, Korean cinema has produced considerably provocative and innovative films. Among them, Hong Sang-su's much acclaimed debut film, *The Day a Pig Fell into the Well,* has received the widest recognition from critics as a radically "new" film.[18] Despite its true-to-life representation of the contemporary Korean urban scene, depicted in a meticulous and detached manner, the film's realism differs radically from that of the previously discussed films. They are films of "traditional" realism, which implicitly assumes a deeper truth or reality that must be presented through representational devices.[19] *The Day a Pig Fell into the Well* manifests a distrust of such an approach; the director's statement that "truth is on the surface" expresses disbelief in absolute truth or grand narratives.[20] The film attempts not to produce realist effects, but to urge the viewer to confront fragments of reality per se. It deconstructs the traditional concept of reality by showing trivial details that ceaselessly collide, intersect, and intermingle with one another in a closed structure. What it constructs, therefore, is not a tapestry of a unitary reality, but its absence.

The Day a Pig Fell into the Well consists of four interwoven but loosely connected parts, the discursive and complicated webs of an interpersonal network. Each part has its own protagonist: Hyo-sup, a novelist; Dong-woo, a white-collar worker; Min-jae, a box-office girl; and Bo-kyoung, Dong-woo's wife. The first segment depicts an ordinary day in the life of Hyo-sup, a novelist of little promise, in scenes ranging from his leaving his house to his futile pleading at a summary court, without narrative causality. He begins by visiting a publishing company only to find that his manuscript does not interest them. The next sequences describe his double date with Min-jae and Bo-kyoung. In the latter half of the segment, as an unwelcome guest at a college alumni party, he becomes entangled in a dispute and finally finds himself before a court.

These sketchy portrayals convey the prevalence of desire. Hyo-sup is described as a man of desires, primarily for sex and recognition. His having midday sex with Bo-kyoung at a cheap "love hotel" in a Seoul suburb expresses his sexual desires. He also seeks recognition as a novelist from the public. He shows up uninvited at the party, because it is supposed to be an event for intellectuals and literary people. However, the point is that his desire is essentially contradictory. He meets Min-jae, who clearly admires him, at a tearoom and hands her his latest unpublished manuscript, which moves her to tears. As they leave, the novelist coaxes some money from her. What makes him more objectionable is that he wants to exhibit his power or masculinity to Bo-kyoung by paying for the hotel room with Min-jae's money. Due to his contradictory desires, he is deeply split within himself. In this sense, he is not so much a hypocrite as a schizophrenic.

A fragmented and disjointed state of being is present throughout the film. In the second part, which traces Dong-woo's business trip to a regional city, Dong-woo is obsessed with cleanliness and doubts his wife's faithfulness. Staying in a motel, he makes a phone call to her in Seoul in order to control her. When he accidentally overhears a couple having sex in the motel, it is disclosed that Dong-woo also has a split self. Becoming aroused, he calls a prostitute, but only after much hesitation. The scene is bizarre: He examines a wallet photograph of his family to suppress his sexual desire, yet he finally surrenders to it and then has clumsy sex with the girl on the bed that he had cursed for its dirty spots. He cannot feel sensual pleasure because of his torn condom, and the act instead becomes a source of worry about venereal disease. The contradictions of his desire—he wants perfect cleanliness but he becomes an adulterer—signify his pathological problem.

In fact, the major characters are more or less schizophrenic without exception. Bo-kyoung is typical. When she recognizes her husband's unfaithfulness—even though she is having a sexual relationship with Hyo-sup—she buys a photograph of her family that had been exhibited at a photoshop and suddenly breaks the frame to tear it up. This sequence depicting the compulsive explosion of a quiet housewife suggests not only that her married life has been an illusion, but that the realist mode of representation manifested by photography is fictitious. It can be read as an attack on the falsity of reality or superficial realism. This quality is more explicitly demonstrated in a scene that shows the brutal murder of Hyo-sup and Min-jae by Min-soo, the theater manager who loves Min-jae. The scene, viewed from Bo-kyoung's perspective, makes us aware that Min-soo's obsessive love for Min-jae borders on madness. This suggests that the self-splits of characters are structural, not accidental.

The prevalence of contradictory desires not only produces internal splits but also disrupts relationships. The disruption of relationships between major characters is the most distinctive feature of *The Day a Pig Fell into the Well*. A series of disjunctions can be observed easily: Hyo-sup is not in love with Min-jae, yet hides his indifference toward her to get some of her money; he has a clandestine sexual relationship with Bo-kyoung, who does not love her husband. No constructive, harmonious relationship between characters exists in the film.

Sex is the film's most important motif for expressing disruption. The protagonists are interconnected through sexual relationships, none of which make any difference to any of them. They merely create an additional source of meaninglessness, confusion, and disjunction. In addition, their sex offers no bodily pleasure at all and is always disjointed and pathological. Every sex scene—one per part—is distorted. For the film's characters, sexual intercourse is like an act of death, not a rejuvenating, energetic one. Hyo-sup and Bo-kyoung's sex sequence in the motel lacks thrilling pleasure. It seems contingent, stale, listless, and pathological. This morbidity can also be observed in a sex scene between Min-jae and Min-soo, who ardently lusts after her.

Another sign of disruption is the telling of lies. Hyo-sup lies to Min-jae, telling her that he will soon repay the money she gave him. For Min-jae, lying is a daily activity. When others ask her about something, she always lies. For example, when a friend asks her about the part-time work payment, she lies about her absence during work time. Bo-kyoung habitually lies to Dong-woo, who tells a lie whenever she talks to her husband over the phone.

Throughout the film, everything conventionally regarded as meaningful, valuable, and unified is under deconstruction. Hyo-sup's clinging to the power of being an author is a prime example. His authorial power is negative in two ways. He exploits Min-jae through his authorial power in both the practical and figurative sense. When Min-jae regards him as a talented novelist, Hyo-sup becomes a powerful author in relation to her; she then is placed in the position of the powerless reader. He takes money from her without reciprocation. When she visits his home to congratulate him for his birthday, she finds Hyo-sup with another woman, Bo-kyoung. As she asks who the woman is, Hyo-sup berates her, shouting, "Don't you distinguish purity from childishness? You're not my type. You're shit!" In one restaurant sequence, Hyo-sup experiences the frustration of clinging to authorial power. A waitress who spills food on Hyo-sup does not make a sufficient apology, regarding him as a mere customer, not an author. Her treatment makes him go berserk. The absurdity of his clinging to authorial power is exemplified in his statement before the summary court judge. Pleading his innocence, he asks, "How dare restaurant attendants whose job is serving roast beef intervene in the talk between literary people?" Significantly, Hyo-sup is a novelist, a profession once honored that now commands little respect.[21] Here the novelist is a metaphor for traditional authority or authorship. Hyo-sup's incompetence signifies not only his lack of talent, but also the decline of authority.

Given that Koreans are often characterized by close familial ties, the total absence of family in the film is quite significant.[22] Despite their marriage, Bo-kyoung and Dong-woo cannot be considered a family. This is symbolized by the couple's failure to appear together within the frame until the last sequence; they communicate with each other

The Day a Pig Fell into the Well,
directed by Hong Sang-su, 1996.

only over the telephone. This family is apparently disintegrating. Also, no family or relatives appear or are discussed. Ironically, Min-jae's sole mention of her mother is a lie: When the head of the theater investigates her absence from work, she uses her mother as an excuse. The family-centered network of relationships, one of the most outstanding features of Korean culture, has no practical meaning in the film.

By the same token, the grand narrative of social change no longer holds true but serves only as the object of cynicism. One example is the scene where a publicity agent to whom Hyo-sup hands over his manuscript informs Hyo-sup of his plan to write about an ex-activist who became a follower of Taoism. It is ironic that the man who talks about the downturn of the movement is in fact a publicity agent, one who stands for crass commercialism. Another scene is more symptomatic. In the restaurant sequence, Hyo-sup gazes at a big photograph hung on the corridor wall. This much-publicized photograph depicting the magnificent top of Mt. Paetku with a large caldera lake is distributed by a newspaper company to evoke popular aspirations for the reunification of the Korean peninsula.[23] Then he enters the room and asks a friend across the table: "How was your trip to Mt. Paektu? Did you swim there?" It turns out that the friend slept through the famous sunrise over the mountain. Here Mt. Paektu is no longer a sacred place of Korean nationalism, but merely a place for fun. In this way, the film deconstructs given social meanings; only amorphous trajectories drawn by atomized individuals are consistently present. This is the typical way in which the film portrays the total disjunction of contemporary Korean life. In this manner, reality conceived as a flawless unity of necessary concatenation is thoroughly deconstructed. To the filmmaker, and even to the characters, reality is the site of struggle between conflicting desires. This is represented by obsession, repression, or distortion of desire, misunderstanding and the closure of communication, and explosions of madness.

The film uses various formal strategies to express disruption and disillusionment. Its episodic narrative structure is a device that effaces temporal linearity. The adoption of a fragmentary narrative structure that enables the shift in protagonists has the effect of suggesting not only the complexity of modern life, but also the disjunction of it. The claustrophobic quality exemplified in Min-jae's room in the theater and the motel room where Dong-woo stays expresses the theme of schizophrenic disjunction. The camera-work is a major means for conveying this. The stationary camera creates a suffocatingly morbid atmosphere beneath the surface. The camera never leads us to a wide-open space, and its movement is kept to a minimum. The view of the camera is emotionless and detached. In addition, the use of seemingly casual editing conveys a sense of disjunction.

The Day a Pig Fell into the Well represents the cinematic achievement of a "Korean" postmodern text that addresses the universality of disruption. It is a dense, multilayered ambiguous text, whose standpoint is deconstructive, grounded in the impossibility of unity. Therefore, the film is not a critique from a privileged perspective, but a deconstruction, which disclaims the primacy of a particular perspective. The film is postmodernist in its attack on modernity, being a text of poststructural metaphysics of a decentered subject, one of whose features is the contradictory nature of human desire.

Nevertheless, the postmodernity portrayed in the film is qualitatively different from "first-world" postmodernity, which is grounded in late capitalism and whose consummation is the consumerist society. The film's postmodernity is inevitably "Korean," in that it is a symptom of South Korea's semi-peripheral position in the world system. It does not glorify the liberation of desire in a Deleuzian manner, nor incline to the delirium of simulacra in a Baudrillardian manner. Rather, the film's postmodernity, expressed through its convoluted narrative and bleak tonality, is represented by the protagonists' marginality. They embody it through the contradiction of their desires and their symptoms of lack. Westernized modernity, uprootedness, and vulgar desires for money and sex intermingle and create total disjunction in Korean urban life.

The Day a Pig Fell into the Well does not address directly the issue of modernization. Nevertheless, insofar as the social reality of modern Korea is considered the outcome of modernization, the film consistently shows how our lives in the postindustrial society have become fragile, dislocated, and confused. Viewed in the context of modernization, the film is a grim portrait of (post)modernity, filled with symptoms of disruption. Thus, the film's critique of or, more properly, cynicism toward modernity is a powerful counter-discourse against modernization/modernity.

Conclusion

I have distinguished three approaches to modernization in these five films. The first is the movement approach, which *Black Republic* and *A Single Spark* employ. Modernization in both films is essentially seen as a process of ongoing alienation, particularly of labor. This discourse emphasizes class conflicts by establishing a firm dichotomy between the bourgeoisie and the working class. The movement's righteousness provides the rationale for their critique of reality. Thus, for today's audience, the movement is depicted not as a creator of social change but as a source of nostalgia.

The second approach employs a perspective based on tradition. In *Sopyonje,* modernization is the force that pushes out, marginalizes, and negates traditional culture. *Festival*, on the contrary, is an attempt to deny the defeat of tradition and to revive it in the present by privileging the reconciling power of tradition. As in the case of the movement approach, the tradition approach is a powerful means of criticizing modernization, but it is clearly no longer viable in the present.

The last approach I have examined is the postmodern. Whereas the two aforementioned approaches critique reality from an assumed vantage point, this one deconstructs reality from within. In *The Day a Pig Fell into the Well*, the reality of modernization is fragmentary, incommensurable, and contradictory.

Overall, the modernization discourses of the films are largely negative in relation to the modernization process itself.[24] Instead of celebrating the nation's "economic miracle," all the films predominantly criticize modernization for its negative effects of alienation and degradation, as Korean literature has done.[25] The protagonists of these films are more or less in conflict with modernization or modernity. In this sense, these films can be seen as counter-discourses on modernization/modernity.

Yet despite their critical view of modernization, they do not provide any practical alternative. That all the approaches fall into the trap of ambivalence ironically results in no path at all. It is intriguing that *A Single Spark* and *Festival,* both of which attempt to claim the positivity of their alternatives and to ignore the negativity of their approaches, each reveal inner contradictions within the text.

This dynamic of the discourses of modernization in recent Korean cinema is deeply rooted in the Korean context; as a result, these films cannot properly be appreciated without ample knowledge of Korean history and culture. Given that "cultural difference marks the establishment of new forms of meaning, and strategies of identification,"[26] investigating national cultural specificities is a necessary step toward overcoming the contemporary cultural hegemony of Western discourse. To accomplish this task, such issues as the relationship between modernization and national culture, between globalization and local economy/culture, must be scrutinized in each nation's concrete context.

Notes

1. These films represent an outstanding achievement of contemporary South Korean cinema. Im Kwon-taek, the director of *Sopyonje* and *Festival,* is acclaimed as the most important and pro-

lific auteur of modern Korean cinema. *Black Republic* and *A Single Spark* are major works of Park Kwang-su, a key figure of New Korean Cinema. When *The Day a Pig Fell into the Well* was released in 1996, it was praised by many critics as the most promising debut in all of Korean film history. Moreover, *Sopyonje* and *A Single Spark*, despite their serious subject matter, were huge successes at the box office, as well as among critics. *Sopyonje* set an audience record for domestic films that held until 1998.

2. In Korean economic discourse, the term *kundaehwa* (modernization) usually means the full-fledged industrialization pursued under governmental leadership since the early 1960s. However, I use the term in a broad sense to designate the whole process of Korea's interaction with the West since its opening up to the West in 1876.

3. Hart-Landsberg, *The Rush to Development*, 224.

4. National Statistical Office, *Illustrated Statistics* (Seoul: National Statistical Office, 1997), 48–49.

5. Chu, *Modernization vs. Revolution*, 10–14.

6. Hart-Landsberg, *The Rush to Development*, 15.

7. Ibid., 17.

8. Ibid., 20.

9. Marx and Mazlish, *Progress*, 1.

10. John Frow, "What Was Post-modernism?" in Adam and Tiffin, *Past the Last Post*, 139–140.

11. Choi, "Discourse of Decolonization and Popular Memory," 350, 353–354.

12. For a better understanding of the South Korean movement, see Hart-Landsberg, *The Rush to Development*, especially chapter 12; Wells, *South Korea's Minjung Movement*; Abelmann, *Echoes of the Past*; Cumings, *Korea's Place in the Sun*, chapter 7.

13. Cumings, *Korea's Place in the Sun*, 371.

14. In the 1980s, the Left in Korea was an amalgamation ranging from neo-Marxism to dogmatic Stalinism to Kim Il Sung's Chuche. Although the movement in the 1980s achieved an all-fronts strategy by adopting Marxism, it appeared equally disunited and factional as the result of differences among leftist groups.

15. Needless to say, the response to *Sopyonje* might be subject to time and place. Just because a text appeals to national memories does not guarantee its success. It must also be determined what constitutes national memories, and to what extent they are subject to change.

16. *Festival* is treated at greater length in my essay "In Defense of Continuity: Discourses on Tradition and the Mother in *Festival*," in *Im Kwon-Taek: The Making of a Korean National Cinema*, ed. David E. James and Kyung Hyun Kim (Detroit: Wayne State University Press, 2002).

17. Paul Willemen, "The Third Cinema Question: Notes and Reflections," in Pines and Willemen, *Question of Third Cinema*, 18.

18. The film was awarded the Dragons and Tigers Award at the 1996 Vancouver International Film Festival and the grand prize at the 1997 Rotterdam Film Festival.

19. Tim O'Sullivan et al., *Key Concepts in Communication and Cultural Studies*, 2d ed. (London: Routledge, 1994), 257–259.

20. "Interview with Director Hong Sang-Su," *Cine 21*, no. 146, 14 April 1998. Available at http://www.hani.co.kr/c21/data/L980330. Accessed May 1998.

21. Until the 1980s, literature, especially the novel, enjoyed the status of a privileged art form in modern Korean culture. Discourses through literature dominated the Korean cultural scene. See Uchang Kim, "The Agony of Cultural Construction: Politics and Culture in Modern Korea," in Koo, *State and Society*, 163–195. This cultural situation changed drastically in the 1990s, and literature was replaced by cinema and television.

22. See Cumings, *Korea's Place in the Sun,* 334, and Tae-Rim Yoon, "The Koreans, Their Culture and Personality," in *Psychology of the Korean People: Collectivism and Individualism,* ed. Geane Yoon and Sang-Chin Choi (Seoul: Dong-A Publishing, 1994), 15–26.

23. Mt. Paektu is the highest mountain on the Korean peninsula. According to Korean mythology the mountain is the birthplace of the North Korean people, so it has become an icon of recent Korean nationalism, particularly the nationalistic aspirations for the reunification of South and North Korea.

24. The negative approach to modernization was very common in Korean cinema. To my knowledge, there are only a few exceptions until the early 1990s, among which *P'altogangsan* (*Sights of the Eight Providences,* 1966) is exemplary. See James Wade, "The Cinema in Korea: A Robust Invalid," in *Korean Dance, Theater, and Cinema,* ed. Korean National Commission for UNESCO (Seoul: Si-sa-yong-o-sa, 1983), 185. In the 1990s, however, some mainstream films began to celebrate the results of modernization. Romantic comedy films are typical. Commonly featuring the sex war between yuppie couples, they unapologetically celebrate the modern and Westernized lifestyle.

25. Uchang, "Agony of Cultural Construction," 177.

26. Homi Bhabha, "DissemiNation: Time, Narrative, and the Margins of the Modern Nation," in Bhabha, *Nation and Narration,* 313.

Selected Bibliography

Abelmann, Nancy. *Echoes of the Past, Epics of Dissent: A South Korean Social Movement.* Berkeley: University of California Press, 1996.

Adam, Ian, and Helen Tiffin, eds. *Past and Last Post: Theorizing Post-Colonialism and Post-Modernism.* Hempel Hempstead: Harvester Wheatsheaf, 1991.

Bhabha, Homi K., ed. *Nation and Narration.* London: Routledge, 1990.

Choi, Chungmoo. "The Discourse of Decolonialization and Popular Memory: South Korea." In *Formations of Colonial Modernity in East Asia,* ed. Tani E. Barlow, 349–372. Durham, N.C.: Duke University Press, 1997.

Chu, Godwin C., et al., eds. *Modernization vs. Revolution: Cultural Change in Korea and China.* Seoul: Sung Kyun Kwan University Press, 1993.

Cumings, Bruce. *Korea's Place in the Sun: A Modern History.* New York: Norton, 1997.

Hart-Landsberg, Martin. *The Rush to Development: Economic Change and Political Struggle in South Korea.* New York: Monthly Review Press, 1993.

James, David E., and Kyung Hyun Kim, eds. *Im Kwon-Taek: The Making of a Korean National Cinema.* Detroit: Wayne State University Press, 2002.

Koo, Hagen, ed. *State and Society in Contemporary Korea.* Ithaca, N.Y.: Cornell University Press, 1993.

Lee, Changsoo, ed. *Modernization of Korea and the Impact of the West.* Los Angeles: East Asian Studies Center, University of Southern California, 1981.

Lee, Young-il. *The History of Korean Cinema: Main Current of Korean Cinema.* Trans. Richard Lynn Greever. Seoul: Motion Picture Promotion Corporation, 1988.

Marx, Leo, and Bruce Mazlish, eds. *Progress: Fact or Illusion?* Ann Arbor: University of Michigan Press, 1996.

Pines, Jim, and Paul Willemen, eds. *Question of Third Cinema.* London: British Film Institute, 1989.

Rayns, Tony, ed. *Seoul Stirring: Five Korean Directors*. London: Institute of Contemporary Arts, 1995.

Wells, Kenneth M., ed. *South Korea's Minjung Movement: The Culture and Politics of Dissidence*. Honolulu: University of Hawaii Press, 1995.

Yi, Hyo-in, Lee Jung-ha, and Kim Kyung-hyun. *Korean New Wave: Retrospectives from 1980 to 1995*. Pamphlet. First Pusan International Film Festival, 1996.

Filmography

Black Republic (Kudul do uri ch'orom), 1990
35mm, 100 min., color
Production: Dong-A Exports
Producer: Lee Woo-suk
Director: Park Kwang-su
Screenplay: Yoon Tae-sung, Park Kwang-su, Kim Sung-soo. Based on a story by Choi In-suk
Cinematography: Yoo Young-gil
Editor: Kim Hyan
Music: Kim Soo-chul
Cast: Moon Sung-geun (Han Tae-hoon, known as Kim Ki-young), Shim Hye-jin (Song Young-sook), Park Joong-hoon (Lee Sung-chul)

The Day a Pig Fell into the Well (Toeji ga umur e ppajin nal), 1996
35mm, 115 min., color
Production: Dong-A Exports
Producer: Lee Woo-suk
Director: Hong Sang-su
Screenplay: Hong Sang-su, Chung Tae-sung, Lee Hye-young, Kim Il-a, Suh Shin-hye. Based on the novel by Ku Hyo-suh.
Cinematography: Cho Tong-gwan
Editor: Park Kok-chi
Music: Ok Kil-sung
Cast: Kim Eui-sung (Hyo-sup), Park Jin-sung (Dong-woo), Cho Eun-sook (Min-jae), Lee Eung-kyoung (Bo-kyoung)

Festival (Ch'ukche), 1996
35mm, 106 min., color
Production: Taeheung Pictures
Producer: Lee Tae-won
Director: Im Kwon-taek
Screenplay: Yook Sang-hyo. Based on the novel by Lee Chung-joon.
Cinematography: Park Seung-bae
Editor: Park Soon-ok
Music: Kim Soo-chul
Cast: Ahn Sung-gi (Joon-sup), Oh Jung-hae (Yong-soon), Han Eun-jin (Mother)

A *Single Spark* (Arumdaun ch'ongnyon Chon Tae-il), 1995
35mm, 100 min., color
Production: Cine 200
Coproducers: Daewoo Cinema, Jeon Tae-il Commemorative Association
Director: Park Kwang-su
Screenplay: Lee Chang-dong, Kim Jung-hwan, Yi Hyo-in, Huh Jin-ho, Park Kwang-su
Cinematography: Yoo Young-gil
Editor: Kim Yang-il
Music: Song Hong-sup
Cast: Moon Sung-geun (Young-soo), Hong Kyoung-in (Jeon Tae-il), Kim Sun-jae (Jung-soon)

Sopyonje, 1993
35mm, 112 min., color
Production: Taeheung Pictures
Producer: Lee Tae-won
Director: Im Kwon-taek
Screenplay: Kim Myung-gon. Based on the novel by Lee Chung-joon.
Cinematography: Jung Il-sung
Editor: Park Soon-duk
Music: Kim Soo-chul
Cast: Kim Myung-gon (Yu-bong), Oh Jung-hae (Song-hwa), Kim Kyu-chul (Dong-ho)

CHAPTER 6

Youth in Crisis: National and Cultural Identity in New South Korean Cinema

Frances Gateward

"New Wave"—the term is used to describe trends in filmmaking that challenge both society and cinematic practice: the nouvelle vague of France during the 1950s; postwar Japanese cinema, the emergence of Britain's Angry Young Man movement, and Cinema Novo in Brazil during the early 1960s; the renaissance of American cinema in the 1970s; and films from Taiwan, the People's Republic of China, and Hong Kong in the early 1980s. To designate a film movement as New Wave denotes a distinct historical and cultural moment, a period of filmmaking characterized by a generation of young filmmakers whose work both reinvigorates and reinvents their respective national cinemas. These are cinematic movements of creation and invention: celebrating cultures, influencing the mainstream media industries, reinvestigating histories, and exploring new avenues of cinematic expression. The films that make up these movements are also, more often than not, the work of committed filmmakers, artists who reveal the disparities between their cultures' ideals and lived social realities. The mid-1980s saw the emergence of another such movement in the Republic of Korea, once known in the West as the "Hermit Kingdom." This term could also be applied to the nation's film industry, for there has never been in place a distribution network by which to export films, and Korean films, at least until very recently, were rarely seen beyond the nation's borders.[1] During the tumultuous eighties, changes in the nation's political, economic, and cultural realms made possible changes in the film industry, resulting in the birth of a new cinematic movement.

The popular and critical success of the movement brought to Korean national cinema the international attention it so richly deserves. In this essay I will discuss this New Wave, locating it within its social, political, economic, and cinematic contexts and noting how one film, Park Kwang-Su's *Chilsu Wa Mansu/Chilsu and Mansu* (1988), artic-ulates the issues and tensions of South Korea in the 1980s. I pay particular attention to youth culture, for as with most New Wave cinemas, this one was born out of youthful rebellion, when the consciousness of the nation was focused on a generation that would lead it through a decade of turmoil toward democratic reform.[2]

A Brief History of Korean Cinema

As many scholars have noted, it is difficult to construct a history of Korean cinema, as most of the documents and films of the earlier periods were destroyed during Japanese occupation and the Korean War. The earliest accounts of motion pictures include the presentation of a short Pathe film in 1898 that was sponsored by an American named Asthouse. According to Lee Young-il, the screening was a marketing ploy, as the price of admission was either a piece of nickel or the empty packaging for a brand of ciga-rettes that had recently been introduced. Other film historians, such as James Wade, in-form us that motion pictures arrived in Korea in 1904 with a private screening for high-ranking government officials, followed by a public screening shortly thereafter. Both were linked to the sweeping changes that were soon to overwhelm the peninsula. The first film was a newsreel documenting the victory of the Japanese navy over the Russian fleet during the Russo-Japanese War. The second film promoted an electric streetcar line built in the capital, Seoul. Together, these two accounts foreshadowed the developments that Korea was soon to experience—the impending annexation by Japan and the rapid, forced modernization that would begin in 1905, and continuing economic transforma-tions that would move the country away from a feudal, subsistence economy to one of capitalism and increased materialist consumerism.

The development of a commercially viable and expressive film culture in the Repub-lic of Korea was a struggle, because for the last century, Koreans have experienced lit-tle political and artistic freedom. Japan's abolition of the Foreign Ministry of the King-dom of Korea, and its subsequent occupation and annexation from 1905 to 1945, resulted in an oppressive and brutal foreign government that abolished all the political, social, and human rights of Koreans. It was also a period of what Jon Byong Je terms "detraditionalization"; under Japanese rule, the aim was to destroy everything Korean.[3] Korean culture was denigrated: The language was outlawed, Koreans were forced to relinquish their family names for Japanese surnames, and all of the creative arts, in-cluding film, were stifled. This was followed by the civil war (1950–53), neoimperialist hegemony from the United States, and a succession of right-wing governments that used national security issues to justify martial law and severe censorship. Yet, despite the strangleholds placed on the society and culture, Ch'ungmuro,[4] the Korean film indus-try, emerged.

Though film was immediately successful as a form of entertainment upon its intro-duction throughout the nation, it was not until 1919 that the first Korean-made film, *Uirijok Gutu/Righteous Revenge* or *Loyal Revenge,* was released. Directed by Kim To-san, it was a kinerama, designed to be combined with a stage performance. The first feature-length release came four years later, *Wolha-Ui Maengse* (Oath under the moon), directed by Yun Paek-nam. But the best-known film of the period was the first box-office smash, *Arirang*, in 1926, produced by actor/director Na Un-gyu. Taking its title from a popular folk song, it celebrated Korean culture and protested Japanese colonialism, getting its politics across not so much in its visual content, but from the performance of the *pyonsa*, who, like the Japanese *benshi*, was a live storyteller who supplied dialogue and narration for the audience. Derived from the Korean tradition of *pansori*, the *pyonsa* made it possible for audiences not only to do without translations of foreign films, but also to enjoy nationalistic sentiments usually not permitted under Japanese censorship.[5] With *Arirang*'s success, the production of films increased to about ten per year, until the colonial Japanese government shut down the industry. From 1938 until the end of World War II, Korean film production ceased; theaters screened only Japanese epics and propaganda films. After liberation in 1945, the film industry retooled, and the first color film, *Yosong Ilgi* (Diary of a woman), directed by Hong Sung-ki, was made in 1949. When the Korean War erupted in 1950, it devastated the developing industry, as it did the nation. It was not until 1955, forty-five years after the invention of the motion picture, that Ch'ungmuro entered its Golden Age, producing one hundred films annually—two hundred per year in the 1960s. Two films which helped stabilize the industry were *Ch'unhyanjon* (The story of Ch'unhyang) in 1955 by Yi Kyu-hwan and *Chayu Buin* (Madame Freedom) in 1956 directed by Han Hyong-mo. These feature films also set a trend for what was to become a staple of the national cinema: films that featured and were marketed to women—the melodrama. According to one film historian, 73.5 percent of all films produced from 1950 to 1960 were melodramas.[6] Many film scholars view the genre—which dealt with such subjects as postwar circumstances and the separation of families, widowhood, and failed romance—as a manifestation of *han*, a uniquely Korean sentiment that Ahn Byung-sup describes as "a frame of mind characterized by sorrowful lament or suffering from heavy persecution. It is a feeling deeply rooted in the heart and reveals itself in resignation, reproaching heaven, and lamenting one's destiny."[7] These films, like all melodramas, exposed gender relations and revealed the constrictions placed upon individuals by societal expectations, but their exaggerated sentimentalism, as well as forced censorship, made them less likely to present overt critiques of Korean politics and society.

This held true for the other dominant genre, the family comedy, which also emerged during this golden age. In literature, theater, and film, comedy is often born of a spirit that celebrates the revolutionary impulse, serving as a cathartic release or a critique of social hierarchy. In Korea, strict censorship outlawed any commentary on the government, its policies, and social conditions, under penalty of imprisonment. Without the freedom to produce social satire and other forms of denunciatory humor, Ch'ungmuro concentrated on domesticity and familial relations in a manner that, though providing some reflections of social change, remained relatively uncritical. All of this changed in the eighties, when dramatic economic, social, and cultural shifts occurred, allowing a handful of filmmakers to use their talents to challenge the forms and ideologies of commercial cinema.

Modernization and Social Upheaval in the 1980s

As with any term describing social phenomena, the notion of "modernization" is defined differently in different disciplines. As Andrew Nahm explains, those in political science define modernization as "the transformation of political systems and practices from those of authoritarianism and feudalism to those of more rational, more functional, highly integrated and efficient, and more participatory democratic systems." Sociologists, on the other hand, link it to urbanization and "the development of an achievement-oriented social and economic way of life." For historians it is a "process by which significant changes in human society that have been taking place in modern times."[8] The Republic of Korea has experienced modernization in all three ways, and then some. Though the history of Korea's modernization is long and complex, the Japanese colonial period and that of post–World War II liberation produced the most swift and radical changes. Scholars such as Jon and Lindauer view this period as the most rapid social change ever noted.

In most countries, modernization is welcomed; for Koreans, it was involuntary. Japan forced massive industrialization and urbanization on Korea, for the benefit of Japan and its empire, transforming it from an agricultural nation to one with developing cities, expanding industries and systems of education, heavy manufacturing, hydroelectric power plants, modern irrigation systems, and textile factories. The process was interrupted by the Korean War but developed at an even faster rate after the conflict. Economics took precedence, with national security a close second. The transformation also included the shift from a practically illiterate nation to one with a literacy rate of almost 95 percent, massive migration into the cities, and expanding mass communications. Indeed, the Republic of Korea experienced its famed "economic miracle," earning its place among the "Asian tigers."

But these changes were not without cost. As the population increasingly migrated toward the urban centers, housing became a serious problem; a large percentage of the urban poor, unable to afford adequate housing, lived in illegally constructed neighborhoods of tin shacks and tents. Kinship and traditional family ties were affected, with a shift from the extended family to the nuclear. As income rose, so did consumerism and materialism. Class differentiation became more distinct. The expanded industrial output had dire consequences for the environment. The economic miracle also brought with it increased dependence on the United States, both militarily, with permanent bases established for U.S. armed forces, and economically. There is, in fact, one definition of modernization that I neglected to list—modernization as Westernization.

Korean culture was assaulted by Western approaches to science and technology, Western customs, institutions modeled on Western structures, Western ways of thinking, and—as the American culture industry successfully continued to dominate the globe—Western popular culture and its ideologies. In addition, the increased mobilization of the population and continual improvement of the mass media helped disseminate foreign popular culture at an unprecedented rate. The past and traditional culture were demonized, seen as backward and primitive.

Scholars such as James Robins note that "exposure to modern culture (that is to say, Western culture) results not in cultural creativity but in conformism and dependency."[9] Others, such as Jon Byong Je, have noted that urban life in modern society creates acute anomie. His landmark study on the impact of urban life on youth revealed that with increased materialism and consumer capitalism came intense inferiority complexes and frustration. All of this was felt by Koreans during the development of the economic miracle. For the nation, the 1980s saw a culmination of all of the economic plans set in motion during the previous decades. But with the increase in Korea's world economic status came an increase in repressive governmental policies. As Nahm comments, modernization was for the "self-preservation of the nation rather than for the improvement of human conditions or the establishment of the rights of man and social justice."[10] The stability of the nation's economy was bought at a high price—the surrender of civil liberties. Repressive government policies, the lack of democratic and human rights, economic inequality, and social injustice put a strain on the nation. It exploded in the 1980s with the strengthening of the *minjung* (people's) movement, a grassroots upswelling led by youth and labor for social and political change.

No longer compliant, the nation experienced more social unrest in only a few years than it had in decades. Working conditions were, and in many ways remain, extremely harsh. According to Lindauer, industrial data suggest that Korea maintained the longest manufacturing workweek of any developed or developing country.[11] Not uncommon were twelve-hour shifts with only short meal breaks and one day off a month. Industrial accidents and fatalities were among the highest in the world, along with a deteriorating distribution of income. Labor protested these conditions, as well as authoritarian controls that favored management over workers and fostered disrespectful treatment by supervisors, an acute sense of relative deprivation among workers, and the perception that wealth was acquired through illegitimate means. The occurrence of labor disputes rose from 265 in 1985 to 276 in 1986 and 3,529 in 1987.[12]

Student and youth movements were also extremely active in promoting social change during the eighties. In fact, historically, every major change in the nation for the past century involved the participation of students: armed resurrection against the Japanese in 1906, the Samil Independence Movement in 1919, the Korean Independence Party in 1930, and the overthrow of Rhee's dictatorship in 1960. Along with labor, the contemporary student movement actively engaged in numerous protests, demanding democratization and unification of the two Koreas and espousing anti-imperialism. It culminated in the spring of 1980 with an event that was to mark the decade—the Kwangju Uprising.

Following the assassination of President Park on 26 October 1979 and the coup shortly thereafter, students of Chonnam National University, located in the southeast city of Kwangju, started movements to promote democracy on campus. In May 1980, their attention shifted to democratization on a national scale. Confrontations with the police escalated, and on the last day of the Grand Rally for National Democratization, May 14, students decided to stage demonstrations off campus, widening the protest to the downtown areas. The street demonstrations, which involved more than seven thousand students, continued for two days. Having voiced their concerns, they voted to cease their activities, waited two days for a government response, then resumed their demonstrations on 17 and 18 May. The response came, and it was both swift and brutal.

On May 17, emergency martial law was instituted across the nation. The military moved into the area, raiding Kwangju's universities and conducting arbitrary mass arrests of students and other civilians. When students gathered at the entrance to Chonnam National University on 18 May, they were met by fully armed paratroopers and police in riot gear. Violence erupted as the number of protestors soared, eventually swelling to more than 200,000. By the fourth day, the citizens of the city joined the uprising, managing to seize arms and eventually driving the military out of the province. They held the city for several days, until 27 May, when military forces surrounded the city and advanced to retake it. Using tanks, armored vehicles, machine guns, and bayonets, the military, backed by the Twentieth Army Division, ended the ten-day uprising, killing more than 2,000 civilians and injuring many more.

This uprising marked the turning point in the movement for democratization, further strengthening the grassroots movement and demonstrating to the nation, and the world, the brutal oppression of the country's military government. This event, more than any other, defined the generation that came of age during the 1980s. This shift was reflected in the motion picture industry, for many of the New Wave directors were active in the student movement.

The New Wave

The economic, political, social, and cultural transformations were reflected in the Motion Picture Law and Regulations that governed the industry. Historically, the mass media, including film, were subject to strict legal statutes and censorship. During the period of Japanese occupation, films presenting a nationalist sentiment were strictly forbidden. *Arirang*, discussed earlier, was able to critique colonialism by making use of the traditional Korean folksong from which it takes its title, and by expressing anti-Japanese thought and action through a character constructed as insane. As incidents of civilian unrest escalated during the 1920s and 1930s, censorship laws were strengthened, and in 1942 all the major studios were forced to close under the Choson Motion Picture Ordinance, which established one production company, the Choson Film Company, Ltd., which produced Japanese propaganda.

Liberation in 1945 enabled a resurgence of Korean filmmaking, yet it was still governed by political decrees. The earlier film regulations aided in the establishment and stabilization of the industry, but stringent laws concerning content continued to severely hamper the expression of cinema artists. All of this radically changed in 1987, with the sixth amendment to the Motion Picture Law. As Elizabeth Buck explains, "In 1985 the Reagan government made movies a trade issue, threatening retaliatory tariffs on Korean videocassette recorders."[13] As a result, the government removed the quota system designed to protect Korean cinema, allowed direct distribution of U.S. films, and—perhaps to make Korean films more competitive— loosened censorship regulations. Here was an opportunity for innovation and experimentation on a level never seen in the industry before; the result was the birth of a new cinematic movement.

Although the films by the directors of New Korean Cinema are marked by individual approaches, styles, and sensibilities, there are recurring themes and subjects that characterize the movement. They include anti–United States and nationalist sentiments (clearly a result of the Kwangju massacre, in which the United States was directly implicated), gender issues, social stratification, alienation in urban landscapes, the destruction of the family structure and community, and a focus on youth and youth subcultures.

Veteran filmmaker Im Kwon-taek, director of nearly one hundred films and considered Korea's first true auteur, experienced unprecedented success during the development of the New Wave; it revitalized his career, which spans three decades, and the national cinema in the process. Not only did his later melodramas became increasingly overt in their social criticism, but also he embraced what was to become another trend of the movement, the increased use of traditional Korean arts as icons of national identity.

> My personal desire has been to capture elements of our traditional culture in my work, and I have been doing so bit by bit. In a world becoming increasingly homogenized—they call it a global village nowadays, don't they?—amid the current of internationalism, what happens to the culture of a people who have kept themselves, for the most part, historically self-contained? The fear is, of course, that most aspects of Korean culture that are not favored by the terms of this new, international, and more aggressive culture may be absorbed, and in the end, disappear. Korean culture is geographically and anthropologically specific, but I believe that it must be revived and brought into the international context; it must make colors visible and find in it what is most unique, what is also the most universal. As Koreans what we can depict best in the medium of film are the very elements of our lives, which will necessarily find their roots in our culture and traditions. If we do not make these visible, who will look? Indeed, who can? Through film, we can, and we must reveal the colors that are our own, and this is particularly important in the global context.[14]

Im's 1981 film *Mandala* concerns Buddhism in modern society; *The Daughter of Fire*, in 1983, depicts shamanism; and his 1993 release *Sopyonje*, one of the most successful films in the history of Korean cinema, focuses on a family of *pansori* artists who struggle to keep the dying art viable in a time when Japanese and Western pop music forms dominate. As he states: "I feel very conscious of my Koreanness, and it has very much been my intention to deal with aspects of Korean tradition and culture. . . . And it's not accidental that many of the traditions I've explored are in danger of being lost. The Korean War and its aftermath did a lot of damage, but the incursion of western influences in the last forty years has been the most important factor."[15]

Another recurring New Wave theme and subject is the white-collar worker. These films examine the experiences of young professionals and the effect of their careers on personal relationships. Examples include Kim Ui-Seok's 1992 *Kyolhon Iyagi* (*Marriage Story*), at the time of its release the third highest-grossing film in the history of Korean cinema; and Jang Sun-Woo's 1998 *Songgong Sidae* (*The Age of Success*), a scathing treatise on the business world and advertising that goes so far as to name its protagonist is Kim Pan-chok, which translates as "good marketing." The name given his love interest, Seong So-bee, means "consumer." In this highly stylized satire of corporate rivalry, the characters engage in corporate espionage, develop consumer goods, and create the television commercials to sell them. The advertisements are as ridiculous as the products themselves, using sex and nationalism to add flavor to cooked foods.

Gender issues are also a major focus of the New Wave, with features that focus on sex roles and gender hierarchies within the family and on romantic relationships. Many concern the plight of the *yogong*, or factory girls. Concurrent with the growth of local textile factories in Korea was the increase in multinational global production, with "export-led industrialization becoming the favored strategy for development, touted by the United Nations Industrial Development Organization (UNIDO), the World Bank and the International Monetary Fund (IMF), along with multinational corporations and banks."[16] Women workers were, and still are, particularly valued as cheap, exploitable labor because they are dextrous, willing to accept lower wages than men, and less likely than men to join labor unions. In South Korea, women between sixteen and twenty-five comprise one-third of the industrial labor force.[17] Most, while working more hours than their male colleagues, earn less pay and are exposed to dangerous, and sometimes deadly, health hazards.[18] One of the most noted films in support of the labor struggles of women is Park Chong-Won's *Kuro Arirang* (1989). The story features a group of female factory workers who attempt to organize a union and suffer personal and public consequences, including a violent confrontation with riot police. Other notable feminist films include Park Chul-Soo's *301, 302* (1995), about two women with eating disorders, their reaction to male expectations, desires, and oppression; and Lee Min-Yong's 1996 film *Gyaegot Un Nalui Ohu* (*Hot Roof*), about domestic violence and the need for collective action against it.

The overarching characteristic of the Korean New Wave, significant in each of the trends described, is the influence of youth. In this respect, the cinematic movement of the 1980s shares some commonalities with other New Wave cinemas. The sensibilities of New Korean Cinema filmmakers differ from their predecessors', as do their concerns and cinematic styles, because they are born of a later generation. They were more heavily exposed to the influence of media than their predecessors; they are the first generation to come of age without direct knowledge and experience of Korea's civil war; and, as noted earlier, they belonged to the student movements that inflamed the nation in the 1980s. Their focus on youth is significant, because, as Henry Giroux points out, "youth simultaneously serves as a symbol of how a society thinks about itself and as an indicator of changing cultural values, sexuality, the state of the economy, and spiritual life of a nation."[19] A film that powerfully articulates youth in crisis is *Chilsu and Mansu*, not only the first feature film directed by Park Kwang Su, the filmmaker considered the initiator of the movement, but also the first Korean feature film released that presents overt social criticism.

Producer-writer-director Park Kwang-su, born in 1955, began shooting Super 8 film while a student of the fine arts at Seoul National University. In the early 1980s, Park founded the Seoul Film Group, a Super 8 collective linked to the student protest movement, and two others, which were involved with labor organizations and underground culture. He traveled to Paris to take a course at the Ecole Supérieure libre d'Etudes Cinématographiques film school and, upon his return, worked as an assistant director to Lee Jhang-Ho. Tony Rayns describes Park's work as characterized by "a coolly analytic detachment . . . trying to find a balance between empathy and analysis. The films' wider perspectives are designed to encourage reflection on [the] wider issues raised."[20] This is certainly true of *Chilsu and Mansu*.

Chilsu and Mansu is the story of two young men—Jhang Chilsu, twenty-two, and Park Mansu, twenty-seven—as they struggle to survive in modern-day Seoul. It effectively reflects the eighties social condition as the two characters experience urban angst, alienation, cultural imperialism, and marginalization from the mainstream as it progresses without them.

Though often described as an offbeat buddy film, a comedy, the film's overall tone is one of pessimism and destruction of the spirit. Park brilliantly defines the aural and visual space of the narrative from the start. The film opens with an assault of sirens. As they wail, the image fades in from black to a shot of Park Mansu, forlorn, gazing out a window over the sprawling city as the sirens continue. Often, in cultures where modernization and urbanization occurs, films emerge in which characters migrate in hopes of realizing dreams of success. Landscapes reveal the wonder of modern technology and power. But as Chungmoo Choi has explained, in Korean cinema: "Disintegrated identities and lost innocence colors the 1980s city in dystopic hues. The cityscape portrayed in 1980 is much more brutal than even that of the 1950s, the period after the Korean War that left the country materially and spiritually devastated. In the 80s it is this brutality of the city that silences people."[21] In *Chilsu and Mansu*, the mise-en-scène reveals urban decay, pollution, and cold stark reality through the use of desaturated colors and the dominant use of blue. The police direct traffic, emptying the streets and sidewalks of Seoul. The sirens signify a civil defense drill, a reminder of the separation between the two Koreas. Park then cuts to the interior of a public bus. Chang Chilsu, also gazing out a window at the city, is thrown off the bus. Immediately we are given two people who have no control over their surroundings. The authorities control the pulse and movement of the city. Chilsu and Mansu are able to look out on the city, yet they remain trapped behind barriers of glass and metal. They are permitted to witness the economic growth, but neither is allowed entry.

The mise-en-scène and framing continue this sense of entrapment and disconnectedness throughout the film, as both Chilsu (Park Joong-hoon) and Mansu (Ahn Song-gi) are lost in their surroundings. The film employs a style of "open framing": Rather than placing Chilsu and Mansu in a centralized, exclusionary film space, the director frequently places them on the periphery. The visual field is redefined so that objects and people that make up part of the mise-en-scène often block our view, passing between the pair of men and the camera. The aural space is similar to the visual space in that surrounding sounds often interrupt or overlap with the conversation of the protagonists. This happens early in the film when Chilsu, angered by the continual verbal and physical abuse he receives from his boss, protests being treated like a dog and quits. Running out of the paint shop, he sees Mansu, an independent contractor, and follows him home in an attempt to secure employment. Throughout this sequence, as they walk along the city streets, their discussion is drowned out by the sounds of traffic, and they are physically boxed in by symbols of modernity—concrete walls, cars, and fences.

In the film, modernity has also separated people and destroyed the sense of community. The two men make little eye contact at first. Only when they begin to rely on each other, becoming a community of two, does direct eye contact ensue. Eventually, the harsh realities of modern life in Korea reveal that community cannot be sustained. Part of the destruction of community by modern life involves a shift from extended to nuclear families, and the progressive breakdown of them, as well. Neither man in the film has a real home. After Mansu hires Chilsu to work for him, Chilsu moves in, claiming it will only be temporary. He is planning to emigrate to Miami Beach, where, he fantasizes, young men drive fast convertibles along the beach. Though Mansu has a place to live, it is not a home but an illegal shelter within a community of such structures. There is no running water and what little furniture exists consists of such things as lawn chairs. Their circumstances and developing relationship exemplify the loss of home and the struggle to reclaim it. Even though they become dependent on each other, financially and emotionally, they continue to keep secrets from and lie to each other. Chilsu lies about his relationship with a college student, Jina, his plan to emigrate, and his family background; Mansu lies about his family, as well.

Through the skilled use of flashbacks, Park reveals the history of the characters, enlightening the viewers as to the motivations and causes of their present condition. Mansu, for example, is disinterested and skeptical about politics, both liberal and conservative, as is revealed in two key sequences when he watches news reports and views political speeches broadcast on television. He drinks heavily and laments a lost opportunity to travel to the Middle East for a lucrative position. The cause, later revealed, is the twenty-seven-year imprisonment of his father for "subversive" political activities, which lies behind the breakup of his family, for he, unlike his mother and sister, has given up all hope for his father's release. Chilsu, we learn, is from the province of Dongduchon, noted for its location near a U.S. army base. As is so often the case, the placement of military bases in both the United States and in other countries affects the local economy, turning the surrounding area into a service industry for the American soldiers.

Chilsu and Mansu, directed by Park Kwang-su, 1988. (Courtesy of the Pusan Film Festival.)

It is not uncommon for some women, in this case Chilsu's stepmother and sister, to become prostitutes. The anti-American theme is emphasized by Chilsu's obsessive infatuation with all things American.

He pastes up images of James Dean and Marlon Brando in the abode he shares with Mansu. He takes his love interest, Jina (Bae Chong-ok), out dancing to a disco with Western music. When they go out to a movie, it is to the fourth installment of Sylvester Stallone's *Rocky* series. We view a portion of the film—the musical number celebrating U.S. culture and all its excess, the prefight spectacle of James Brown singing "Living in America." Chilsu frequents a Burger King where Jina is employed. Drinking the symbol of U.S. cultural dominance, Coke, he spends a lot of time in the restaurant, which pipes American pop music over the speakers. As Rayns points out, Chilsu does not need to move to America; America is already there.[22] We hear Korean music only in a montage sequence in which the pair ride their bike through crowded city streets on their way to work. It is significant that this montage marks a shift in the film from light comedy to a much darker tone.

The song in that sequence was written and sung by Kim Soo chul, a popular singer of the period. A staple of the New Wave, Kim worked with directors Lee Jang-Ho and Bae Chang-Ho as a composer, and sometimes as an actor. He is renowned throughout Korea for his incorporation of traditional folk music into rock 'n' roll. It is a moment of high irony, for the visuals and musical style suggest an upbeat mood. The lyrics however, reveal something else:

Urban skyscrapers keep emerging and blocking the fair sky.
The ones whom I miss so much have already left and are no longer here.
Streetside trees, worn out by city life, speak no more.

In the thick urban air, I see only shadows [of the trees].
Ah, is it me who has changed? Is it the world which has changed?
Now that people sound foreign, I find myself with a longer way to go.
In the home of my youth there used to be a beautiful mountain and clean river.
As time goes by, they become forgotten and disappear.
Where have all gone, whom I miss so much?
The deeper the night becomes, the more bitter my heart gets.

The bicycle is an important motif in the film. Mansu, upon Chilsu's agreement, with his own hands adapts his one-seater into a bicycle for two. Later, as a foreshadowing of events to come, the men fall in the street as they ride home in the rain.

The film closes with a scene that reduces the government and politics to absurdity. The economic survival of the pair is tenuous, but Mansu manages to find them work — painting a billboard advertising Glamour Whiskey. (The sales pitch uses sex — the bottle is held by a distinctly non-Asian, buxom blonde.) High atop a skyscraper, providing us with more visual sweeps of the city as the men look out, Chilsu decides to get a better view, climbing even higher to a perch atop the billboard. Mansu follows, and here, in a moment of revelation and closeness, they reveal the secrets they have kept from each other. In a bizarre turn of events, authorities confuse them for suicidal protestors, mistaking their beer bottle for a Molotov cocktail. The situation escalates. The head of the advertising agency arrives, as do armed troops. Seeing no way out of the situation and resigned to his guilt by association with his father, Mansu jumps, copying the actions of a protestor he saw on the news. Chilsu is arrested, and the film ends with a shot of him looking out the back of the police car as he is driven away. The film ultimately depicts a culture that denies the material success and personal security it tries to create.

Chilsu and Mansu contains many of the themes and characteristics that define the new Korean film movement as unique and exciting. This film, and the others that make up the New Korean Cinema, not only has forced great change upon Ch'ungmuro but also has effected change in the wider society and culture. These dynamic and courageous filmmakers, by constructing controversial narratives in new cinematic forms, have for the first time made it possible for Korean national cinema to receive the worldwide recognition that it so rightly deserves.

Notes

1. Though two Korean nation-states exist, I will be using the term "Korean" here as shorthand when referencing the Republic of Korea (South Korea). This is not to suggest that the People's Republic of Korea (North Korea) is not Korean.

2. The term "youth culture" is used in the tradition of cultural studies — to define a subcultural social group determined by particular positions, ambiguities, and contradictions within the wider society. Youth culture is determined by the age, styles, and activities of particular subcultures within the specific historical and cultural moment that represent a response and resistance to the dominant culture.

3. Jon, "Republic of Korea," 133.

4. The film industry takes its name from the district in Seoul where it is located.

5. *Pansori* is a traditional folk art form involving classical tales told in song.

6. Lee, *History of Korean Cinema*, 116.

7. Ahn Byung-Sup, "Humor in Korean Cinema," *East West Film Journal* 2, no. 1 (1987): 95.

8. Andrew C. Nahm, "Modernization Process in Korea: A Historical Perspective," in Lee, *Modernization of Korea*, 26, 30.

9. James Robins, "Modernization from Varied Perspectives," in Lee, *Modernization of Korea*, 83.

10. Nahm, "Modernization Process in Korea," 27.

11. David L. Lindauer, introduction to Lindauer et al., *Strains of Economic Growth*, 7.

12. Ezra F. Vogel and David L. Lindauer, "Toward a Social Compact for South Korean Labor," in Lindauer et al., *Strains of Economic Growth*, 105.

13. Elizabeth Buck, "Asia and the Global Film Industry," *East West Film Journal* 6, no. 2 (1992): 129.

14. "Between Blockbusters and Art Films," *Harvard Asia Pacific Review*, summer 1997, http://www.hcs.harvard.edu/hapr.im/html.

15. Quoted in Rayns, *Seoul Stirring*, 26.

16. Fuentes and Ehrenreich, *Women in the Global Factory*, 9.

17. Ibid., 16.

18. In March 1988, a fire broke out at the Green Hill Textile Company. Because of locked doors and exits blocked by product, twenty-two women lost their lives.

19. Giroux, *Fugitive Cultures*, 10.

20. Rayns, *Seoul Stirring*, 13.

21. Chungmoo Choi, "The Magic and Violence of Modernization in Post-Colonial Korea," in Chungmoo, *Post-Colonial Classics*, 11.

22. Rayns, *Seoul Stirring*, 50.

Selected Bibliography

Choi, Chungmoo, ed. *Post-Colonial Classics of Korean Cinema*. Irvine: Department of East Asian Languages and Literatures, University of California–Irvine, 1998.

Fuentes, Annette, and Barbara Ehrenreich. *Women in the Global Factory*. Boston: South End Press, 1983.

Giroux, Henry. *Fugitive Cultures: Race, Violence, and Youth*. New York: Routledge, 1996

Jon, Byong Je. "Republic of Korea." In *Youth in Asia: Viewpoints for the Future*. Association of Asian Social Science Research Council. New Delhi: New Statesman Publishing, 1988.

Lee, Changsoo, ed. *Modernization of Korea and the Impact of the West*. Los Angeles: East Asian Studies Center, University of Southern California, 1981.

Lee, Young-il. *The History of Korean Cinema: Main Current of Korean Cinema*. Trans. Richard Lynn Greever. Seoul: Motion Picture Promotion Corporation, 1988.

Lindauer, David L., Jong Gie Kim, Joung Woo Lee, Sop Hy Lim, Jae Young Son, and Ezra F. Vogel, eds. *The Strains of Economic Growth: Labor Unrest and Social Dissatisfaction in Korea*. Cambridge: Institute for International Development/Harvard University Press, 1997.

Rayns, Tony, ed. *Seoul Stirring: Five Korean Directors*. London: Institute of Contemporary Arts, 1995.

Wade, James. "The Cinema in Korea." In *Korean Dance, Theater, and Cinema*. UNESCO. Arch Cape, Ore.: Pace International Research, 1983.

Selected Filmography of the Korean New Wave

Black Republic/They Like Us, Park Kwang-su, 1990
Deep Blue Night, Bae Chang-Ho, 1985
Farewell My Darling, Park Chul-Soo, 1996
Life and Death of the Hollywood Kid, Jhung Ji-Young, 1994
Lovers in Woomuk-Baemi, Jang Sun-Woo, 1989
My Love My Bride, Lee Myung Se, 1990
Our Sweet Days of Youth, Bae Chang-Ho, 1987
Our Twisted Hero, Park Chong-Won, 1992
A Petal, Jang Sun-Woo, 1996
Seoul Jesus, Jang Sun-Woo, 1985
A Single Spark, Park Kwang-su, 1996
Three Friends, Yim Soon-Rye, 1996

CHAPTER 7

The Fragmented Commonplace: Alternative Arts and Cosmopolitanism in Hong Kong

Hector Rodriguez

This essay proposes the category "culture of the fragmented commonplace" to describe a cluster of recent works of Hong Kong theater, literature, film, and video. This culture is not so much an organized artistic movement as a loose tendency comprising a cluster of narrative subject matter, methods of formal construction, and thematic concerns. It developed in a historically circumscribed period that began around 1975 but mainly encompasses the 1980s and 1990s. This culture does not embrace the whole of Hong Kong artistic production; its core examples were often produced in avant-garde cultural contexts outside mainstream commercial institutions influenced by international modernism.

The culture of the fragmented commonplace rests on two salient characteristics. First, it contains specific references to well-known Hong Kong streets and landmarks, historical events and situations, vanished architecture, old popular songs, local slang or myths or folktales, disposable everyday objects, and other concrete elements that produce a strong sense of place. The works I have in mind invariably establish a link to the historical memory and everyday reality of Hong Kong by drawing on and reasserting a recognizably local culture.

Second, these various referential contents are depicted as an assemblage of fragments. The artists in question produce a collage effect, an impression of intense heterogeneity, by drawing on diverse or unrelated subject matter and employing abrupt shifts in mood, location, and point of view. Video artworks like *Image of a City* (May Fung and Danny Yung, 1990), *She Said Why Me* (May Fung, 1989), *Project No. 9064* (Kwan Pun Leung, 1990), *95/23 Ninety Five/Two or Three* (Ernest Fung, 1995), *Love* (Hung Keung, 1997), *Happy Valley* (Mark Chan, 1997), *Diary from the Hard-Boiled Wonderland* (Ip Yukyiu, 1998), *Invisible City "Wall"* (Rita Hui, 1998), and *Song of the Earth: "The Farewell"* (O Sing Pui, 1998) generate an effect of fragmentation by juxtaposing archival footage or black-and-white photographs with fictional or documentary images in the present, and sometimes with written material superimposed on the screen. Novelists like Leung Ping-Kwan (*Cutting Paper,* 1977) and Xi Xi (*My City,* 1976) employ a "multi-perspectival" method: The authors shift between the standpoints of two or more characters, producing an inclusive and many-sided image of the city out of an accumulation of multiple particular experiences.[1] The idea of collage has also been explicitly theorized. Video and installation artist Jamsen Law, for instance, has described video making as a collage activity that generates new meanings through the juxtaposition of diverse material.[2]

These artists seldom employ classical methods of narrative organization; they tend to avoid goal-oriented protagonists who face obstacles or conflicts and achieve a clear-cut resolution. The typical strategy is to abolish or attenuate causal chains and to rely on ambiguous or "open" endings. The culture of the fragmented commonplace sometimes shows an intense attachment to those "dead" or "trivial" instants normally excluded from classical narrative as irrelevant to the main dramatic conflict. Instead of offering the resolution of a "well-constructed" plot, such novels and films conclude by seeming arbitrarily to cut off a potentially limitless accumulation of random everyday moments. Novels and films with a stronger narrative framework, such as Evans Chan's *To Liv(e),* construct several intersecting, crisscrossing stories that shift between documentary and fiction in order to bring forth a strong effect of stylistic heterogeneity. These various methods produce the impression of a random and open-ended collage of highly diverse materials. The everyday domain splinters into broken fragments of history and daily life, or into multiple impressions or experiences. This collage effect allows artists to fulfill two basic aims: to retain some form of social reference and at the same time to adhere to the stylistic self-consciousness characteristic of international modernism.

Artists are sometimes drawn toward the compression or brevity of the poem or the sensuous immediacy of the photograph, aiming for the maximum possible concentration of meaning or expression. The short story or video art piece are ideal forms to achieve this abbreviation and intensification, but longer novels, films, and stage performances often seem to be a loose assemblage of relatively brief passages that could to some degree stand on their own as short stories or vivid vignettes. The artwork becomes a scrapbook of small moments, memories, and gestures. These variegated elements retain their autonomy as fragments, refusing wholly to subsume their distinct particularity into any general artistic structure.

In a few cases, this assertively fragmentary quality is the consequence of a collaborative production process. The forty-three-minute avant-garde video *The Song of the Earth: "The Farewell"* (1998), for instance, was created by six video makers (Rita Hui, Jacky Siu, Veronica Law, Eugene Mak, and Jack Cheung, along with O Sing Pui, who coordinated the project and retains final directorial credit), some of whom worked independently on different segments that can stand on their own as separate projects. The video is clearly divided into discrete blocks or units with distinct formal characteristics that range from a montage style reminiscent of silent city symphonies to a long-take approach. Another example of a collaborative creative process that leads toward an impression of stylistic heterogeneity is the 1998 multimedia stage performance adapted from Dung Kai-cheung's novel *The Atlas*. In addition to the music of Chan Ming-chi composed for percussion and traditional Chinese instruments, the performance also featured dance and video art prepared by various artists associated with the local avant-garde groups Videotage and Flowery World.

Such a collaborative approach, however, remains relatively uncommon. In most cases, the collage effect arises out of the personal aims and interests of an individual artist responsible for the whole work. This essay employs the term "background" in a technical sense to denote the frameworks of assumptions and concerns that supply a motivation for the choices that artists make. In my account, a background comprises the reason or reasons why one or more artists at a given time act as they do in creating their works. My discussion of the culture of the fragmented commonplace considers five backgrounds that contributed to the rise of this culture: (1) the influence of cultural studies, especially the "post-structuralist" reworking of semiotic theory; (2) a "revisionist" understanding of history that privileges small-scale everyday objects, places, and activities rather than "epic" or heroic events; (3) a modernist interest in intertextuality, defamiliarization, impermanence, and the nonrational; (4) an interest in the city as a distinct phenomenon, based on the assumption that urban space is not only an objective datum but also an "expressive" or "phenomenological" space comprising memory, desire, and imagination; and (5) a renewed interest in the lyrical trends of classical Chinese art and some of its more contemporary heirs.

This essay does not contend that every work of the culture of the fragmented commonplace partakes of all five backgrounds. Some artists were influenced by only one or two of these factors, and few of the works discussed here are "pure" instances of the culture of the fragmented commonplace. Sometimes only particular scenes or segments of a work partake of the characteristics I am considering. The scope of my project is to identify broad areas of intersection between individual works or artists, not to provide the final word on any of them. My examples remain very different from one another, and it would be misleading to impose a unity that does not exist. The culture of the fragmented commonplace forms nothing more than a node in a broader network of intersecting, overlapping, but also heterogeneous works and genres.

Backgrounds

The Semiotic Consciousness

The expression "semiotic consciousness" denotes the assumption that the social environment is mainly or completely comprised of "signs," broadly defined as artifacts that express or embody meanings. Signs in this sense are not only words but also (and perhaps more importantly) such visual artifacts as billboards and photographs. The semiotic consciousness involves a tendency to treat the world as an encoded text. This text nonetheless appears strangely oppressive or at best ambivalent, because established structures of meaning putatively conceal the concreteness and complexity of flesh-and-blood human experience.

Italo Calvino remains an influential literary model for this semiotic consciousness. Discussing the aims of his novel *Invisible Cities,* Calvino has remarked that he chose the city as a symbol of "the tension between geometric rationality and the entanglements of human lives." This mismatch between the systematic order of semiotic structures and the concrete "entanglements" of human experience remains a widespread concern of many contemporary theorists in the so-called post-structuralist tradition. Teresa de Lauretis, for instance, has drawn our attention to the gap between mainstream representations of women and the everyday lived experiences of actual women. Calvino himself has observed that the work of Roland Barthes brings out the tension between language and experience: "All of [Barthes's] work . . . consists in forcing the impersonality of the mechanisms of language and knowledge to take into account the physical nature of the living, mortal subject."[3]

Although not always directly influenced by Calvino's work, many Hong Kong artists regard their daily culture as a collage of prefabricated and stereotypical visual signs. These clichés have cemented "a solid and compact" image of the city that (in their view) should be highlighted and resisted. While Hong Kong filmmakers and writers often retain a strong attachment to everyday places, objects, and mass media images as a source of identity and an alternative to official history, they also understand that prevalent signs merely repeat hegemonic ways of seeing and speaking. These signs fail to do justice to the texture and depth of actual human life in Hong Kong. The mismatch between meaning and experience defines one of the key thematic concerns that underpin the works I am discussing.

Some artists respond to their awareness of this gap by employing modernist techniques to defamiliarize commonplace objects and places, thus seeking out fresh devices to capture the texture of daily urban experience. The systematic defamiliarization of the commonplace is meant to achieve freedom from established styles of seeing and describing Hong Kong. Mark Chan's video *Happy Valley* assembles an assertively heterogeneous collection of visual materials pertaining to the district of Happy Valley: black-and-white photographs and archival footage of old Hong Kong, moving shots of contemporary streets, government documentaries, city maps, street signs, billboards, computer icons, and so on. Most of those images depict socially constructed representations that embody meanings. This "semiotic" consciousness is intensified by the video's literary references, particularly the use of written quotations, which exemplify a modernist taste for intertextuality. A superimposed text from Calvino's *Invisible Cities* describes the imaginary city of Tamara as a place full of streets thick with signboards: "The eye does not see things but images of things that mean other things. . . . However the city may really be, beneath this thick coating of signs, whatever it may contain or conceal, you leave Tamara without having discovered it."[4] This quotation cues the viewer to interpret the images as a commentary on the opaqueness of signs. Mainstream representations cannot encompass everyday experience. By juxtaposing many different kinds of images into a variegated collage, the visual design of *Happy Valley* not only highlights the pervasiveness of images and their status as "constructed" signs, but also defamiliarizes and fragments those visual materials in an effort, perhaps, to find a new point of view on urban life. Mark Chan sometimes "breaks" an otherwise fluid camera movement through the use of insert shots, particularly archival footage and old Hong Kong photographs. Superimpositions, split-screens, color distortions, rhetorical intertitles, and words shown over the visual images help to intensify this collage effect and to produce "busy" frames overloaded with information. Hong Kong appears to be a forest of disorienting, unfamiliar, and dreamlike signs.

Noting that anybody who has lived in Hong Kong will readily recognize their city in Calvino's novel, a character in Evans Chan's film *To Liv(e)* also reads a passage from *Invisible Cities*, replacing the name of the imaginary city of Aglaura with that of Hong Kong: "So if I wished to describe Aglaura to you, sticking to what I personally saw and experienced, I should have to tell you that it is a colorless city, without character, planted there at random. But this would not be true either: at certain hours, in certain places along the street, you see opening before you the hint of something unmistakable, rare, perhaps magnificent; you would like to say what it is, but everything previously said of Aglaura obliges you *to repeat rather than say.*"[5] A few endlessly repeated clichés have, we are told, created "a solid and compact image" of the city. Although deeply implanted in the conscious awareness of its inhabitants, this image differs sharply from their concrete experience. The desire to "say" something new about this experience rather than "repeat" prefabricated discourses provides an impetus behind *To Liv(e)*. As the voice-over recounts the story of Aglaura/Hong Kong, a tracking shot discloses a nocturnal view of Hong Kong streets, capturing perhaps "the hint of something unmistakable, rare, perhaps magnificent" of which Calvino's novel speaks. The movements of the camera give a visual experience of the city, not as it is customarily described or shown in hegemonic signs but as it lives "on the ground," showing the cinema's power to document an urban experience that lies beyond the descriptive powers of language. The moving shot is ambiguous; while it is possibly readable as the point-of-view shot of a character who (we later find out) is riding the Hong Kong tram, the lack of reaction shots throughout the sequence also suggests an "impersonal" perspective on the city. The standpoint of the character merges with the rhetorical voice of the filmmaker, producing something like an objective experience not clearly attached to the consciousness of any given character.

The film's basic story premise brings out the tension between the concrete experiences of actual Hong Kong people and the widely disseminated mythologies that purport to describe or judge them. The narrative takes off from a current event: European "art cinema" star Liv Ullman's highly publicized criticisms about Hong Kong's treatment of Vietnamese boat people. Angered by those comments (and more generally, by the tendency of outsiders to speak of Hong Kong without acknowledging the city's multilayered historical predicament), Ruby, the film's outspoken protagonist, writes a series of letters to Liv Ullman. *To Liv(e)*, probably inspired by *Letter to Jane*, partakes of a familiar characteristic of Jean-Luc Godard's cinema aptly pointed out by David Bordwell:

the recurrence of certain broad types of scenes that become "paradigmatic" blocks throughout the film. The narrative alternates between Ruby reading her letters to Liv Ullman, ordinary conversations between friends and lovers, documentary images of the city and its people, family visits, and artistic performances and other public events.[6] The accumulation of heterogeneous narrative materials helps to produce the kind of collage effect that distinguishes the culture of the fragmented commonplace.

Different paradigmatic blocks are organized according to different rules. For instance, sequences depicting everyday conversations or family visits stand out not only from the rest of the film but also from other examples of the culture of the fragmented commonplace in their relative kinship to classical narrative cinema. They contain goal-driven protagonists that enter into dramatic conflicts and confront the need to make momentous decisions. In contrast, when Ruby reads her letters to Liv Ullman, *To Liv(e)* adopts a more intensely self-conscious style, inserting archival footage and newspaper clippings while maintaining a stylized mise-en-scène: Ruby faces the camera directly, sitting against an austere, theatrical black background with symbolic props like an American flag. These moments are by far the most insistently essayistic and self-consciously rhetorical of the entire film, and perhaps of the entire culture of the fragmented commonplace. Almost completely lacking in playfulness, the letters contain strong conclusions and somewhat loose but frequently convincing arguments about local and international politics. Nondiegetic insert shots are sometimes used in an argumentative manner; thus, when Ruby quotes from the *New York Times,* the film proceeds to show us a clipping of the paper, as if presenting evidence on behalf of a scholarly claim. There is no self-parody or ambiguity here: The filmmaker has put forth a thesis that viewers are expected to take very seriously.

The film's tendency to use actual historical material (including not only newspaper reports but also archival footage and documentary images of contemporary Hong Kong) gives several sequences a strong nonfictional component that once again recalls Godardian filmmaking. The line between fact and fiction is also blurred when fictional characters converse with actual political figures like Elsie Tu about their real past experiences. In accordance with Evans Chan's "paradigmatic" approach, those moments are differentiated from the rest of the film because they follow distinct narrative rules. Lacking any overtly rhetorical nondiegetic insert shots and a stylized set design, they do not partake of the extreme self-consciousness of the letter-writing sequences, but they are also less conventionally classical than the family sequences because of their striking combination of fiction and nonfiction. In other sequences, however, Chan draws on another strategy of European art cinema, which Bordwell terms "the realism of concrete behavior and locales," showing fictional protagonists simply strolling in actual locations like the Star Ferry.[7] The narrative thus accumulates "dead" or "transitional" moments that do not further any line of action but provide a documentary record of particular times and places. Like the best examples of postwar European art cinema (including, for instance, Antonioni and Rossellini), Evans Chan sometimes expresses a sense of isolation and crisis through the concrete presentation of nonpurposeful behavior in actual everyday locations.

Josephine Koo as Teresa in *To Liv(e)*, 1992. (Courtesy of director Evans Chan.)

Despite its strong effect of fragmentation, the film is unified by an enveloping sense of impending historical and existential crisis. This thematic aim is not simply a matter of content; it also supplies the dominant principle of narrative form. The overall structure of *To Liv(e)* is designed to compare and contrast the diverse responses of various characters to Hong Kong's (then) impending reunification with China. Thus Evans Chan creates minor characters like Michelle who appear only briefly to express their views and concerns about the political and social future of Hong Kong and then vanish from the narrative. These characters largely function to demonstrate that the people of Hong Kong do not respond to the end of colonialism in a homogeneous manner. Their presence is realistically motivated, insofar as they are friends or acquaintances of at least one of the protagonists, whom they meet in a restaurant or at a party. Thus the sense of crisis is embodied in a realistic depiction of everyday life. Indeed, despite the strongly Godardian self-consciousness of the letter-reading sequences or the modernist combination of documentary and fiction, the bulk of *To Liv(e)* remains reasonably realistic.

Evans Chan is not interested in calling attention to artistic form as an end in itself so much as in advancing thematic meanings about the human condition in relation to the immediate historical predicament of Hong Kong. Like Bergman (whose work is referenced in one of Ruby's letters to Liv Ullman) and other international art-cinema auteurs, Chan writes dialogue that frequently mentions grand existential questions, in particular the search for a home and the fundamental unreliability of the world. One of Ruby's letters describes the predicament of Hong Kong people as an "anonymously threatened existence," highlighting the sense of existential insecurity that pervades the film. Thus

the English title *To Liv(e)* is meant to evoke not only Ruby's response to Liv Ullman but also the difficulty of survival. The story is organized, first, to facilitate the explicit communication of this theme to the viewer and, second, to show how uncertainty pervades the normal life of Hong Kong people. The film underscores not only the quotidian insecurity experienced by individual characters as they struggle to keep their emotional and ethical commitments alive, but also the uncertain future of artists working precariously in Hong Kong's independent public spheres. The presence of Hong Kong avant-garde culture highlights the fragile consolidation of a cultural space devoted to independent artistic production in the midst of a shifting and uncertain reality.

As if to situate the film within an ongoing genealogy of radical artistic activities, Evans Chan calls attention to recent avant-garde productions in Hong Kong. The "commonplace" references of the film largely belong to the local artistic community. Characters and situations make reference to the theater of Zuni, the video art of Ellen Pau, the dance of Karen Suen and South ASLI, and of course the City Contemporary Dance Company, whose founder, Willy Tsao, produced the film. These references are, on the whole, diegetically motivated. For instance, Evans Chan does not simply interrupt the narrative by inserting an unmotivated avant-garde dance performance but rather justifies its presence by following Ruby as she enters the theater and finds her seat. The filmmaker does not include a segment of a video art piece by Ellen Pau as a nondiegetic insert shot; rather, the images appear on a television set in Ruby's apartment. While the narration is often strongly self-conscious during the letter-writing scenes, this self-consciousness is hardly consistent throughout the film. *To Liv(e)* includes modernistic sequences in the midst of an otherwise realistic depiction designed to highlight existential and social themes. A content-driven filmmaker, Chan does not pursue artistic self-consciousness for its own sake.

History as a Montage of Vernacular Materials

The culture of the fragmented commonplace aims to "reflect" Hong Kong history and experience, and sometimes also to express a vision of what history is. This interest is underlain by a modernist understanding of history as a montage of commonplace materials. It erects an archive of the local past not on the basis of large-scale political events but out of the perishable products of everyday life. Thus old television programs, fashions, and songs are treated as receptacles of historical memory about everyday popular culture. This attachment to the everyday vernacular pervades works of theater in Hong Kong. Rozanna Lilley has described the performances of the avant-garde theater group Zuni Icosahedron as "bits and pieces of history, scraps of culture, [and] silent gestures."[8] In a similar vein, the City Contemporary Dance Company's 1997 dance production *Lost in a Melodramatic City* was constructed out of heterogeneous references to the popular films, television shows, music, and political events of Hong Kong's recent past.

We might trace this idea of history back to the work of one of China's greatest contemporary writers, Eileen Chang (Zhang Ailing), whose essay "From the Ashes" had already expressed the hope that historians "might concern themselves a little more with irrelevant matters" rather than impose an overarching interpretation on the essentially formless flux of historical materials: "That thing we call reality is without structure, a confusion of gramophones playing in chaotic cacophony, each singing its own song. . . . [I]f history insisted on her own artistic wholeness, she would become fiction."[9] Chang suggests that history lacks the aesthetic unity and order that properly belong to the sphere of fiction; but many writers and artists in Hong Kong believe that fiction should also reflect the "cacophony" of society and history by accumulating detailed references to commonplace things, places, and events that project a strongly local flavor and an impression of looseness or randomness. In his epochal poem "Images of Hong Kong," local poet and cultural critic Leung Ping-Kwan has expressed an understanding of history as an assemblage of everyday fragments:

> history . . . is a montage of images
> of paper, collectibles, plastic, fibres,
> laser discs, buttons.[10]

This understanding of Hong Kong reality and historical memory as a montage of images and ordinary popular culture objects has inspired artists like Leung to produce literary works with a strong attachment to the concrete vernacular, and especially to the presence of mass-produced images.

International Modernism

The influence of Godard on Evans Chan's *To Liv(e)* exemplifies a third background that shaped the culture of the fragmented commonplace: the influence of international modernism. Hong Kong artists sometimes indulge in rather heavy-handed intertextuality, inserting explicit or implicit references to fashionable novelists and cultural theorists, as well as more venerable literary and philosophical sources. Calvino seems to be the most popular author. In addition to *Happy Valley* and *To Liv(e)*, he is quoted in Dung Kai-cheung's 1997 novel *The Atlas*. Xi Xi's short story "Marvels of a Floating City" also contains references to Magritte, Plato, and Hegel, while *My City* self-consciously alludes to the influence of Garcia Marquez and Godard on the composition of the novel itself. Xi Xi was a key member of a new generation of young film critics like Law Kar and Sek Kei who started writing influential reviews in magazines like *Chinese Student Weekly* throughout the 1960s. Their shared sense of mission combined a preference for international art cinema with the conviction that Hong Kong cinema should reflect local reality.

The impact of international modernism can be illuminated by comparing the culture of the fragmented commonplace with the practice of avant-garde photomontage. Artists working within such modernist movements as Dada, surrealism, and constructivism often advocated photomontage as a method that can readily reconcile the tension between artistic autonomy and social reference. As it has often been used, avant-garde photomontage is meant to avoid the two horns of a crucial modernist dilemma: either to embrace the ivory-tower detachment from concrete life that distinguishes purely abstract or "nonobjective" art, or to fall back into outmoded norms of nineteenth-century European realism. Photographs, the raw materials of photomontage, obviously have a particularly close and obvious connection to reality, although exactly what this connection might consist in is not always easy to put into precise words. By relying on photographs as basic raw materials, the artist retains a concrete connection to the actual world, instead of producing purely autonomous or self-referring works. (These comments describe only some salient uses of photomontage; they are not meant as generalizations.) Rather than presenting a consistently lifelike story world, however, montage often manipulates these fragments of reality to generate fantastic or dreamlike or intellectual images that reassert a high degree of artistic autonomy.[11] This practice manifests a compelling impulse toward social reference and an equally strong aversion to the traditions of realist painting and drama. Modernist photomontage refers to ordinary reality but at the same time highlights the power of art to transfigure that reality.

Although the culture of the fragmented commonplace seldom relies on actual photomontage or collage techniques, a comparable artistic aim sometimes underlies its basic formal strategies. On the one hand, the references to Hong Kong popular culture and everyday life (what I have termed "the commonplace") reassert the connection between art and life. On the other hand, artists produce an impression of fragmentation in order to render the commonplace unfamiliar. Like photomontage, the culture of the fragmented commonplace aims to transfigure concrete subject matter, preserving the tension between social reference and self-conscious stylization that distinguishes many instances of modernist photomontage. Everyday materials are made strange through their presentation in a fragmentary and sometimes disorienting or perplexing manner. Collage often calls attention to the formal structure and the autonomy of the artwork qua artwork, without wholly sacrificing referential meaning. This modernist ambivalence toward the commonplace is readily compatible with the "semiotic" awareness of the conflict between signs and experience. By defamiliarizing ordinary objects, places, and activities, the modernist hopes to express a fresh and novel way of seeing or describing everyday life different from mainstream words and images. Defamiliarization is thus connected with the semiotic consciousness that has shaped the culture of the fragmented commonplace. Perhaps one of the earliest and most impressive literary examples of the culture of the fragmented commonplace, Xi Xi's *My City*, adopts modernist techniques to render ordinary objects, places, and situations strange. The most obvious method is the manipulation of point of view. The novel alternates between the first-person narration of the young protagonist, Ah Guo (Fruits), third-person descriptions of the thoughts and impressions of his aunt Liberty, and other chapters with a more ambiguous point of view. Although both Fruits and Liberty face everyday tasks and live in a recognizably lifelike world, these two characters are also designed to fulfill the purely artistic aim of providing a fresh and unusual narrative perspective that projects a disorientating and detached view of ordinary life. The world depicted is at once recognizably quotidian yet self-consciously literary. The characters' language is often playful and illogical. Fruits freely inserts short sentences from government commercials and popular songs into descriptions of places and events. He also substitutes the proper names of well-known

Hong Kong landmarks with simpler descriptive labels: thus the Botanical Gardens become the Big Tree Garden, while the Peak Tram becomes the Hill-climbing-car. Liberty sometimes modifies the names of places to acknowledge Hong Kong's historical experience, referring for instance to Tsim Sha Tsui as Fat Sha Tsui, because the original Tsim (sharp or pointed) no longer reflects the reality of that district after the government's extensive land-reclamation project. Names are thus transformed to reflect the fleeting nature of everyday reality. Reference becomes a problem: Readers must actively discover just what actual places are being described by the characters' unusual and roundabout expressions. The novel's "semiotic" awareness of the gap between signs and experience is enhanced by the author's refusal to name the city in the novel as Hong Kong, although the locations described leave no doubt as to the intended reference.

Other defamiliarization strategies involve the ludic repetition of words and phrases, and the construction of ungrammatical sentences. A similarly ludic approach underpins Fruits's anthropomorphic impulse to describe houses using human adjectives like "plump," "lively," "happy," "dull" or "stupid." Descriptions are often elliptical or obscure even when that information is obviously clear to the novel's protagonists. The narration may, for instance, introduce a character like Merry Mak (chapter 6) without identifying the nature of his relationship to Fruits until his reappearance in the story at a later point (chapter 8). The use of Fruit's first-person perspective does not produce a consistent impression of cognitive intimacy with the protagonist, but rather the reverse, highlighting the gap between what the character knows and what is communicated to the reader.

In addition to the choice of point of view, *My City* fulfills the modernist aim of rendering the everyday unfamiliar through two additional and interconnected methods, ambiguity and stylistic heterogeneity. In this respect, the novel partakes of a well-known modernist tendency to challenge epistemic objectivity. Modernist movements like surrealism challenged the idea of scientific knowledge and redeemed the value of mysticism, "primitivism," and the irrational. Modernists often strove to depict (what are assumed to be) the simplest, most direct, childlike, or instinctive areas of human experience, those presumably least bound by stultifying artistic or cultural conventions.[12] In a related vein, Latin American magical realism celebrated folk myths, outrageous historical events, and other manifestations of the marvelous in everyday life. While surrealism strove to create imaginary objects through bizarre and fantastic combinations of ordinary objects, magical realism sought out the marvelous elements that were already embedded in the quotidian fabric of popular life, without relying on strange juxtapositions.

An example of the influence of magical realism in *My City* is the account of torrential rains falling over the city. Although not clearly labeled a character's dream or fantasy, this chapter contains strongly fantastic or marvelous elements. The visual motifs of this portion loosely recall the dream recounted in the previous chapter, but there are important discontinuities between the two segments. In the latter chapter, the city is no longer empty, and the narrator employs the third rather than the second person; the events now appear equally strange and fantastic, equally marvelous, but not attached to the consciousness of any single character, providing instead a general picture of a whole city permeated by the marvelous. We are no longer simply in the presence of someone imagining or dreaming something unusual; we are confronted with a city where imaginary elements organically grow out of the objective setting itself, its everyday culture, its natural environment, its buildings, and its people. Strikingly "magical" details enhance this effect. Xi Xi recounts how, faced with torrential rains, the staff of a large library makes a reservoir by piling old volumes of Chinese classics onto four walls. Additional references to a city historian and to journalists recording the events suggest documentary objectivity in the midst of otherwise marvelous events, a mixture of history and legend typical of magical realism. (Despite its origin in a specifically Latin American context, magical realism has become an international style. Its influence pervades the literary work of, for instance, Salman Rushdie, Toni Morrison, Derek Walcott, and Tahar ben Jelloun.) The novel is not, however, consistently magical realist. Other chapters present the playful activities and imaginative projects of different characters without suggesting that their objective environment is itself pervaded by the marvelous. *My City* briefly adopts the conventions of magical realism while confining them largely to this one chapter, "quoting" these literary norms "out of context." This stylistic diversity heightens the effect of heterogeneity and collage.

My City captures the ephemeral or fleeting quality of ordinary materials. This aim is widespread among Hong Kong and international modernist artists. Robert Shapazian has noted how, for instance, "photographers imbued with the Modernist spirit saw in a sudden and intense way . . . that in photographic imagery the world seemed at once solid and intangible, present yet ephemeral."[13] Modernist photographers manifest both a close affinity for concrete sensuous reality and an interest in expressing an experience of ghostly impermanence. This attempt to render the fleeting quality of ordinary subject matter also pervades many instances of Hong Kong's culture of the fragmented commonplace. Underpinned by the awareness that Hong Kong reality is in danger of being irretrievably lost, they unfold an archive of fleeting, momentary, and vivid images. In this vein, *My City* contains long descriptive passages of commonplace objects and locations that bring out the colors, shapes, and odors of the urban environment and project a shifting collage of errant, evanescent, yet extremely concrete images. This approach enhances the effect of ordinary reality by producing a dense and vivid world full of life-like details that refer to everyday Hong Kong experience.

Xi Xi begins chapter 9, for instance, by describing a man calculating property profits, moves on to discuss an antique car in a car showroom across the road and the everyday routine of the street market, then seamlessly picks up one of the novel's major characters in order to follow her actions and thoughts. A striking example of Xi Xi's immaculate literary technique, this free-floating passage projects a feeling of spatio-temporal freedom, a flowing combination of heterogeneous impressions, and an encompassing urban experience that is not confined to the experience of any single character. *My City* highlights the evanescent quality of this ordinary world by referring to things disappearing and people dying. The chapter initially recounts a seemingly irrelevant detail, advancing from one concrete description to another, gradually producing an enveloping atmosphere of loss and evanescence that seems to inhere in the minute visual details of the everyday urban setting. Xi Xi brings out the presence of the city as an ephemeral, dreamlike, and almost illusory world.

The extraordinary artistic merit of the novel lies in its magisterial interweaving of "realist" references to concrete everyday places and activities in Hong Kong within an otherwise assertively fictional, imaginary world, producing a striking combination of artistic autonomy and social relevance that recalls many works of modernist photomontage. A similar tendency to flaunt ambiguity and self-consciousness for the purpose of rendering everyday life strange pervades works like Xi Xi's "Marvels of a Floating City" or Dung Kai-cheung's *The Atlas*, both of which bring together imaginary events, historical descriptions, and essayist interpretations in order to challenge established genre distinctions between fiction and nonfiction. Organized as a series of extremely concise discussions around circumscribed clusters of thematic labels, *The Atlas* combines concrete descriptions of places and maps with abstract reflections about some of the salient topics of post-structuralist theory and cultural studies. In this context, it would be inaccurate to deny that the novel makes knowledge claims. References to well-known landmarks, districts, historical events, and popular legends about the city produce a strong sense of urban culture, while many of the author's discussions about the politics of representation and the philosophy of meaning are meant at the very least as half-serious claims. *The Atlas* accumulates intertextual references to familiar themes of structural linguistics (the arbitrariness of the sign, the difference between syntax and semantics) and continental critical theory (copies and simulacra, power and desire), explicitly alluding to Latin American and European authors (Calvino, Borges, Eco). The novel also embodies a strong "semiotic" consciousness. Through careful analyses of Hong Kong maps, the author treats the textual representation of urban space as a network of signs that embody desires, hopes, and anxieties. Maps are treated not as objective or transparent representations of reality but as "constructed" meaningful texts that call for analysis and interpretation.

By juxtaposing commentary, history, and imagination, the author nonetheless produces an assertively unreliable narration that systematically undercuts the boundary between reality and imagination. It becomes difficult to evaluate the seriousness or sincerity with which knowledge claims are put forth. Thus, the detached third-person narrator at times informs readers that an event may not have happened in the manner recounted, or descriptions make constant references to gossip and legend. *The Atlas* reconfigures actual materials into an imaginary "photomontage" of ghostly places and events, the fantastic landscape of a city of mind, an urban topography halfway between history and myth. Theories and places sometimes appear to be mere raw materials assembled into a marvelous, surreal world. In a manner that recalls "magical-realist classics like *One Hundred Years of Solitude*, Dung Kai-cheung's novel carries out a historical inversion that redeems genres of popular culture excluded from colonial history and grand epic literature, and often makes explicit comments about the relationship between colonialism and urban space. The result is a consistent defamiliarization of ordinary reality. *The Atlas*, like Xi Xi's *My City*, employs self-conscious conventions in order to create an inconsistent and ambiguous literary product. Dung Kai-cheung achieves this effect by taking on, and sometimes playfully masquerading as, the analytical voice of a cultural theorist.

Afa Chiang has described his own initial idea for the ultimately mediocre multimedia stage version of *The Atlas* (1999) in these terms: "(Individual or collective) stories formed a city, the space in which we dwell. . . . What was dealt with were images and bodies, moving in warm fluidity on the stage."[14] During the performance, percussion musicians sometimes change position on the stage, grouping and regrouping themselves as they continue playing their instruments. Movements on the stage highlight the relationship between the human body, the imagination, the ground, and the sky: Dancers move about in different ways, sometimes heavily anchored on the ground, sometimes weightlessly rising up a ladder. A succession of video images (some transmitted from a specially designed web site, others broadcast live from a video camera inside the auditorium) are intermittently projected either onto a screen in the center of the small studio theater or onto the white floor where dancers or musicians continued their performance. The content of those images was often very difficult to make out. The stage had become an imaginary and extremely fluid, ghostly space where live images and sounds, actual bodies, and recorded images came together in a flow of impressions at once ethereal and intensely corporeal. Although some of the video images were derived from recognizable public locations (such as the escalator to the midlevels in Central district) or community settings (the Videotage office in Oil Street), those places had been defamiliarized and reconfigured into a fantastic, poetic space inside the auditorium.

Expressive Space and the Lyrical Tradition

Influenced by Calvino's work, an additional background regards the "city" as an "imaginary" phenomenon. The representation of Hong Kong as an imaginary city may also have been influenced, directly or indirectly, by ongoing discussions in urban theory that emphasize the active role of desire, feeling, fantasy, and memory in determining the lived experience of urban space: "A place is dead if the physique does not support the work of imagination, if the mind cannot engage with the experience located there, or if the local energy fails to evoke ideas, images, or feelings."[15] This emphasis on imagination and ambiguity partly grows out of a renewed awareness of urban space as a container of human experience rather than a mere objective phenomenon. In other words, this culture, which forms the fourth background to the commonplace, shows a distinct awareness of the city as a sui generis phenomenon that demands a phenomenological depiction.

A fifth and final background to the culture of the fragmented commonplace arises out of well-known trends in traditional and modern Chinese culture. Although the impetus behind the fragmentation of the commonplace was to a large extent derived from international modernism, some artists also drew their inspiration from Chinese aesthetic sources. The line between indigenous and foreign influences is often very difficult to mark. The "empty space" in classical painting, for instance, supplies an indigenous precedent for the minimalist stage design employed by such local groups as Zuni Icosahedron. The use of titles written over images or banners hanging from the stage derives from the more analytic tendencies of Brechtian epic theater, as well as from the combination of calligraphy and painting in traditional Chinese art and the stylized conventions of Chinese opera (which of course influenced Bertolt Brecht in the first place). The use of minimalist theatrical devices to create a "poetic" atmosphere may also find justification in the "imagistic" preference of some Chinese poets to embody expressive content through the visual description of landscapes.

While some instances of the culture of the fragmented commonplace—particularly Evans Chan's *To Liv(e)*—follow a resolutely modernist paradigm, the search for cultural identity, as well as some of the similarities between Chinese art and Western modernism, have encouraged other Hong Kong artists to take an interest in Asian cultural traditions. The culture of the fragmented commonplace sometimes demonstrates the creative fruitfulness of local culture, particularly when traditional aesthetic concerns are treated as flexible sources of inspiration rather than rigid rules. Afa Chiang and Chan Ming-chi have noted the influence of the Confucian *Book of Changes* on the music for their theater production of *The Atlas*, which reframed the stage as a small-scale paradigm of cosmic space: "The movement of sound in space will be distributed as with Yin and Yang and the Five Elements. There will be positive and negative, first and last, top and bottom, front and back, southeast and northwest." Combining Western percussion with classical Chinese instruments, Chan's music acquires an obscure symbolic content clarified only by the undeniably pretentious program notes: "The extraordinarily drawn-out sound of the sheng pipes represents the Cosmos resting in frozen womb-time."[16]

The culture of the fragmented commonplace sometimes employs a lyrical approach to evoke classical Chinese culture. At stake is the question of asserting a Chinese identity built not only by drawing on the urban space of Hong Kong, but also by dialoguing with the traditions of national poetry and painting. Sinologist Jaroslav Prusek has identified a subjective, expressive, or broadly "lyrical" tendency in classical Chinese poetry; this tendency has been extended and modified by such modern writers as Yu Dafu, who treat fiction as confessional expression.[17] According to Prusek, the influence of socialism on Chinese literature undermined the development of this lyrical mode. Expanding on this argument, literary theorist David Der-wei Wang has noted that, while literature in the People's Republic of China after 1949 was characterized by an "epic sensibility, i.e., a sense of shared communal fate at a changing historical moment," many mainland (and Taiwan) writers of the eighties have brought about "a resurgence of the lyrical in Chinese narrative discourse," even in stories and novels that deal with traditionally "epic" political events or social phenomena.[18] This resurgence of the lyrical often manifests an ambivalent or hostile attitude toward the politics of nationalism and the culture of propaganda. The rise of the culture of the fragmented commonplace can be understood, at least in some instances, as an effort to renew the lyrical tradition of Chinese literature.

Although lyricism is a loose category rather than a uniform artistic method, its practitioners often assemble a collection of perceptions, memories, and mental associations in order to depict a flow of ephemeral and contingent impressions. Thus the production of a fluid imaginary world in the stage production of *The Atlas*, the videotape *Song of the Earth*, and *My City* may be described as examples of this lyrical mode. Emphasizing his own link to Chinese lyricism, Leung Ping-Kwan has praised traditional men of letters for writing "occasional poems . . . that show how one relates to people, to their environment, and to the outside world in general" in a concrete place and time.[19] This assertively impressionistic outlook can be interpreted as a reaction against the view held by many modern Chinese writers that literature should serve a pedagogic function by promoting patriotism, self-sacrifice, and large-scale social change. The line between modernist and traditional practices thus becomes blurred throughout the culture of the fragmented commonplace. A modernist emphasis on ambiguity may encourage artists to recover traditional Chinese poetry and painting, but awareness of local traditions may also shape the reception of modernism, particularly the tendency toward producing a poetic and impressionistic chain of ambiguous images.

Such recent works of video art as *Happy Valley* and *Song of the Earth* convey a dreamlike, lyrical impression of evanescence, unreality, and isolation that seems to inhere in the urban space of Hong Kong as a whole. Consider the latter example. The "Farewell" section of Mahler's *Song of the Earth*, which supplies the title of the videotape, intermittently insinuates itself into the soundtrack, only to be occasionally replaced by diegetic sound or voice-over commentary. Taken from classical Chinese poetry, the lyrics of this composition make implicit reference to an established interpretative schema of Chinese lyricism, that poetry or painting should be seen as a direct representation or embodiment of mind. The rigorous avoidance of daytime locations produces a consistent tone of unreality and solitude that facilitates this interpretation of the video as a journey into an inner world. One of the first images, an excruciatingly long take of the sun setting over the harbor, marks a threshold into a steadfastly nocturnal universe, an imaginary city.

Throughout the exterior street sequences that follow, the use of a shaky handheld camera generates blurred images that, while depicting recognizable Hong Kong landmarks and districts, also resemble fantastic painterly visions. Crowds and buildings sometimes come clearly into view only to disappear out of focus, generating an indistinct nonobjective montage of shifting lights, lines, colors, and shapes that only fleetingly stand out from the enveloping nocturnal darkness. Other sections employ relatively longer takes to capture anonymous people riding the tram in the night or an elderly woman collecting garbage on an isolated bridge. Given that most of the figures shown are either alone or lost in thought, the images project an experience of isolation and withdrawal into the self. The nocturnal setting contributes to this overall tone of unreality, suggesting a ghostly city lived in an imaginary mode by isolated people retreating into their inner shells. Whether half-deserted or crowded with anonymous strangers, the urban spaces shown in *Song of the Earth* are sepulchral, alienating, and fantastic.

What the video emphasizes is the diversity of temporal experiences that intersect in Hong Kong, all of "the inner cities that exist in people's minds" increasingly detached from objective reality.[20] This videotape depicts Hong Kong as an urban space lived, as it were, in a multiplicity of heterogeneous, individual time zones. One segment comprises a single, static, long take in the main office of the Zeman Media Center in the Hong Kong Arts Center building. The stationary camera, the presence of a large mirror in the background, and the movement of characters in and out of the frame—all foreground the off-screen space and also the audience's confinement to a static viewing position. The aimless movement of anonymous young people captures an experience of isolation and empty time, foregrounding pure duration in a single location. (The choice of location in one of the key production and exhibition centers for independent video also self-consciously marks the video as a product of a particular milieu.) A rather different temporal consciousness pervades other segments constructed out of a series of black-and-white photographs that display old districts and buildings in old Hong Kong now lost or vastly modified, highlighting the melancholy evanescence and forgetfulness that seem to envelop the entire city.

The occasional onscreen presence of an anonymous female photographer and the occasional off-screen clicking sound of a photo camera to some extent organize the images as a photographic portfolio of urban sights. Her function within *Song of the Earth* is that of a protagonist of sorts, a "minimal" character lacking specific personal traits who nonetheless provides the impression of a tenuous narrative thread. But it is worth recalling just how tenuous this point of view remains. She does not appear throughout the tape. We are sometimes attached to the consciousness of additional characters. One particularly revealing segment includes both exterior facades and interior scenes in large apartment buildings, accompanied by the alternating and overlapping dialogue of an anonymous male character speaking to a wall about questions of self-identity and memory (the ideas of time and selfhood provide broad thematic concerns that unify the various sections of this extremely disparate video). The terse and solemn dialogue departs from the poetic tone of the rest of the film, thus strongly differentiating this segment. While *Song of the Earth* does manage to express a generalized urban experience of isolation, loss of history, uncertain identity, and withdrawal into the self, its component segments project an impression of autonomy from the whole tape. This tension between the parts and the whole pervades the culture of the fragmented commonplace.

The Problem of Order

The tendency to produce an impression of fragmentation heightens the tension between individual elements and a whole artwork. The main challenge for artists involves finding ways to produce this effect of "brokenness" or dispersal without the result degenerating into a chaotic collection of random everyday materials. How can a sense of artistic order arise out of a wide variety of assertively heterogeneous elements? T. W. Adorno's discussion of modernist montage calls attention to this interplay between order and dispersal: "Montage disavows unity by stressing the disparity of its parts while at the same time affirming unity as a principle of form."[21] The problem involves finding artistic techniques that unify the various materials into an ordered whole without surrendering the heterogeneity and independence of its various raw materials. I propose to label this task "the problem of unity and dispersal." Overarching thematic materials often supply this principle of order.

The use of philosophical and cultural themes partakes of a widespread tendency of international modernist literature and cinema: Jorge Luis Borges, Italo Calvino, and Jean-Luc Godard weave abstract philosophical concerns and larger social questions into concrete plots. This method goes hand in hand with a tendency toward fragmentation and an assertive awareness of the impossibility of writing a complete novel or a self-contained plot. Borges often wrote commentaries of imaginary books in order to side-step the task of actually writing those books, and Calvino created his novel *Invisible Cities* out of extremely short stories arranged under broad thematic headings. Citing Borges's influence, Calvino has confessed his own preference for narrative brevity and his interest in constructing vivid plots and images that embody grand philosophical concerns. His stories are designed to achieve a "maximum concentration of poetry and of thought" and give "narrative form to abstract ideas of space and time."[22] Calvino's example led many Hong Kong artists working within the culture of the fragmented commonplace to combine concrete descriptions of actual places, events, and customs with more abstract or intellectual thematic meanings. The voice-over dialogue in Mark Chan's video piece *Happy Valley,* for instance, makes explicit reference to existential themes concerning the relationship between space, memory, time, and desire.

A typical unifying strategy employed in the video piece *Videotable* (Danny Yung and Jim Shun, 1984), the Super 8 short *Journey* (Danny Yung, 1981), and the video documentary *Journey to Beijing* (Evans Chan, 1997) mobilizes spatial metaphors such as the "journey" or the "center" to highlight the quest for cultural identity relative to the political future of Hong Kong. However minimal, the dialogue often helps viewers to interpret the images as a social commentary. In *Videotable,* the languorous sound of two voice-over commentators repeats and recombines a few words and ideas into new patterns, making explicit and playful references to the Hong Kong Arts Center, the spatial vocabulary employed in political discourse (left, center, right), and the very name of China (*zhongguo,* the "central" or "middle" kingdom).

The emphasis on collage sometimes enables video artists to express a mood of cultural disorientation in the midst of an uncertain quest for meaning. The very fragmentation of style emerges as a principle of unity: It embodies a consistent experience. Stylistic disjunction typically reasserts how the tissue of habits, norms, memories, and places comprising everyday life and identity in Hong Kong can no longer be taken for granted. Home, understood in its wide cultural sense as a space of belonging, has become a problem, the target of a quest the outcome of which remains uncertain. An experience of marooned or shipwrecked selfhood, an existence lived in the midst of broken or ephemeral fragments that do not come together as a stable home, pervades, for instance, *She Said Why Me* (May Fung, 1989). An anonymous young woman walks among Hong Kong temples, streets, landmarks, and stylized interior spaces. The journey once again functions as a metaphor for the quest for identity and meaning. The woman is sometimes blindfolded and often shown in full shot, although the tape finally ends with her looking directly at the camera. By making use of a blindfold and (later) direct address, video-

Journey to Beijing, 1998. (Courtesy of director Evans Chan.)

maker May Fung highlights the gaze of the character and the role of images within Hong Kong culture and history: The actions of this anonymous protagonist are consistently intercut with black-and-white archival footage of old Hong Kong and childhood photographs. The presence of this minimal character, as well as the title of the tape, fosters the impression that we are witnessing the painful inner quest of a single person. An intensely subjective structure is of course characteristic of many international avant-garde filmmakers, from Jean Cocteau's *Blood of a Poet* and Maya Deren's *Meshes of the Afternoon* to Stan Brakhage's early shorts. But *She Said Why Me* also adds archival historical footage to assert the role of visual images in shaping the sense of history and identity, building bridges between the videomaker's personal past and Hong Kong's collective past.

Other works of video art employ a fragmentary collage of both fictional and archival images to bring about an intensified expressive quality. The videotape *Love* (Hung Keung, 1997), for instance, combines historical photographs with intensely sexual and obsessive animated scenes that depict sketchily drawn bodies falling apart to the physical and pulsating beat of African drums. The intensity and physicality of this video, as well as the intimate connotations of its title, help to connect the general history of Hong

Kong with the more particular aspects of a nonrational experience, exemplifying in the heterogeneity of its raw materials the strong collage effect that distinguishes the culture of the fragmented commonplace.

Conclusion

The culture of the fragmented commonplace generates an impression of dispersal and diversity by assembling heterogeneous raw materials drawn from the everyday culture, history, and politics of Hong Kong. This artistic practice manifests a twofold impulse: a reaction against the abstract tendencies of nonobjective art, and an equally intense urge to avoid "classical" norms of objective realism. Fragmentation thus becomes a method of referring to the commonplace in a manner that renders it unfamiliar. In thus describing the culture of the fragmented commonplace, however, I am not promoting this tendency as the only proper path for Hong Kong artists to follow. My aim is descriptive rather than normative. I am highlighting a particularly widespread tendency, outlining its principal characteristics and artistic problems, scrutinizing a range of textual examples, and providing some of the backgrounds behind its rise and development.

Notes

1. Poet, novelist, and cultural critic Leung Ping-Kwan has discussed multiperspectival literature in "Urban Culture," in *The Metropolis*, 41.

2. Law, "Nietszche, Deleuze, and Video Art," 2.

3. Italo Calvino, *The Uses of Literature*, trans. Patrick Creagh (San Diego: Harcourt Brace Jovanovich, 1982), 71, 301–302.

4. Italo Calvino, *Invisible Cities*, trans. William Weaver (San Diego: Harcourt Brace, 1974), 13–14.

5. Ibid., 66–67 (emphasis added).

6. David Bordwell, *Narration in the Fiction Film* (Madison: University of Wisconsin Press, 1985), 317.

7. Ibid., 314.

8. Rozanna Lilley, "Treading the Margins: Performing Hong Kong," in Evans and Siu-mi, *Hong Kong*, 143.

9. Eileen Chang, "From the Ashes," *Renditions* 45 (spring 1996): 47.

10. Leung, *City at the End of Time*, 33.

11. Dawn Ades, *Photomontage* (London: Thames and Hudson, 1976), 66.

12. For a discussion of primitivism in international modernism, see Robert Goldwater, *Primitivism in Modern Art* (Cambridge: Harvard University Press, 1938), and Colin Rhodes, *Primitivism and Modern Art* (London: Thames and Hudson, 1994).

13. Robert Shapazian, "The Modern Movement," in *The Art of Photography, 1839–1989*, ed. Mike Weaver (New Haven: Yale University Press, 1989), 228.

14. Program notes, *The Atlas*, Hong Kong Arts Festival Society, February 1998, 9.

15. Eugene Victor Walter, *Placeways: A Theory of the Human Environment* (Chapel Hill: University of North Carolina Press, 1988), 204.

16. Program notes, *The Atlas,* 10, 13.

17. Prusek, *The Lyrical and the Epic,* 14.

18. David Der-wei Wang, "Afterward: Chinese Fiction for the Nineties," in *Running Wild: New Chinese Writers,* ed. Wang and Jeanne Tai (New York: Columbia University Press, 1994), 249.

19. Leung, *City at the End of Time,* 168.

20. Program notes, *Invisible Cities,* Hong Kong Arts Center Festival NOW, 1998, 8.

21. T. W. Adorno, *Aesthetic Theory,* trans. Robert Hullot-Kentor (London: Athlone Press, 1997), 222.

22. Italo Calvino, *Six Memos for the Next Millenium* (Cambridge: Harvard University Press, 1988), 51, 49.

Selected Bibliography

Cheung, Martha, ed. *Hong Kong Collage: Contemporary Stories and Writing.* Hong Kong: Oxford University Press, 1998.

Evans, Grant, and Maria Tam. *Hong Kong: The Anthropology of a Chinese Metropolis.* Honolulu: University of Hawaii Press, 1997.

Law, Jamsen. "Nietszche, Deleuze, and Video Art." Master's thesis, University of Hong Kong, 2000.

Leung, Ping-Kwan. *City at the End of Time.* Trans. Gordon T. Osing. Hong Kong: Twilight Books and the Department of Comparative Literature, University of Hong Kong, 1992.

———. "Urban Culture: Space, Identity, and the Politics of Representation." In *The Metropolis: Visual Research into Contemporary Hong Kong, 1990–1996.* Hong Kong: Photo Pictorial Publishers and Hong Kong Arts Centre, 1996.

Pau, Ellen. "Development of Hong Kong Video Art." *VTEXT,* June 1997, 54–57.

Prusek, Jaroslav. *The Lyrical and the Epic.* Ed. Leo Ou-fan Lee. Bloomington: Indiana University Press, 1988.

Tai, Jeanne, and David Der-Wei Wang, eds. *Running Wild: New Chinese Writers.* New York: Columbia University Press, 1994.

Xi Xi. *My City: A Hong Kong Story.* Trans. Eva Hung. Hong Kong: Chinese University of Hong Kong, 1993.

Part II

Postmodernism and Its Discontents

CHAPTER 8

Immediacy, Parody, and Image in the Mirror: Is There a Postmodern Scene in Beijing?

Dai Jinhua
Translated by Jing M. Wang

Marginality

Conspicuous on the Chinese postmodern skyline in the 1990s is the emergence of a particular cultural immediacy, the sense of "being on site." With its crude and rich texture, strong sense of presence, and fragmentation, such immediacy presents a cultural narrative different from that of the 1980s, as if narrating a world whose center has disappeared or at least scattered. Various kinds of rock 'n' roll music, suddenly popular behavior, pop arts, avant-garde or experimental drama performed in small theaters, and the new documentary movement are among the central scenarios and the most culturally symptomatic art forms. It is this cultural scenery that Chinese postmodernists have defined as Chinese postmodernism. It is also this very scenery that was later used as strong evidence of postmodern culture in China.

As if to complement the new discourse of fragmentation, this on-the-spot art is the staging of a cultural aspect that remained invisible in the late 1980s. At the same time, the emergence of such a culture of immediacy was closely related to a particular artist community formed in the late 1980s. These artists were a metropolitan marginal group related not only in terms of cultural discursive context but also interpersonally; they had a common origin in the roaming-artist group Yuanmingyuan Painters' Village.[1] Although the official/elite intellectual-centered culture in China was repeatedly shaken toward the end of the 1980s, it remained powerful and effective. Because important cultural groups and their events could happen only within the system of mainstream culture, the roaming-artist community doubtless existed on the margin of society. Indeed, this dubious, transgressive community was the frequent target of distrust from the system as well as of harassment by the police. But the social crises at the end of the 1980s turned out to be a historical opportunity for this cultural group, allowing it to mount a stage suddenly left empty by the mainstream and to occupy its center, from certain perspectives. What made this cultural opportunity possible was not only the decentering after 1989 of the Chinese elite cultural community but also the shifting and restructuring of margin and center in political and cultural discursive contexts worldwide.

First, in the late 1980s and early 1990s, some marginalized populations, including the roaming artists and Beijing's foreign residents (from embassies and consulates and various foreign organizations, and journalists of overseas presses), another privileged but marginalized group, began to form a special connection or even alliance.[2] The latter introduced the works of Chinese artists to the world via the Western media and funds from international cultural organizations. Yuanmingyuan Painters' Village was for a while a site of interest for Western tourists, which helped buyers find the artists' works. The artists subsequently caught the attention of art traders, collectors, screeners of international film festivals, and overseas scholars. Foreign institutions in Beijing and hotels, pubs, and cafés frequented by foreigners provided locales for exhibiting avant-guard and pop arts, staging experimental plays and rock 'n' roll concerts, and showing underground films and documentaries. Like the films of Zhang Yimou and Chen Kaige before 1995, such cultural groups and their artistic practices became, in Western eyes, representatives and symbols of Chinese contemporary culture that remained invisible in China. This special cultural bonding not only opened a narrow venue to the world but also made the artists rich. Many first- and second-generation villagers left their cottages in the vicinity of Yuanmingyuan and joined the crowd that, in Deng Xiaoping's words, "got rich first." Yuanmingyuan Painters' Village relocated to Eastern Village, a newly established, respectable residential area near foreign embassies. The artists became the models of success in the age of money worship and were ranked among the wealthy of the 1990s, forming a new center. At the same time, part of this mobile population made its way into, and even dominated, the exploding mass media, especially TV, which became one of the new centers of power in the 1990s. Participants upped both their social status and their income.

When Chinese postmodernists identified this cultural phenomenon as postmodern art practice, their criteria were the artists' marginalized social status and their means of representation, not the artistic structure and expression of their work. Relying on those artists, critics completed the mapping of a Chinese postmodern topography and announced the end of elitist culture and the beginning of a new epoch—not a misreading but a narrative necessary to keep the tragic end of the 1980s out of sight in the neo–new era. The coincidence of the death of the poets and the emergence of performance art added to the postmodern narrative. Although these phenomena happened simultaneously, they were treated sequentially (a game of turning stories into plot) to fill out China's postmodernist narrative. First, campus poet Haizi, well loved by students, committed suicide in 1989 by throwing himself in front of a train. Poetic circles claimed that the young poet who aspired to epic poetry found it impossible to live with the current dispersed sense of history in China. Then, during the national modern arts exhibition in 1989, a performance artist shot off a gun to climax his work—a shocking cultural incident, as the use of weapons is forbidden in China. Following this, an obscure poet, Gu Cheng, committed murder-suicide with his wife, an act regarded as a symbol of the new age of enlightenment ("Night gives me dark eyes, yet I use them to seek light").[3] The posthumous publication of his work, *Ying Er,* caused chain reactions in Chinese cultural circles and the mass media. Meanwhile, avant-guard arts, especially political pop (such as the "culture shirt" event in 1991) and diverse performance arts, became extremely popular. In the narrative of the Chinese postmodernists, the death of these poets symbolizes the pathetic and thorough end of the elitist, modern culture in the 1980s, and the emergence of performance art, the debut of a decade characterized by a robust postmodernism that bridged the chasm between high-brow and popular cultures.

Of course, we can create an opposite or at least different narrative without much trouble. Actually, poetry was one of the first literary genres to lose its attraction in the 1980s. In 1986, when the new generation of poets declared a determination to "surpass Beidao," poetry had already been transformed into an inner-circle art, along with avant-garde arts, rock 'n' roll, and the new documentaries; they received little attention except from overseas. Self-sponsored underground journals and occasional funds from international cultural foundations gradually became their main means of existence.[4] As a matter of fact, what constituted the narrative of the death of the poets toward the end of the 1980s is that the young poets who took their own lives, such as Haizi, Gemai, and Kedou, were all campus poets, as opposed to popular/mass poets. It was this circle of poets that first hoisted the banner of postmodernism. In the 1990s, all literary, artistic, and cinematic practices labeled postmodern were intimately related to various groups of poets. Furthermore, in the process of discussing and naming the postmodern, from 1990 to 1994, the arts and cultural phenomena with which postmodernism was identified shared the elitism characteristic of contemporary poetry .

Immediacy

I do not mean that Chinese culture in the 1990s did not undergo any change from the previous decade. On the contrary, the difference is obvious. I am trying to show that the situation at the end of the 1980s was not the only social and cultural ingredient that made the difference possible, nor was such change a natural ten-year periodization. There was a qualitative break. In 1984, Professor Fredric Jameson gave a series of talks on postmodernism and cultural theory at Beijing University that caused a sensation in Beijing and led to changes in Chinese intellectuals' scope of vision and knowledge.[5] China certainly saw radical changes in the production, circulation, and consumption of culture in the 1990s, in the sense that these processes became more related to the global cultural context instead of operating in isolation. Culture, literature, and the arts all were marginalized and commercialized. In the course of this change, cultural space became fragmented and consequently pluralistic. But, given the Chinese cultural transformation, it is more relevant to discuss the modernity and postmodernity of Chinese society than the postmodernism in Chinese literature and art. Perhaps "postsocialism" is a more accurate term.

The culture/art scene that emerged in the 1990s differed significantly from the elitist culture of the 1980s—anti-mainstream, official mainstream, and enlightenment. A counter-argument spearheaded by the marginal art groups in the 1990s against the "five-thousand-year" culture of the 1980s aimed at discovering, recording, and constructing scenes of the here and now. Unexpectedly, the first representative work is a film that is also the first work of the new documentary movement, *Roaming the Streets of Beijing: The Last Dreamers* (Wu Wenguang, 1990). The making of this film bridged the 1980s and 1990s. The director's initial motivation was to participate and record a process and represent a scene. The significance of the completed work lies in its making visible a cultural site that remained obscured in the grand cultural spectacle of the 1980s. The film depicts the life of some of the roaming cultural population who emerged during this time of change and who struggled daily to keep themselves alive: Are they in search of a dream, or are they avoiding reality? The work adopts a naked and almost naïve visual style and creates, with its detail and intimacy, a sense of imminence so strong that it becomes almost oppressive. As the director, Wu, says: "I think everything that has just happened on the spot is the most essential thing. It has the most sense of texture. Nothing can be more essential than what happens on the spot, no matter what you add and subtract from it through mise-en-scène."[6] Following *Roaming the Streets of Beijing*, a more refined work, *I Graduated* (Shi Jian, 1990), was produced which exhibits quite a different scene. Its time frame is the two weeks in 1992 when the undergraduates of Beijing University and Qinghua University were graduating and leaving their campuses. The social turmoil of 1989 traumatized those who witnessed it. But rather than a record of the experience of that generation, this film is a transition point— a wound, a numbing pain, hopeless and indifferent expectation, sundry but monotonous beckonings and temptations in the individuals' lives: Make money? Go abroad? Participate in society? Undergo rites of passage?

If Robert Rauschenberg's installation art exhibition in China in 1981 came as a shock to the audience, pop art and performance art became trends in the 1990s. In fact, as the best form of on-the-spot demonstration, performance art participated in and constructed the postmodern episodes and images and has even come to symbolize social existence in China in the 1990s. Therefore, it frequently appears in the literature of the decade. Performance art, in the hands of popular novelist Qiu Huadong, is a necessary adornment that highlights a philosophy of life and a sense of absurdity. It is adopted as the title as well as the object of ridicule in one of the works by female writer Fang Fang. In this piece, a young woman in despair tries to commit suicide by throwing herself from a skyscraper. However, caught by a huge parachute that opens at the climactic moment, she completes a piece of performance art. The police, in the name of artists, put her in detention. The first-person male narrator in the text never figures out if his relationship with the female artist is just another piece of performance art.

However, this main cultural trend, the emergence of the postmodern scene, did not mean the construction of a simulacrum in the Baudrillardian sense. Rather, it meant truthfulness, naked texture, witness, and evidence. It was, at the same time, an intervention of reality, a cultural subversion and deconstruction. But this pursuit of truth in relation to official discourse became a particularly Chinese cultural performance, a performance piece, in the 1990s during the confrontation and exchange of ideologies between China and the West and during the fever of naming the postmodern.

Some examples may help illustrate the cultural vision of these marginal artist groups that were called postmodern. Between the spring and summer of 1993, small-theater director Mou Sen, after his dramatic attempts such as *Frogs Troupe*, was running a short-term theatrical performance–training program in Beijing. The trainees came from all over China—young people who had ambitions in the arts but had never had the opportunity for formal art education. They paid their own fees. Their education consisted of performance and body training, and in mid-summer 1993, they staged a small-theater drama, *The Other Shore*, in a classroom at the Beijing Institute of Film. By Gao Xing-jian, a modern playwright of the 1980s, the play was revised for this performance by poet Yu Jian, who added the subtitle *A Postmodern Poetic Drama*. This play demanded high performance skills from the actors. A lack of funds limited the choice of performance locale, and actors and audience were so close to each other that bodily contact was unavoidable. Seizing this opportunity, the director designed two dramatic actions. One was smearing watercolor on the faces of the audience to arouse their disgust, in the hope that they would become involved in the play. The other was killing a chicken on the spot, symbolizing the murder of people who held different opinions, also in the hope of provoking the audience to protest and participate. The director thought that if the audience remained silent during the killing of the chicken (thus, of people), it would reflect their numb and passive social attitude. In other words, they would still be the onlookers identified by Lu Xun. But the director's expectation and the audience's reception proved a subtle mismatch. Although most of the audience members were young people in the arts, they (including myself) were acclimated to being onlookers, not performers, once they were in the theater. Therefore, they remained an audience in the conventional sense, in spite of their disgust and polite dodging. If the director's intention was realized to some extent—that is, the audience did respond— to the audience, a traditional play was being staged: The actors recited their lines (with the director as prompter) and played out their designated roles. If the audience had taken part, these amateur actors with less than high school educations might not have been able to come up with the improvisation necessary to finish the play.

During the seminar that followed the play, advocates of postmodernism in China enthusiastically announced that the night on which this play was staged marked the death of traditional drama and the birth of its postmodern counterpart. The play signified the "death of meaning, deep structure, and ultimate concern," claimed Zhang Yimou. Yet, explaining his intentions at the seminar, Mou Sen emphasized the significance of drama as education, enlightenment, and moral instruction for his undereducated troupe. He cited the example of the drama school or troupe in an African American community in the United States, most of whose young participants abandoned their gangs and criminal actions and "successfully entered society."

At the performance of *The Other Shore*, there appeared a mirror image characteristic of the new documentary movement and what was later called "new state" fiction. Mou Sen, director of *The Other Shore*, played a main character in *Roaming the Streets of Beijing*; Wu Wenguang, director of the film, filmed the performance of the play. This was more than a so-called friendship performance: Some scenes from *The Other Shore* appeared in Wu's new work, *All Places Are Homes*. The same scenes appeared in the documentary of the same title by film producer Jiang Yue. In this documentary, Jiang filmed the entire process of crew training and rehearsals of the play *The Other Shore*. After the play was performed twice, the drama troupe graduated its students. Jiang followed up with a film of what happened to some of the students, revealing some unanticipated results from their experience. Their few months of training and performing turned out to be the most magnificent moment in the lives of these students from remote provinces and small towns. Mou Sen's classes and ideals pumped up their idealistic enthusiasm. After their short performance career, they had to return not only to their previous social status and fate but also to a society in which idealism was wiped out by commercialization and money-worship. The students were reluctant to return to the reality of grim, isolated small towns. They dreamt of drama, the stage, and performance. If this had been their secret dream, performing *The Other Shore* had made it come true. They tried to follow Mou Sen, hoping for a chance to continue their dramatic careers to benefit society. Mou Sen's idealism lodged deep in their minds, like a promise never actually made yet demanding to be fulfilled. The director certainly could not take responsibility for such an ending. Consequently, the students dispersed feeling almost cheated and betrayed, because it seemed probable that Mou Sen could work with professional troupes in the future. Some of them, believing that they were the real followers of Mou Sen's ideals, returned to their hometowns to carry on experimental drama. Under circumstances when even state-supported theatrical troupes were disbanded because of the cultural transformation and economic pressure, theirs was a doomed aspiration. In Jiang's film *The Other Shore,* this episode has a touch of the intensity of Balzac's stories.

This scene can be variously described, depending on one's perspective. Is it the enlightening practice of modernism? Is it the artistic practice of postmodernism? Is it complex, ambiguous, and characteristically Chinese mirror imagery? Is it the weight of realism, the lightness of postmodern discourse, or perhaps a scene common to traditional Chinese plays? On the other hand, when the new documentary movement caught the attention of the West, such films began to be banned by the Chinese government, and their producers were forbidden to make any more films.[7] This was a continuation of the rules of the political games common during the cold war. But before long, as part of a different game, China Central Television (CCTV) initiated a show called *Time and Space in the East* in 1993.

Unprecedented in many ways, this show was the turning point in the development of TV culture and the rapid expansion of mass media in China in the 1990s. It was an independent production for which the producer raised all the funds, and the show was supported by the income from commercials. It was broadcast in the morning, a previously unfilled time slot. This show consists of four parts: "Offspring of the East" (high-profile people), "Life Space" (daily events and characters), "A Moment of Focus" (in-depth news), and "Golden Tunes" (Chinese popular songs). Shortly after its debut, it became one of the most popular shows in China. Of particular interest, those who established *Time and Space in the East* were on the government blacklist of advocates and filmmakers of the new documentary movement. Subsequently, the principles of new documentary were invariably carried over to these programs. More amusingly, shortly after the debut of *Time and Space in the East,* a program devoted to news called *Focal Interviews* was created as a spin-off of "A Moment of Focus." This new program, shown during prime time, became one of the TV shows that directly impacted society, especially through its exposure of so-called "bad people and bad things."

Telling It Like It Is, a spin-off of "Out of Life Space," is one of China's first talk shows. Its theme (telling the stories of ordinary people), subject matter, ways of interviewing and framing, camera movements, and mise-en-scène, soon afterward imitated by local television stations, became characteristic of new mainstream Chinese TV shows. But it is in this form that the potential problems of the new documentary movement began to appear. In this show, the emphasis on narration and dramatic elements began to blur the relative boundary between documentation and performance, not to speak of the use of narrative modes typical of documentaries, such as real-life shooting versus reenactment, real-life versus performance elements, and daily life versus the presence of the camera. It is hard to distinguish the original look of real life from reenactment, performance, and other artificial factors. Ordinary Chinese soon became accustomed to the presence of the camera, not so much ignoring it as presenting themselves with ease. In other words, in this show, which captures the viewers' attention with its realness, the making of simulacrum began to be a common phenomenon.

When CCTV reported the return of Hong Kong from the British in 1997 as the event of the century, the frontline journalists were all from the independent production team of *Time and Space in the East* and *Focal Interviews;* such reporting had previously been the exclusive territory of CCTV's own news broadcasters. If the new documentary movement identified with the marginal and the unofficial, CCTV represented the central and the official. But at this point, they merged. In other words, the margin marched at an amazing pace and in an amazing manner toward the center. In my view, this is important evidence of the shared space in Chinese culture in the 1990s. As another cultural site, while revealing so-called postmodern characteristics, television demonstrates a complex depth model: the power of elite intellectuals/masses/people; reality/fabrication/simulacrum; margin/center/mainstream; subversion/construction/norms;

official/unofficial media. Therefore, the cultural scenery of China in the 1990s is much different, or at least much more variegated, from the simplistic picture drawn by Chinese postmodernists.

The Naming of Chinese Postmodern

Rather than agree that postmodern culture was an important episode in the Chinese cultural vista in the early 1990s, I argue that the introduction of the postmodern became one of the parapolitical practices in this transformative period. As if an irony on postmodern irony, the significance of this political practice comes not from an analysis of the covert political nature or double-sidedness of postmodern artifacts, but from occasionally deliberate misreading and misappropriation as a self-conscious participation in a political culture.

To a certain extent, it was in the early 1990s that translation, introduction, and application of postmodernism mounted to a pitch that added color to the grimness and goriness that followed the 1989 shock. This time around, the translation and introduction of new Western theory was no longer characterized as the sacred Promethean fire. It was a new game with a new set of rules. Indeed, it attempted to lift or replace the stagnant weight of reality with its gamelike lightness. Interestingly, a typical Chinese postmodern misreading was the introducers' joyous announcement of the arrival of a postmodern era. Thus, for China, postmodernism was used to evidence new progress in the linear narrative of history. If the year 1979 ushered in the great historical process of modernization, we should announce with gusto that we have taken leave of the modern age and made a great leap forward into the postmodern period. We were not stunted, we were not stalled; we gradually caught up with the world step by step. What is absurd is that the introduction and discussion of postmodernism in China in the 1990s not only severed postmodernism from its theoretical and social contexts, but also emptied it of its critical reflection on modernity. The postmodern decade of the 1990s consequently became very different from the modern decade of the 1980s, a successful shift after the sudden break at the end of the 1980s.

As a matter of fact, this was a recurrence of the political and cultural logic and strategy that existed at the turn of the 1970s. Then, the successful concealment of the complex history of modernization in China made it possible to construct the year 1979 as the beginning of Chinese modernization. The negation and criticism of feudalism (the Cultural Revolution or traditional dictatorship) prevented us from investigating more deeply the history of contemporary China, especially the history of the Cultural Revolution. But in the 1990s, the clear naming of the postmodern enabled us to let go of the history of the 1980s without a qualm, especially the wound and trauma of the late 1980s, and to turn away from this history. In so doing, we did not have to burden ourselves with reflecting on the culture of the 1980s, nor did we need to look directly into our wounds and the abyss.

Rather ironically, the enthusiastic propagation of postmodern theory, artistic practices, and the frantic naming of the Chinese postmodern turned out to be an authoritative mainstream narrative. China not only bade farewell to the modern period and marched into the postmodern age in the linear description of history but also categorized as postmodern all the new people and new phenomenon that surfaced on the cultural horizon of the 1990s. Apart from the marginal and avant-garde arts mentioned earlier, the following art forms were lumped together as postmodern: pessimistic realistic fiction, labeled "new state," "new experience," and "new generation"; sixth-generation feature films of widely diverse quality; TV serial dramas characteristic of popular culture; women's autobiographical writings; popular novels produced in large quantities under the supervision of cultural brokers—and the list goes on. However, the so-called postmodern decade of the 1990s and the modern decade of the 1980s coincided in a cultural humanitarian value judgement: the 1990s equaled real, humane, beautiful; the 1980s equaled false, evil, ugly. Therefore, this postmodern narrative accomplished a monolithic panoramic view, not a picture of a pluralistic, diversified, and decentering cultural reality.

Perhaps unexpectedly, this view called postmodernism successfully concealed the most prominent cultural realities of China in the 1990s: globalization (in the form of commercialization and commodification of the cultural market), the entry of international capital, the formation of a new power structure, rapid stratification of classes, and the establishment of a cultural leadership.

Magic and Parody in the Transformation Period

The absurdity of the postmodern discussion and the promiscuity of postmodern art practices to some degree refract, as if in a magic mirror, postmodern or postsocialist characteristics of China. Perhaps the colorful postmodern horizon was revealed through Chinese social life rather than through art practices: from the skyscrapers juxtaposed with traditional-style roofs in the streets of Beijing to the huge commercial billboard shared by the sign that read "Socialism" in Chinese characteristics and the sign that read "Hennesey XO"; from Zhang Yimou, whose films were banned but who was awarded the May 1st Labor Hero medal by the Department of Labor, to the busy streets in the Chaoyang district, where pictures of labor heroes from the 1950s and 1960s and a Coca Cola advertisement stood side by side. Furthermore, around the late 1980s and early 1990s, the music of Cui Jian, the father of Chinese rock 'n' roll, was made a core symbol of elite culture. And yet along both sides of highways dotted with fast-food restaurants extends the countryside, where ancestral halls and religious temples are reconstructed.

As for the literary and artistic practices of the 1990s, relatively pure postmodern attempts took the form of fantasy and parody in literature and films (as is true of other third-world and Latin American countries). In my opinion, the absurdity of real life during the process of globalization was not the only cause of the use of postmodern techniques. More importantly, fantasy and parody provided an avenue for Chinese artists to effectively process their social experience, which is a combination of the premodern, modern, and postmodern. Such practices started in China in the mid- and late 1980s, originating in the search-for-roots literature in the so-called movement of historical and cultural reflections. We could read most of the works that Fredric Jameson called national allegory, but they were not so much the practice and evidence of Jameson's theory as an interesting coincidence, because the writers were writing in the manner less of Sherwood Anderson than of Garcia Marquez. It is not hard to find proof in the early works of Mo Yan and in the works of avant-garde novelists such as Ge Fei, Yu Hua, and Su Tong.

What characterized the field of literature in the late 1980s and early 1990s was a cultural trend toward what I call political parody. One of the first representative works of the fifth-generation filmmakers, *The Black Cannon Incident* (1987), was partly a parody of the anti-espionage films of the past seventeen years. There was also the enormous compelling force of Cui Jian's rock 'n' roll music, extremely popular in the late 1980s, which was partly derived from rock 'n' roll, partly from elements of political parody. A Cui Jian concert would often reach its climax with the rock 'n' roll–style "Nan Ni Wan" and "A Piece of Red Cloth"; he sang the latter with his eyes hooded under a piece of red cloth.[8] Onstage, Cui Jian wore the traditional outfit of the Cultural Revolution: a People's Liberation Army green uniform. The stage was set up after the fashion of a political meeting room in the 1950s and 1960s, with six red flags lined up symmetrically. What is more, Cui Jian's collections were titled *Rock-and-Roll in the New Long March* and *Eggs Under the Red Flag*. During this time, political pop became a symbol of the art forms of Yuanmingyuan Painters' Village, which included such parodies as the standard portraits of political leaders, but wearing pigtails pointing to the sky, or the superimposition of the "Game Over" message from a video game over images of revolutionary heroes of the Cultural Revolution.

Wang Shuo's novels, and TV film adaptations of his works, which served as a cultural pontoon bridge between the late 1980s and early 1990s, constituted a popular topic of conversation in the late 1980s. Wang Shuo became the first best-selling writer and high-profile figure in the cultural marketplace since 1949. His success had to do with his smooth narration, rebellious spirit, and romantic love stories, but more popular, especially among readers and viewers in northern Chinese cities, were the delirious talk and unrestrained political jokes and parodies in the Beijing dialect. During and toward the end of the 1980s, the magic and parody in literature and art together accomplished a process of cultural apoliticization: Rebellion and resistance were turned into ridicule, mockery, and satire, conspicuous in their ideology.

By the mid 1990s, when the generation of writers born in the 1960s came onstage, parody in literature and art had become relatively pure and mature. If the literature and art of the early and mid-1980s were mostly structured in a fine weave of intertextuality understood by author and reader, this shared memory quietly disappeared in the literary texts of the 1990s. In its stead reemerged the cultural memory that was marginalized throughout the 1980s. If the history that surfaced in the magic and parody of the literature and art of the 1980s accomplished the historical and cultural break between the new era of the 1980s and the past, then history in the parodic form of the literary and filmic texts of the 1990s achieved through the act of writing a new narration and continuity, in spite of the fact that this continuity reflects a deeper break and reintegration.

What first appeared in films was a tendency to recover childhood memories of the Cultural Revolution. In two important films, *In the Heat of the Sun* (Jiang Wen, 1994) and *Growing Up* (Lu Xuechang, 1997), there coincidentally appeared a mixture of the Cultural Revolution, childhood memory, initiation stories, and a parody of the revolutionary classic text *How Steel Was Tempered*.[9] As a revolutionary cultural classic of the Soviet Union in the 1950s and of socialist realist literature and art, *How Steel Was Tempered* (as novel and film) can be regarded as one of the most important signifiers of the socialist culture of China.[10] An examination of the society and culture of the 1950s, 1960s, and even early 1980s reveals that a strange combination of *How Steel Was Tempered, The Gadfly*, and *John Christopher* formed the foundation for the cultural construction of revolutionary heroism (collective?)/heroism (individual?), of revolutionary idealism/idealism, in China in the 1950s and 1960s. Among these, *How Steel Was Tempered* was certainly the best known, best received, and most legitimized. Aided by the effective ideological apparatus and occasionally by the popular film, the story and characters in this work were familiar to everyone in Chinese cities and towns during those decades. We could use the reversal of the cultural order between *How Steel Was Tempered* and *John Christopher* as a metaphor for the social, political, and cultural transformation at the turn of the 1970s and 1980s: Revolutionary heroism and collectivism were replaced by individualism (that is, cultural heroism or elitism); communist revolutionary idealism gave way to humanitarian idealism. Therefore, *How Steel Was Tempered* successfully effected in the 1980s a cultural relocation from the center to the margin. Liu Xiaofeng, one of the representative cultural figures of the 1980s, published in *Book Reading* an essay called "In Loving Memory of Dongnia," which discusses the inner journey of Chinese intellectuals in the 1980s and for the first time associates memories of reading *How Steel Was Tempered* with memories of the Cultural Revolution.[11]

A parody of *How Steel Was Tempered* appears in two scenes of the film *In the Heat of the Sun*, a rewrite by director Jiang Wen.[12] But this time around, the novel's reappearance did not represent, as it had in the 1980s, an epoch, a period in history, a cultural violence that swallows the individual and throttles love. On the contrary, the parody represents a personal memory of the Soviet film and a self-conscious attempt by the director at postmodern artistry. In an adaptation faithful to the original work of Wang Shuo, Jiang Wen's most important rewriting came from his memory of films he had seen in adolescence. It is these parodies that enhanced the postmodern flavor of *In the Heat of the Sun*. It was also in this film that the once-ignored initiation story in *How Steel Was Tempered* was brought to light for the first time. As an initiation story itself, *In the Heat of the Sun*, like *How Steel Was Tempered*, reveals the psychology of the protagonist Ma Xiaojun, who attempts, drawing on many scenes from *How Steel Was Tem-*

pered, to transform his traumatized feelings, frustrations, and futile impulses of violence during adolescence into a break from the once-legitimized class differences in and political standpoint of the film. Also noteworthy about *In the Heat of the Sun* is the cultural expression of its music, a patchwork of Cultural Revolution songs, including the "Internationale," and music from Giacomo Puccini's *Cavalleria Rusticana.*

In *Growing Up* (originally titled *Steel Was Thus Tempered*), from sixth-generation director Lu Xuechang, *How Steel Was Tempered* becomes the object of parody, the pretext, for the entire film; the political significance of the original work is more or less destroyed. The protagonist in *Growing Up* learns the Soviet story through a children's picture book that he comes across. He claims that his first spiritual mentor as he was growing up was a charming, idealistic young man named Zhu Helai.[13] However, following the example of Zhu Helai, he tried not so much to grow up to be a hero like the protagonist in *How Steel Was Tempered* as simply to become an adult. This mentor disappears early in the film. When the protagonist, who becomes a rock 'n' roll youth, eventually locates him, he learns that Zhu Helai had been blinded by bandits during a rebellion and has wandered destitute, far from home. In the two versions of the film (as censorship required), the main characters cannot meet their respective Zhu Helais or "grow up" in the true sense of the term. Between the original text and the parody, the film represents two eras, two lives and value systems that could not possibly cross paths. Heroes, even individualistic heroes, had withdrawn from the stage. Yet, what they left behind was not a peaceful world. Contemporary China was not ready for a scene from the post-industrial age, in which alienated souls live serenely in an alienating world.

The Mirror of Reduplication and Parody

The film *Mr. Wang Incinerated by His Desire* (1996), by the post-fifth-generation director Zhang Jianya, another 1990s Chinese postmodern text of reduplication and parody, demonstrates a further dilemma of postmodern culture in contemporary China.[14] The character is adopted from *Mr. Wang,* a series of works by famous cartoonist Ye Qianyu of Shanghai in the 1930s. Hinged upon an affair of Mr. Wang, a typical nobody in Shanghai referred to as a tenant thrice removed, the film pieces together parodied episodes from diverse films and other artistic texts. Such episodes include parodies of well-known scenes from Zhang Yimou's films (lovemaking in the wild in *Red Sorghum* and the ritual of foot massage), meant to reveal Mr. Wang's daydreams. Also included are episodes from the 1960s revolutionary classic *Eternal Life in the Raging Fire* and from the model drama of the Cultural Revolution, *The Red Lamp.* The climax of the film, which is an open fight between two tycoons of the underground society, is borrowed from scenes in the world classic *Battleship Potemkin.*

Yet the audience reception fell far short of the filmmaker's expectations. When viewing this postmodern film in which not one single word is without an allusion, the young audience mostly recognized episodes from Zhang Yimou's films and repeatedly responded with laughter. But they were at sea about other episodes; they had not seen enough films. Some film critics even questioned the presence of the navy during the tycoons' fight. Likewise, middle-aged viewers, who identified strongly with the parodies of sixties films, had little knowledge of the origins of other scenes.

The cartoon character Mr. Wang was adapted for film with the help of Ye Qianyu as early as the 1930s. A film series with Mr. Wang as the main character later appeared in Shanghai during the Japanese occupation in the 1940s and again after China won the war of resistance over Japan. But Zhang Jianya's works are not reproductions or parodies of these popular film series. Neither the filmmaker nor the critics mentioned Mr. Wang's film history, possibly a small oversight to allow Zhang to claim credit for originality. But more likely, this fact of film history is accessible to few people except film historians. To a certain extent, Chinese and world films made before 1949 represent prehistory for the contemporary audience, with the exception of a small number of leftist films of the 1930s and 1940s. The unexpected failure of *Mr. Wang Incinerated by His Desire* in the marketplace testifies to the dilemma of postmodern film writing in China today. The changed times, the intrusion of political cultural violence, and the repeated rewriting of cultural logic caused a fragmentation and discontinuity of Chinese people's culture, including their film-viewing experience. Even obsessed fans find it impossible to fully appreciate such postmodern filmic texts. Therefore, at the level of its reception, *Mr. Wang Incinerated by His Desire* is less a postmodern landmark in Chinese film history than a reincarnation phenomenon in China in the 1990s, an attempt to reconstruct the regional culture of Shanghai.

It is in this context that literature, as compared to film, proved a better site for postmodern parody. In 1990s China, where grim realist writings and popular literature produced in batches flooded the market, the parodic works of Wang Xiaobo, Li Feng, and Cui Zi'en were distinctive. As a writer who made his name late in life, Wang Xiaobo was the first to experiment with postmodern treatments of the history and experience of the Cultural Revolution. Most of the works in his collections *Age of Gold* and *Age of Silver* are parodies of the wounds literature (or scar literature) of the late 1970s, of political reflective novels, and of some 1980s search-for-roots literature, as well as of Soviet political dissident writer Alekandr Solzhenitsyn's works. Wang Xiaobo structures the cruelties of the Cultural Revolution in sadistic and masochistic sexual scenes. In sad yet funny descriptions, he insinuates the structure of power, politics, and violence, using a logic similar to that of abusive love. The three novels in his collection *Bronze Age* are postmodern rewritings of Tang short stories. Using his original work *Peerless* as a wedge, Wang Xiaobo with his fantastic story touches on another aspect of Cultural Revolution experience—fascist mass psychology, violence, and selective remembering and forgetting.

In rewrites of classical Chinese literature, Li Feng represents another success story. Although not all of his works are of the same quality, at least three are exquisite, refined pieces. *Another Voice* is an ingenious continuation of the classic novel *Journey to the West*. *A Young Oil Vendor in the Sixteenth Century* is a unique retelling of a vernacular story, *The Young Oil Vendor Had the Call Girl All to Himself. My Heroic Life as Wu Song* is another version of *Water Margin*. It is from these witty and clever retellings that the reflected cultural scenery in the 1990s emerged. Their reflective and critical awareness—lacking in most literary and art works in the 1990s—help to throw into relief the social and cultural problems of the time. At Li Feng's hands, when Sun Xingzhe in *Another Voice* returns from his quest for "the sacred word from the West," what he comes home with are not honor and truth but extreme physical and mental exhaustion, despair, and perplexity. The protagonist will experience a more distant and more torturous journey to recover lost memories, identity, and self, so as to be reconciled to the existence shared by all ordinary people.

In *A Young Oil Vendor*, the oil vendor, in trying to ransom his beloved, becomes obsessed with the game of making and hoarding money. Wu Song, in despair in *My Heroic Life*, falls into a series of violent and murderous acts that he realizes are meaningless but that are beyond his control. In such cases, postmodern duplications and parodies serve less as a bridge between premodern and modern Chinese culture than as a magic mirror that allows one to look into 1990s Chinese society while still avoiding the dazzling light that offends the eye.

In this series of authors and their works, Cui Zi'en's writings were the first queer texts in China. His novels *Rose Bed* and *A Clown Comes on Stage* are fraught with parodies and patchworks of Chinese classical literature and European literary masterpieces, as they glide through a multitude of literary texts. By virtue of postmodern duplication, Cui Zi'en unfolds and exhibits the ambiguous gender identities of diverse characters in literary classics, thereby subverting gender order, gender norms, and the institution of gender power. His writings are at once a conspiracy against gender culture and a carnival of a culture of difference.

In the 1990s, postmodern texts and the writing of such texts represent individual cases in the cultural vista. They both imply the possibility of escaping the new institutions of oppression and reveal the futility of trying to change reality. *Weekend Lovers* (Lou Ye, 1993), a representative sixth-generation film produced by Fu Jian Film Productions, employs postmodern parody to demonstrate the impossibility of a happy ending. After scenes of cruelty, meaningless, and violence among contemporary youths, the film draws to a happy silent-film ending, after the fashion of classic Hollywood melodrama. Protagonist Lala is released after serving his sentence in prison. In bright sunlight, his friend from former days waits for him at the prison gate in his Cadillac. Lala's girlfriend stands there hand in hand with a child, Lala's namesake. Father and son, husband and wife, and friends eventually get back together. But this reveals the grimness of reality more than it reflects end-of-the-century contentedness.

The only postmodern or quasi-postmodern film that brims over with warmth and tenderness is a sixth-generation film titled *Love Talk* (Li Xin, 1995) produced by Shanghai Film Productions. Its parodies of heroic ambition and love mythology open up a space of fairy-tale happiness even while it declares the end of the age of idealism. For instance, after closet doors open with the uncanny squeaking sounds of a horror film, a mysterious bombshell appears out of which colorful candies pour. At the end of the film, an elephant comes running down a busy street in Shanghai. This is an imagination, a smile, as well as an absurdity.

A corner in the jumbled and multicolored cultural public space. A phase in the heterogeneous cultural skyline. Between the hardship of premodernism, the processes of modernization and globalization, and the game of postmodernism, where do Chinese intellectuals position themselves?

Notes

1. The entire group became famous thanks to the painters, although it included writers and poets who never published a piece of work, youths who dreamt about experimental drama and filmmaking, and musicians and singers. Because they had no "unit," no residence registration in Beijing, and no regular source of income to feed and clothe themselves, they had to rent peasants' houses in a nearby suburb of Beijing. They used to live in community in the vicinity of Yuan Ming Yuan Park.

2. The term "mobile population," which refers to the "roaming artists," appeared at the end of the 1950s and became widely used in the 1960s, when it referred to homeless victims of natural calamities who begged for food. In recent years, this term came to refer to a population without residence registration that eked out a living in cities.

3. Cheng Gu, "Black Eyes," in *Black Eyes* (Beijing: Renmin Wenxue Chubanshe, 1986).

4. Unlike *Today,* a privately sponsored literary journal in the 1970s and 1980s, the self-sponsored poetry journals that spread across the country around this time were not engaged in political protest and were not politically subversive. They circulated only among poets and provided a space for the publication of their works.

5. Jameson's talk was transcribed and translated into Chinese by Tang Xiaobing. Its book version, *Postmodernism and Cultural Theory,* edited by Tang Xiaobing and published by Shan'xi Normal University Press, deeply impacted Chinese humanities in the 1980s.

6. Interview by author, 5 August 1993, Beijing.

7. After *MaMa* (1990) directed by Zhang Yuan won the Jury Award and a Special Mention at the Festival Des Trois Continentes in Nantes, France, feature films made outside the official system became hot spots in Euro-American film festivals; see my book *Scenery in the Fog.*

8. "Nan Ni Wan" is a famous revolutionary historical song, a eulogy of the mass-production movement in the Shan Gan Ning area during the Yan'an period. It was a household song from the 1950s to the 1970s. Singing it in a rock 'n' roll style, Cui Jian led the way in performing "revolutionary songs" in the style of popular music.

9. *In the Heat of the Sun* was adapted from Wang Shuo's novella "Animal Fierce"; *Growing Up,* produced by Beijing Film Productions, was finished in 1995 but not released for two years, after several revisions.

10. The film was based on Soviet writer Nikolay Ostrovsky's autobiographical first novel, which portrays a worker's son participating in the war and reconstruction of the early Soviet Union and becoming a young Bolshevik. Like the protagonist, the author became blind and paralyzed from old wounds (but under this handicap, he wrote a second novel, *Born in the Storm*). *How Steele Was Tempered,* translated into Chinese in the 1950s, became one of the most widely

read books among city youths in the 1950s and 1960s. The film adaptation was also soon trans-lated into Chinese.

11. This essay was published in a journal called *Reading* in April 1994 and later included in *The Love and Fear of a Generation,* a miscellaneous collection of Liu Xiaofeng's works (Hong Kong: Oxford University Press, 1994).

12. In the home version of *In the Heat of the Sun,* the two episodes that were parodies of *How Steel Was Tempered* focus on the romantic relationship between the protagonist in the novel and Dong Niya, a young girl of aristocratic origins. These were inserted between love scenes of the protagonists of the film, Ma Xiaojun and Mi Lan. But in the overseas version, both parodies were taken out, because these were cultural memories from a socialist period and in a socialist camp, impossible to share with the world.

13. Zhu Helai is an important character, a mature Bolshevik, and Paul's spiritual father in *How Steel Was Tempered.* In *Growing Up,* this character, played by the director Tian Zhuangzhuang himself, is his namesake.

14. *Mr. Wang Incinerated by His Desire* was a product of Shanghai Film Productions. Zhang Jianya made an earlier film, *The Story of San Mao as a Soldier,* in a similar style. He subsequently was labeled a "postmodernist."

Selected Bibliography

Ahmed, Sara. *Differences That Matter: Feminist Theory and Postmodernism.* Cambridge: Cambridge University Press, 1998.

Dai, Jinhua. *Scenery in the Fog.* Beijing: Peking University Press, 2000.

Foucault, Michel. *Power, Truth, Strategy.* Ed. Meaghan Morris and Paul Patton. Sydney: Feral Publications, 1979.

Jameson, Fredric. *Postmodernism and Cultural Theory: A Transcript of Jameson's Speech.* Trans. (into Chinese) and ed. Tang Xiaobing. Shan'xi: Shan'xi Normal University Press, 1986.

Siebers, Tobin. *The Subject and Other Subjects: On Ethical, Aesthetic, and Political Identity.* Ann Arbor: University of Michigan Press, 1998.

Tang, Xiaobing. *Chinese Modern: The Heroic and the Quotidian.* Durham, N.C.: Duke University Press, 2000.

Watt, Stephen. *Postmodern/Drama: Reading the Contemporary Stage.* Ann Arbor: University of Michigan Press, 1998.

Xu, Ben. *Disenchanted Democracy: Chinese Cultural Criticism After 1989.* Ann Arbor: University of Michigan Press, 1999.

CHAPTER 9

Terms of Transition: The Action Film, Postmodernism, and Issues of an East-West Perspective

Chuck Kleinhans

> The way in which the American system itself undertakes to incorporate exotic elements from abroad—samurai culture here, South African music there, John Woo films here, Thai food there, and so forth.
> —Fredric Jameson, "Notes on Globalization as a Philosophical Issue"

At first glance, the ultraviolent action films made in the United States and Hong Kong since the mid-1980s seem a perfect case study for considering postmodern culture as an allegory of late/global/finance capitalism.[1] Some key elements of a transnational genre are definitely present:

- The films are produced and circulated within capitalist commercial culture.
- They are reciprocally exchanged and widely exported on the world market.
- They have a generic identity that combines similar styles and themes.
- They share an emphasis on violent spectacle and allegorical narrative.
- They have influenced each other.
- There are actual relations, most obviously the move of Hong Kong directors John Woo and Ringo Lam and stars Chow Yun Fat, Jackie Chan, and Jet Li to Hollywood.

I do not want to argue against these films' similarities and relations, though they need qualification and elaboration. Rather, it is unsatisfactory to project this genre as an instance of postmodern culture if we think of the postmodern as a completely new moment. The ultraviolent action films are more than simply an expressive form of a new global capitalism. In particular, their appeal to audiences and the way they deal with their subject matter draw on older aesthetic currents, especially from European Romanticism up through the twentieth century.

The Action Film as Cultural Type

In *Irma Vep* (Olivier Assayas, France, 1996), a movie about the making of a movie, Maggie Cheung (Zhang Manyu) plays herself cast in a made-for-TV remake of the silent serial *Les Vampires* (Louis Feuillade, France, 1915–16). On the set, the Hong Kong star is interviewed (in English) by a French television "journalist who loves John Woo" (Antoine Basler), as he is identified in the credits. The interviewer immediately reveals himself as not concerned with the star but obsessed with action films, which he sees as vastly superior to the kind of "intellectual cinema" that the director within the film, René Vidal (Jean-Pierre Léaud), makes. The reporter esteems John Woo, Jean-Claude Van Damme, and Arnold Schwarzenegger as true cinéastes. Cheung, throughout the film, exhibits a courteous, gracious professionalism while the characters around her project their own desires on her. She politely demurs at the reporter's questions and assertions, explaining that she has not worked with Woo, who in any case excels with male actors. She says that variety in cinema is a good thing.

These comic ironies dramatize some of the contradictions at the heart of contemporary transnational commercial culture. The action film is triumphant in the international market, and in a world in which commercial success trumps any other aesthetic concern, that says it all. In the film *Irma Vep*, when director Vidal meets with his star before filming, he shows her an action clip from *The Heroic Trio* (Dongfang sanxia; Hong Kong, Johnny To and Ching Siu-tung, 1992) and explains that he cast her because of her graceful movement. She replies that stunt doubles did that sequence. Even the most knowledgeable specialist, in this case a burned-out nouvelle vague director, uses Hong Kong action film to project his own fantasies. So not only the character "Maggie Cheung" but also the whole category "Hong Kong action film" are repositories of Western desire. This orientalist vision contributes to the legend that U.S. independent upstart directors such as Quentin Tarantino recirculate Hong Kong action elements—first as fans of a "low" genre, and later as filmmakers in their own right, borrowing Hong Kong style and imagination to invigorate U.S. commercial cinema. Just as *Irma Vep*'s television journalist finds John Woo "strong,"[2] so the fan cult endorses, with a self-congratulatory twist, a special version of the boys' fantasy world of action cinema. A college or cinematic education does not change the fantasy; rather it widens the range of consumption, allowing a more cosmopolitan or exotic taste.[3]

But by now this story is well known, and here I am less concerned with simply retelling it than with drawing out a correlative point, which I think addresses a much more lasting issue in East-West relations. Specifically, how do we analyze postmodern capitalist culture? Probably the most influential statement of this problem has been in the various works of Marxist critic Fredric Jameson. He argues that three stages of culture—realism, modernism, and postmodernism—are expressive forms of three stages of capitalist production: industrial capital, advanced monopoly/Fordist capital, and late or global capital. In opening the discussion of postmodernism about twenty years ago, Jameson stressed the remarkable changes from a culture of modernism to postmodernism to make the point that we have arrived at a new stage of culture. Subsequently, he and others have concentrated on the differences, on the changes. And as other cultural analysts have gone back and extended this kind of analysis, "modernism" has been redefined and fleshed out in relation to "modernity."

Thus the artistic/cultural movement (modernism) is linked more decisively to modernity, a more general social condition. This has given scholars a certain productive purchase on thinking through the art-and-society relation that surpasses the limits of the crudest base/superstructure model or the limited terrain of, for example, Lukacs's denouncing modernism while celebrating realism. But Jameson's framing of aesthetic and cultural stages has also led to an impasse in thinking, because in using the concept of a decisive break between realism and modernism, or modernism and postmodernism, a cultural analyst is forced to stress the antinomies of difference rather than the unity of a contradiction, or the unresolved and evolving nature of cultural, social, political, and economic transformation.

I want to argue that on a global scale we cannot arrive at the best analysis by assuming the separation of these moments/movements. Rather, to understand the cultural production of the capitalist era, we must first see the cultural process as a whole, as a changing and shifting sequence not of successive phases but of overlapping ones, waves which change and transmit. I make this claim most decisively because in my own field of literary and visual communications, popular commercial culture today is not simply "postmodern" and different, but also "modern," and "realist," and especially "romantic." In other words, if we look at the field of cultural production as a social as well as an aesthetic phenomenon, we can see much deeper and persistent structures—structures that change, to be sure, but structures that remain essential to accounting for contemporary culture. For example, the dominant narrative forms of Hollywood cinema today are the dominant forms of nineteenth-century European/North American theater. Today's commercial screenwriter writes with exactly the same principles of Eugene Scribe's *pièce bien faite*. Which might remind us that Scribe was so successful in mid-nineteenth-century Paris that he actually farmed out much of his well-made playwriting to hired hands, saving the smoothing out and the sale for himself—not much different from the traditional studio system or the Hollywood blockbuster film process today.

The Action Genre

"Action films serve the same function as Westerns—they present morality plays, albeit with cursing, a lot more blood, and violence, and tits," comments actor Bruce Willis. "In my mind, a big, exciting, thrilling, scary, violent film is no different from the newest ride at Disney World. You're sitting in a darkened room with 100 or 200 people, and these little flashing points of light on the screen are able to scare you, thrill you, make you jump. That's the trick. That's the art form."
—Marshall Julius, *Action!*

Without analyzing the international action film genre in detail (a monographic specialist project that would obscure my main point here), I want to outline what such a project would involve. In particular, I want to forestall assumptions that this is an "easy" thing to do, or that the task's outcome can be predicted in advance because we are dealing with a "vulgar" form—mass culture at its most commercially triumphant. The intellectual and academic prejudice against action film, in some cases even within film studies, has prevented a deeper analysis.

So, what would we have to do to compare and contrast Hollywood and Hong Kong action films in order to offer a comprehensive analysis of their uniqueness and their relation? There is no proper first step to such a project but, obviously, defining terms and finding a tentative basis for comparison is a start. For my purposes I will (tentatively) lop off some forms we might include on the Hong Kong side, such as the earlier martial-arts examples and the Chinese ghost stories and the comedies. On the Hollywood side, we can bracket for the time the earlier action form of the western and the disaster film (Towering Inferno, Titanic). But these are simply movements of critical efficiency, and any second thoughts immediately become productive in another direction.

Hollywood does produce a series of films that combine the supernatural and action, usually in a horror/fantasy/near-future sci-fi form, but those seldom receive substantial critical attention. So, let's say we have trimmed the field to films with contemporary settings, predominantly masculine adventures, cop and criminal stories, and high levels of "operatic bloodshed." A typical way a film critic might proceed would be to develop a cross-national genre description through the comparison and contrast of specific films, accounting for changing genre conventions. Since generic analysis involves both stylistic and subject matter analyses, the elaboration of narrative themes and the figures of visual style, editing (sound and visual), dramatic pace, and so forth would then be worked out. The obvious themes include: cop/criminal relations; codes of honor among thieves; codes of knights/warriors; situations of females, especially female fighters; patterns of undercover investigation; importance of urban settings; ineffectuality of the justice system; foreign or exotic settings, et cetera. These themes are embodied most acutely in key moments that depict gunfights and their aftermath, explosive detonations, and massive destruction of property and people. These moments function not only to advance the story line but also to articulate generic style elements. That is, it is not only the presence of such moments that marks the genre, but also the particular way they are presented visually. For example, we commonly see the once new, now worn "bulletcam" shot (the bullet's point of view shot rushing forward to the target), as well as the "Mexican standoff" (a suspended moment with figures in close quarters, guns drawn and pointed at each other). Probably the single most characteristic visual style element in the action genre is the shot of an expanding orange fireball with a silhouetted figure in the foreground running toward the camera. The shot expresses violence, danger, our own position as spectators, and our emotional tie to the threatened hero, who is barely escaping death. Just in time. Thrills and chills.

So, for a tentative working definition of the genre: a male-oriented narrative (if there is a central woman, she takes a masculine role) featuring violent combat, especially with gunplay, whose earlier and other forms include martial arts ranging from hand-to-hand combat to swashbuckling swordplay to technological combat (for example, Top Gun).

There is an emphasis on the hero's body, especially as it is punished, and sometimes the films feature an excessive body, as in the Terminator or cyborg forms (an aspect that oscillates between anxiety about and assertion of masculinity).[4]

Having assembled our projection of what comprises the field, we might then begin to examine the genre further by considering authorship—that is, directors well noted in the genre and stars who appear in it. And we could begin to look at influence and reception. In this stage of analysis, we might see influences as reciprocal. Hollywood as the dominant global form of cinema obviously shapes other cinemas, but in the case of Hong Kong action film, we also see the influence of Hong Kong action on a generation of younger U.S. directors such as Tarantino and Rodriguez (*El Mariachi*).

Economically, we would need to also consider questions of film import and export, noting that Hong Kong action films initially entered the United States as cinema for the Chinese diasporic audience—via theaters in some communities, but more importantly on video, a far less transient and site-specific means of diffusion. Obviously, we would note the presence of John Woo and Ringo Lam in Hollywood in the 1990s, as well as Chow Yun Fat's Hollywood debut in *The Replacement Killers* (1997), and perhaps Jean-Claude Van Damme's appearing in Hong Kong settings, if not Hong Kong films.[5] But to say this, perhaps we are not saying anything new. Hollywood has always been willing to import directors and stars for financial gain.[6] And after a certain point in the development of film finance and evolved production processes, Hollywood often films abroad. So, an adequate study of transnational "genre" films could not simply rely on analyzing the most direct actual relations (*rapports du fait*). We would soon see the need to consider larger institutional and economic issues in order to define the action film genre.

For that kind of institutional analysis, which considers the relation between marketing and film style, I turn to another term, "High Concept." High Concept refers to a general strategy for marketing Hollywood film.[7] Developed in the mid-1970s, High Concept aims not at making art, but at making money. The essence of a High Concept production and marketing strategy is that a film should have a simple pitch (a description of the story) that can be summed up in a single image (for example, *Independence Day*—alien invaders blow up the White House). Such films are star powered; saturation advertised, especially on television, before release; and saturation released, opening everywhere the same day. Above all, high-concept films are aimed at a specific, but very large, audience—youth and the moviegoing mass audience. The films are presold by being generic and thus instantly familiar, or they may recycle comic books, television series, and so on. Furthermore, they are often successfully connected to merchandising and tie-ins (Disney is the master of this), even though violent action seldom finds an easy merchandising tie-in except for the superhero subgenre (*Batman*) or animals (*Jurassic Park*).

High Concept is the general strategy, driven by marketing, which then decisively shapes the contemporary action genre. In Hollywood, money is made on hits. As a contemporary capitalist institution, film finance capital seeks the blockbuster and thus shares many aspects of speculative capital, such as that invested in wildcat oil well drilling. At the same time, through media/entertainment conglomerations, the system tries to smooth out speculation at the delivery end. U.S. capital invested in the culture industries colonizes new areas of consumption. Examples range from Disney turning children into consumers to Rupert Murdock purchasing baseball and soccer teams while trying to dominate satellite television delivery and product to China and the Asian subcontinent. Although a genre study of U.S. and Hong Kong action cinema and their interrelationship would seem to start by talking simply about films and cultural texts, sooner rather than later, the analysis must consider global capitalism. But let me return to that point further on.

High Concept massively changes dominant fiction films, and the action film in particular, especially in style. The High Concept feature rests on a high level of technical achievement, especially in terms of digital special effects and production design, and this technical apparatus for production cannot be matched by smaller cinemas. For such films as *Terminator 2*, *Independence Day*, and *Mission: Impossible*, there is no competition. Style includes both image and sound track, and today sound and image are closely related, as in music videos. It is no accident that the first-time-out director of *The Replacement Killers*, Antoine Fuqua, had a background in commercials and music videos: The only thing he had to "prove" with a debut feature was that he could apply his established skilled style to a full-length narrative; he needed to concern himself only minimally with directing actors in spoken dialogue. Sound is important, but on the sound track, music and sound effects dominate over dialogue. Bold images predominate over character psychology, and character is already a given because character and star image fuse. Thus, narrative is fused with spectacle, telling a story with pictures, physical stunts, special effects, and music. A full and integrated production design fused with highly coordinated cinematography and rapid editing become the most expressive parts of the whole. The form becomes much like the Hollywood musical genre, with sequences and "numbers" as the dominant elements.

From this vantage point, we can see the sense of John Woo's frequent statements in interviews that his own filmmaking was especially influenced by the Hollywood musical. His "bullet ballet" work meshes exactly with the High Concept action genre in a choreographing of heroic bloodshed.

Face/Off: Romantic Heroes in a Melodramatic Narrative

As new as High Concept filmmaking is, one of the most striking characteristics of ultraviolent action films, be they made in Hong Kong or in the United States, is the persistence of older patterns alongside new expressive forms. The characters who hold the most advanced weapons embody cultural types who first appeared on the world stage about two hundred years ago. To provide an example of this phenomenon of mixed forms, I will sketch in an aspect of John Woo's *Face/Off* (1997) to set up my conclusion about the political implications of mixed aesthetics across generations.

In *Face/Off*'s title sequence, master criminal Castor Troy (initially Nicolas Cage), working in the service of international terrorism, prepares a special high-tech chemical biological bomb that will kill millions of people in Los Angeles. This advanced urban terrorism is right out of the headline news. The crazed criminal derives from the figure of the amoral man of action, a superman beyond the ordinary, from the early nineteenth century, who like Balzac's Vautrin hurls himself against a bankrupt society "like a cannonball." Only the weaponry is updated. Castor Troy reiterates the power of the nineteenth-century gothic as a blasphemous, even satanic, figure posing as a priest in this opening scene and also in the final shootout in a Catholic church, where he is explicitly perverse in mimicking the pose of Jesus on the cross.

Troy's opponent is an alienated romantic antihero, FBI agent Sean Archer (initially John Travolta), embittered and obsessed with catching Troy since the criminal killed the cop's young son six years earlier while trying to assassinate Archer himself. Again, in a replication of Romanticism's fascination with the doppelgänger, the film shows not simply the metaphoric equation of cop and criminal as fundamentally linked or increasingly alike as the pursuit continues, but literally produces this identity switch with each taking on the other's face (thanks to high-tech surgery) and then carrying on his business and personal life, in disguise, on the other's turf. For all the emphasis on computers, advanced medicine, and repeated shootouts in the contemporary urban environment, *Face/Off*'s story line is deeply embedded in the family, both in Archer's domestic space and in Troy's criminal family. While the criminal double invades Archer's middle-class family, the undercover cop ends up saving Troy's son and finally adopting that child, replacing his own lost son. Both protagonists enact different but overlapping aspects of romantic masculinity. We see them firmly located within a contemporary setting while the plot line plays out a nineteenth-century melodrama.[8]

Face/Off's pattern displays extreme parallels following the two protagonists which reaches its most spectacular high point in the FBI raid at the hideout. Sean Archer (looking like Castor Troy) escapes prison and arrives at drug dealer Dietrich's warehouse-sized place. Treated as friend and hero, he's obliged to take drugs, and he meets Dietrich's sister Sasha. Earlier in his FBI role, he threatened her with loss of her child if she didn't help capture Troy. Now in an astonishing twist on the recognition scene, Sasha reveals that Castor is the father of five-year-old Adam. Archer flashes back to his own son, killed at age six by Castor. While he hugs the boy, the FBI attack directed by Troy-as-Archer begins. In the mayhem and gun battle that follow, Archer acts to protect the child.

Using an elaborate variation on the famous set piece standoff and shootout in Woo's *The Killer* (Hong Kong, 1990) in which a blind woman is caught between the cop and the hitman, unable to know what is going on during the gunfight, the child wears earphones and is the audience's subjective sound point of view during the battle. The music swells as the gunfire fades, and an elaborate slow-motion montage sequence begins with the kid's Walkman (and the audience soundtrack) hearing Olivia Newton-John's version of "Somewhere over the Rainbow." The sequence proceeds with intense visual action counterpointed by the dreamy musical lyricism. All pretense of realism disappears while epic operatic spectacle takes over.

The second stage of the shootout presents the film's most dramatic "face-off" as the two protagonists meet in a circular room of mirrors, reminiscent of Orson Welles's famous set in *Lady from Shanghai* (1948). On opposite sides of a mirror partition, the cop and criminal prepare to shoot it out.

> TROY-LOOKING-LIKE-ARCHER (played by Travolta). (Sigh) I don't know what I hate wearing worse, your face or your body. I mean, I enjoy boning your wife, but—let's face it—we both like it better the other way. Yes. So why don't we just trade back?
>
> ARCHER-LOOKING-LIKE-TROY (played by Cage). You can't give back what you've taken from me.
>
> TROY. Oh, well, plan B. Let's just kill each other. (The gunfight begins again.)

The pair face each other (spatially), with each looking at back-to-back mirrors, and thus each faces an image of himself—which is itself a false image, since each is literally wearing the other's face—and fires his weapon at the other, who is spatially on the other side of the set of mirrors. This dizzying reflexive and ironic play of image and identity is further multiplied by our knowledge of each actor's star persona and previous roles. Each actor is obviously also enjoying playing with the characteristic signature actions of the other. The result is a commercial version of Romantic irony of a high order indeed.

Almost all the characteristics commonly ascribed to Romantic heroes apply to one or both of the leads: the individual, exceptional hero's exhibiting either introversion or exhibitionism; narrative pathos, with the script's concentration on emotions, passions, and inner struggles; the characters' melancholy, nursing a grievance, suffering to the point of madness, and fearing loss of identity; the visual style's dramatizing the monstrous, diseased satanic and grotesque, enacting cruelty and egotism; the protagonist's and antagonist's marking of the double, a shadow self; the male leads' inability to communicate with others and misrecognizing their own environment. This is a world first explored in nineteenth-century melodrama. It is a moral universe populated by clearly identifiable villains and victims, with open confrontations between good and evil. It is also a world of the patriarchal family in which male authority and family security are threatened and in which the prime motives for actions are familial relations. Melodrama's plots and situations revolve around secrets and aspects of the past that produce suspicions and misrecognitions, and the plot's final revelations try to restore innocence and justice. From the nineteenth-century theatrical tradition, suspenseful narratives and scenes of rescue are enacted in body-oriented performance, heightened with music and sound effects, and theatricalized by set and lighting. Remarkable spectacles have long combined with the drama of real life to produce strong emotional responses in the audience. In *Face/Off,* it is all there: romantic heroes face off against each other in a highly melodramatized story and setting.

Romanticism/Postmodernism
in the Asian/Western Moment

Capitalism by its nature drives beyond every spatial barrier. Thus the
creation of the physical conditions of exchange—of the means of communication and transport—the annihilation of space by time—becomes
an extraordinary necessity for it.
—Marx, *The Grundrisse*

How should we understand contemporary cultural transitions between East and West?
What is the nature of the relations we are witnessing between Asia and the West in popular cinema? Is the local, the regional, being lost and absorbed into the transnational,
the global, with postmodern Hollywood triumphant? If we look at the leading edge of
cultural change, particularly in mass-mediated culture, we can easily accept the apparent fact of postmodernism, whether we celebrate it as wonderful (in global capitalist triumph), accept it as inevitable (in a kind of Baudrillardian frenzy), regret it (in a nostalgia for high culture and national tradition), or face it with anxiety. Considering the
action film with specific reference to Hong Kong, we can easily imagine it transformed,
with post-1997 Hong Kong film production absorbed within China, losing its dialect,
losing its characteristic forms and themes, and even losing its major directors and some
of its stars to Hollywood. Gone, absorbed elsewhere, diced and blended in the postmodern space/time compression.

I want to argue against that kind of analysis. To assume postmodernism is the cultural expression of a new stage of capitalism is appealing because the idea contains an
important and profound truth. But to leap to the conclusion that postmodernity or capitalism is in the process of a complete transformation, that cultural expressions are
changing with it (in some ways in advance of it), or that we are at a different stage is
deceptive and precipitous. The business people, politicians, and intellectuals who see the
world while flying from one airport to another seldom observe the millions of children
doing stoop labor in the rice paddies and fields below, living at or below subsistence,
and deprived of an education. In the United States and Europe, relocating apparel sweatshops, electronic manufacturing, and heavy polluting industry to global free-enterprise
zones removes the most visibly exploited part of the workforce from the nation, but it
does not erase its global existence. Capitalism depends on extractive and exploitative
relations between people and with nature—be that fishing and polluting the seas or re-
moving fuel and forests from the land. These are facts, and no amount of pious triumphalism about the "failure of communism" can change them. (And with the current situation in Russia and the Asian economies, should we be talking about the "failure of
capitalism"?)

We should try to understand and analyze new trends and new developments, whether
by Jameson's considering postmodern/global architecture, cinema, or literature, or the
ongoing work of a new generation of scholars such as those writing in the major Asian

studies cultural journal *Positions*. But we should also realize that, especially with mass-mediated popular culture forms, changes on the leading edge do not effect a total transformation.

As I have tried to show with the example of the ultraviolent action film today, and in the very recent past, the move to a cinema of spectacular effects is more "universal," but only in a certain direction—such spectacle creates a larger potential market but at the loss of character and psychology that seem too local, too specific. Action film can demonstrate and play with deep anxieties about masculinity, especially as in the case of *Face/Off*. This masculinity, which cannot really protect the family, cannot be effectively patriarchal. This is, of course, the anxiety created by capitalism itself—that the father, the wage earner, the worker, cannot protect the family from the unnatural disasters of unemployment, personal crime, and an increasingly heartless world. These cultural forms that play with the precariousness of gender roles and the family first appear in a substantial way in the West with the rise of capitalism, with the expansion of industrial capital, the factory system, urban concentration, political democracy, new and expanded technologies of transportation and communication. But these changes, marking the transition from feudalism to capitalism, are still going on in the developing world (and at times reversing the trend, as with the Taliban period in Afghanistan). And capitalism in the industrial/commercial/financial core is still seeking to control even more of life, turning what was private, familial, separate, a haven, into something from which money can be made. Television's entering the U.S. home in the 1950s is only one of the most visible markers of that change. In the United States today, formerly familial and socially organized services such as healthcare and eldercare are being transformed into commercial operations. Formerly "independent" professionals such as doctors are brought into the commercial healthcare system. Every site—hospital, school, kitchen, or bedroom—is transformed into a profit center.[9] And thus it also becomes a potential locus of class conflict.

On a global scale, we have to see contemporary late capitalism as expanding both in the former periphery and also in the core. But this means that the same old struggles of transformation seen in early and mature capitalism are also present as active processes in this expansion aspect of late capitalism. The old struggles exist alongside new forms of conflict and contradiction caused by transformations in the most advanced sectors and sites. So, postmodernity, as the cultural expression of a globalized late capitalism, must be understood as containing within it earlier cultural forms as well as newer postmodern ones. Many of the aesthetic and cultural expressions of European Romanticism appear in contemporary cultural forms, though not all and certainly not in exactly the way they originally appeared. And that is because the economic and social transformations that gave rise to such expressions are still going on.

Thus Romanticism, realism, and modernism can be viewed as the cultural forms of emergent, industrial, and Fordist capital, but only if we also understand that they remain a significant part of the mix. Postmodernism does not displace these previous forms. It absorbs them and transforms them into something still possible, still expressive, still speaking to the audience.

Notes

1. The reference is to the ongoing work of Fredric Jameson.

2. He is speaking English and bluntly translates from the French *fort*, adding another irony for the bilingual members of the audience, perhaps reminding us that *Irma Vep* initially circulates within the European Economic Community, and that Cheung passes through the film knowing only English, with French as virtually a "background" language—another comment on current cultural shifts. At the same time, the scene repeats/references an interview by Jean-Marie Melville with Jean Seberg in Godard's *A Bout de souffle* (*Breathless*, 1959).

3. Reviewing Woo's *Hard Target*, Georgia Browne notes a cadre of New York City fans who whoop "Woo! Woo!" during his films, including retrospectives of his Hong Kong work. "Let It Bleed," *Village Voice*, 31 August 1993, 51.

4. An excellent analysis of these aspects of U.S. action film is Yvonne Tasker's *Spectacular Bodies: Gender, Genre and the Action Cinema* (London: Routledge, 1993).

5. For an extended discussion of Woo in international context, see Ann T. Ciecko, "Transnational Action: John Woo, Hong Kong, Hollywood," in *Transnational Chinese Cinemas: Identity, Nationhood, Gender,* ed. Sheldon Hsiso-peng Lu, 221–237 (Honolulu: University of Hawaii Press, 1997).

6. For example, Austria, which never had a substantial film industry, provided a series of directors in the classical Hollywood period: Eric von Stroheim, Fritz Lang, Joseph von Sternberg, Edgar G. Ulmer, Otto Preminger, Billy Wilder, and Fred Zimmermann.

7. Justin Wyatt, *High Concept: Movies and Marketing in Hollywood* (Austin: University of Texas Press, 1994).

8. I have discussed melodrama and the action hero in "Class in Action," in James and Berg, *The Hidden Foundation*, 240–263; "Realist Melodrama and the African-American Family: Billy Woodberry's *Bless Their Little Hearts*," in *Melodrama: Stage, Picture, Screen*, ed. Jacky Bratton, Jim Cook, and Christine Gledhill, 157–166 (London: British Film Institute, 1994); "Notes on Melodrama and the Family Under Capitalism," in Landy, *Imitations of Life.*

9. The introduction in the United States of a new oral drug, Viagra, for male impotence (at ten dollars a dose) puts a pricetag on (some) males' sexuality. It is already embroiled in controversy over how many a physician can prescribe in (capitalist) "managed care" health plans and in the government-sponsored subsidy for the retired and the poor.

Selected Bibliography

Arroyo, José, ed. *Action/Spectacle Cinema: A Sight and Sound Reader.* London: British Film Institute, 2000.

Chow, Rey, ed. *Modern Chinese Literary and Cultural Studies in the Age of Theory: Reimagining a Field.* Durham, N.C.: Duke University Press, 2000.

James, David, and Rick Berg, eds. *The Hidden Foundation: Cinema and the Question of Class.* Minneapolis: University of Minnesota Press, 1996.

Jameson, Fredric. *Postmodernism, or the Cultural Logic of Late Capitalism.* Durham, N.C.: Duke University Press, 1991.

Jameson, Fredric, and Masao Miyoshi, eds. *The Cultures of Globalization.* Durham, N.C.: Duke University Press, 1998.

Landy, Marcia. ed. *Imitations of Life: A Reader on Film and Television Melodrama*. Detroit: Wayne State University Press, 1991.

Yau, Esther C. M., ed. *At Full Speed: Hong Kong Cinema in a Borderless World*. Minneapolis: University of Minnesota Press, 2001.

CHAPTER 10

Consuming Asia: Chinese and Japanese Popular Culture and the American Imaginary

David Desser

Hong Kong has gone Hollywood: For three seasons on CBS, Hong Kong superstar Samo Hung starred in *Martial Law;* famed Hong Kong director John Woo continues to produce hits in Hollywood, most recently, *Mission: Impossible 2* (2000); Tsui Hark released two films starring Jean-Claude Van Damme (*Double Team,* 1997; *Knock Off,* 1998); Jackie Chan starred in another major Hollywood release, *Shanghai Noon* (2000), following the tremendous success of *Rush Hour* (1998); Chow Yun-Fat appeared opposite Mira Sorvino in a big-budget crime thriller, *Replacement Killers* (1998), opposite Mark Wahlberg in *The Corruptor* (1999), and as a romantic lead opposite Jodi Foster in *Anna and the King* (1999); and Michelle Yeoh starred opposite James Bond (*Tomorrow Never Dies,* 1998). Meanwhile, as Kurosawa Akira and Satyajit Ray receive Oscars for lifetime achievement from the American Academy of Motion Picture Arts and Sciences; as video stores across the United States devote separate large sections to Japanese animation, and a package of Japanese animation is offered for sale on television commercials in the United States; and as the producers of the all-American *Independence Day* (1996) follow up that blockbuster with a megabudget film called *Godzilla* (1998), it is time to acknowledge that something profound has changed across the popular-culture terrain.

The standard map of the pop-culture landscape would doubtless be a series of tentacles emanating from the United States and spreading across the Atlantic, south across Latin America and out over the Pacific. U.S. cultural imperialism, a branch of U.S. economic imperialism, in an effort to create new markets for American ideals, imposes Hollywood film and television programming, along with a host of other symbols, images, and products, ranging from Walt Disney's cartoon creations to Coca-Cola, McDonald's, Michael Jordan, and Nike. There is certainly much to commend this view of the international pop-culture scene. Hollywood cinema often dominates local movie theaters; U.S. television is ubiquitous in international markets; Americans overseas can always count on a Big Mac and Coke when the local cuisine begins to wear on their untrained palates; Michael Jordan is as instantly recognizable a figure as Mickey Mouse. As John Lent notes in his introduction to the anthology *Asian Popular Culture:* "US mass media products account for 75 percent of broadcast and basic cable TV revenues, 85 percent of pay TV revenues, and 55 percent each of all theatrical film rentals and home video billings worldwide." Such a profound dominance has led to "fears about what C. J. Hamelink termed cultural synchronization—the process in which cultural products go only in one direction, damaging the variety of cultural systems worldwide."[1]

But such a view is at best partial; in certain ways it is no longer even correct. Popular culture has never really been a unilateral influence. At the very least, the exchange has been back and forth, give and take, but more accurately, popular culture circulates, available for both producers and consumers to mediate, extend, rework, rethink, reinvent. Popular culture is both product and outcome, mass culture and folk culture, and we can no longer afford our knee-jerk anti-Americanisms or ignore the very real and palpable influence of other cultures on the U.S. entertainment and leisure industry, however powerful it may continue to be. Across the world, other popular cultures are achieving the international prominence once reserved for U.S. productions, such as the worldwide appeal of Japanese *manga* (comic books) and anime, the international superstardom of Jackie Chan, or the ever-increasing popularity of Hindi cinema, while in the United States itself, the pop-culture canon has been irrevocably invaded by works from across the seas. ("Anime" is shorthand for animation, now used in English to refer specifically to Japanese animation, which for a short while was called "Japanimation.")

Of course, U.S. culture has long been "in process," and no one could claim that U.S. popular culture has evolved in a vacuum of American nation and identity formation. Take the case of American films: Imagine the Hollywood cinema without the influence of British, French, German, Austrian, and Scandinavian talent in the 1920s and 1930s. Imagine, perhaps even more fundamentally, the growth and development of Hollywood without the Irish, Italian, and Jewish immigrants and their offspring. If American movies became the world's cinema, it might have something to do with this as much as with any economic or political context. America's increasingly multicultural landscape may help account for this continued American success as pop-culture provider to the world: African American, Latino, and Asian American dimensions to U.S. culture are realities whose influences are clearly detectable across the vast terrain of cultural products and movements. Yet this notion of pop-culture provider to the world must be amended, and amended in ways perhaps even more profound than emigration or importation of European talent to Hollywood.

With little fanfare and scholarly notation, there has been a profound influx of Asian popular-cultural texts and forms into U.S. and international culture. For John Lent,

Asia's contributions (or what he calls "cultural gifts") to worldwide popular-cultural forms include "karaoke, Go, and Asian-type motion pictures."[2] Though I am not sure how popular the board game of Go really is (or if board games are part of popular culture), karaoke and Asian cinema (in various forms) are now part of entertainment practices worldwide. But there is far more to these Asian contributions than singing along to laser discs in nightclubs and bars or viewing Japanese anime or Hong Kong martial arts films in college-based screening rooms. From the cartoons and video games viewed and played by children through the food consumed by trendy yuppies, Asian culture is an integral part of the landscape of culinary and entertainment pastimes across the United States. While this is not an especially new phenomenon, the last fifteen years have seen profound influences and dominances.

Made in Japan

The idea that it was Kurosawa's 1951 surprise sensation *Rashomon* that opened up the Japanese cinema to the Western world is too familiar, indeed clichéd, to need rehashing. It was invoked yet again in the director's obituaries in September 1998. What the West responded to in *Rashomon*, what elicited the claim for many, many years following that Kurosawa was "Japan's most Western director," remains obscure. Did the West respond to *Rashomon*'s postwar angst, its existential cri de coeur, its acknowledgment of the relativity of truth and certainty in a world where nuclear energy had changed man's relationship to nature and to God to which the Western world responded? Or to Kurosawa's raw cinematic energy and power, his dynamic camera moves and montage editing, the exotic yet recognizable characters embodied in Mifune Toshiro (who himself would become Japan's best-known actor in the West) and Kyo Machiko, and the vaguely familiar orientalist patina that surrounds the film?

The Japanese certainly believed the latter had the most appeal for the West, for Japanese filmmakers, particularly at Daiei studios, embarked on a campaign of filmmaking for Western consumption. This produced the orientalist period dramas familiar to scholars of Japanese cinema in the 1950s, the works especially of Mizoguchi Kenji (*Ugetsu monogatari, Saikaku ichidai onna* [*The Life of Oharu*], *Sansho dayu* [*Sansho the Bailiff*], *Yokihi* [*Yang Kwai-fei*]); Inagaki Hiroshi (the *Miyamoto Musashi* trilogy, known in the West as *The Samurai Trilogy*); and Kinugasa Teinosuke (*Jigokumon* [*Gate of Hell*]). For audiences less familiar with these atmospheric costume films, Kurosawa's samurai films typify Japanese cinema of this era, especially *Shichinin no samurai* [*Seven Samurai*], *Yojimbo,* and *Sanjuro.*

That so many of Kurosawa's films have been remade, especially as Westerns, lent credence to the idea that Kurosawa was somehow already a Western director and that the samurai film had somehow been influenced by the Western, which accounted for Kurosawa's immediate popularity and appeal. The seeming familiarity of samurai films was part of a discourse of Japanese imitativeness; that the Japanese were great borrowers and adapters of other cultures (Chinese, Korean, American) was a common motif in much postwar sociological and anthropological analysis in the West. Of course, Japanese cinema was influenced by Hollywood, just as Japanese prewar and postwar culture has been greatly influenced by U.S. culture. That U.S. culture had itself undergone a significant shift in midcentury was less talked about, less acknowledged. For Kurosawa's films found their significant appeal in a postwar world that had to come to terms not only with "the Bomb," but also with an ever-increasing reliance on technology, on bureaucracy, and on group interaction and dynamics. In other words, Japanese cinema found a home in a West that had come to resemble Japan as much as Japan had come to resemble the West.

The notion (also something of a cliché) that Japan is group oriented and America more individualistic, that Japan is vertically oriented and America more horizontally relational, must be seen as a matter of degree. The group dynamics of *Shichinin no samurai* translated well to *The Magnificent Seven* in 1960, a film which betrays the increasing recognition of shifting personal and communal relations in postwar America. The World War II combat film was the first Hollywood genre in which the group took precedence over the individual or the couple. It reflected the war experience itself, where armies of men and material would win the war; where the individual had to learn to work as part of a team; where technological skill (as a fighter pilot or bombardier, submarine commander, artillery officer, radio electrician or even cryptographer) would be as important as individual initiative and heroic bravery. Postwar American society similarly became reliant on ever-greater group efforts. The corporation replaced the entrepreneur; the planned community replaced the anarchic, atomized city. Even the genre par excellence of the U.S. experience, the Western, shifted its focus from the classic loner-heroes like William S. Hart and Gary Cooper to the group in such crucial films as *Red River, My Darling Clementine,* and *Rio Bravo* all the way up to *The Wild Bunch.* It was in this atmosphere that films like *Shichinin no samurai* and *Kakushi toride no san akunin* (*The Hidden Fortress*) found so receptive an audience in the West. Similarly, the increasing democratization of Japan and its greater exposure to Western values and culture might be said to have "individualized" Japan to a greater degree, making loner-heroes like the wandering swordsman played by Mifune in *Yojimbo* and *Sanjuro* more familiar, more responsive, to postwar Japanese audiences.

Kurosawa's influence on contemporary world cinema is almost incalculable, from the numerous remakes of *Shichinin no samurai* and *Yojimbo* (in Westerns, science fiction, fantasy, even contemporary action/adventure), to the director's stylistic and thematic inspiration of directors like Steven Spielberg, Sam Peckinpah, Francis Ford Coppola, George Lucas, Walter Hill, John Milius, John Sayles, and others too numerous to mention, though perhaps John Woo might be one more to acknowledge.[3] Yet Kurosawa's 1950s films were by no means the most popular Japanese films of their day, in Japan or, shortly thereafter, in the West. That distinction belongs to a series of films inaugurated by one of Kurosawa's protégés at Toho, Honda Inoshiro, whose 1954 *Gojira* (Godzilla) became the most recognized film ever made in Japan. Released in the United States in 1956 as *Godzilla, King of the Monsters,* it was the first Japanese film ever to be reworked for U.S. distribution, dubbed into English, with some Japanese footage deleted and extra footage added with then B-level star Raymond Burr. This would set a pattern for reworking and releasing a host of Japanese films and television programs for the next four decades.

Gojira became the flagship film not only for the twenty-one films to follow featuring the giant Tyrannosaurus-like creature who wreaks havoc time after time, sometimes attacking, sometimes defending the Japan that gave him birth, but also for a whole genre of films known as *kaiju-eiga* (monster movies). Director Honda and special-effects wizard Tsuburaya Eiji followed *Gojira* with *Rodan* in 1956, again drawing inspiration from dinosaurs; the pterodactyl monster would appear in a few more films. Meanwhile, Honda was not finished directing havoc-wreaking monsters. *Mosura* (Mothra) in 1961 was yet another oversized creature that found itself destroying any part of Japan that stood in its (in this case, her) way.

The appeal of Godzilla, Rodan, and Mothra in Japan is not hard to explain. Godzilla is the by-product of nuclear energy, "awakened" by atomic explosions, perhaps the A-bombs dropped on Japan at the end of World War II, perhaps the more recent atomic testing at Bikini atoll. While the appearance of Rodan and Mothra is not attributed to the atomic age specifically, the havoc they wreak is clearly derived from the same sort of imagery—the fire bombings of Tokyo and the atomic bombings of Hiroshima and Nagasaki. Though the Japanese have not been overly anxious to explore "the Bomb" through cinema (one exception was Kurosawa, whose *Ikimono no kiroku* [*Record of a Living Being*] was made at Toho at the same time his assistant Honda was working on *Gojira*), there is certainly a legacy of trauma to be worked through, as kaiju-eiga and, later, anime demonstrate. For Ron Tanner, these monsters need not specifically have derived from nuclear paranoia: "For the Japanese, the enemy is not technology, but nature, especially nature out of control. The Atomic bomb was nothing but nature gone mad, and monsters like Rodan or Mothra show this sort of fear."[4] Perhaps that is so. More importantly for our purposes here, Godzilla and the other giant monsters struck a nerve with U.S. audiences similarly caught in the grip of atomic fever and nuclear paranoia. The oversized ants of *Them!* (1954), similarly the product of nuclear testing, this time in the desert Southwest of the United States, clearly paved the way for the appearance of the oversized creatures from Japan. The almost concurrent release of *Godzilla* with *It Came from Beneath the Sea* (1955), in which a giant octopus menaces San Francisco, shows how Japanese cinema was capturing the zeitgeist of the era. Of course, the United States itself had a precedent in an oversized creature running amok in a major city in *King Kong* (1932), one of the few classic Hollywood films which was well known to postwar audiences in the pre–video cassette age. Godzilla, Rodan, and Mothra were thus familiar enough to U.S. audiences and easily assimilated in the cold-war era, readily available to young audiences especially through the ever-expanding medium of television. Surely there is not a baby boomer around who cannot recall the Saturday afternoon viewing of these made-in-Japan monsters.

Concomitant with the appearance of all these monsters was the generally science-fiction (SF) atmosphere in which they appeared. SF, of course, was a major genre new to world cinema in the postwar era, but whereas much American SF was dedicated to paranoid visions of alien invasion (*The Day the Earth Stood Still, It Came from Outer Space, Invasion of the Body Snatchers,* and so forth), the Japanese were relatively optimistic about the benefits of technology and its future good. This showed up in the kinds of toys being manufactured in Japan and the strides made in Japanese industry in robotics and other forms of automation.

At the time of *Gojira* and the other kaiju-eiga, Japanese manufacturing had reestablished its industrial footing and the Japanese economy had already achieved "the economic miracle." In the United States, however, the label "Made in Japan" connoted inexpensive if ingenious gadgets. The kaiju-eiga, with their clever if not always convincing special effects, seemed to fit right into that pattern. One sector in Japan that had achieved substantial success in the years after World War II was toy making, where the Japanese specifically targeted the U.S. market. As Tanner notes, "almost all Japanese-made toys (80–90 percent in the first 25 years after the war) were exported to the United States, which was the only viable market at the time." The toy market was both an offshoot of and an inspiration for televisual and cinematic programming. Japanese-made toys in the United States owed their success to the popularity of kaiju-eiga and, in the 1960s, the increasing popularity of Japanese animated programming. Like kaiju-eiga, these televised anime were SF oriented. Popular children's animated shows imported from Japan and dubbed into English, like *Astro Boy*, introduced in 1963, and *Gigantor* in 1966, were a far cry from American-produced children's programming. Says Tanner, "While Japanese children were watching cartoons of the boyish 'Tetsuwan Atom' [Astro Boy], 'the pure hearted child of science,' a robot do-gooder who first appeared in 1951, American children were watching cartoons with 'Roy Rogers' and 'Superman.'" Though I am not familiar with a Roy Rogers cartoon, Tanner's point is well taken. Programs like *The Mickey Mouse Club* or other Disney-produced shows like *Davy Crockett* reflected prewar and war-era values. For grown-ups in the period 1957–1964, the most watched genre on television was the Western, and this popularity carried over into children's programming and U.S.-made toys. Dolls were still ubiquitous in U.S. culture (made more so by the introduction of Barbie in 1959), while six-guns, rifles, and cowboy hats dominated the toy shelves. During this period, the Japanese cornered the worldwide toy market, their toys reflecting the popularity of kaiju-eiga and the new SF anime: "By 1958, Japan was the world's largest exporter of toys . . . one-half of the $1.3 billion in American toy sales during that year were sci-fi related—robots, flying saucers, ray guns, rockets—and . . . most of these were made in Japan."[5]

While it is doubtful that many of the youngsters watching programs like *Astro Boy, Marine Boy, Speed Racer, Gigantor,* and *Kimba the White Lion* knew they were Japanese in origin, the sensibilities and practices of Japanese popular culture made significant inroads into the U.S. visual and thematic landscape. Links between technology and the body, the body in nature, the body in space (anime was always more popular with youngsters than NASA's space program), and shifting relationships between humans and aliens became part of the American consciousness. Similarly, Godzilla and his offspring—misunderstood monsters created by a blind and cruel adult world—continued to be popular on television, especially among children. *Ultraman,* created for Japanese television in July 1966, shows the hybridization of kaiju-eiga and anime as the live-action, body-armored Ultraman does battle with Godzilla-like creatures in a science-fiction setting. From *Astro Boy* to *Ultraman* in a few short years, Japanese televisual SF was on a course that would culminate in the mind-boggling anime of the 1980s. In the States, however, Gene Rodenberry's *Star Trek* television series (whose first episode aired 8 September 1966) was surely the culmination of SF anime for the postwar generation up to that point.

Meanwhile, Japanese cinema of a more traditional sort, with the likes of Kurosawa, Mizoguchi, Ozu Yasujiro, and Teshigahara Hiroshi as staples of the international art cinema, continued to exert an impact on U.S. audiences in the 1960s, particularly the very large baby-boom generation becoming ghettoized on college campuses. Japan's feudal and traditional culture was visualized in compelling and memorable ways, and audiences developed a greater appreciation for Japanese aesthetic practices like the tea ceremony, Zen painting, and flower arranging (ikebana). (How much of the counter-culture's interest in Zen meditation and in other Eastern religions, for instance, might have been the result of its presentation in the art cinema?) Kurosawa's samurai enabled the likes of Okamoto Kihachi, Gosha Hideo, and the film series devoted to Zatoichi the Blind Swordsman to further impact U.S. audiences with their visions of wandering swordsmen engaged in stylized violence and justifiable mayhem. Though the films were shown in specialized theaters (art theaters and theaters in Japanese neighborhoods on the West Coast and Hawaii), audiences developed an appreciation for Japanese cinema, at once familiar yet startlingly original.

Made in Hong Kong

Another Asian culture, that of Hong Kong, also made a significant pop-culture splash on U.S. shores. In a cultural analysis of the popularity in Hong Kong and Taiwan of Hong Kong–made gangster films, Barbara Ryan asks: "But how many viewers of non-Asian descent know the international hit *Better Tomorrow* (1986) or the genre to which it gave rise? Although many people could describe Bruce Lee kung fu films frame by frame, Hong Kong gangster films such as *Rich and Famous, City on Fire,* and *True Colors* have not found many non-Asian fans."[6] This must come as something of a surprise to the numerous admirers of John Woo and Ringo Lam, both working comfortably in Hollywood precisely because of their Hong Kong hits like *A Better Tomorrow* and *City on Fire.* One is hard-pressed to know how Ryan could so badly have misread the popularity of Hong Kong's contemporary action thrillers. We might ask Chow Yun-Fat, the superstar of this Hong Kong genre, if these films are popular in the West. You can find him in Los Angeles, too, working in the Hollywood film industry. Hong Kong film in the 1990s was perhaps the most popular foreign cinema in the United States, and this is not the first time that this has been the case.

One is not sure if the presence and popularity of Japanese period films, kaiju-eiga, and animated children's shows, paved the way for the entry of Hong Kong cinema into the

United States in the early 1970s, but for all the popularity of Japanese programming, the Hong Kong cinema proved its equal, first on movie screens, then through independent and cable TV stations, and finally through home video. Indeed, the Bruce Lee kung fu films inaugurated the first U.S. and international craze for Hong Kong martial arts movies, but their popularity extended well beyond Lee's handful of films and his too-short life.

I have written elsewhere that the appearance of martial arts in Hollywood cinema and the Hong Kong martial arts film on U.S. movie screens coincides with U.S. troop withdrawals from Vietnam in 1972 and 1973.[7] Unlike its celebration of World War II, Hollywood had done virtually nothing in support of the Vietnam War, America's most unpopular overseas venture. Thus, when Richard Nixon announced the gradual withdrawal of U.S. troops beginning in 1972 (along with the virtual end of the military draft), followed by the removal of all troops and the closing down of the American embassy in Saigon in 1973, there was a sigh of relief on the home front. Yet the sense that the war had been lost (Nixon's advisors told him in his second term as president, declare victory and get out) was a bitter pill for many Americans to swallow. The legacy of Vietnam would not show up in the Hollywood cinema until 1976 or so. It might have been ironic, then, or all too appropriate, that for the first time in U.S. history, mainstream theaters were flooded not simply with foreign films, but with Asian films, and not just Asian films, but Hong Kong films, which burst on the American screen with all the fury of Bruce Lee's lightning-fast fists.

On 16 May 1973, the Hong Kong films *Fists of Fury, Deep Thrust—The Hand of Death,* and *Five Fingers of Death* were number 1, 2, and 3 respectively on the *Variety* list of the week's top box-office domestic draws. Both *Fists of Fury* and *Deep Thrust* were on the charts for the first time. *Five Fingers of Death,* however, was in its seventh week on the charts and would stay there for a few weeks more. *Five Fingers of Death* would remain on the charts for almost three months. The box-office performance of both *Fists of Fury* and *Deep Thrust* is hardly less impressive.[8]

The presence of three foreign films at the top of the U.S. box-office charts in May 1973 went unremarked. Indeed, the whole kung fu phenomenon caught industry analysts by surprise. This inability, which seems like a genuine unwillingness, to recognize the popularity and power of Hong Kong films might have something to do with the primary audience to which they appealed: not to mainstream audiences struggling with the legacy of the Vietnam War, but precisely to those subcultural, disillusioned, disaffected audiences who had opposed the war or who were more radically and generally alienated from much of mainstream culture. That is to say, martial arts movies appealed to inner-city and rural audiences; to African-American, Latino, and Asian American youth nationwide; and to the younger remnants of the counterculture who had already evinced an interest in Asian culture (if not necessarily Asian popular culture, for example, Zen Buddhism). This appeal to black audiences in particular led, unacknowledged of course, to the critical denigration of the genre. But for audiences of color, the sight of Asian men and women starring in action-packed movies filled with attractive and dynamic heroes and suave and sophisticated villains was a welcome relief from years of stereotypical characterizations and outright exploitation of their like. Similarly, the Hong Kong films' plots of exploited workers and subaltern peoples resisting the forces of exploitation and colonialization doubtless struck an allegorical nerve. It was precisely this subcultural appeal, along with the marginal and fly-by-night companies that often released the films, that led to the rather sudden decline of Hong Kong imports, at least until later in the decade when local and cable television institutionalized kung fu much as local television had earlier reveled in the kaiju-eiga.

Still, the year 1973 found Hong Kong movies raking in U.S. dollars. In the week of 20 June, no fewer than five Hong Kong kung fu films appeared in the Top 50. To *The Chinese Connection, Deep Thrust,* and *Fists of Fury* were added *Duel of the Iron Fist* and *Kung Fu, the Invisible Fist.* That same week *The Hammer of God,* yet another Hong Kong film, opened; it was number 1 for the week of 27 June. Since the quiet release of *Five Fingers of Death* at the end of March, seven Hong Kong films had hit the U.S. box-office charts. By the middle of August, two more films from Hong Kong found their way to box-office success: *Shanghai Killers* and *Fearless Fighters.* By year's end, such films as *Lady Kung Fu* and *Deadly China Doll* would hold the top spot on the U.S. charts at least for a week and often longer, and Hong Kong imports such as *Fists of the Double K, Seven Blows of the Dragon, The Thunder Kick,* and *Queen Boxer* also found significant success.

The death knell of the first kung fu craze sounded by late November 1973, when *Variety,* reviewing *The Sacred Knives of Vengeance,* wondered if "the cycle may well be on its way out." It was. While one could typically find five Hong Kong films in the weekly Top 50 in the last months of the year (though rarely near the top), on 2 January 1974, there was only one such film. A month later, no Hong Kong film made the charts. By the time Bruce Lee's Hong Kong–made *Return of the Dragon* (aka *Way of the Dragon*) was released—almost one year to the day after the release of *Enter the Dragon* —its powerful box-office performance (over $1 million in New York City alone in its first five days) was unique to Hong Kong imports.

The Hong Kong films that entered the U.S. theatrical market throughout the rest of the 1970s almost always were released through minor distributors. By this time, martial arts movies were exclusively the province of inner-city theaters, second-run houses, small-town double bills, and drive-ins. To attract inner-city audiences in Los Angeles, it was not uncommon to find English-dubbed kung fu films with Spanish subtitles in neighborhood or downtown theaters. Still, the occasional gem, like *The One-Armed Boxer vs. the Flying Guillotine,* opened quietly in neighborhood or minority theaters.

The craze for Hong Kong kung fu films also returned Japanese films to the public consciousness. Japanese imitators of Hong Kong films, like Sonny Chiba's *Streetfighter* series, entered the kung fu fray shortly thereafter, as did some samurai films such as part three of the *Kozure Ookami* (*Lone Wolf with Child* series, dubbed into English as *Lightning Swords of Death,* 1974). That film was released with the tagline, "Raise a kung fu fist and he'll chop it off," although there is no kung fu/Hong Kong component to the film whatsoever; the Japanese original was made in 1972; the video version is entitled *Lupine Wolf.* Another was Gosha's *Goyokin* (1969), released as *The Steel Edge of Re-*

venge in 1974. (Gosha's film was remade as a combination samurai film/Western by Tom Laughlin as *The Master Gunfighter,* 1975). Some years later, interestingly, part two of the *Kozure Ookami* series was more carefully reworked for U.S. distribution as *Shogun Assassin,* doubtless to capitalize on the popularity of the television adaptation of James Clavell's novel *Shogun* in 1980 (itself a reflection of America's continued interest in Japanese/Asian culture).

Meanwhile, the Hong Kong martial arts film remained in circulation because of the explosion of programming demands that came with the rise of satellite-delivered cable television in the early 1980s, along with local television programming needs. It was not uncommon to find "Kung Fu Theater" or some variation thereof in UHF outlets surrounding major cities; in the late 1980s through the early 1990s, the USA Network ran *Martial Arts Theatre* on weekend afternoons. Meanwhile, Bruce Lee had never lost his cult appeal, and his Hong Kong films and the Hollywood-made *Enter the Dragon* (1973) retained their enormous popularity. Even *Game of Death* (1978), incomplete at the time of Lee's death, found significant box-office appeal despite its clearly unfinished form. By the late 1970s, Hollywood itself began the production of martial arts films, first with the rise to stardom of Chuck Norris, then with the gradual emergence of other martial arts stars, including Sho Kosugi, Michael Dudikoff, and, later and more significantly, Jean-Claude Van Damme and Steven Seagal. The Hollywood martial arts film, though it speaks to American cultural particularities, overt and covert, derives the most of its characteristics from these 1970s Hong Kong films. Later martial arts efforts in Hong Kong, such as the films of Jackie Chan and Tsui Hark, would influence continuing Americanization of the Hong Kong genre.

Though the martial arts film remains the dominant draw for Western audiences of Hong Kong cinema even today, it was the gangster/police thrillers of the middle 1980s through the early 1990s that caught the attention of cult audiences, who demanded that, at the very least, the films appear in Chinese, preferably the Cantonese dialect in which they were originally released in Hong Kong. This lent greater artistic integrity to Hong Kong films, always previously released in hastily dubbed formats, often with the same recognizable voices in dozens of Hong Kong imports. (Though Hong Kong movies played regularly for years in Chinatowns in New York, Toronto, San Francisco, Los Angeles, and Honolulu, where Hong Kong– made Mandarin-language films predominated, shown with Chinese and English subtitles, it was the rare *gweilo* (white ghost/white person) who ventured into such theaters.) Whatever the appeal of the martial arts films however, the gangster films struck an even more responsive chord with contemporary U.S. audiences. As with Kurosawa's films of the 1950s, these gangster films, films noirs, and policiers spoke to American audiences as they might have spoken to Chinese ones. The films of John Woo and Ringo Lam fit comfortably into patterns of male-oriented action and buddy films such as those made by Howard Hawks or Sam Peckinpah, or the works of French master Jean-Pierre Melville, who had extended the film noir and gangster film into new realms of existential angst and stylish violence. As with Kurosawa's films of the 1950s and 1960s, Woo's films of the 1980s and 1990s were both familiar and pleasingly unique. And as with Kurosawa, the influence of Woo is clear across the body of Hollywood cinema; unlike Kurosawa, however, Woo is now working in

Hollywood. While few find his American films like *Hard Target, Broken Arrow,* or *Face/Off* as artistically successful as *A Better Tomorrow, The Killer,* and *Hard Boiled,* he has brought his unique stylings to an ever-larger audience than the more cult-oriented Hong Kong efforts.

Turtles and Rangers and Mario, Oh My!

Interest in Japan following World War II was understandable, as Japan shifted from powerful enemy to devoted cold-war ally. War with Japan and the U.S. Occupation had exposed Americans firsthand to Japanese culture. So, too, the Korean War brought Asia to America's attention as cold-war fever ran hot. From the 1950s on, trade with Japan became a major component of U.S. consumerism, especially in toys and electronics. Though it would provoke problems and concerns, the increasing success of Japanese automobiles in the U.S. market starting in the 1970s and Japanese purchases of U.S. real estate (not to mention Hollywood studios in the 1980s) continued to bring Japan and Japanese culture to America's consciousness. Similarly, American interest in China rose with the U.S. alliance with China against the Japanese in World War II, more negatively after the founding of the People's Republic of China and throughout the tense cold-war era. A more positive spin on China was detectable following Richard Nixon's visit to the People's Republic in 1972. In a separate development, the Hong Kong film industry established itself as a world power with the rise to prominence of the Shaw Brothers Studio and the reliance on Mandarin-language productions, enough to bring Hong Kong films onto U.S. screens. In general, U.S. interest and concern with Asia following the trauma of Vietnam made Japanese and Chinese culture particularly compelling.

To this might be added the increasingly vocal and politicized presence in the United States of Asian Americans (the solidification of Japanese Americans into the middle class, continued out-migration of Chinese from Chinatowns, increases in immigration from Korea and, of course, Southeast Asia). Changes in U.S. immigration laws in the mid-1960s and a new influx of Southeast Asians following the Vietnam War added Asian American cultural legacies to an ever-increasingly multicultural United States. U.S. culture was shifting inexorably, still struggling with racialized images of Asia and Asian Americans to be sure, but possessed of a new generation free not only of the traumas of World War II (free, too, just as significantly, of the triumphalism of World War II), but also of the trauma of Vietnam. It was this generation that would not only embrace the films of John Woo and his Hong Kong cohorts, but also create a space for Japanese culture unprecedented in U.S. history. For all of Japanese cinema's prestige as art cinema starting in the 1950s, nothing compared to the popularity of another sort of Japanese cinema.

The Japanese popular-culture texts that I have in mind here are what I think of as interrelated phenomena: anime, children's SF television programming, and video games. Though Japanese television cartoons have long been both popular and influential on American television, as discussed earlier, what came to be called anime was a pop-culture phenomenon of the late 1970s that slowly built on an increasing fan base throughout the 1980. Its rise was driven by a combination of increased interest in and availability of manga in the United States; the production of Japanese theatrical, televisual, and direct-to-video (OAV) anime for release in Japan; and the increasing availability of the VCR and the home computer in both Japan and the United States. The circulation of manga and anime was a bottom-up phenomenon, driven almost entirely by fan culture through exchange of tapes, self-subtitling, college anime clubs, and the Internet. By the time scholars and critics began paying attention to anime, it was already ensconced within a large network of international fans, many of whom had the passion of the collector and the knowledge of the scholar. Companies in the United States like AnimEigo (a combination of the words "anime" and "eigo," Japanese for "English") and magazines like *Manga-jin, Anime, Animerica,* and *Giant Robot* were produced by and for fans.[9] The editors of *Eastern Standard Time* claim that the first U.S. anime fan convention was held in 1991, long before scholars and critics had even noted the phenomenon.[10]

The target audience for anime in Japan was children and adolescents, the same audience that would take anime to its heart in the West. While there is a great range of anime, some directed almost exclusively to young children and some not suitable for those under seventeen, the bulk of anime is aimed at and appeals to adolescents thirteen and older, especially youth of high school and college age. Young characters predominate in anime texts, children and teenagers especially, and the major thematic issues of gender confusion or gender bending, role playing, bodily and sexual anxiety, and relationships to family and peers, are associated with youth, and with adolescence in particular. Thus the characteristics of anime in Japanese popular culture revolve around those arenas of stability vs. change, cultural and physical anxiety, the modern and postmodern condition, all sifted through the psychosexual development of the adolescent. In post-Vietnam, post-Watergate, postfeminist America, such anxieties are common to adolescents of both genders.

There can be little doubt that *Akira* (1989) is the best-known example of anime in the West.[11] A crossover hit into the realm of the international art film *Akira* derives from a manga, but it was a manga geared toward the male youth market.[12] Its complex animation, its post-apocalyptic setting, its SF and horror elements, and its focus on a male protagonist earmarked it for cult status among emerging anime fans. Indeed, *Akira* may have been the catalyst for the anime fan cults in the West. Its themes of rebellious youth breaking free of authority yet pursued by it and banding together for protection and a sense of family, and the adolescent allegory of transformation reflected in the process of morphing, found a receptive audience the world over as well as in Japan.

Akira is a direct outgrowth of war and postwar experiences. From the atomic bombings to the economic miracle to Japan's rise as a major economic power in the world, to overcrowding and overachieving, *Akira* speaks to a young generation in Japan. Freda Freiberg quotes a description of the stress under which Japanese exist: "Apart from the experience of the atomic bomb, . . . the Japanese nation's 'collective psyche' has endured . . . [the] pressure of living in a high-tech, collectivist but commercial society; the nation's lack of natural resources; the overcrowded living conditions; and the ever-present threat of earthquake, typhoon and fire."[13] Dan Fleming notes what he calls the imagination of apocalypse, specifically, "the Bomb"—anime and manga are filled with images of physical destruction, post-apocalyptic cities, and weird hybrid bodies.[14] I would also point out the pressures of the nuclear family on Japanese youth and the omnipresence in particular of the mother. Freiberg notes with great insight the absence of the Japanese family in *Akira* (though this is not an absence ubiquitous in anime by any means). And it is not just the family that is absent, but specifically the mother. This lack of the traditional family is common in anime, where substitute families predominate. But even when there is one parent around, it is more often than not the father. Breaking away from family in general and from mother in specific is one hallmark in the move from childhood to adolescence and from adolescence to adulthood. It is a universal phenomenon, but it takes on particular poignancy in Japan, which is so mother centered. That anime is a youth phenomenon in Japan helps explain the interaction of text and audience.

What is most striking in anime, especially the anime popular with U.S. fans, is the predominance of female characters. If one's knowledge of anime is based almost solely on *Akira*, then this feature of anime will not be evident. But such popular multipart series as *Urusei Yatsura, Dirty Pair,* and *Bubblegum Crisis* all have female characters in the leading roles, as does another popular series, *Sailor Moon* (a show geared to children that has broken out of its child slot into the adolescent fan market). *Urusei Yatsura* also has a male character of importance, but other shows in which the male character is supposed to dominate find the female characters prominent and, I suggest, more the objects of cult followings and certainly more the objects of identification: *All Purpose Cultural Cat Girl Nuku Nuku* and *Oh! My Goddess!* come to mind in this category. That is, while anime in the United States has fans of both genders, a mostly male-dominated fan culture has made anime a pop phenomenon and has taken to its collective heart, soul, and psyche so many female characters. This represents to me a significant shift in American images of masculinity that I would argue is owed precisely to the post-Vietnam context in which this fandom has arisen.

Bubblegum Crisis, described as focusing on a "sexy all-girl vigilante force known as the Knight Sabers [who] use armored power-suits," belongs generally to the mecha-anime subgenre, where robots, androids, mechanized beings, and the like prevail.[15] It is also may be linked, as Annalee Newitz points out, to the "magical girl" subgenre. For Newitz, the linking of these two subgenres is important, demonstrating "the way male and female bodies are largely indistinguishable once wedded to mecha technologies."[16] In this immensely popular series, all but one of the main characters is a woman; the only recurring male character is important, but the heroics of the plot and the emotional investment of the audience is with the women. There is a certain fetishization of the female body, it is true, in now-classic "male gaze" terms, but I would suggest that here, as in the other numerous anime with female leads, the boy audience is identifying with the girl protagonist. She may be both idealized lover and ego ideal, but it is this latter hypothesis that is so intriguing for understanding the appeal of anime to boys in the West. As Carol J. Clover points out, the predominately male audience of slasher films is not necessarily identifying with the killer, or at least not solely with the killer, but with the (usually) female victim. And in the rape-revenge subgenre of horror, the male audi-

ence is asked to condemn the rape of the heroine and root for her often literal emascu-
lation of her attackers.[17] Thus we need to point out that for anime and its related genres,
identification between audience and protagonist can cross not only cultural lines but
also gender lines.

The best example I can think of to demonstrate that anime's fans are attracted to the
form's allegories of gender identity and gender confusion is *Ranma 1/2*—the story of a
teenage boy who, when doused with cold water, turns into a teenage girl. That the boy's
father, when similarly exposed to cold water, turns not into a woman (not into his
mother, that is) but into a panda, is surely an absence, a lack, to be noted. For Newitz,
Ranma 1/2 may be allegorical of all of anime: "While quite racially mixed as a group,
otaku [anime fans] are overwhelming male, particularly in the United States. For this
reason, it is important to understand that what is at stake for Americans watching anime
is certainly bound up with gender identity, especially masculine identity." In the subgenre of magical girls (of the large genre she calls "romantic comedy"), "the men in
these anime are young, bewildered, and sexually inexperienced." This "subgenre features women who are simultaneously powerful and traditionally feminine." Ranma, as
both a boy and a girl, is a trained martial artist, thus reminding us of the continuity between anime and the older Japanese (and Chinese) popular-cultural forms already predominant in the West, a link of great significance. For Newitz, *Ranma 1/2*, and presumably other anime, has a clear reading: "Quite simply, *Ranma 1/2* demonstrates to
the young man who enjoys romantic comedy anime that he is constantly in danger of
becoming a girl. . . . Like Ranma, the male anime fan has a 'feminine half' who enjoys
passively consuming animated fantasies about love. His attachment to non-sexual romance might be said to feminize him." I will amend this a bit and point out that non-
sexual romance is not necessarily a woman's, a female, characteristic, though it might
be culturally claimed and desired that it is. I would say that it is a latency-age characteristic, not an adolescent one. Thus I disagree with Newitz's contention, suggestive and
insightful though it is, that "when American fans consume magical girl anime, partly
what they enjoy about the genre is its historical incongruence with American mainstream culture. Or, to put it another way: they are enjoying depictions of women which
take for granted that women are subordinate to men. . . . Americans consume magical
girl anime as a form of nostalgia for the kind of social situations made possible by traditional gender roles."[18]

I would say instead, in more psychoanalytic terms, that latency or even infantile sexuality is the preferred mode, a union with the all-powerful mother, a sense of longing
for wholeness, an unwillingness to acknowledge sexual difference, and a fear of the gendered self. Thus *Ranma 1/2*, with its appeal to children as well as adolescents, is closer
to an allegory of the transition from latency to adolescence than to the transition from
adolescence to adulthood. The infantalization of the Japanese man may be the roots of
this dominant strand in anime, but it is clearly a strand with cultural tendencies across
the West, too. However, the psychoanalytic model I proposed should also be seen in con-
gruence with the cultural shift I indicated earlier, that the "nostalgia" for traditional gender roles may be less important than the shift these roles have undergone, a shift where

a man might more easily identify with a woman under the sign that all gender roles are social constructions.

The motif of a magical girl and a young male appears in another anime that I think is archetypal: *All Purpose Cultural Cat Girl Nuku Nuku*. The family set-up, as in *Ranma 1/2*, is a father and son, though in *Cat Girl*, the boy's mother is a major character. The predominant character, however, is the cat girl—an android who has the brain of a cat but who can speak. The young boy's reliance on her is clearly as an all-powerful mother who, ironically or not, protects him for his actual mother and from other women in the service of his mother. Because she is not his mother, however, Nuku Nuku can be eroticized, not so often for him but very often for the audience. I would suggest that the audience for this anime, as for many others, can identify with both the boy and the cat girl, especially if we allow the *otaku*'s relative lack of social skills and physical prowess as an allegory of an outsider, the cat girl, who is a superhero.

If the gender bending of anime is not yet convincing, perhaps a reminder of the martial prowess of women and the women stars of the Hong Kong cinema can further delineate this cross-gender or transgender appeal. Fans of the contemporary Hong Kong cinema have made cult favorites of not only the John Woo/Chow Yun-Fat gangster films, but also the new generation of martial arts films. (I am claiming, let us recall, that fans of anime and martial arts films not only are part of the same demographic, but also are often one and the same—fans of anime, fans of Hong Kong, and, as we will see, fans of Mario). In this constellation of stars of the martial arts films, we find the likes of Brigitte Lin Ching-hsia, Maggie Cheung Man-Yuk, and Michelle Yeoh (aka Khan), whose stardom in the States as cult figures is every bit as significant as their careers in Hong Kong; indeed, Michelle Yeoh is aiming for U.S. stardom. Popular films in the United States include *The Heroic Trio, The Executioners,* and *Wing Chun,* in which there is no significant male heroic presence, and the gender-bending *Bride with White Hair* and the gender-defying *The East Is Red* are part of every respectable Hong Kong video collection.

Anime and Hong Kong film fans' ability to identify across cultural, racial, and gender bounds bespeaks the fluidity of identity within the postmodern context. Similarly, the prevalence of pop-culture intertextuality in anime elicits the same sort of appeal as the works of Quentin Tarantino, an icon for some but by no means all anime fans. I would, however, contradict Newitz: Anime is not an example of "cultural imperialism in reverse," and Americans are not in fact "being colonized by Japanese pop culture."[19] For Newitz, the fact of being colonized makes American fans anxious, makes them feel disempowered and dependent and hence feminized. If this is true, it must mean either that anime fans outside of America in the West—in Canada, Great Britain, and the other places where anime has found a receptive audience—are similarly experiencing anxieties over cultural imperialism, or that the issue of Japan vs. America is not a salient one for understanding anime's appeal in the contemporary context.

Japanese and Hong Kong popular culture in the form of anime and new-style martial arts films were only part of the late 1980s and early 1990s infusion of Asian popular-cultural forms. We need also think of "hybrid" forms such as *The Teenage Mutant*

Ninja Turtles and the *Mighty Morphin Power Rangers,* both of which had a popularity and an impact even anime has barely matched. These phenomenon deserve greater detailing than I can manage here, but no survey, however brief, can afford to ignore what is arguably the most sensational sign of Asia's impact on U.S. culture (along with video games, discussed later).

SF anime like *Astro Boy* and the live-action *Ultraman* paved the way for the acceptance of *The Teenage Mutant Ninja Turtles* and the *Mighty Morphin Power Rangers.* The Turtles grew out of shifts in action/adventure comic books, especially those from the Marvel Comics group, which had felt the impact of martial arts movies and of manga. By the 1980s, kung fu, ninjutsu, and bushido (Japanese martial arts and spirituality) had found their way into such cult comics as *Daredevil, Dr. Strange,* and *The X-Men,* among others. American comic books and Asian martial arts would merge in 1984 to create *The Teenage Mutant Ninja Turtles.* A cult success from the start, the Turtles attained a level of popularity few could have imagined. What Marsha Kinder calls a "supersystem" of Turtlemania emerged in the late 1980s, culminating in the 1990 feature film that remains the highest grossing martial arts film in history, taking in over $135 million in the domestic U.S. box office.[20] The much-inferior 1991 sequel grossed almost $80 million in the United States, making it the fifth-highest-grossing martial arts film of all time.

Even before the films reached such unprecedented success, the Turtles appeared in an animated television series and had been marketed in a wildly successful line of toys. Dan Fleming notes the circulation of this hybrid form that became the Turtles supersystem:

> The Youli Toys factory in Guangzhou was . . . where many of the successful plastic *Teenage Mutant Ninja Turtles* figures were manufactured for Playmates Toys Inc., a major operation with a Californian address. But the parent company, Playmates Holdings, is a Hong Kong business that had already successfully sold to the nationalistic Japanese an electronic talking doll, cleverly marketed as a language-learning aid. Fortified by having proved that such markets are not impregnable to outsiders, Playmates licensed the Turtles from the writers of a very minor US comic book, because they liked the martial-arts element, and then marketed the whole concept back into the United States. . . . The big US and European-based toy companies could only look on while the Turtles dominated the 1988 Christmas market and continued to achieve considerable worldwide success for the following three years.

As with robot toys in the 1960s, Asian manufacturers had a clearer sense than American ones of what children would buy and buy into. Fleming: "Just why the prominent martial arts or kung fu features of *Teenage Mutant Ninja Turtles* were so well received by children at the time is an intriguing question. That aspect of the original comic clearly attracted Playmates Holdings of Hong Kong."[21]

But, as we have seen, martial arts movies from Hong Kong and Japan had found a receptive audience in the United States in the 1970s and found an even more receptive audience in the 1980s (when Hollywood was developing a martial arts genre of its own with much inspiration and co-optation from Hong Kong cinema).[22] And if martial arts movies from Hong Kong and Japanese films of an earlier generation demonstrate something of the increasing Westernization of Asia, so, too, they continue to demonstrate shifts in Western culture: Martial arts dramatize the tension between individualism and collective discipline. For the Chinese and Japanese, martial arts reflect shifts in the old notion of obedience to the "collective spirit"; for the West it reflects a growing awareness of the limitations of "individual will."[23]

Teenage Mutant Ninja Turtles is what I have called a hybrid form. Clearly influenced by Japanese and Hong Kong cinema of an earlier generation and reformulated for U.S. consumption (the Turtles have a "Japanese" rat master but are coded as California surfer dudes, despite their alleged New York City locale). This idea of a supersystem imported, adapted, and transformed for American use reached its height in the *Power Rangers* phenomenon of the early 1990s. Sci-fi fantasy, martial arts, and cheesy special effects never had it so good as on the Fox Television program derived from a popular Japanese children's series. "Shown six days a week on US television in late 1993 and 1994 . . . the Power Rangers series at its peak was reaching 57 percent of 6–11-year-olds in the United States. . . . All told, industry analysts believe, sales of Ranger toys and other paraphernalia could approach $1 billion [by 1995]—what the Turtles generated at the peak of their popularity."[24] Toys, Halloween costumes, a spurt in enrollment in martial arts classes for children, and the inevitable feature film were only some of the offshoots of the phenomenon. It was a hybrid form in that it combined the special effects and fight sequences of a Japanese live-action SF program with new footage of a multicultural, multiracial, dual-gendered group of all-American teens.

The basis of the *Mighty Morphin Power Rangers* was *Kyoryuu Sentai Zyuranger* (Dinosaur Task-Force Beast Ranger) produced by Toei Studios, in which five Japanese young adults—Geki (Tyrannoranger), Goshi (Mammothranger), Dan (Triceraranger), Boi (Sabertigerranger), Mei (Pteryoranger)—are released from suspended animation to combat a villainess named Bandra. The *Power Rangers* went on the air in Japan in 1992 and ran for fifty episodes. It was a typical, if popular, kind of show called *sentai*, which means task force or battle group. These shows typically revolve around a team of spandex-clad, helmet-wearing, karate-wielding heroes, each dressed in a different color, who also have their own fighting machines to defeat monsters originating from an evil alien force. Fleming understands that the *Power Rangers* was an outgrowth of popular Japanese children's programming:

> Since the 1960s, and in particular the animated films of Tezuka Osamu . . . Japanese television has developed several hugely popular genres of highly stylised animated or live-action series, mixing martial arts, science-fiction and traditional Japanese romantic adventure narratives. . . . In anime . . . and manga . . . Japanese popular culture has explored its own distinctive universe of apocalyptic imagery . . . robot-human hybrids, deformed characters, martial arts and traditional warrior-caste themes (ninja, samurai, etc.) and an ever-present fascination with technology.[25]

One can trace a direct line from animated series like *Mobile Suit Gundam* (1979–), *Bubblegum Crisis* (1987–), and the film *Akira* (adapted from a manga) to such sentai shows. Similarly, the use of "zords" (dinosaur-like machines that can combine to form a Megazord) may be related to "Transformers"—rocket ships, space tanks, and other vehicles disguised as robots. Though there are precedents in Japanese literature and mythology, Tanner suggests that the immediate inspiration came from Go Nagai's anime *Mazinger Z* in 1972. These new-style transformers became popular toys not only in Japan, but in the United States and were in turn the inspiration for an American-made 1970s television series, *The Transformers*. Tanner also notes that the imagery in shows like *Power Rangers* was familiar both to Japanese and American audiences through the impact of blockbusters like *Star Wars*: "Was it only coincidence that the Jedi Knights and the Imperial Storm Troopers of the *Star Wars* trilogy looked so much like samurai and Shogun-era warriors, who had long been the mainstay of Japanese comic books and animated cartoons and who, during the late 1960s and early 1970s, were making their appearance on the toy market as futuristic warriors?"[26] It was not just Kurosawa's *Hidden Fortress* that provided the Japanese-derivation and inspiration for *Star Wars*, the most popular trilogy in film history. *The Mighty Morphin Power Rangers* was easily assimilable into this ongoing intercultural system.

A typical internet fan page for the *Power Rangers* relates how Haim Saban (producer, chair, and chief executive officer of Saban Entertainment) was traveling in Japan and saw a series of sentai television programs. Saban realized an immediate opportunity to import the concept, since the helmets and suits cover the faces and bodies of the actors and thus it would be simple and inexpensive to hire likable, no-name, inexperienced, nonunion actors and actresses to pose as teenagers and dub their voices over the original Japanese footage. Attempts to sell the project to network television were unsuccessful until the president of the Fox Kids Network bought Saban's idea in 1993.[27]

For Dan Fleming, *Power Rangers* continues to demonstrate the ongoing cultural melange of Japanese and American characteristics: "The persistent theme through all of this is the uneasy balance between individuality and teamwork. The American high-school kids . . . are individuals, their differences exaggerated in part by ham acting. . . . But the masked Japanese fighters are a team, their identities wholly submerged. . . . In super-hero mode they become a hierarchy . . . and their ultimate destiny is to become cogs in the Megazord machine." This motif has a particularly potent to appeal to children struggling with identity and attendant issues of conformity, role playing, confusion, competition, and so on, Fleming suggests.[28] As the appeal of anime to adolescents may be seen as an allegory of sexual maturity, so *Power Rangers* appeals to childlike urges to be absorbed into a group, a team, and to feel empowered by these mergers as well as through technology.

Both the Turtles and the Power Rangers were implicated in an even larger Asian investment in U.S. popular culture and must thus be seen as part of a supersystem that involves not only manga, anime, and feature films but also, and perhaps most importantly, video games. Perhaps the primary engine of the Asian impact on American culture came not through cinematic or televisual sources, but through the introduction of the Nintendo Entertainment System to the United States in 1985. It may be coincidental that this introduction coincided with the 1980s boom in U.S. martial arts films—such as the films of Chuck Norris and Sho Kosugi, and *The Karate Kid*—but the relationship between martial arts and home video would be one of mutual influence and impact. Similarly, the introduction of video games is part of the rising popularity of anime, which it resembles in form and, to some extent, function. Video games, in arcades and then in the home, had been a fact of life since the early 1970s, breaking through in 1979 with the introduction of hardware from the likes of Atari, Midway, and Mattel, among others.[29] But a video bust occurred in 1982, mostly for lack of software. As with robot toys and transformers, the Japanese had a better take than U.S. industry on the meaning and impact of home video: "The Famicom, or 'Family Computer,' which Nintendo started selling in 1983, is now often cited as having changed the face of entertainment (it would be called the Nintendo Entertainment System in the West)."[30]

Breakout hits like *Donkey Kong* and, most significantly, the *Super Mario Brothers* (both invented by Miyamoto Shigeru for Nintendo) would allow home videos in a few short years to overtake movies as the major form of mass entertainment: "In 1992 Japanese video game giant Nintendo for the first time made profits that exceeded the earnings of Hollywood movies in total for that year: a phenomenally sudden reorientation of what we think we mean by the term 'popular culture.'"[31] U.S. retail sales for video games in 1997 reached $5.5 billion, and while not every video game is of Japanese origin, virtually every unit on which video games are played is: Nintendo's N64 and Sony's PlayStation dominate the market, with Sega in third place. The Top 25 best-selling games are all played on either PlayStation or Nintendo 64.[32]

Links between home video and Chinese and Japanese martial arts movies show how bound up these seemingly discreet forms are: Though the Mario Brothers games are among the most popular video games, martial arts, especially for older players, is one of the dominant genres. *Street Fighter* and *Mortal Kombat*, for instance, are ubiquitous both in arcades and in home systems. Both have been turned into feature films. *The Teenage Mutant Ninja Turtles*, which began as a comic book and evolved into an animated series, spawned arcade and home video games. In the other direction, *Goldeneye*, based on a recent entry in the long-running James Bond series, spawned one of the most currently popular video games. Much as was the case with anime, whose visual imagery is the foundation for video games, some of the gender-bending potential may be found in video games. Among the most today are *Tomb Raider*, which features a female protagonist but whose primary appeal is to male players. The release of *Lara Croft, Tomb Raider* (2001), the feature film version of this game, shows the continuation of the circular interaction among these interrelated pop-cultural texts.

In the slightly more than four decades from Kurosawa's *Rashomon* to *Tomb Raider*, Japanese and Chinese popular culture have had an impact on U.S. culture that is almost impossible to measure. The list goes on unabated, it seems. The whole Pokemon phenomenon, for instance, continues to demonstrate the openness of American society to Japanese pop-culture imports and the Japanese ability to map and predict global culture. Here I hope I have at least sketched in some of these cultural transmissions and some of why they have occurred. I take heart in what I see as a genuine opening up of U.S. culture and society to these Asian influences, especially on the part of today's youth.

Notes

1. Lent, introduction to *Asian Popular Culture*, 3.

2. Ibid., 4.

3. In addition to *The Magnificent Seven (1960)*, overt remakes of *Shichinin no samurai* include *Battle Beyond the Stars* (1980), *Steel* (1980), *Uncommon Valor* (1983), and *Dune Warriors* (1990); significant borrowing can be detected in *The Wild Bunch* (1969) and *Conan the Barbarian* (1992), to name but two. Interestingly, *Seven Samurai* was also remade in Hong Kong as *Zhan shen tan (Beach of the War Gods,* 1973). The most famous remake of *Yojimbo* (Bodyguard) is Sergio Leone's spaghetti Western, *A Fistful of Dollars* (1964), but other remakes include *Omega Doom* (1996) and *Last Man Standing* (1996). Though not a remake of *Yojimbo, The Bodyguard* (1992) references the film to the extent that Kevin Costner's character watches it during the course of the movie.

4. Ron Tanner, "Mr. Atomic, Mr. Mercury, and Chime Trooper: Japan's Answer to the American Dream," in Lent, *Asian Popular Culture,* 81.

5. Ibid, 80, 84–85, 80.

6. Barbara Ryan, "Blood, Brothers, and Hong Kong Gangster Movies: Pop Culture Commentary on 'One China,'" in Lent, *Asian Popular Culture,* 61.

7. David Desser, "The Martial Arts Film," in *Film Genre 2000: New Critical Essays,* ed. Wheeler Winston Dixon (Albany: SUNY Press, 2000).

8. The discussion of Hong Kong cinema's impact on the U.S. box office starting in 1973 is drawn from David Desser, "The Kung Fu Craze," in *The Cinema of Hong Kong: History, Arts, Identity,* ed. Poshek Fu and David Desser, 19–43 (New York: Cambridge University Press, 2000).

9. *Giant Robot* is by no means devoted exclusively or even primarily to anime. Its success represents the overall appeal of Asian and Asian American culture not only to Asian Americans but to many non-Asians as well.

10. Yang et al., *Eastern Standard Time,* 55–56.

11. The discussion of anime is adapted from Desser, "Anime," 21–34.

12. Freiberg, "*Akira* and the Postnuclear Sublime," 94.

13. Ibid., 97.

14. Fleming, *Powerplay,* 181–182.

15. Yang et al., *Eastern Standard Time,* 59.

16. Annalee Newitz, "Magical Girls and Atomic Bomb Sperm: Japanese Animation in America," *Film Quarterly* 49, no. 1 (fall 1995): 8.

17. See Clover, *Men, Women, and Chain Saws.*

18. Newitz, "Magical Girls," 4, 6, 5.

19. Ibid., 11, 12.

20. Kinder, *Playing with Power,* 122.

21. Fleming, *Powerplay,* 113, 140.

22. See Desser, "The Martial Arts Film."

23. Fleming, *Powerplay,* 141–142.

24. Quoted in ibid., 19.

25. Ibid.

26. Tanner, "Mr. Atomic," 96, 99.

27. See http://www.cyberverse.com/~piero/mmpr/faq5.html.

28. Fleming, *Powerplay,* 22–23, 27.

29. Kinder, *Playing with Power*, 88.

30. Fleming, *Powerplay*, 180.

31. Ibid., 56.

32. See http://www.techweb.com/investor/stort/INV1998 and http://www.videogameheaven. com/vgslhipr.htm.

Selected Bibliography

Clover, Carol J. *Men, Women, and Chain Saws: Gender in the Modern Horror Film.* Princeton, N.J.: Princeton University Press, 1992.

Desser, David. "Anime: Its Origins in Japan and Its Appeal to Worldwide Youth." In *Pictures of a Generation on Hold: Selected Papers,* ed. Murray Pomerance and John Sakeris, 21–34. Toronto: Media Studies Working Group, 1996.

Fleming, Dan. *Powerplay: Toys as Popular Culture.* Manchester: Manchester University Press, 1996.

Freiberg, Freda. "Akira and the Postnuclear Sublime." In *Hibakusha Cinema: Hiroshima, Nagasaki, and the Nuclear Image in Japanese Film,* ed. Mick Broderick, 91–104. London: Kegan Paul, 1996.

Kinder, Marsha. *Playing with Power in Movies, Television, and Video Games: From Muppet Babies to Teenage Mutant Ninja Turtles.* Berkeley: University of California Press, 1991.

Lent, John A., ed. *Asian Popular Culture.* Boulder, Colo.: Westview Press, 1995.

Weisser, Thomas, and Yuko Mihara Weisser. *Japanese Cinema: The Essential Handbook.* Miami: Vital Books, 1996.

Yang, Jeff, Dina Gan, Terry Hong, et al. *Eastern Standard Time: A Guide to Asian Influence on American Culture, from Astro Boy to Zen Buddhism.* Boston: Houghton Mifflin, 1997.

Part III

Women in Modern Asia

CHAPTER 11

Of Executioners and Courtesans: The Performance of Gender in Hong Kong Cinema of the 1990s

Augusta Lee Palmer and Jenny Kwok Wah Lau

Hong Kong's contemporary electric shadows, taken collectively, project a cinematic world of gendered contradictions onto global screens. If the female protagonists of Hong Kong cinema could be united in a single celluloid world, what images would their encounters, their juxtaposition, produce? In an imaginary Chungking Mansions arcade, a resurrected Ruan Lingyu (the tragic 1930s screen star remembered in Stanley Kwan's 1991 *Actress*) raises her eyes forlornly toward heaven, while the androgynous Asia the Invincible (the transgendered hero/ine of the *Swordsman* series) gallops by, shooting down her foes with sewing needles. Asia dismounts and ducks into a phone booth, disguises herself in a trench coat, blonde wig, and dark glasses, replaces her lethal needles with a mere revolver. A few miles away, the doomed reincarnation of Golden Lotus (the lead character in Clara Law's *The Reincarnation of the Golden Lotus*), the "most famous whore in Chinese history," drives her car off a cliff—waving to Thelma and Louise on the way down. The aging hard-bitten party girl of Wong Kar-wai's *Days of Being Wild* rebukes the mournful ghost of the prostitute who drives the plot of Stanley Kwan's *Rouge* for her naiveté, while the Heroic Trio sweeps down on motorcycles to save the world. Meanwhile, Huang Feihong's Thirteenth Aunt and fiancée—the female lead in the *Once upon a Time in China* series—dutifully cranks away, capturing the whole scene on her turn-of-the-century movie camera.

This is a random catalogue of a few of the contradictory images of women in contemporary Hong Kong Cinema. This essay will take the form of a bricolage of images of women in Hong Kong cinema while examining the provenance and significance of those images.[1] In particular, we examine some surprisingly regressive portrayals of gender in the "art films" of Hong Kong's second wave. We look at the work of Wong Kar-wai, Clara Law, and Stanley Kwan in terms of its portrayal of women, which is incommensurate with the complex reality of women's lives in Hong Kong. We will also look at a few representations of gendered subjects in contemporary popular cinema texts that, in some cases, actually reveal a more nuanced approach to gender. Our examples comprise Asia the Invincible from *Swordsman II,* the women of *Executioners,* and Thirteenth Aunt from the *Once Upon a Time in China* series. Finally, we will question the incongruity of these two groups of films in terms of their representation of women. Why this discrepancy? And, why have popular genres been more permeable in some ways to a renewed vision of gender than supposedly progressive and postmodern art films?

Women in Hong Kong—Triple Unhappiness: Capitalism, Patriarchy, and Paternalism

Even a cursory look at sociological and anthropological studies of Hong Kong quickly reveals that women there have long faced a triple bind. In Hong Kong, the traditional Chinese patriarchy was underwritten and supported by a paternalistic British imperialism which preferred a hands-off approach to governing the territory in order to foster burgeoning capitalist interests.[2] Thus, the frequently made assumption that the oppression of women in the colony is solely derived from a "traditional" Chinese patriarchy is a gross oversimplification. Yet, despite this triple oppression, the status of women in Hong Kong is high in relation to that of women not only in other nations in Southeast Asia, but also in the "first world."[3]

Gender equality in Hong Kong has a mixed and contradictory history largely due to the British approach to administering the territory, which depended on the compliance of Chinese elites to ensure stability and productivity. To minimize change, the British "froze" much of Hong Kong law in its nineteenth-century form, which reflected a period in which England as well as China regarded women as chattel. Thus, while Britain later rejected some of its "traditional" patriarchal baggage as part of its alliance with that famous behemoth, progress, internal and external orientalists insisted that "Chineseness" must remain tied to patriarchy. Thus, concubinage, for example, remained legal in Hong Kong until 1971, decades after the practice was illegal on the mainland. Only in the late 1980s did women in the New Territories begin to demonstrate against the antiquated laws that prevented them from inheriting property, winning that right only with the repeal of the laws in 1994.[4]

Yet women are paramount to the economic success of Hong Kong. Indeed, Hong Kong's economic miracle was largely accomplished by the cheap labor of female factory workers. And, now that Hong Kong has shifted from a blue-collar economy and developed a large middle class, that labor has merely been farmed out to a different set of young, underpaid female workers in Southern China.[5] Hong Kong women are largely well educated and sometimes achieve high positions in government and industry. However, as in most industrialized centers of the world, sexism is still apparent in both daily life and cinematic representations.

Women in Hong Kong Cinema

Just as the nimble fingers and long hours of underpaid female workers were essential to the backstage labor which produced Hong Kong's public economic miracle, women have played a crucial role in Hong Kong filmmaking, not only as actresses but also as screenwriters and directors. The Hong Kong New Wave that burst onto the international scene in the early 1980s was preceded by woman director Tang Shu Shuen. Her first film, *The Arch* (1970), shot expressionistically by Satyajit Ray's cameraman, was "the standard-bearer of art films produced in the territory."[6] Unfortunately, the talented Tang was able to make only four films in her career.

Although most of the first wave's filmmakers were male, Ann Hui, one of the leaders of the New Wave, has forged a career for herself and in her films has consistently pursued critiques of Hong Kong society and modernity, often via female protagonists.[7]

The second wave of the late 1980s included a few more women directors, among them, Clara Law and Mabel Cheung, as well as directors trained by Ann Hui such as Stanley Kwan. In the late 1980s and early 1990s, a number of popular and art films centered on female characters appeared, making use of the charismatic screen presence of Maggie Cheung and Brigitte Lin. These "woman-centered" films ran the gamut from exploitation films to high art, and they produced just as wide a range of representations of women.

This small body of films prominently featuring female characters, along with the emergence of a few more female directors, generated a simplistic optimism about gender representation not necessarily merited by the content of the films themselves, as Stephen Teo's reaction demonstrates:

> These new developments regarding the representation of gender have to some degree deflected the criticism often made of Hong Kong films that they are fearful of and hostile to women. It is perhaps the most popular manifestation of the new thinking which takes into account the growing role women play in Hong Kong affairs, not least in the film industry. That women's role is emphasized in the male-dominated genre of martial arts films is the clearest sign yet of the more mature direction taken by Hong Kong cinema from the late 80s onwards, mainly by the second wave of new filmmakers. Hong Kong is defined and felt through the heartbeat and perspectives of women in the films of Stanley Kwan and others.[8]

Teo's brief rendering of gender representation in Hong Kong film begs the questions of this essay. First, is the representation of women in the late 1980s and early 1990s really a "new development" that manifests women's changing roles? Second, are the representations of gender in martial arts and other popular films actually similar to the representations of gender in second-wave art films? Third, are the second-wave directors primarily responsible for a "progressive" representation of gender? Finally, in the films of Stanley Kwan and other second-wave directors, is Hong Kong's being "defined and felt through the heartbeat and perspectives of women" a sign of the importance and "progressive" quality of female characters, or merely the familiar use of female characters to symbolize political and cultural crises?

Like the issue of gender equality in Hong Kong, the representation of gender in Hong Kong cinema is an ambiguous and complex issue that deserves closer attention than it has been given thus far. Although many woman-centered texts appeared in the late 1980s and early 1990s, narrating a woman's story does not necessarily indicate a feminist or even a progressive attitude toward gender. Additionally, many of the depictions of women in contemporary Hong Kong cinema draw on earlier traditions of representation—both negative and positive. So, although the quantity of women's stories in this period is an interesting phenomenon, they might be better represented as a new spin on old ideas, rather than classified as an entirely "new" development.

Teo is right to draw attention to the importance of women in martial-arts films, but not because those films have always been male dominated. The earliest Shanghai cinema featured *nuxia* (female knight-errant) heroines drawn from the pages of popular fiction, and, although martial-arts films have more commonly had male protagonists, female martial-arts performers like Feng Hsu in King Hu's *Touch of Zen* have been memorable. We would argue that much popular filmmaking draws on a long tradition of popular female heroines. In contrast, the art films of the second wave have tended to be allegorical melodramas that focus perceived cultural crises in the bodies and stories of women. This tendency also has plentiful antecedents, in both spoken drama (as opposed to operatic drama) and 1930s Shanghai film production. Thus, these two modes of representation are quite distinct from one another and, regardless of whether one assigns a "positive" or "negative" value to either, should not be conflated.

Despite the relatively advanced social status and education of Hong Kong women, many second-wave filmmakers have portrayed women in a surprisingly atavistic manner largely because of their tendency to use women as the focus of conflicts between past and present, tradition and modernity, and more specific geopolitical conflicts between Hong Kong and mainland China. We agree that it is precisely "through the heartbeats and perspectives of women" that Hong Kong is portrayed in many second-wave art films. The choice of the word "through" is crucial, as it makes clear that the films are not about women, but about Hong Kong. This idea is certainly nothing new. Ackbar Abbas and many others have interpreted Hong Kong cinema from 1984 onward as an allegorical cinema which mourns the "disappearance" of Hong Kong before the fact. However, what we want to explore here is the kind of gender economy produced by these allegorical constructions. In terms of representation, these films are both about gender and about the conflict between Hong Kong and mainland China. Though gender issues cannot be entirely disentangled from political tensions, for the most part issues of gender representation have been ignored once a political allegory has been established. Using several textual examples, we want to explore how political allegory and nostalgic melodrama inflect gender representation.

By way of contrast, we will also explore the representation of women in some more popular Hong Kong film texts from the same period that in general present more positive as well as more ambiguous portrayals of gender. As our examination of these texts will indicate, some of this openness may be derived from precedents in Chinese literature. Drawing on the tradition of knight-errant fiction and earlier depictions of women warriors, as well as other generic conventions, the popular texts we have chosen also display a willingness to "play" with elements of past representations and are less fixed in their notions of gender than the second-wave art films we discuss.

Unidimensional Types and Historical Heroines: Tradition and Modernity, Part 1

The aesthetic innovation and lush photographic beauty of the films of the second wave are not matched by their fairly retrograde representations of women and gender politics. Films by second-wave directors have often represented women through the use of unidimensional "types" that are rarely explored critically. The fact that many of these types represent demeaning roles for women is not just elided but often celebrated for its pure artifice. Despite his recent foray into more politically correct territory with the alternately lyrical and bitter gay romance *Happy Together* (1997), the films of Wong Kar-wai are an excellent example of the preference for sharply drawn types of women. *Days of Being Wild* (1990) follows the story of a playboy named Yuddy (Leslie Cheung) as he seduces a stadium concessions operator (Maggie Cheung) and later takes off on a doomed search for his mother in the Philippines. The women in this film are as flat as paper dolls. Maggie Cheung's ingenue spends her time mooning over Yuddy, long after he has replaced her with the less demanding Mimi. Yuddy's adoptive mother is an aging party girl from Shanghai who seems to have very little under her cosmetic carapace. *Fallen Angels* (1995), scorned women resort to stereotypical hysteria or cleaning binges as well as masturbation to mourn their lost loves. The argument can be made that there is a sense of gender reciprocity in the airport/airplane philosophy of love elaborated in *Chungking Express*, in which some partners in love affairs land only in order to take off again, while others represent safe havens, waiting for someone else to land and make their lives complete. This philosophy is reflected in Wong's other films as well. A sad policeman in *Days of Being Wild* (Andy Lau) moons over Maggie Cheung's lovelorn ingenue, while she is besotted with the unresponsive Yuddy. However, more screen time as well as more sympathy is almost always given to the ruminations of male characters; female characters are frequently as mysterious as Yuddy's missing biological mother or as cruelly drawn as his adoptive one.

Gayatri Spivak's words on Indian widow sacrifice have been appropriated more than once to describe the relationship between women and modernity in China.[9] Spivak's notion that "the figure of the woman disappears, not into a pristine nothingness, but into a violent shuttling which is the displaced figuration of the 'Third World Woman' caught between tradition and modernization" is indeed useful for looking at the representation of women in Hong Kong cinema.[10] Most astute is her idea that the woman does not disappear into a "pristine nothingness," since women in Hong Kong cinema have particularly cluttered "disappearances" and "violent shuttlings" when an overlay of allegories of geopolitical conflict between Hong Kong and mainland China is added to their representational burden.

The tendency to burden female characters with the allegorical weight of the nation, the people, or cultural identity seems especially strong in art films.[11] These allegories use female protagonists as stand-ins for Hong Kong (in rape narratives) and for the mainland (in motherland narratives), or as mediators of the conflict between tradition and modernity. The analysis of gendered roles within these allegories has had to wait for later, much like the rights of real women have had to wait until the problem of the nation or culture in crisis was (never) solved.[12]

Farewell China. "It is the uneasy tension and mutually constituting relationship between the bodied (as index to women's oppression as commodified and exploited bodies) and the socialized (as index to political and cultural complexes) that I see as central to the examination of gender issues here," writes Shih Shu-mei in "Gender and a Geopolitics of Desire."[13] This conflict between the "bodied" and the "socialized" is exemplified by *Farewell China,* a 1990 Clara Law film which depicts the travails of a mainland woman who immigrates to the United States and her ensuing descent into madness. The film has not received much critical attention, possibly due to its hyperbolic and histrionic political content. Precisely because of this, it provides an excellent case study for the interaction of gender and political tensions.

After introducing its characters at home in mainland China, Farewell China's narrative takes the form of a detective story, as Zhou (Tony Leung Ka-fai) travels to New York illegally to search for his missing wife, Li (Maggie Cheung). Abandoned by his legal immigrant friends, who fear repercussions for aiding him, Zhou is befriended by a Chinese American teenage runaway and prostitute, who helps him in his search. The film repeats some modernist tropes of 1930s Shanghai films, which portrayed "woman as a quintessential figure of the city, and the city as a discursive construct with which to capture (that is, figure out) woman."[14] This time, the city is New York and the woman is an enigma largely because the trauma of living in a new land has forced her to split into several personalities, only one of which remembers the husband and child she left behind in China. After she is finally "found," Li reverts to another personality (who makes her money bilking other immigrants for fictitious projects in the old country) and, believing her husband is an unknown assailant when he calls out to her, kills him in front of a model of the "Goddess of Democracy," or Statue of Liberty, that stood in Tiananmen Square.

Law shot the film from a script written by her husband Eddie Fong, who was not afraid to tell the story in broad strokes—as evidenced by the ending. *Farewell*'s political metaphors are both readily apparent and relatively confused: the destruction, spiritual pollution, and loss of a formerly pure China to the West is clearly marked by Li's descent into madness on the mean streets of New York and is echoed by the hardness of Zhou's teen prostitute accomplice. The slaughter of innocents in Tiananmen by those who should have "recognized" them is more than evoked by the ending. Maggie Cheung's portrayal of Li is histrionic yet somehow believable, emphasizing the bodied over the socialized. Her supposedly socialized contamination is countered by her inherent drive and desire to leave China, which prompt her to apply for visas multiple times and finally to have a child in order to become unattractive after she was refused a visa because she was "too pretty." This early and seemingly "unnatural" drive is necessary to accomplish the political allegories of contamination and destruction, but it also undermines them by locating the blame for the tragedy in Li's transgressive ambition. Both *The Reincarnation of the Golden Lotus* (Law, 1989) and *Temptation of a Monk* (Law, 1993) repeat the narrative of the self-destructive woman who chooses to transgress social mores and is therefore punished.

Cheung's acting also foregrounds the performance of self as she morphs from a mainland mom into a fashionably dressed New York businesswoman, from a frightened, lost immigrant to a gutsy and thoughtful wife who can carry a purloined mattress from Brooklyn to the Bronx on her bicycle so her husband will have a place to sleep when he joins her in the land of milk and honey. Perhaps the film's most poignant moment comes when, through a random twist of fate (Zhou has given up on finding Li and is delivering Chinese food to one of her neighbors), Li meets Zhou. She pulls him into a small room where she is dwarfed by the upended mattress, turns on a tape of songs from the Cultural Revolution, and begins to relive the traumatic days of their romance, which began in the turbulent mid-1970s when everyone feared that all their actions were subject to Party scrutiny. This kind of tearful and, for the spectator, masochistically inflected moment is a kind of set piece for some second-wave art films.

Rouge. The tendency toward melodramatic hyperbole is also pronounced in the woman-centered second-wave films with period settings. Though the romance of these settings allows films like Stanley Kwan's *Rouge* and *Ruan Lingyu* (also known as *Actress* and *Center Stage*) to escape criticism as histrionic and excessively melodramatic, closer examination shows similar structures of gender representation and melodrama at work. To open her discussion of melodrama and masochism, Rey Chow invokes the oft-repeated story of the Chinese translators of *La Dame aux camelias,* whose sympathy for the title character was so great that, as they worked, their loud weeping could be heard outside the house. This story illustrates the sheer power of melodrama itself and, as Chow goes on to explain, the crucial connection between fictional female suffering and masochistic readers/spectators. This masochism is spectatorial identification with the woman as a figure of suffering and humiliation that reflects or embodies societal ills.[15] Chow does not remark upon the hybrid nature of the particular form of melodrama the translators created.

Stanley Kwan has been called the contemporary master of the *wenyi* melodrama genre, a hybrid of Chinese theatrical drama influenced by the West introduced into mainland films in the 1930s and 1940s.[16] Kwan's *Rouge* (1988) lodges its heroine in the interstices between East and West, tradition and modernity, nostalgia and remembrance. The story is about a 1930s courtesan named Ruhua (Anita Mui), the victim of an unsuccessful suicide pact, who returns to 1980s Hong Kong after waiting fifty years for her lover's arrival in the netherworld. When she arrives at a Hong Kong newspaper to place a classified ad, she meets a modern Hong Kong couple who help her to complete her quest.

Gender performance is foregrounded in *Rouge.* The star-crossed lovers meet when Twelfth Master (Leslie Cheung) is captivated by Ruhua's performance in male drag of a Cantonese song from the 1910s. Ruhua's gift for artifice is her most charming qual-

Maggie Cheung as Ruan Lingyu in *Center Stage*, directed by Stanley Kwan, 1992.

ity. Twice in the film, Twelfth Master takes note of the seductive power of Ruhua's "many looks": heavily made up, lightly made up, made up as a man, and not made up at all. When he idly wonders which is the "real" Ruhua, she answers that the real one is quite ugly. This emphasis on artifice through makeup and performance is not limited to Ruhua. Twelfth Master himself becomes a minor actor in Cantonese opera. But his aptitude for performance and artifice is less developed than Ruhua's.

The interest in Cantonese opera and the life and times of 1930s courtesans reveals the film's concern with both Hong Kong history and a "sociology of prostitution."[17] Kwan is clearly preoccupied with detailing the disappearance of historical Hong Kong at the hands of progress and, by extension, presaging the disappearance of present-day Hong Kong culture that was expected to accompany the handover of Hong Kong to the People's Republic. The modern couple, Chen and Chu, become sleuths looking for evidence of Ruhua and Hong Kong's fifty-year-old past. They comb through ancient newspapers and listen to Ruhua's reminiscences. They discuss her *chiqing* (excessive capacity for love), leaving viewers to find their modern lives and modern romances a bit dull in comparison to Ruhua's Technicolor past. The city is once again the key to capturing the mysterious woman, but in this case, Ruhua is also the key to (re)capturing the city of Hong Kong.

What is ultimately disappointing about *Rouge* is that its immersion in nostalgia and its fascination with forgotten artifices become mere candy coating for 1997 anxieties. However, when the candy melts, the residue of misogyny and humiliation remains. The interest in the sociology and history of a 1930s prostitute is a desire merely to resurrect the surfaces of the 1930s rather than to get inside or understand them. Because Ruhua is constructed as an unknowable mystery and elusive ghost, the film shows no real interest in understanding either what might have motivated a woman like her, or that sacrificing everything for love appears so attractive to her because her real life would have been filled with misery. Further, the film emphasizes the predictable humiliation of Ruhua in front of the wealthy parents of Twelfth Master, as well as her eventual abandonment by her (less than) ideal lover.

This is the site where the film cathects with the masochistic spectatorship mentioned earlier. Ruhua's suffering and loss is portrayed as hyperbolic and excessive, as when her weeping for Twelfth Master is heard from the next room by the modern couple. Yet, she is clearly marked for spectatorial identification by the number of subjective shots assigned to her. This marking is further underscored by the modern couple's attempts to identify with Ruhua, as if they were modeling this masochistic identification for the spectator.

In a discussion of *Rouge*, Rey Chow posed the question: "Perhaps nostalgia is a feeling looking for an object?"[18] If so, what is *Rouge*'s nostalgia searching for? Is it what exactly is yet to be lost, somehow more identifiable in the past than in the present? Clearly, a large part of the appeal of *Rouge*, *Ruan Lingyu*, and other second-wave films with period settings like Mabel Cheung's *The Soong Sisters* (1997) is their nostalgic setting, which celebrates the minutia of past lives in the form of rouge lockets and yellowing newspapers that reported on the life of courtesans. Yet, there are parts of daily life in the past that may not be so appealing, especially to women, as to deserve resurrection. Surely, women may have a different feeling about those fetching cheongsams. As Pia Ho, a member of the Hong Kong performance group Zuni Icosahedron, said about the choice of cheongsams as costumes for the troupe's performance of *Chronicle of Women*: "The cheong sam represents a kind of formalism. When a woman is wearing one she has limitations on her actions. She has to be very elegant and very graceful when she moves around. So, to an extent, it's a kind of bondage."[19] Thus, nostalgia and recycled images become mere imprisonment, restricting the movements and agency of female characters with their obsessive entanglement with objects. The performance of woman becomes the performance of making up, with no attempt to find the real Ruhua, let alone to question the codes of gender representation at work in 1930s imagery.

Women in Popular Cinema: Tradition and Modernity, Part 2

If one finds unsatisfying the heroines of high-minded political allegories and melodramas with period settings, another set of heroines with a history presents much more satisfying fare. Several representations of women within the popular martial-arts genre present quite a bit more grist for the analytic mill. Women warriors are no novelty in the history of Chinese fiction and film. The story of Hua Mulan, the girl who took her father's place in the army, dates from the sixth century. In the early years of the century, *nu xia* (female knight-errant) heroines were popular in fiction and film. Part of their appeal is precisely their juxtaposition of male and female qualities: martial skill combined with feminine grace, and death-defying feats performed by blushing maidens. This is the same multiplicity of looks (or performed roles) Twelfth Master finds so appealing in Ruhua.

Asia the Invincible. Asia the Invincible, the sympathetic but lethal villain of *Swordsman II* (Ching Siu-tung and Tsui Hark, 1992), pushes the envelope of the gender boundaries seen in *Rouge* much further. Brigitte Lin Ching-hsia portrays Asia, who, over the course of the film, goes through a kind of spiritual sex change that results in an ambiguous portrait of cross-dressing, mistaken identity, and tragic love. Teo describes Asia as an example of "the female as a dangerous, elusive creature," which would seem to place her in a role similar to the mysteriously psychotic Li Hong in *Farewell China* or the beautiful and inscrutable Ruhua of *Rouge,* whose deep love causes her to add sleeping pills to her lover's suicide cocktail just to make sure he joins her in the underworld.[20] However, Asia is entirely unlike these two characters. First, her lethality does not result from either her powers of seduction or from being scorned in love, but rather from her greed for power and her martial-arts skills. Second, and much more important, Asia is neither male nor female. S/he has given up her maleness to attain greater martial-arts power, but s/he is clearly a hybrid being.

Despite being the villain, Asia is the most fascinating character in the film, far outpacing the supposed hero, Lingyu Chong (played by Jet Li). Asia is appealing because, while she is neither clearly male nor female, she is clearly human in her desire and love (revealed only in the final sequence) for the bumbling Lingyu Chong. She is also appealing because she is so obviously a formidable opponent. She is able to entice Lingyu Chong with her beautiful looks, kill people at twenty paces with those devilish embroidery needles, and aim for a craftily achieved total domination. However, she is unable to attain Lingyu Chong either sexually or romantically because of her biological male status.

Swordsman II certainly has its own essentializing attitudes toward gender. The ability to do needlework and love excessively, coded as feminine, is Asia's ultimate undoing. But more importantly, her transgendered identity is a result of her insatiable lust for power, and her ability to frustrate her male and female lovers could be construed as a less than progressive view of a transsexual identity. Nonetheless, the ability to imagine and perform a character whose gender is only partially assigned by biology indicates a more nuanced approach to gender as a nonessential category that cannot always be successfully applied. In addition, the appeal of Brigitte Lin's performance and the fascination the character may hold for spectators also undermine the more narrow visions of this villainy.

Brigitte Lin Ching-hsia as Asia the Invincible in *Swordsman II,* directed by Ching Siu-tung, 1992.

Executioners. Executioners (Ching Siu-tung and Johnny To, 1993), the sequel to *The Heroic Trio* (Johnny To, 1993), plays fast and loose with many gendered tropes of Hong Kong cinema. An action film with an apocalyptic setting, scenes of mass protest, and a struggle to free the world from the machinations of a demented and scarred villain and his henchmen, *Executioners* clearly falls into the Hong Kong hand-over anxiety film genre. Yet, its three heroines make it more interesting than one might expect from its plot. After the action of *The Heroic Trio,* the three female friends have gone their own ways. Chat (Maggie Cheung), the party girl perfectly at home throwing grenades in seamed thigh highs, has become a mercenary. The more puritanical Ching (Michelle Yeoh), dressed in leftovers from *Red Batallion of Women,* has joined a kind of resistance movement. The formerly invincible Wonder Woman, Tung (Anita Mui), has promised her police commissioner husband to focus on being a mother and to avoid "superheroing" around. She uses her powers only occasionally to amuse her daughter, Tungching. Fate, not to mention the apocalypse and some nasty villains, quickly dispatches Tung's husband into the hereafter, and the girls are reunited in the good fight.

Elements of the family melodrama—set into play by the supposed conflict between Tung's life as Wonder Woman and her responsibilities as a wife and mother—quickly build as Tung's husband twice asks her, "What kind of mother are you?" But this is a generic red herring, which is fractured by the death of Tung's husband and Tung's imprisonment. While Chat is stuck with the cute Tung-ching, Tung languishes in prison long enough to do an impression of Ruan Lingyu's icon of sacrificing motherhood in *The Goddess*. But Anita Mui's goddess is not content to stare forlornly heavenward for long; soon she is sucking the blood from a live mouse to get the strength for a violent jail-break and to reassert her Wonder Woman identity.

Meanwhile, Ching is protecting a phony president with her life, and Chat and Tung-ching are on an expedition to find an uncontaminated fresh-water source. Despite the usual obstacles, the three are reunited at the end, when Ching sacrifices herself to help the other two women defeat the nefarious and hideously deformed masked villain. When the president's aide thanks Chat and Wonder Woman their trouble, Chat says, "We didn't do it for you, we did it for friends." In this way, the remaining heroic duo refuses to be co-opted by the spinmasters of male authority. Finally, the two women and Tung-ching wander off together, forming a new kind of female family in lieu of Tung's earlier and unsatisfying union with the police commissioner.

If the Heroic Trio is the fictional descendant of *nu xia* fiction, it has substantially changed the paradigm. *Executioners* defies the earlier tradition by its formation of a female community. Perry Link notes that the female knight-errant in early-twentieth-century popular fiction is not subversive because she is so exceptional that her exception proves the rule.[21] But, to have three such women working together begins to undermine the exceptional nature of their forcefulness. In addition, Chat and Tung's eventual forming of a female family unit marks their refusal to support the status quo.

Executioners is by no means an ideal text, whatever that might entail. The film is quite open about enjoying the occasional soft-core exploitation moment—like the Heroic Trio giggling through a not very revealing bubble-bath scene. Its characters are less than three dimensional—perhaps it is hard to imbue a machine-gun battle with any degree of intellectual or emotional depth. The film does not represent a lesbian utopia, as Chat and Tung's relationship is depicted as strictly platonic.[22] However, the way in which it subverts the maternal melodrama is by allowing the mother figure to become a super-heroine on her own terms instead of caring for her family first and foremost. The film also refuses to kowtow to male physical superiority and suggests tentative female community building. In this way the film's subversive portrayal of women exceeds its predecessors and many of its contemporaries.

Huang Feihong's Thirteenth Aunt. Thirteenth Aunt (also known as Aunt Yee and played by Rosamund Kwan), though by no means a traditional woman warrior, is another popular female character by first-wave director/producer Tsui Hark. Although Aunt Yee has been dismissed as just another passive foil to a mythic martial-arts hero, her role in the *Once upon a Time in China* series deserves more attention. Kwai-cheung Lo has written about the emergence of technology in the series and notes the importance of Aunt Yee in what he calls the "outward-focus" of the series. He dismisses her character as a less than feminist representation. Yet to take the third film of the series as an example, Huang Feihong's Thirteenth Aunt and fiancée plays a crucial role in the film. Though she is not a martial-arts heroine, meaning that she does not fight, she manages to dupe the Russian villain into a bait and switch: He follows her hoping to retrieve a motion picture camera loaded with film that shows an attempted execution of a Chinese official by the Russians.

She is an ambiguous character, viewed as "foreign" by fellow Chinese because of her Westernized attire, but viewed as exotic by the foreigners who sometimes pursue her. She is "modern" and Westernized but puts modern invention to the service of tradition, as when she arranges for the repair of the steam engine used to manufacture the homeopathic remedies made by Huang Feihong's father. She is the master (or mistress) of motion picture technology. She shoots, develops, and projects her own films, using the technology to record "traditional" magical spells, to figure out a mystery, or to record a crime. Although she often defers to Huang verbally, her actions skirt around her promises. Her smooth and assured manner often provides comedic contrast to Huang's bumbling outside the realm of gong-fu fighting. She is the one who makes their untraditional marriage plans clear to Huang's father, just as she is the one to manage useful but possibly scheming foreigners and unwieldy or unfamiliar technology. Thirteenth Aunt negotiates the terrain between tradition and modernity without making sacrifices and lives in a world of (male) violence without being either destroyed or co-opted by it.

In many ways, Thirteenth Aunt is the female character most in tune with the actual position of Hong Kong women. She is by turns accommodating and intimidating. She is non-Western but Westernized by her education and experience living abroad, yet she still feels the need to appease traditional patriarchy. She treads a careful path of negotiation with male authority in order to carve out her own place.

Conclusion

In an article about female symbols of resistance during another period of more violent cultural crisis—the Japanese invasion and occupation of China during the 1930s and 1940s—Hung Tai-chung cites two types of heroine used to bolster national sentiment in popular spoken dramas. These female types, the courtesan with a patriotic heart of gold and the woman warrior who fights to save the nation, are both rewritings of earlier traditions of representation. One of the courtesans, Pan Jinlian (sometimes translated as Golden Lotus), is drawn from a minor adulterous character in a fourteenth-century novel, *The Water Margin*. But one of the female warriors, Hua Mulan of recent Disney fame, is much older. And, as Hung points out in a comparison to the strategic portrayals of Joan of Arc by the French Resistance and the Vichy government, neither the types nor their utilization for multiple causes in times of cultural crisis is specific to China.

Interestingly, in the years before the handover, a time of cultural crisis for Hong Kong, these two types reappear in Hong Kong cinema. A courtesan is the heartbeat of *Rouge*, while woman warriors appear as both villains, like Asia the Invincible, and heroines, like the women of *Executioners* and *The Heroic Trio*. In one case, the same character re-curs—the *Water Margin*'s Pan Jinlian, whose story was adapted into a popular stage play in the 1930s, reappears in Clara Law's 1989 *Reincarnation of the Golden Lotus*, reincarnated just in time for the Cultural Revolution and fated to repeat most of the patterns of her twelfth-century life. Killing herself in a flaming car crash presages not only the more liberated leap of Thelma and Louise, but also the impending "death" of Hong Kong itself.

Just as in the 1930s, images of women and the practical lives of women are undergoing drastic changes in contemporary Hong Kong. However, the anxieties surrounding both gender and cultural crisis were more diffuse and ambivalent in the 1980s and 1990s than in the 1930s, which is reflected in the variety of contradictory representations of women in the film texts we have examined. But the gap between courtesan and woman warrior seems to have widened in these recent texts, forming a schism between art film representations and popular representations not elucidated in Hung's study of 1930s spoken drama. How is it that films like *Executioners* and the *Once upon a Time in China* series provide more satisfying representations of women than those of *Days of Being Wild* or *Rouge*?

There are several answers to this question. One is that the woman warrior is now the more progressively inflected image of the two types of female symbol of resistance available in the fictional canon. Another explanation may be the distinction between the pure fantasy of an action film and the nostalgically inflected verisimilitude of a period melo-drama. The focus of *Rouge* is a historical footnote, so we expect reality and are disappointed at the paper-thin image of Ruhua. On the other hand, a film like *Executioners* initially seems to promise a cathartic round of ass-kicking violence, so we are pleasantly surprised when its representation of gender roles is less retrograde than expected. In addition, *Executioners* never hints at a "sociology of super heroines" in the way that *Rouge* hints at a "sociology of prostitution." Relinquishing the expectation of verisimilitude may give action filmmakers more room to play with female iconography and stereotype than their nostalgic counterparts who are excavating the past for art film subject matter.

There is another more complex way to understand the multiple layers of contradiction in the representation of women in contemporary Hong Kong cinema. On the one hand, there are "art films," which some might expect to be more modern by virtue of their creation by younger directors who have been exposed to progressive ideologies and are actively engaged in finding "new" aesthetics, but who are nonetheless regressive in their depiction of women. On the other hand, we have observed "popular" *wuxia* films, products of traditional Chinese folklore that often support patriarchal values, yet that contain depictions of stronger, more self-determined female protagonists. Our explanation here will encompass a web of interlocking conditions and traditions that link literary tradition and film practice to class and gender.

As we mentioned earlier, despite the prevalence of the patriarchal in Chinese literary and cultural history, there have long been literary and theatrical genres, particularly the wuxia or martial-arts genre, that depict strong and exceptionally self-directed female protagonists. However, these strong female protagonists are always treated as exceptions. Not only are they always in the minority among a majority of male warriors, but they are also exceptions because of their skill in the martial arts and their ability to beat the men at their own game in a man's world. In modern Hong Kong, martial-arts stories derived from folklore have been revitalized by high-tech special effects. Scenes that create a powerful sense of the fantastic, as compared to the more primitive optical effects used in the same genre during the 1960s and 1970s, are attractive to a young and largely middle-class audience. These films are popular precisely because they are a masterful mixture of both traditional folklore characters and modern cinematic presentation. Because of the accepted generic tradition of wuxia and contemporary class practice, the strong and sometimes lethal female protagonists in these films do not necessarily offend the male Hong Kong audience or create a controversy over supposed male bashing in the way that films like *Thelma and Louise* did in the United States.

Though patriarchal societies throughout the world share basic similarities, each cultural and temporal context produces its own modes of patriarchal practice. Thus, patriarchy is practiced differently in other parts of the world than in Hong Kong. As most of the population of Hong Kong has consisted of refugees, survival has been a major concern. The insecurity of life in exile has encouraged Chinese pragmatism to reign supreme. Under British rule, education was mandatory for children of both sexes, and employment—particularly government employment, which offered better pay—was relatively open to both sexes. Thus, some families would support any child, regardless of gender, who showed the ability to achieve academically, as academic achievement was and still is a relatively guaranteed route to upward mobility in Hong Kong. This practice was viewed as a kind of family investment, since the child's later career success would, due to both the practice of filial piety and economic networks based on familial relationships, directly benefit the family, especially the parents.

Similar survival needs on the societal level also facilitated (relatively) nondiscriminatory practices in a broader arena. The period between the 1950s and the end of the 1970s was one of intense struggle for Hong Kong, first for survival, and later for economic leadership in the global marketplace. This spirit of competition encouraged the job market to take in anyone who could do a good job. The history of Hong Kong's film and television industries naturally reflects this larger societal trend. The tendency to hire women who could get the job done became especially apparent when men were perceived as failing to accomplish needed corporate or societal goals. In the 1970s for example, the first strong woman in the field of television, Leung Suk-yee, was appointed to head TVB (one of only three television stations in Hong Kong at the time) only after several male predecessors had failed.[23] Under Leung's leadership, TVB reached a high point in market dominance that has yet to be surpassed. Another strong woman, Cheung Man-ye, was appointed top program supervisor in the drama section at RTHK (another of the three major stations). Her unique philosophy and style of leadership led to RTHK's dominance in the field of television drama. Many directors of these RTHK TV dramas later became key figures in the Hong Kong New Wave; among them, Ann Hui also became one of the strong women in media. The accomplishments of these female television executives was so impressive that the term "strong woman" was created by the print media in the 1970s to describe them and then came into popular usage, which led to greater public acceptance of women in business and society. The strong-woman phenomenon expanded into the realm of politics with women like Chan Fong An-sung, who has been the chief secretary for administration since 1993, that is, the head of the government's administrative branch, and Fan Tsui Lai-tai, a member of both the legislative and the executive councils during the eighties, who became president of the Hong Kong Legislative Council in 1997. An important addition to this list of strong, self-directed women is the precursor of the strong woman in Hong Kong politics, Yip Shek-yan. A British woman who served on Hong Kong's legislative council, Yip has spoken up for the local Chinese, women, and the working class for decades.

Hong Kong Chinese middle-class professional women, because of their education and career accomplishments, tend to have more presence in both social settings and workplaces than their U.S. counterparts. Relative gender equality is more recognizable in the middle class than in either the upper or lower classes. Since these middle-class women are only midlevel professionals, their authority in the workplace and in society at large is still quite limited when compared to that of their male counterparts. High-profile and high-status positions are available only to a handful of "lucky" professional women, who are as much an exception in Hong Kong's contemporary reality as they have been in folklore and in the literary tradition. Like martial-arts heroines, successful female executives remain exceptions that simultaneously challenge and uphold the general rule of patriarchal dominance. (Research indicates that some upper-level women executives tend to protect their special status and collude in a sexist attitude).[24]

Unfortunately, this class-based partial gender equality is quite fragile, subject to change whenever an environment or tradition that encourages gender hierarchy asserts itself. For example, in the realm of secondary education, even though the proportion of women professionals is relatively high (about 45 percent), the percentage of male teachers promoted to administrative positions is disproportionately high. According to 1991 statistics, men hold approximately 70 percent of school principals, subject chairs, and other administrative positions.[25] In the civil service sector, which is seen as a model for employment relations, only 31 percent were female and only 5 percent held directorate-level positions as late as 1993.[26]

In the film industry, one finds that film production—despite its tradition of exceptional strong women—follows the generally sexist rule. Female stars and directors have often been subject to discrimination. It is commonly believed that Tang Shu Shuen, the first woman director in Hong Kong, who made such outstanding films as *The Arch* (1970) and *China Behind* (1974), might have had a better chance to succeed had she made her appearance ten years later.[27] As if the general societal tendency toward discrimination were not enough, there is a long tradition of regarding women in the theatrical and entertainment industries as in some ways equivalent to prostitutes.[28] The contemporary directors of Hong Kong art films have studied the filmmaking traditions of Shanghai, Hollywood, and Hong Kong, all of which are entrenched in sexist practice despite occasional lip service to the contrary. Not surprisingly, the majority of these directors are male, which reduces the likelihood of a personal investment in changing the existing gender hierarchy. Furthermore, there is still no strong opposition to the sexist tradition. There has been little consistent feminist film or media criticism in Hong Kong. The feminist critiques that exist are often drowned out before their message can be heard, let alone absorbed. For example, in 1992 the Women and Media Concern Group of the Hong Kong Association for the Advancement of Feminism published in *Women's News Digest* a list of ten sexist television advertisements. Other than a very brief mention on radio news, it was basically ignored by the larger society.[29] In addition, if one refuses to consider the self-sacrificing female characters in melodrama as strong women because of their complicity with the patriarchy, there are very few precedents for strong female characters outside of the wuxia tradition. In light of this, it hardly seems surprising that Hong Kong art films rarely depict female characters out of sync with both the melodramatic tradition and the culture of film production in Hong Kong.

Returning to the imagery we mentioned at the beginning of this essay, we could look for contradictions in the negotiation of gender roles epitomized in the performances of a single actress, Maggie Cheung. Her many looks draw the spectator to Cheung's own star image as surely as Twelfth Master was drawn to Anita Mui's Ruhua in *Rouge*. Setting aside our knowledge of the separation of star and role for a moment, we can wonder whether Cheung (or for that matter any woman) is the pampered but charismatic international female star of contemporary world cinema immortalized in *Irma Vep*. Or is she the recreated Ruan Lingyu of *Actress/Center Stage*, sadly killing herself over gossip and lying still as death itself in the background while a procession of male directors relate their memories to the audience? Is she *Farewell China*'s intrepid mainland mom who emigrates to America to make a better life for herself and her family, the consummate New Yorker bilking other emigrants, or the psychotic convergence of the two? Or is she Chat, the party girl, mercenary, and savior of the universe she plays in *Executioners*? More importantly, as both Hong Kong itself and the Hong Kong film industry are transformed, what roles will Hong Kong women play in the years to come?

Notes

1. When we began work on this essay in 1999, there were not many works available on the representation of gender in Hong Kong cinema. Happily, that has already begun to change. Essays that tackle the subject and some of the films we discuss here, in greater detail and from a variety of viewpoints, include Shuqin Cui's "Stanley Kwan's *Center Stage*: The (Im)possible Engagement Between Feminism and Postmodernism," *Cinema Journal* 39, no. 4 (summer 2000): 60–80; on *The Heroic Trio* and *Executioners*, Anne T. Ciecko and Sheldon Lu's "*The Heroic Trio*—Anita Mui, Maggie Cheung, Michelle Yeoh—Self-Reflexivity and the Globalization of the Hong Kong Action Heroine," in *Post Script: Essays in Film and the Humanities* (special issue on Hong Kong cinema) 19, no. 1 (fall 1999); and in the same issue of *Postscript*, Amelie Hastie's "Fashion, Femininity, and Historical Design: The Visual Texture of Three Hong Kong Films."

2. For a more detailed exposition of this tripartite patriarchal structure, see Pearson and Leung's introduction to *Women in Hong Kong*.

3. See, for example, Theresa W. N. Tsang, "The Women's Movement at the Crossroads," in Pearson and Leung, *Women in Hong Kong*, 135, which indicates that 88 percent of teenage girls in a Hong Kong sample planned to go to the university, as opposed to 45 percent in a U.K. sample. In addition, 88 percent of the U.K. sample expected to be married with children and not working by age twenty-five, while 88 percent of the Hong Kong sample expected to be single and pursuing careers at the same age.

4. These demonstrations to change the property laws of the New Territories present a fascinating and ambivalent process of negotiation between New Territories women, Hong Kong intellectuals and feminists, Chinese patriarchy, and British colonialism. See Evans and Tam, *Hong Kong*.

5. See Salaff, *Working Daughters of Hong Kong*, for a series of case studies on Hong Kong's working women in the early 1970s and a 1995 overview of the changes made since then.

6. Teo, *Hong Kong Cinema*, 138.

7. For a discussion of Hui's films in terms of their social critiques and progression toward a feminist viewpoint, see Elaine Yee Lin Ho, "Women on the Edges of Hong Kong Modernity," in Yang, *Spaces of Their Own*, 162–190.

8. Teo, *Hong Kong Cinema*, 202.

9. See Chow, *Woman and Chinese Modernity*, opening aphorisms, and Lilley, *Staging Hong Kong*, 181.

10. Gayatri Spivak, "Can the Subaltern Speak? Speculations on Widow Sacrifice," *Wedge* 7/8 (1985): 128.

11. For a similar interpretation of the representation of women in political allegories based in handed-over anxieties and gender deconstruction, see Lilley, *Staging Hong Kong*.

12. This perceived need to wait until national issues are resolved before gender issues are broached, and the consequences of that waiting, are a trope of writing on women's rights in Hong Kong. See, for example, Pearson and Leung's introduction and Tsang's "Women's Movement," both in Pearson and Leung, *Women in Hong Kong*.

13. Shih Shu-mei, "Gender and a Geopolitics of Desire: The Seduction of Mainland Women in Taiwan and Hong Kong Media," in Yang, *Spaces of Their Own*, 283. Shih explores in detail the depiction of mainland women in films from both Hong Kong and Taiwan.

14. Yingjin Zhang, *The City in Modern Chinese Literature and Film: Configurations of Space, Time, and Gender* (Stanford, Calif.: Stanford University Press, 1996), 186.

15. See Chow, *Woman and Chinese Modernity*, chapter 4, "Loving Women: Masochism, Fantasy and the Idealization of the Mother."

16. Teo, *Hong Kong Cinema*, 208–211.

17. Chow, *Woman and Chinese Modernity*, 64.

18. Ibid., 61.

19. Lilley, *Staging Hong Kong*, 202.

20. Teo, *Hong Kong Cinema*, 201.

21. Link, *Mandarin Ducks and Butterflies*, 214.

22. There is a body of films that do strive for a lesbian utopia, while freely acknowledging the value of lesbianism as an exploitation-film commodity. Category Three films (Hong Kong version of NC 17) such as the *Naked Killer* series and films like *Portland Street Blues* deserve further scholarly attention.

23. Names in this section follow Chinese tradition of placing the family name first, since this is how the Hong Kong public recognizes them.

24. Robert I. Westwood, "The Politics of Opportunity: Gender and Work in Hong Kong," in Cheung, *Engendering Hong Kong Society*, 17.

25. See Po-king Choi, "Women and Education in Hong Kong," in Pearson and Leung, *Women in Hong Kong*, 101–132.

26. See Westwood, "The Politics of Opportunity," 68.

27. Shing-hon Lau, "Shu Shuen: The Lone-Rider in Hong Kong Cinema in the '70s," in *Hong Kong Cinema in the Seventies: Special Issue of the 8th Hong Kong International Film Festival* (Hong Kong: Hong Kong Urban Council, 1984), 106–109.

28. For a historical perspective on the slippage between actresses and prostitutes as well as a discussion of how actresses began to effect social change, see Weikun Cheng, "The Challenge of the Actresses: Female Performers and Cultural Alternatives in Early Twentieth-Century Beijing and Tianjin," *Modern China* 22, no. 2 (April 1996): 197–233.

29. Cheung, *Engendering Hong Kong Society*, 228.

Selected Bibliography

Abbas, Ackbar. *Hong Kong: Culture and the Politics of Disappearance.* Minneapolis: University of Minnesota Press, 1997.

Barlow, Tani, ed. *Gender Politics in Modern China: Writing and Feminism.* Durham, N.C.: Duke University Press, 1993.

Cheung, Fanny M., ed. *Engendering Hong Kong Society: A Gender Perspective of Women's Status.* Hong Kong: Chinese University of Hong Kong Press, 1997.

Chow, Rey. *Woman and Chinese Modernity: The Politics of Reading Between East and West.* Minneapolis: University of Minnesota Press, 1991.

Evans, Grant, and Maria Tam. *Hong Kong: The Anthropology of a Chinese Metropolis.* Honolulu: University of Hawaii Press, 1997.

Lilley, Rozanna. *Staging Hong Kong.* Honolulu: University of Hawaii Press, 1998.

Link, Perry. *Mandarin Ducks and Butterflies: Popular Chinese Fiction in Early Twentieth-Century Chinese Cities.* Berkeley: University of California Press, 1981.

Pearson, Veronica, and Benjamin K. P. Leung, eds. *Women in Hong Kong.* New York: Oxford University Press, 1995.

Salaff, Janet W. *Working Daughters of Hong Kong: Filial Piety or Power in the Family?* New York: Columbia University Press, 1995.

Teo, Stephen. *Hong Kong Cinema: The Extra Dimensions.* London: BFI, 1997.

Yang, Mayfair Mei-hui, ed. *Spaces of Their Own: Women's Public Sphere in Transnational China.* Minneapolis: University of Minnesota Press, 1999.

CHAPTER 12

The Woman with Broken Palm Lines: Subject, Agency, Fortune-Telling, and Women in Taiwanese Television Drama

Lin Szu-Ping

This essay focuses on popular television in Taiwan and its interwoven relations with culture, gender politics, and subjective agency. I am convinced that women in different parts of the world are situated within unique social conjunctures, within particular local cultural practices and discourses. With a focus on the subjectivity of Taiwanese women, I examine a specific constituent of social and cultural construction—the concept *of nu ming* (the fortune of a woman)—activated in the fortune-telling system of folk beliefs and practices in Taiwan. Through the examination of the gender-biased nu ming, especially in the myth of "women with broken palm lines," I explore the agency in a Taiwanese prime-time television show that works against the way the fortune-telling system constitutes women.

When it comes to the constitution of the subject, it is often argued that subject is constructed by cultural, social, political, and historical contexts.

> To claim that the subject is constituted is not to claim that it is determined; on the contrary, the constituted character of the subject is the very precondition of its agency. For what is it that enables a purposive and significant reconfiguration of cultural and political relations, if not a relation that can be turned against itself, reworked, resisted. . . . We need to ask, what possibilities of mobilization are produced on the basis of existing configurations of discourse and power? Where are the possibilities of reworking that very matrix of power by which we are constituted, of reconstituting the legacy of that constitution, and of working against each other those processes of regulation that can destabilize existing power regimes?[1]

These possibilities are the essence of the concept of agency. Therefore, as Judith Butler points out here, it is crucial to question the condition of agency, not to take it for granted. Agency, and its ability to resignify, works against power because the subject is never outside of power: "Construction is not opposed to agency; it is the necessary scene of agency, the very terms in which agency is articulated and becomes culturally intelligible."[2]

With these concepts of subject and agency in mind, I examine the television show *Shun-Niang: The Woman with Broken Palm Lines,* and grapple with the construction of Taiwanese women by nu ming in the fortune-telling system, and the possibility of reconstructing it in the social sphere.[3] In the process, I offer a lens through which to look at the possible social maneuvers and operations that the concept of agency exercises, and the meanings they may convey to women.

Nu Ming and the Construction of Women

Fortune telling has long been a popular folk cultural activity in Chinese and Taiwanese societies; its basic concepts can be traced back thousands of years to traditional Chinese philosophical thought like *ying/yang wu hsing,* the major principles in the interpretation of the cosmic and human worlds in ancient China. In the 1990s, traditional fortune-telling beliefs and practices showed no signs of dwindling but on the contrary seemed to be on the rise in Taiwan, through books, newspaper columns, television programs, and even Internet web sites.[4]

With the social changes occurring in Taiwan, including opportunities for work and education that empower women with more knowledge, assurance, and economic independence, Taiwanese women have come a long way from the time when the fortune-telling beliefs controlled their lives. However, as fortune-telling is still common, many women continue to be constructed by its beliefs and practices; they constitute most of the people who seek guidance and predictions through fortune-telling, especially concerning matters of love and marriage.[5] The credibility of folk customs and fortune-telling practices, or the social/cultural/psychological underpinnings of their popularity, is not the focus of this essay; rather, my concern from a feminist perspective is for fortune-telling's grave gender bias. The theories and practices of the fortune-telling belief system were established in a firmly grounded ancient patriarchal society. Today, there are still women who live under its discriminating and suppressive influence, and my case study will demonstrate this by examining the television phenomenon regarding women with broken palm lines.

This is where the meaning of agency in feminist politics comes to bear: not necessarily for breaking out of the construction of fortune-telling in folk cultural customs and beliefs once and for all (a question still under debate), but for breaking out of its unequal and discriminating constitution of women. In contemporary Taiwan, the feminist movement has gained much momentum since the late 1980s, thanks to the tremendous efforts of many women's movement activists.[6] Because of their dedication and hard work, myriad issues of gender equality and antipatriarchy have been brought to public attention in society and undergone discussion and debate—including concerns about equal employment opportunity; women's status in the civic laws of kinship; women's welfare during pregnancy, childbirth, and child rearing; and problems of marital violence, sexual harassment, and other forms of gender discrimination. An examination of some of the traditional beliefs established under the patriarchal structure could not come at a more appropriate time.

In all the branches of traditional fortune-telling (*suan ming*), the term "nu ming" refers to judging a woman's fortune. One major traditional theory of nu ming describes eight special patterns of a woman's fortune: *chun* (pure), *ho* (gentle), *ching* (clean), *kuei* (noble), *cho* (indecent), *lan* (excessive), *chang* (dissolute), *yin* (lascivious).[7] These eight patterns divide women into two groups: those endowed with the first four patterns of "good fortune" who are fit to be virtuous and dutiful wives, and those who are not. Under these rules, judgments of fortune are prescribed from the male perspective to maintain the continuity of the family system—to choose "good wives" (pure, gentle, clean, and noble) who are able to take on and pass down the responsibilities of women—caring for the household and bearing children to continue the family line. Women with good fortunes are therefore regarded as beneficial for the family, able to *wang fu wang tzu* (bring honor, prosperity, and glory to their husbands and sons). Nu ming, a woman's fortune, thus becomes the social symbol of a woman's meaning and value to a society established upon the patriarchal family system.

Women with the four evil patterns of nu ming—*cho, lan, chang, yin*—not only are regarded as having bad fortunes because of those patterns, but also and more importantly are viewed as bringing ill fortune to *ke* (jinx) their husbands and children. When we examine the descriptions of women whose bad fortunes categorize them as indecent, excessive, dissolute, or lascivious, and who are said to jinx their husbands, we realize these descriptions apply, in modern terms, to women considered independent, ambitious, intelligent, and sexually attractive or active.

When the ancient fortune-tellers prescribed these rules, women whom they presumed to defy and deviate from the ideal social norm of the "gentle, virtuous woman" who helps maintain the patriarchal family structure were thus labeled women of ill fortune. And the misfortunes that these women were presumed to bestow on others have come to serve as excuses for their male counterparts' anxiety about their maintenance of power. Under this construction, being women of good fortune is an honor, while being women of ill fortune is a curse.

Palmistry: Women and Broken Palm Lines

According to books on palmistry, the principle of the method of fortune-telling that involves nu ming is, as in physiognomy, based on the belief that people's "internal elements" are always in accord with their external features, that one can discover and judge people's temperament and character from outward appearances—including the statement and configuration of facial features and palm lines—and thus predict their fortune

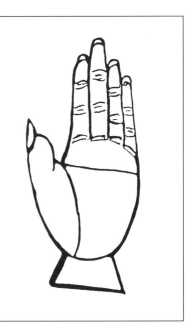

Drawing of broken palm lines.

in life.[8] Even today, palmistry is one of the most popular fortune-telling methods in Taiwan.[9]

The most famous judgment based on nu ming in palmistry, and probably in all the traditional fortune-telling practices regarding women, is the reading that involves women with broken palm lines. According to palmistry writers, there are three groups of palm lines to look at when telling fortunes—the major lines and the secondarily important rising lines and significant lines.[10] The major palm lines consist of three fundamental lines that foretell a person's "predetermined" fortune in life: the line of life, the line of reason, and the line of emotion. When the line of reason and the line of emotion merge into one line across the palm, the pattern is called *tuan chang wen* (broken palm lines), which is said to be hereditary.[11] Because of the belief that a woman with broken palm lines would jinx her husband and her son, that throughout her life misfortune would befall her family, a woman with broken palm lines in traditional society would often be feared and despised; she would be shut out by the community, especially in terms of marriage. If she got married, she would probably be mistreated and detested by her husband's family because of the pernicious fortune she might bring.

With ideological constructions in the fortune-telling system rooted in a patriarchal structure, men and women with the same outward attributes receive entirely different readings. In palmistry, men with broken palm lines are considered to be favored with auspicious prospects in life, and to succeed more easily than others.

In some books on palm reading, a woman with broken palm lines are not "feminine looking" (read: does not look or act like a woman who fits traditional norms), will try to control her love life, but will still fail to have a happy marriage. Other writings suggest that people with broken palm lines should be heedful because they are prone to beating others to death, and the women will "have the psychological tendency to kill their husbands."[12]

The Discourse of Fortune-Telling

Michel Foucault points out in his discussions of power and the knowledge of truth that "(truth) is produced only by virtue of multiple forms of constraint, that each society has its regime of truth, its 'general politic' of truth: that is, the types of discourse which it accepts and makes function as true; the mechanisms and instances which enable one to distinguish true and false statements, the means by which each is sanctioned; the techniques and procedures accorded value in the acquisition of truth; the status of those who are charged with saying what counts as true."[13]

The truth under discussion here is not "the ensemble of truths which are to be discovered and accepted," but rather "the ensemble of rules according to which the true and false are separated and specific effects of power attached to the truth." Therefore, truth is a system of ordered procedures for the production, regulation, distribution, circulation, and operation of statements, linked in a relation with systems of power which produce and sustain it, and to effects of power which it induces and which extend it.[14] A "regime" of truth is a discourse and a mechanism of power.

Fortune-telling is a major discourse in folk customs and beliefs, a system of convictions and statements deeply ingrained in traditional Chinese and Taiwanese societies—one that large numbers of ordinary people believe in and abide by. A system of belief whose status approaches a regime of "Truth," fortune-telling for centuries governed ordinary people's daily lives from birth to death. The phrase "The fortune-teller says . . ." was and to some extent continues to be a critical influence on people's outlook on life. The fortune-telling system is complex, with detailed ideas and practices that can be traced back in ancient philosophies and medical beliefs and written works passed down for generations. It is a discourse that has the ability to operate with the hegemony of knowledge and power in the arena of telling fortunes and fates. It prescribes what counts as truth and what does not, especially, for my purposes, regarding nu ming—the fortune of a woman. Women, especially in the traditional society, were subjugated to its truth in the sense that it produced the discourse that could decide, disseminate, and expand upon the effects of power—the unequal gender relations in a highly patriarchal system. On the one hand, patriarchal power reproduces and transmits the truth regarding nu ming within the fortune-telling discourse. On the other hand, the construction of women whose fortunes were determined and classified into good and bad was a function of the discourse of truth, which further bears the effects of power and reproduces power.

From a feminist outlook, the concern regarding the construction of women in the fortune-telling system is "not a matter of emancipating truth from every system of power . . . but of detaching the power of truth from the forms of hegemony, social, economic and cultural, within which it operates at the present time."[15] The construction of women within the fortune-telling discourse can be challenged and reworked, and it is the ful-crum women should use to bring down the patriarchal gender bias within the fortune-telling discourse and its regime of "truth."

Today, there are ever more people trying to debunk the gender bias in the discourse of nu ming. More importantly, there are women writing books with the aim of de-bunking it and intervening in the fortune-telling system, by pointing out that the con-structions of nu ming were concocted within a system established upon a patriarchal structure and should be reexamined and challenged in modern society.[16] These writers point out that telling a person's character and temperament is the key to the practice of palmistry, and that these constituents of character and temperament are actually the source of biased judgments toward nu ming. Palmistry books claim that the traits of character and temperament of a person with broken palm lines include being ambitious, self-assertive, and obstinate; being unwilling to accept others' opinions and unconcerned with what other people think; being resolute, tough, and hard headed, determined to persevere through difficulties and achieve goals; being solitary, eccentric, and idiosyn-cratic; being self-centered, impulsive, and ill-tempered. These descriptions of a person with broken palm lines, of course, describe a person with a more unrestrained charac-ter in a traditional sense.

In palmistry, this temperament in a man indicates a tendency to succeed in life. In-deed, all the readings for a man with broken palm lines indicate that they will bring him great fortune. The broken palm lines are even said to be the palmistry pattern of *tien tzu* (the emperor) and *hsiang kuo* (the prime minister), and it is claimed that some fa-mous political leaders from Japan, Europe, and the United States had broken palm lines.[17] However, for women with broken palm lines and thus with the same disposition and temperament, it is a totally different story. When a traditional society demanded that a woman be gentle, obedient, and self-effacing for the good of the family, the un-restrained temperament of a woman with broken palm lines became an aberration from the social norm and was thus condemned. The power to put certain meanings into dis-course and to repress others is a social technology parallel to the power to produce cer-tain bodily patterns and behaviors as normal and to repress others as abnormal—we see the operation of both of these techniques in the discourse and practice of reading nu ming in women with broken palm lines.

Shun-Niang: The Woman with Broken Palm Lines

In the Taiwanese prime-time television drama *Shun-Niang: The Woman with Broken Palm Lines*, we look for agency through a new regime of truth against the false fortune-telling belief—its configuration, its operations, and its effect on the attempt to keep building a new discourse.

The serial is based upon the novel of the same title by Peng Hsiao-Yen, a professor and writer. Juan Chien-Chih started producing the show in 1993. From the beginning, Peng recognized the difference between writing a novel and writing a television show and granted total control of the adaptation to Juan.[18] As the producer, Juan guided the adaptation of the novel and oversaw the writing of the screenplay by playwrights in her production company.

The television screenplay of keeps the basic structure of the novel but alters details of the story. In the novel, the narrative not only dwells upon Shun Niang's tenacity in leading a big family through decades, but also elaborately deals with stories of her daughters-in-law and their subtle interactions. However, the television screenplay develops all the major plot lines around Shun-Niang and the myth about women with broken palm lines. It becomes a story entirely about her endeavor to break the bonds of the fortune-telling belief, a significant change from the novel. For Juan, the story of Shun-Niang was an exemplary one about a strong and tenacious woman who was determined to go against all odds to achieve her desires and goals.

According to Juan, this is the theme she has tried to repeat in all the television shows about women that she has produced, because it is this conviction that has supported her performance. Juan entered the entertainment business in the early 1970s at the age of eighteen as a television actor with only a few dollars borrowed from her sister. She transformed herself into a producer and ended up heading her own company and producing television shows to her liking. Juan is one of the few examples of successful women producers in Taiwanese television. Before producing the one-hour series *The Woman with Broken Palm Lines*, Juan had produced four half-hour drama serials, almost all stories of strong, enduring women. Often asked about why this is, she explains that she values the opportunity to produce something encouraging and inspiring for the female television audience.

Around the time when *The Woman with Broken Palm Lines* aired in August 1996, Shun-Niang and her endeavors to overcome discrimination became the focus of entertainment news coverage. More than thirty items appeared in the newspapers, outpacing the coverage of any other prime-time show of that year or the recent past. This heightened interest is understandable. This fortune-telling myth has a long history in Taiwanese society but at the same time has been a taboo subject. When a prime-time television drama cast a spotlight on it and offered an opportunity to bring it out in the open and into people's consciousness, it drew intense responses.

Of course, long before the airing of the show, the topic had been an issue of concern for women with broken palm lines in real life. There were three waves of responses from these women. In the pre-production phase, when an announcement about this show-in-the-making was released to the newspapers, Juan's production company and the CTV network (China TV) received calls from more than a dozen women with broken palm lines. According to newspaper reports and Juan's accounts, the women implored the producer and the network not to make a television show about this issue.[19] For these women, the myths had already had negative influences and caused enough emotional pain. To their minds, bringing this issue to television would only worsen their feelings of shame and cause them more psychological apprehension and distress. The producer explained that the show was meant to break this hostile and unfounded belief, and to prove that no matter what pattern of palm lines women have, they can lead lives of happiness and success. However, after receiving these negative responses from the women, the network asked the production company to remove "woman with broken palm lines" from the title and change it to simply *Shun-Niang*.[20]

The show kept this simplified title until a week before its premier, although Juan was reluctant about the change all along. She felt that *The Woman with Broken Palm Lines* conveyed the message she intended for the show. It turned out the new female network president agreed, considering the title *Shun-Niang* too weak, according to the *China Times* of 4 August 1996. Therefore, the title was changed back, as subsequent publicity reflected. During this time of publicity and promotion, Juan urged the women with broken palms who had called in to watch the show so they could see that it was about fighting prejudice and breaking with detrimental beliefs.

Once the scheduled air date of the show was released, Taipei's *China Daily* reported on 7 August 1996 that "dozens of phone calls from women with broken palm lines swarmed into the CTV network office. It seems the number of the women with broken palm lines in Taiwan is much larger than people have imagined." Within less than two weeks, the show had become the object of heated discussion. Seizing the opportunity, CTV advertised the show's thesis—"break the superstition and dissolve the prejudice"— and the network sponsored a series of promotional activities, as Taipei's *Independent Daily* reported on 4 August 1996.

At the press conference on the pilot episode, the network program manager emphasized that the female protagonist in the show was speaking against prejudice for the sake of all women with broken palm lines, and that the show would surely elicit in them great confidence in their futures (*China Times* and *China Daily*, 8 August 1996). Thus, with huge publicity and numerous responses from the audience even before the premier, and with higher production values compared to other prime-time dramas, *The Woman with Broken Palm Lines* beat the other prime-time shows in the ratings and did tremendously well from the first episode on, as the *China Daily* recorded on 14 August 1996. Subsequently, a third wave of intense response poured in. The *United Daily* on 23 August reported that women with broken palm lines called into the television station to divulge their grievances after the airing of the show: failed marriage plans, a husband's suspicion, and so on.

According to the producer, she indeed received phone calls in which agonized women told her about their sufferings. One caller was preparing to get married and had tried to communicate with her future husband's family about her broken palm lines; however, the airing of the show made broken palm lines a hot topic again, and the family decided to cancel the wedding. There was also a married woman whose mother-in-law cast her out of the house for her broken palm lines, after the neighbors kept talking about this fortune-telling belief. Another married woman with broken palm lines was beaten by her husband, simply because she had the same last name as the female protagonist, Shun-Niang, in the show. Juan said that she feels sorrowful even today when she thinks about the experiences of women with broken palm lines.

In the meantime, Juan again urged the audience to keep watching the show to its end to understand its ultimate message. According to Juan, during the airing of the forty-seven episodes, there were calls to the production company every day from women talking about how they could identify with the female protagonist. The staff members in her production company became amateur counselors, talking to women with broken palm lines.

On the other hand, there were many responses from women with broken palm lines who said they had not been affected by the discriminating fortune-telling belief. Instead of talking about sufferings, they talked about their blessings in life and the fact that they had attained happiness and fulfillment. Other women said they had turned away from the negative influences of the fortune-telling belief and had been able to lead happy and successful lives. Still others stated they were glad to see a show dealing with the issue and hoped it could help other women drive away the shadow cast by the belief.

Foucault proposes that power must be analyzed as something that circulates and functions in the form of a chain, employed and exercised through a netlike organization.[21] In the case of *The Woman with Broken Palm Lines,* power and agency (in Butler's sense) worked together in a complex fashion in the production and promotion of the show on the institutional level. The production was an initial point of agency, when the original novel was rewritten into a screenplay entirely about the female protagonist who endeavors to break out of her ill-fated role. However, the maneuver of agency regarding the show extended beyond the intentions of the production team, when the show was released through the large-scale operations of a television network with multiple mechanisms to publicize and promote it.

Agency became a social event as it involved a television drama that not only provided an opportunity to discuss a popular belief, but also generated fervent responses and public attention. Consequently, the nature of the television event as a social phenomenon brought with it more resources for the maneuver of agency in the discourse, in the attempt to find ways to destabilize the existing power of fortune-telling beliefs. In the social discourse against nu ming, the reconstituting agency no longer resided simply in the production company. As heated responses from women helped to shape and frame the issue of women with broken palm lines, the maneuver of agency moved to an ever-more-public arena. In addition to the producer, the collective agency comprised the executives that ran the television network, including the female president who supported and scheduled the show, and the female program manager who planned a series of activities to promote it and repeatedly emphasized the need to "break the superstition." Agency was exercised by the lead actress, Yueh Ling, in her statement of support, and by the actor Chen Sung-Yuan, who spoke in the advertising trailer as a male with a conscience. Furthermore, the wide publicity surrounding the show and the message it carried was largely distributed through newspapers. Around the time when the airing of the show was a hot news topic, the discourse regarding fortune-telling and women was shaped in newspaper reports with the "break the superstition" motto at the center. Agency was exercised in the "break the superstition" discourse presented in the newspaper reports when a term like "feminism" was inserted in articles to describe the ambience of the show. In this way, a collective social agency was mobilized in the discourse, as a seemingly emerging new "regime of truth" was presented in the media.

In the case of the social event surrounding *The Woman with Broken Palm Lines,* social agency was not simply a product of individualism, but a product and activity of a collective social maneuver. The new regime of truth intended by the show merged with the commercial nature of the television network, especially with its high profitability in the prime-time slot. And it brought about an event of social agency with a discourse that was less likely to emerge as prominently as it did if not for the specific nature of the operations of the commercial television network and the significance of a show in a prime-time slot. The motivation for the maneuvering of the different parties involved is, of course, ambiguous. For instance, the television network was certainly motivated by money—commercial success was inextricably involved with circulating the motto "break the superstition." As we can see, any collective social maneuver involves different group agendas, different positions, and different ways of operating.

Meanwhile, this maneuver of social agency involving the reconstitution of women also exposed the deeply ingrained nature of their traditional constitution—in the fervent responses from the women with broken palm lines. It was through the channel of discourse around the show that these undercurrents of women's anxiety, apprehension, and pain gushed out to be publicly recognized as an on-going cultural and social problem that often had been ignored. Furthermore, while the maneuver of social agency helped to further the discourse of breaking the fortune-telling belief about women, it simultaneously activated the ingrained oppositional forces within this constitution. These ingrained forces strongly influenced some of the women and pulled them back into hurtful situations The forces of the fortune-telling constitution were exemplified through the distressing positions the women callers were situated in—losing a marriage engagement, being cast out of the family by a mother-in-law, or being beaten by a suspicious husband.

The persistence of the ingrained forces within the construction of women by nu ming also suggests that the work of building a new discourse is a long-term one. As it is difficult to incorporate the issue of agency for individual women with broken palm lines in this essay, the focus of this discussion is the agency surrounding the show on the social level.[22] However, we have to remember that the phone calls of protest and pleas from the women against the airing of the show are in fact a form of agency exercised by the women themselves, in order to prevent further harm to their already disadvantaged position. At the same time, the protest exposes the need for assistance and channels of communications for women dealing with these issues.

Searching for the Possibility of Agency— The Textual Level

As the title suggests, *The Woman with Broken Palm Lines* develops the major plot lines around Shun-Niang and the fortune-telling myth. The show is set in a town near Taipei earlier in the twentieth century, and the setting, props, and costumes create a period ambience in which a Taiwanese woman is trapped by local folk beliefs and customs. Analyzing the show's scripts demonstrates how agency—the breaking away from fortune-telling beliefs in nu ming to improve women's social position—is revealed through the text.

The narrative opens with the birth of Chen Shun-Ying (Shun-Niang's formal name). Her father, an idler who spent all his time and money on gambling and women, has died in an accident near the whorehouse he frequented even on the eve of his child's birth. At Shun-Niang's birth, a painful exclamation bursts from her aunt: "Sister, it's broken palm lines again!" Immediately, the three sets of broken palm lines—of the newborn Shun-Ying, her mother, and her aunt—appear together in close-up. This shot significantly indicates the "curse" into which these women are said to be born—the broken palm lines hereditary in the Chen family for generations.

After giving birth to Shun-Niang, the devastated mother hangs herself from a big tree on the Chen estate, hoping that this sacrifice will ensure a better life for her daughter. The next scene jumps to Shun-Niang twenty-four years later, getting ready to marry into the established Lai family. Twenty-four is very late for a girl to marry in traditional society. However, instead of joyously welcoming the bride, the Lai family, led by the matriarch, storms into the Chen family launching a tirade.

Shun-Niang, breaking the traditional taboo that a bride should not unveil herself and speak in public on her wedding day, says to her aunt and the elders in the family, who are still trying to save the engagement: "I am more than willing to cancel this marriage haunted by superstition. Please grant me this wish."

After the wedding is cancelled, Shun-Niang talks to her aunt, conveying her determination for the first time in the show to fight the hurtful fortune-telling belief:

SHUN-NIANG. Aunt Hui, why don't you fight it?

AUNT HUI. Fight? Fight how? How can people fight with fate?

SHUN-NIANG. Fate? Does a pattern of palm lines change my fate? If I cut my hands off, can I cut off the fate said to be brought by my broken palm lines?

The show continues with a series of plot lines that draw upon Shun-Niang's struggle. She is mocked and humiliated repeatedly and brutally wherever she goes because of the broken palm lines, especially after the wedding engagement with the Lai family is broken. Undaunted, Shun-Niang enters the competition posing as the Goddess of Mercy (a major female deity in folk custom) in the parade of the Ghost Festival on the fifteenth of the seventh month. It is a highly honored position from which the daughters of the Chen family for generations have been banned because of their broken palm lines; their names were not allowed even on the candidate list. Shun-Niang is determined to break the taboo. To her family's warnings that "gossip should be feared," Shun-Niang replies: "Gossip should be feared—my mother was forced to kill herself because of this fearful gossip, and I grew up with it. If I am afraid of the rumors, I can only hide in the house crying all my life and can never be who I want to be."

In the face of her persistence, the temple master finally grants Shun-Niang the chance to be considered—by the Goddess of Mercy herself through Chih Chiao, a commonly

Shun-Niang posing as the goddess in *Shun-Niang: The Woman with Broken Palm Lines*, 1996. (Courtesy of producer Juan Chien-Chih, CTV, Taiwan.)

used method of divination that consists of throwing two shards of woods on the ground to see which side turns up. Through divination, the Goddess of Mercy chooses to confer on Shun-Niang the honor of posing as the deity in the festival procession. Shun-Niang thus proves the legitimacy of women with broken palm lines. The attainment of this honor means that the women of the Chen family can feel proud after all the years of humiliation and mockery by the people in the town.

After breaking off the wedding engagement with the Lai family, Shun-Niang meets an orphaned traveling grocery vendor, Wu-Chiu, who falls in love with her. When Shun-Niang is mortified by the townspeople, he defends both her and the Chen family. He considers the beliefs about broken palm lines to be sheer rubbish and thinks that the mockery and humiliation are unfair to Shun-Niang. Wu-Chiu finally plucks up his courage to discuss marriage with aunt Hui, Shun-Niang's guardian. However, the aunt is strongly opposed to the match because Wu-Chiu is merely a traveling grocery vendor, while the Chen family is a well-established and wealthy clan in town. Acting against the traditional custom that a girl has no say in her marriage, Shun-Niang persuades her aunt to support her own wish.

Her aunt finally agrees to the marriage on one condition—since Shun-Niang is the only heir of the Chen family, the Chen family will *chao chui* Wu-Chiu in this marriage, that is, Wu-Chiu must marry into the Chen family, and he and their children must bear the Chen name. Wu-Chiu agrees.

As the plot moves along, there are myriad portrayals of Shun-Niang being mortified and vilified because of her broken palm lines. She is humiliated by the members of the Lai family in the temple, who slap her face and force her to kneel in front of the deities because they blame their son's continuing illness on Shun-Niang's thoughts of marrying him. When malaria breaks out in town, the townspeople throw things and spray water at Shun-Niang and her family as a type of exorcism; they believe that the woman with broken palm lines, posing as the Goddess of Mercy in the festival procession, has infuriated the gods, and the disease is a punishment. When she goes out, people point at her behind her back or to her face, talking about the fearful curse and the pernicious fortunes of broken palm lines. By the middle of the series, when Shun-Niang is pregnant and the family business she takes charge of is running smoothly, she says: "I have married a good husband, we have a business, and the Chen family is going to have a child. This is the best rebuttal to the gossip and unfounded rumors."

However, several years after the birth of their son, Wu-Chiu disappears through foul play by the Chen family's nemesis, Li-Hung. Again rumors surface, this time accusing Wu-Chiu of leaving his wife and son to elope with another woman. Despite the rumors, Shun-Niang firmly believes that Wu-Chiu would never desert them. A year after his disappearance, her son is still constantly taunted by other children for being deserted by his father. Shun-Niang, who still believes in her heart that Wu-Chiu is alive, nevertheless decides to announce to the town that Wu-Chiu is dead and to bury an empty coffin in the Chen family cemetery. Shun-Niang's family and friends strongly oppose this idea, arguing that announcing the (fake) death of her husband does even greater harm to herself. Shun-Niang disagrees: "I have to protect my son and my husband from the unfounded rumors people heap upon them. . . . When I bury a coffin that is empty, I know I have conquered the curse of bringing a jinx to my husband. I have overcome my own fate." With the discursive power of the empty coffin, the show attempts to cast off the shadow cast by the fortune-telling myth.

The narrative is thus built upon Shun-Niang's struggles against the hurtful fortune-telling belief. However, many discursive elements come into play. For a woman with broken palm lines, the discursive tension appears most significantly when she and her family are concerned. Shun-Niang's inner struggle over her determination to overcome the malicious fortune-telling belief and her love and sense of responsibility for her family, comprises the development and the tension within the character. To defend the reputation of her husband, to protect her son from the myth, and to keep the image of the family intact, she buries the empty coffin. This act furthers her wish to conquer the myth in her own heart. However, near the end of the show, the love and responsibility she feels for her family members gradually move her in the opposite direction—toward the collapse of her endeavor and the waning of her strength to fight the fortune-telling belief.

Shun-Niang wavers when rumors arise concerning her son's epilepsy, blaming it on her broken palm lines. As she does everything she can to help with her son's illness, including diligently studying medical books, she begins to consider more seriously the rumors about her palm lines. In the last part of the show, with the deaths of her aunt and cousin (deaths clandestinely related to malicious schemes set up by the family's enemies, including Li-Hung and another villain, Chou), the rumors about Shun-Niang's broken palm lines spread ever more intensely, even with Wu-Chiu's dramatic return to the family two years following his disappearance. Faced with the accusation that she has brought misfortune to her family members, Shun-Niang has gradually lost confidence. Meanwhile, Li-Hung poisons Wu-Chiu's medicine, endangering his life, and then accuses Shun-Niang of jinxing Wu-Chiu and asks her to sign divorce papers to save her husband. (This is Li-Hung's scheme to get Wu-Chiu for herself.) Losing her aunt and her cousin, and seeing her husband lying unconscious in bed, Shun-Niang's strength crumbles. Signing the divorce papers, she collapses in sobs, blaming herself for her broken palm lines. After Shun-Niang signs the divorce papers, Li-Hung stops putting poison in Wu-Chiu's medicine, and he recovers.

It is highly unsettling and intriguing to see the character of Shun-Niang collapse and her determination fail. Her fight against the false palm-lines belief is diminished in the discursive struggles, when the sense of love and responsibility for family members is presented as her ultimate priority. What is argued here is not that the sense of family love and responsibility is not important, but that within the tensions of the discursive configuration in the show, a woman's struggles and endeavors meet their limit when her obligations for her family's well-being is at stake. Meanwhile, Shun-Niang's sacrifice reveals the immense difficulty women with broken palm lines confront in real life. When the false beliefs are so intricately embroiled with the well-being of family members—when the issues of fate, fortune, and jinx arise—it is indeed a tough construction to break and requires continuous endeavor and strength.

But in spite of all the ideological tensions, struggles, and twists within the discourse, the show eventually returns to its uppermost motif: breaking the fortune-telling belief about women with broken palm lines. In the narrative, after recovering, Wu-Chiu rejects both the divorce papers and the myth about broken palm lines, works together with Shun-Niang, and finally discovers and discloses the malicious scheme of Li-Hung and her collusive partner. The rumors about broken palm lines are actually the result of human foul play. In the end, Shun-Niang is reunited with Wu-Chiu. In the final shot, with her husband, her son, and her best friend, Yen-Chih, by her side, a woman with broken palm lines has persevered.

In the 1990s in Taiwan, television representations of women have become a multifaceted arena of discourse. Some are confined to women's traditional social images: gentle, submissive, and self-effacing. Others try to rewrite the traditional images and engage with discursive reconstructions to re-present women as more self-conscious, confident, and independent. Therefore, it is important to keep in mind that, as Butler points out, agency is always and only a political prerogative, and it is crucial to question the conditions of its possibility, not to take it for granted as an priori guarantee.[23] In this light, investigating such a case as *Shun-Niang: The Woman with Broken Palm Lines* helps to think about the process of the emergence of agency: from the original novel to the production of the television show, from the discursive intentions in the texts to the mobilization of the collective social force in promoting the show and the idea it conveys. We consider this process with a sense of hope. The television show offers a valuable lens for examining the possible maneuvers and operations regarding the concept of agency, and the meanings they may convey to women. It demonstrates that there *are* shimmering possibilities for Taiwanese women to gradually rework the power configuration and to reconstruct it, even with all the extant configurations of women in traditional patriarchal structures.

Notes

1. Judith Butler, "Contingent Foundations," in *Feminists Theorize the Political,* ed. Judith Butler and Joan W. Scott (New York: Routledge, 1992), 12–13.

2. Judith Butler, *Gender Trouble: Feminism and the Subversion of Identity* (New York: Routledge, 1990), 147.

3. My sources include the texts of the television show itself and the secondary texts generated by it, including newspaper reports and audiences responses, the materials regarding fortune-telling beliefs and nu ming—specifically fortune-telling books—and an in-depth interview that I conducted with the producer of the show.

4. Any middle-to-large chain bookstore in Taipei today, for example, offers hundreds of titles on methods of traditional Chinese fortune-telling, as well as another dozen on Western astrology, a hot fortune-telling trend among the younger generations. On the Internet, web sites related to traditional and Western fortune telling include www.tisnet.net.tw, msdn.acer.net, and www.ee.hwh.edu.tw; see Lee Szu-Chuang, "Fortuneteller on the Net," *China Times Weekly,* 4 April 1998, 90–91. Beginning in 1993, numerous television shows appeared that were based on fortune telling. See Lai, *Genre Analysis,* and Lai Kuo-Chou, ed., *A Preliminary Look at the Regulation of Programs on the Paranormal* (Taipei: Committee of Television Culture Research, 1997).

5. Shih and Chen, *Modern Nu Ming,* 1. Sometimes today, women are still referred to as *hou ming* (born with good fortunes) or *dai ming* (born with bad fortunes).

6. See Lee Yuan Jen, "How the Feminist Movement Won Media Space in Taiwan," in Yang, *Spaces of Their Own,* 95–115.

7. Lin Po-Yu, *The Book on Women's Pa Tzu* (Taipei: Yi Chun, 1995), 8–39; Shih and Chen, *Modern Nu Ming,* 84–85.

8. See Lin Tung-Hua, *The New Palmistry* (Tainan: Northwest, 1970), 1–5; Fan Ting-Tsan, *Learning About Life from Palmistry* (Taipei: Wu Ling, 1997), 14–39; Asano Hachiro, *The Most Scientific Guide to Palmistry* (Taipei: Shang Yen, 1998), 10–13.

9. Any medium-to-large bookstore in Taipei usually carries at least twenty to thirty titles on palmistry. The reference books on palmistry and fortune-telling here are available in libraries and bookstores in Taiwan; their authors are mostly fortune-tellers. Many call themselves *shan jen* or *chu shih,* Taoist or Buddhist devotees or hermits, with strong connotations of folk religions or beliefs.

10. See Li Da-Wei, *The Mystery of Palmistry* (Taipei: Chung Wen, 1994), 3–8; Lin, *The New Palmistry.*

11. Fei-Yun Shan Jen, *Fortune Is in Your Hands* (Taipei: Shih Pao, 1997), 53; Yung Shih-I, *Fortune and Life* (Taipei: Yung Chih, 1994), 52.

12. Hsia-Hsiang Chu Shih, *Palmistry by Hsiao-Hsiang* (Taipei: 1997) 222.

13. Michel Foucault, *Power/Knowledge: Selected Interviews and Other Writings, 1972–1977* (New York: Pantheon, 1980), 131.

14. Ibid., 132, 133.

15. Ibid., 133.

16. Yung Shih-I, *Fortune and Marriage* (Taipei: Yung Chih, 1996); Fei-Yun, *Fortune Is in Your Hands;* Lin Shu-Jung, *Woman! Do Not Resign Yourself to Fate* (Taipei: Crown, 1996); Shih and Chen, *Modern Nu Ming.*

17. Fan, *Learning About Life from Palmistry,* 136–137; Hachiro, *Most Scientific Guide to Palmistry,* 100–101, 252–253.

18. Peng Hsiao-Yen, tape-recorded interview by the author, 10 November 1998, Academia Sinica, Taipei. Juan Chien-Chih, tape-recorded interview by the author, 18 November 1998, Yarn Channel Communications, Taipei; all of the references to Juan's accounts come from this interview.

19. Juan interview; also see *China Daily* (Taipei), 4 August 1996; *China Times* (Taipei), 12 August 1996; "*Shun-Niang: The Woman with Broken Palms* Finally Revealing Her Face," *TV Weekly* (Taipei), 25 August 1996.

20. Juan interview; also see *China Times* (Taipei), 4 August 1996.

21. Foucault, *Power/Knowledge*, 98.

22. Personal information of the women with broken palm lines who called the production company and the network was not recorded. Turning to organizations which help women deal with difficult issues in life, I also encountered difficulties in attaining personal information regarding women with broken palm lines in society. However, it is a long-term topic greatly worth investigating.

23. Butler, "Contingent Foundations," 13.

Selected Bibliography

Barlow, Tani. "Theorizing Woman: Funu, Guojia, Jiating" (Chinese women, Chinese state, Chinese family). *Genders* 10 (1991): 132–160.

Chen, Cheng-Kuang, and Sung Wen-Li. *The New Social Movements in Taiwan*. Taipei: Chu Liu, 1989.

Chen, Mei-Yen. "'Superstitions' and Folk Religions: A Critical Reflection and Analysis of a Discourse." Ph.D. diss., Hsing-Hua University, 1988.

Grewal, Inderpal, and Caren Kaplan. "Transnational Feminist Cultural Studies: Beyond Marxism/Poststructualism/Feminism Divides." *Positions* 2, no. 2 (1994): 430–445.

——, eds. *Scattered Hegemonies: Postmodernity and Transnational Feminist Practices*. Minneapolis: University of Minnesota Press, 1994.

Hu, Yu-Hui. *Three-Generation Living: Myth and Pitfall*. Taipei: Chu Liu, 1997.

Lai, Kuo-Chou, ed. *The Genre Analysis of Programs on the Paranormal, Fortune-Telling, and Fengshui*. Taipei: Committee of Television Culture Research, 1995.

Lai, Tse-Han. "Organization, Power Structure, and the Evolution of Women's Position in the Chinese Family." In *Essays in Social Sciences,* ed. Chen Chou-Nan, Chiang Yu-Lung, and Chen Kuan-Chen, 383–404. Taipei: Academia Sinica, 1982.

Shih, Chi Ching, and Chen Hua. *Modern Nu Ming: Women's Haven away from Fortune-Telling*. Taipei: Teacher Chang, 1997.

Women's Studies Association, ed. *White Book on Taiwanese Women*. Taipei: China Times Publishing, 1995.

Yang, Mayfair Mei-hui, ed. *Spaces of Their Own: Women's Public Sphere in Transnational China*. Minneapolis: University of Minnesota Press, 1999.

Zito, Angelo. "Ritualizing *Li*: Implications for Studying Power and Gender." *Positions* 1, no. 2 (1993): 321–348.

About the Contributors

DAI JINHUA is professor of comparative language and culture at Peking University. She is a major scholar of contemporary Chinese popular culture and has authored numerous articles and books in Chinese on the topic, including her most recent work, *Scenery in the Fog* (2000). In the past ten years, she has lectured at a number of universities in the United States, including Harvard University and Duke University.

JEROEN DE KLOET, who completed his Ph.D. at the Amsterdam School of Social Science Research with a dissertation titled "Red Sonic Trajectories: Popular Music and Youth in Urban China," is an assistant professor at the University of Amsterdam's Department of Communication Studies. His research focuses on the globalization of popular music, as well as on the cultural, political, and technological implications of computer hacking in Indonesia, China, Europe, and the United States.

DAVID DESSER is professor of cinema studies at the University of Illinois. He has authored and edited numerous books on Japanese, Hong Kong, and U.S. cinema, including most recently *Ozu's "Tokyo Story"* (1997), *The Cinema of Hong Kong* (2000), and *Hollywood Goes Shopping* (2000). He is the former book review editor of *Film Quarterly* and a former editor of *Cinema Journal*.

FRANCES GATEWARD teaches courses on cinema and popular culture in the Center for Afro-American and African Studies and the Program in Film and Video at the University of Michigan. She is the editor of *Zhang Yimou: Interviews* (2001) and coeditor of *Sugar, Spice, and Everything Nice: Cinemas of Girlhood* (2002). Her current research projects include a cultural history of African American cinema and an anthology on contemporary Korean cinema.

CHUCK KLEINHANS is coeditor of *Jump Cut: A Review of Contemporary Media* and professor and director of graduate studies in the Radio/Television/Film Department at Northwestern University. He is currently writing a study of the institutional structure of experimental film.

HAN JU KWAK is a doctoral candidate at the School of Cinema and Television at the University of Southern California. His main area of interest is the relationship between mass culture and society, particularly Korean popular cinema in relation to Korean society. His most recent essay, "In Defense of Continuity," is included in *Im Kwon Taek: A Making of Korean National Cinema* (2002).

JENNY KWOK WAH LAU teaches film in the Cinema Department of San Francisco State University. She specializes in contemporary Chinese cinema and culture and has published widely in journals and books, including her recent chapter in *The Cinema of Hong Kong* (2002). Some of her writings have been translated into Chinese and German.

LIN SZU-PING received her doctorate in media and cultural studies in the Department of Communication Arts at the University of Wisconsin at Madison. She is currently assistant professor of journalism at Shih Hsin University in Taipei, Taiwan. Her research interests include media/cultural studies and women's studies. She is currently working on a book on women, representation, and prime-time television drama in Taiwan.

AUGUSTA LEE PALMER is a doctoral candidate in Cinema Studies at New York University's Tisch School of the Arts, where she is writing her dissertation. She has taught film history and criticism at various film schools and has published film criticism and interviews.

HECTOR RODRIGUEZ is associate professor and BA program leader at the School of Creative Media, City University of Hong Kong. He has published essays on the philosophy of film and Asian cinema history in numerous journals and books. His video work has been shown on Radio Television Hong Kong (RTHK), at Hong Kong City Hall, and in the Parasite exhibition space. His current research concerns algorithmic art and digital culture.

YOMOTA INUHIKO, film historian and critic of literature, is a professor at Meijigakuin University, Tokyo. He has published nearly seventy books, including *Japanese Cinema in Asian Context* (2001), *Li Xianglan and East Asia* (2001), *100 Years of Japanese Cinema* (2000), *Radical Wills in Japanese Cinema* (2000), *Mizoguchi Kanji the Director* (2000), and *Exile in Morocco* (1999). He has also translated into Japanese works by Paul Bowles, Edward W. Said, and Pier Paolo Pasolini.

MITSUHIRO YOSHIMOTO is associate professor of East Asian studies at New York University. He is the author of *Kurosawa: Film Studies and Japanese Cinema* (2000). His teaching and research focus on the questions of representation, media, and urban space.

Index